Ragae Ghaly
Krishna Kothapalli

# SAMS Teach Yourself

# EJB

# in 21 Days

**SAMS**

*201 West 103rd St., Indianapolis, Indiana, 46290 USA*

# Sams Teach Yourself EJB in 21 Days
## Copyright © 2003 by Sams Publishing

International Standard Book Number: 0-672-32423-7

Library of Congress Catalog Card Number: 2002102795

Printed in the United States of America

First Printing: October 2002

05   04   03   02            4   3   2   1

## Trademarks

## Warning and Disclaimer

**ASSOCIATE PUBLISHER**
Michael Stephens

**DEVELOPMENT EDITOR**
Mark Renfrow

**MANAGING EDITOR**
Charlotte Clapp

**ACQUISITIONS EDITOR**
Carol Ackerman

**PROJECT EDITOR**
Andy Beaster

**COPY EDITOR**
Mike Henry

**INDEXER**
Aamir Burki

**PROOFREADERS**
Abby VanHuss
Julie Cook

**TECHNICAL EDITORS**
Chad Fowler
Mike Altarace

**TEAM COORDINATOR**
Lynne Williams

**INTERIOR DESIGNER**
Gary Adair

**COVER DESIGNER**
Aren Howell

**PAGE LAYOUT**
Susan Geiselman

**GRAPHICS**
Oliver Jackson
Tammy Graham

# Contents at a Glance

## Appendixes 539

# Contents

# About the Authors

**RAGAE GHALY** has more than 25 years of experience in both academic research and industrial fields. He is an independent consultant, and he has worked in different capacities for large enterprises such as SHL Systemhouse, General Motors, Proxicom, and WellPoint Health Network. He has been working with Java and J2EE since their inception. His areas of interest include distributed systems, object-oriented modeling, middleware, design patterns, enterprise architecture, and EAI. He gained a masters degree in computer science from Florida International University. He has published a handful of papers about real-time object-oriented databases and J2EE application servers. Ragae lives in California, and in his free time he likes to study human languages. He also likes to travel and spend precious time with his family.

**KRISHNA KOTHAPALLI** has 10 years of experience in the software industry in different roles as a developer, consultant, and architect. He has worked in small, medium, and large companies such as SHL Systemhouse, Sapient Corporation, Xerox Corporation, General Motors, and CacheEdge. His areas of interest include distributed object-oriented systems, Internet systems, and biotechnology. He gained a masters degree in computer science from the Indian Institute of Technology, Madras. He has published articles in the areas of distributed algorithms and Enterprise JavaBeans. In his free time, he plays with his children, helps organize research for autoimmune diseases, and develops Web sites for non-profit organizations. He believes that anything under the sun can be mastered in 21 days, with the exception of the GNU Emacs editor with its unlimited capabilities. Ever since he dreamed of retiring rich at the age of 30, he has started to feel younger with every passing year.

# Dedications

*To my wife Mary, for all good reasons,*

*to Raymond, for his sparking thoughts,*

*to Rudy, for starting to do the right things,*

*to Laura, for her honesty and openness,*

*and to Lillian, for her compassion and love.*

*—Ragae*

*To my wife Sunitha for love, support, and understanding.*

*—Krishna*

# Acknowledgments

*From Ragae Ghaly:*

To those who inspired me and still ignite my mind with thoughts. To my parents for their love, guidance, and support. To the memory of Raouf Ghaly, who is the source of inspiration and human values. To the memory of Prof. Yakoub Gayed, who taught me how to respect time. To Prof. Fatin Fahim and Prof. Rushdy Amer, who lit the candles in my career path from engineering to computer science. To Prof. Tzilla Elrad, Prof. Prabu Prabhakaran, and Prof. Naphtalie Rashe, who sparked my mind with new ideas. I would also like to thank my wife Mary, and my daughters Laura and Lillian for their love and support during the writing of this book.

*From Krishna Kothapalli:*

To my parents for lifetime care, affection, and support. To my young kids Abhiram (age 4) and Tejasvi (age 2), for making life interesting and memorable with their cute little acts, spilling water on my laptop, and teaching me the ABCs of life's priorities.

*Special Thanks:*

The authors would like to thank Carol Ackerman for her encouragement, support, and guidance.

The authors would like to thank the following Sams editors: Mark Renfrow, Mike Henry, Andy Beaster; reviewers Mike Altarace, Chad Fowler, and Mike Fogarty from Princeton Solutions Group, and Keith Magnant from Element K for their insightful remarks on the manuscript and for being patient in answering our queries.

Very special thanks to Raymond Ghaly and Raghava Kothapalli for helping us in writing this book. Raymond and Raghava were instrumental in streamlining the code examples, and had great insights for setting up and testing both the WebLogic and JBoss servers. Without their help, this book would not have seen the light of day.

# We Want to Hear from You!

As the reader of this book, *you* are our most important critic and commentator. We value your opinion and want to know what we're doing right, what we could do better, what areas you'd like to see us publish in, and any other words of wisdom you're willing to pass our way.

As an Associate Publisher for Sams, I welcome your comments. You can email or write me directly to let me know what you did or didn't like about this book—as well as what we can do to make our books better.

Please note that I cannot help you with technical problems related to the *topic* of this book. We do have a User Services group, however, where I will forward specific technical questions related to the book.

When you write, please be sure to include this book's title and author as well as your name, email address, and phone number. I will carefully review your comments and share them with the author and editors who worked on the book.

Email:      feedback@samspublishing.com

Mail:      Michael Stephens, Associate Publisher
           Sams
           201 West 103rd Street
           Indianapolis, IN 46290 USA

For more information about this book or another Sams title, visit our Web site at www.samspublishing.com. Type the ISBN (excluding hyphens) or the title of a book in the Search field to find the page you're looking for.

# Introduction

With the introduction of Java in the mid-1990s, its portability was obvious on the client side. Java has quickly become the language of choice for writing applications. Most browsers support Java, and Java applets and Java applications can run on any machine or operating system. But this is not enough for enterprise applications, which require server-side Java support. Writing applications for the enterprise is usually a difficult task. Enterprise applications must be scalable, portable, and secure. That's what Java 2 Platform, Enterprise Edition (J2EE) is all about: a complete architecture and framework for developing and deploying server-side Java components. Enterprise JavaBeans (EJB) is the heart of the J2EE platform. It enables simplified development of distributed Java applications. Other J2EE run-time services, such as JNDI, JDBC, and JMS, are vital in completing the full picture of server-side component architecture.

Since the EJB 1.0 specification was introduced by Sun Microsystems in 1998, it quickly gained industry momentum among application developers and vendors. Today, more than 25 application server vendors support EJB technology in their products. Charles Stack, president and CEO of Flashline, states, "The EJB component architecture allows vendors to simplify application development, [and] speed the delivery of high-quality products to market...The market for commercial EJB technology-based components is rapidly growing as more corporations adopt the J2EE platform as their primary development architecture." More than 20 companies collaborated with Sun Microsystems to finalize the EJB 2.0 specification in 2001. This demonstrates the industry's support of and commitment to building enterprise applications using EJB technology.

This book focuses primarily on teaching the EJB technology, but it also covers other J2EE technologies that are essential to understanding EJBs. You'll be introduced to all aspects of EJB development using the most current version of the specification.

The book helps you learn concepts and the reasoning behind them by using simple, under-the-hood diagrams. In addition, it focuses on step-by-step instructions for developing components and then running them.

You'll learn how to write portable applications that can run on multiple application servers and databases. For demonstration purposes, we provide step-by-step instructions for running the examples in two different application servers: WebLogic Server and JBoss. WebLogic Server is the most widely used commercial application server today, and JBoss is an emerging open source, small footprint, J2EE application server. We also use multiple databases: Pointbase (a lightweight Java database to run the examples with WebLogic Server) and Hypersonic (to run the same examples with JBoss).

This book does not depend on any Java development tools or IDEs. It requires only the use of a text editor. You'll be introduced to all aspects of developing, compiling, packaging, deploying, and running your components and applications in easy and simple methods. By the time you're done with this book, you'll be acquainted with the reasons why EJB is the choice of serious enterprise application developers.

# How This Book Is Organized

During your 21-day journey to learn EJB, each day discusses a major EJB type or a J2EE service used by an EJB. Each day's concepts are illustrated with code fragments. A real-life example is given in most of the days, and you're provided with different scripts to run on both WebLogic Server and JBoss. Each chapter ends with a "Best Practices" section that helps you become more familiar with the subject matter. A few questions are given at the end of each day for review purposes.

Examples in this book are based on an online university registration system. Each week you'll learn about and develop the components needed for the system. On Day 21, you build the complete enterprise application using the components you built in previous days.

In the first week, you're introduced to the main concepts of EJB, and given a few examples to illustrate how to register and find your components. This week also explains how to package and run your simple components in application servers. In summary, you'll learn the following:

- Day 1 gives you an overview of the EJB architecture, and discusses the benefits to the enterprise of both EJB and the EJB container. You also learn about the roles and responsibilities in developing enterprise applications.

- On Day 2, you look at the EJB fundamentals and explore all types of EJBs. You examine the packaging mechanism used in deploying EJB applications.

- Day 3 covers the fundamentals and characteristics of session beans, both stateful and stateless. Here you cover the life cycle, instance pool, and the concepts of activation and passivation.

- Day 4 fully explores the JNDI services. It covers the concepts of naming and directory services. You're introduced to the JNDI API's classes and interfaces, and shown how to use JNDI to support other J2EE services.

- On Day 5, you start getting down to the details of developing a stateless session bean. You learn how to develop, package, deploy, and run a real-life example.

- Day 6 focuses on the development of a stateful session bean example. You take a closer look under the hood of this type of EJB.

Week 2 discusses the concepts of persistence and asynchronous messaging. It starts by giving you an overview of Web applications, and ends with the development of a message-driven bean.

- Day 7 sheds light on the MVC architecture pattern in designing Web applications. You explore Web tier components such as servlets, JSPs, and tag libraries, which are common clients to access EJBs.
- On Day 8, you explore the fundamentals and characteristics of entity beans and how they are used in object persistence.
- Day 9 introduces the concept of JDBC, and how you can use both declarative and programmatic approaches in connecting to any tabular databases.
- Day 10 focuses on developing a real-life example of bean-managed persistence entity beans. You learn how to develop, package, deploy, and run the bean into two application servers' environments.
- On Day 11, you continue to learn about entity beans by developing a container-managed persistence entity bean.
- Day 12 covers the development of relationships among entity beans using the advanced feature of container-managed relationships.
- Day 13 explores the fundamentals of JMS, and discusses its two main paradigms: point-to-point and publish-and-subscribe. You're introduced to the message-driven bean and how to use it as a JMS consumer.
- On Day 14, you develop a real-life example of a message-driven bean. You learn how to package, deploy, and run the message-driven bean into two application server environments.

Week 3 includes advanced topics, such as J2EE transactions, security, and JavaMail. It starts with a full introduction to J2EE application and J2EE design patterns. It ends with the discussion of the complete enterprise application: University Registration System.

- Day 15 covers aspects of J2EE architecture, and is an umbrella chapter for learning about the J2EE tiers—specifically, the client, Web, EJB, and EIS tiers. It briefly discusses the J2EE design patterns.
- Day 16 begins 3 days of coverage of J2EE transactions. It explores the fundamentals of both local and distributed transactions. You learn about the JTA API and how to use it in developing transactional applications through the development of a real-life example.
- On Day 17, you learn by example how to develop an enterprise bean with container-managed transaction, and how to set transactional properties into the bean's deployment descriptor.

- Day 18 concludes the coverage of J2EE transactions with the study of bean-managed transactions. You develop a step-by-step example of BMT and learn how to package, deploy, and run it in two different application servers.

- Day 19 covers the concepts and mechanisms of J2EE security. You explore the JAAS architecture and learn how to implement security into enterprise applications.

- On Day 20, you learn how to use the JavaMail API to send email messages from enterprise applications. You develop a complete enterprise application with the primary focus on JavaMail.

- Day 21 finishes the development of a complete enterprise application. You spend the day studying how to design, develop, deploy, and run the University Registration System.

There are also a few appendices, which are vital in installing and configuring WebLogic Server and JBoss application servers. Both UML and XML are used in the book, and an appendix is dedicated to each subject. A glossary of terms is provided at the end of the book to act as a quick reference to the many abbreviations used in the book.

# About This Book

This book teaches you about Enterprise JavaBeans and Java 2 Enterprise Edition. Its primary focus is to show you how to create an EJB, and how to use EJBs in the context of J2EE services. By the time you finish *Sams Teach Yourself EJB in 21 Days*, you'll have a good understanding of the EJB APIs and J2EE services, both classes and interfaces. You'll also have a well-rounded knowledge of how to deploy an enterprise application into a J2EE-compliant application server. You'll also learn how to configure EJB, JMS, JDBC, and JavaMail to work under the WebLogic Server and JBoss application servers.

You learn by doing in this book. You develop EJBs and applications that demonstrate the topics being introduced, and the usage of those concepts. The source code for all the working examples, along with other supplemental material such as how to configure and run each day's example in the WebLogic Server and JBoss server environments, is available at http://samspublishing.com. Type 0672324237 in the search field to find the page you are looking for.

# Who Should Read This Book

This book teaches EJB to the following audience:

- Java programmers of all levels who want to know how to develop enterprise applications using EJB and the J2EE platform.

- Beginning-to-intermediate users of EJB, such as developers, technical managers, and system integrators.
- Advanced EJB developers who want to know how to run their components and applications on WebLogic Server and/or JBoss.
- Experienced component-based developers in other paradigms, such as CORBA or .NET. A basic knowledge of the Java programming language is enough to understand this book.

If you're an experienced developer with knowledge of another object-oriented programming language, such as C++, and have a little background of Java, you can grasp EJB and learn each step from developing to running those examples in application servers.

# WEEK 1

# Enterprise Java Architecture

1

2

3

4

5

6

7

# DAY 1

# Understanding EJB Architecture

Developing enterprise applications has become a daunting task. Enterprise applications are complex, used by many users, developed by multiple teams, and deployed on heterogeneous systems that might span multiple environments. In addition, enterprise applications have to be distributed, secure, transactional, reliable, scalable, flexible, expandable, reusable, and manageable. Moreover, enterprise applications must be integrated with existing systems, and leveraged against the existing infrastructure.

Enterprise JavaBeans (EJB) is a component-based architecture for developing, deploying, and managing reliable enterprise applications in production environments. EJB architecture is at the heart of the Java 2 platform, Enterprise Edition (J2EE). With the growth of the Web and the Internet, more and more enterprise applications are now Web based, including both intranet and extranet applications. Together, the J2EE and EJB architectures provide superior support for Web-based enterprise applications.

The following is a summary of today's target in exploring both the EJB technology and J2EE architecture. You'll learn

- What EJB is, and its benefits in simplifying the writing of enterprise applications
- How EJB is different from ordinary JavaBeans
- About the big picture of the J2EE, and where EJB fits into it
- What flavors of beans are available, and the characteristics of each
- The importance of the EJB container, and the available common services provided to your beans
- More about the roles and responsibilities in developing and deploying J2EE applications—who does what

# The Challenges of Developing Enterprise Applications

Enterprise applications are facing many challenges, such as portability, reusability, interoperability, and application integration. Since the inception of Java in 1995 as a simple object-oriented and portable language, its main focus was on the development of portable client-side applications. The challenges of developing portable Java enterprise applications remain due to the lack of server-side application development framework and tools. By *server-side computing*, we imply the design of small, location-transparent components that work together to fulfill enterprise service requirements. In many cases, these lightweight components can work as both client and server.

Enterprise computing is rapidly changing in both hardware and software. New applications are required to meet with the emerging user demands, and are still required to interface with existing applications. It's not practical to throw out the huge investment in applications written in older-generation languages that already work to maintain data in legacy systems. This dictates a need to integrate new applications with the existing systems. Today, server-side software offers the corporate world many opportunities to rethink its enterprise-wide computing infrastructure. With the acceptance and growth of Java in recent years, software portability, reuse, and application integration have become important and accepted for many client applications spread throughout the enterprise.

Enterprise applications are complex, and in many cases require the development of several teams, which might span multiple domains. Today's applications are required to have faster time to market to compete and to fulfill user demands. Another challenge facing the enterprise is interoperability with other environments, which might be heterogeneous in hardware, software, or network architectures.

1

In facing such challenges, enterprise application architectures have undergone an extensive evolution. The first generation of enterprise applications was centralized mainframe applications. In the late 1980s and early 1990s, most new enterprise applications followed a two-tier architecture approach (also known as the *client/server* architecture). Later, the enterprise architecture evolved to a three-tier, and then to a Web-based architecture.

One of the solutions for these challenges is the J2EE technology, which was developed by Sun Microsystems. The following sections describe the J2EE architecture and, as a major participant, the EJB technology of developing component-based enterprise applications.

# What's an EJB?

Let's first understand the meaning of component and server component model, and then examine the meaning of EJB. A *component* is a piece of code that implements well-defined interfaces. Typically, it lives in a runtime environment and takes advantage of the services offered by the environment. For the component to live in a runtime environment, it must follow the rules of the runtime environment. This ensures the proper functioning of the runtime environment and the portability and scalability of the component. A component is not a complete application. An application consists of multiple components working together.

Generally, developing server-side objects is more difficult than writing graphical user interface (GUI) or client components. This is because in addition to writing business application logic, the developers must also take care of system-level issues such as multi-threading, access to databases, efficient management of resources, transactions, security, access to legacy systems, and so on. A *server component model* or *architecture* provides support for server-side components. This simplifies the development of server-side components and allows developers to focus on developing business application logic.

An *enterprise bean* is a server-side component that implements the business logic of an enterprise application and adheres to the rules of the Enterprise JavaBean architecture. Enterprise beans live in an EJB container—a runtime environment within a J2EE server. The EJB container provides multiple services to support the enterprise beans.

**Note**

The Enterprise JavaBeans specification states, "The Enterprise JavaBeans architecture is a component architecture for the development and deployment of component-based distributed business applications. Applications

written using the Enterprise JavaBeans architecture are scalable, transactional, and multi-user secure. These applications may be written once, and then deployed on any server platform that supports the Enterprise JavaBeans specification. The Enterprise JavaBeans architecture will make it easy to write applications: Application developers will not have to understand low-level transaction and state management details, multi-threading, connection pooling, and other complex low-level APIs." The entire 500+ pages of the specification, meant for application server vendors to digest and implement, can be accessed at
`http://java.sun.com/products/ejb/docs.html`.

**Note**

EJB is an overloaded name. Depending on the context, it represents either a server-side component, or component-based architecture. We'll use the terms *EJB*, *Enterprise Bean*, and *Enterprise JavaBean* interchangeably in this book. Unless otherwise mentioned, we'll use the term *bean* to mean EJB.

The following are the characteristics of EJBs:

- They contain business logic that operates on the enterprise's data.
- They depend on a container environment to supply life-cycle services for them. EJB instances are created and maintained by the container.
- They can be customized at deployment time by editing the deployment descriptor.
- System-level services, such as transaction management and security, are described separately from the enterprise bean.
- A client never accesses an enterprise bean directly; the container environment mediates access for the client. This provides component-location transparency.
- The EJB is designed to be portable across EJB servers provided by different vendors.
- They can be included in an assembled application without requiring source code changes or recompilation of them.
- Beans are always single threaded; you never have to write thread-safe code. You design your threads as single-threaded components, and the EJB container handles multiple client requests by load balancing and instantiating multiple instances of the single-threaded components.

# EJB Architecture Overview

The J2EE architecture is a consolidation of standards, specifications, frameworks, and guidelines to provide Java capability on the server side for the enterprise. These standards and frameworks consist of classes and interfaces to be implemented by both service providers and developers. The EJB API is at the heart of the J2EE architecture. The other APIs are used as services to the EJB API. Many middleware vendors have been delivering implementations of the server-side APIs for the last few years.

A J2EE implementation can be obtained from many vendors today. The implementation of the J2EE specification is realized through a Java application server, a product that offers the infrastructure-base solutions to the enterprise needs. The most common application servers today are BEA's WebLogic Server, IBM's WebSphere, and the open source JBoss.

**Note**

J2EE offers enterprise applications a higher level of abstraction. Not only does it offer portability of server-side component-based applications, but it also offers built-in common services to support all aspects of an infrastructure.

**Tip**

The company Flashline provides an application server comparison matrix for an up-to-date look at the current and future releases of all application servers. You can access the comparison matrix at
http://www.flashline.com/components/appservermatrix.jsp.

Figure 1.1 depicts how Java benefits both the client and the server. The Java Virtual Machine (JVM) abstracts applications on the client from the underlying environment and operating systems. On the server side, the J2EE application server offers common infrastructure services to enterprise applications.

The J2EE technology addresses the following enterprise component types (which could certainly be expanded in future releases of its specification):

- Application clients. These are standalone client-side Java applications, which are hosted on client machines, and can use any relevant J2EE server-side functionality.

- Applets. These are tiny client-side components hosted by a Web browser, and are mainly convenient to use in initiating services and then displaying the results to the user.

FIGURE **1.1**

*Java on the client and
on the server.*

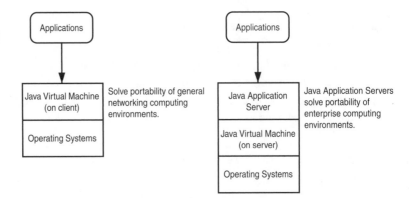

- Servlets and JavaServer Pages (JSP). Servlets are server-side Java components that process requests on behalf of the users. Servlets invoke arbitrary services and process the results through the generation of HTML output to be displayed on a Web browser. JSP is a convenient API for embedding Java within HTML pages, from which the JSP implementation generates servlets.

- Enterprise JavaBeans. EJBs are server-side components for encapsulating an application's business logic. An EJB can offer specific enterprise service either alone or in conjunction with other EJBs. EJBs can be packaged together to be available to deliver transactional and secure enterprise applications over the network to other J2EE applications or services.

These components span multiple tiers, and a full coverage of multitier architecture and the J2EE architecture will be discussed on Day 15, "Understanding J2EE Architecture." It's worth noting here that the introduction of browser-based clients, such as applets and form-based JSPs, has contributed to accessing application functionality that's hosted on a remote server through a unified form-based interaction. This shift from providing core corporate functionality at the PC and workstation level to the server via remote access has intensified the focus on server-side software.

Note    Web-based applications have contributed to increased portability from a user-interface point of view. You can access your application functionality and data using a unified client agent (Web browser).

## Comparing EJB with JavaBeans Components

The JavaBeans concept was developed to support reusable components in the Java programming environment. Because JavaBeans are used to build GUI components,

1

JavaBeans components might be thought of as a client-side technology. However, JavaBeans are not required to be visual and they can be used in server environments.

JavaBeans are Java classes that have the following characteristics:

- Support visual software development tools: The class must expose variables (called *properties*), methods, and events.
- Customizable: This includes support for default property editors or provision for unique custom routines. Customization permits developers to change the behavior of a bean without changing the source code.
- Support introspection: This refers to disclosing properties, methods, and events to other classes.
- Persistent: This permits a bean to be saved in its customized state.

> **Note**
> JavaBeans are not part of the J2EE architecture. They're being used for a while as a data bean to transfer data from EJB components to Web components. JavaBeans are also used in a few J2EE design patterns.

JavaBeans are used in the J2EE applications as either a view bean or as a data bean. The most common examples of a view beans are in designing a GUI. For example, a GUI button widget could be developed as a JavaBean. Development tools can use introspection to examine the button bean's properties such as label and color. You also can use these tools to set the bean's behavior to respond to the user event of clicking on the button. A data bean can be used as a data container to transfer data between a servlet and an EJB. To process a user request, a servlet invokes an EJB with the request, and business data is populated into a data bean to be displayed as a response to the user.

The only similarity between an EJB and a JavaBean is that both are components. An EJB does not have the same structure as a JavaBean. An EJB consists of two interfaces and two classes, whereas a JavaBean consists of only one Java class. A JavaBean is local to a single process and can't be shared by multiple users, while some types of EJB are shareable.

> **Note**
> It's important to understand that Enterprise JavaBeans are different from ordinary JavaBeans. Unfortunately, the use of the term *JavaBeans* causes much confusion. EJBs, servlets, and JSP components have more in common with each other than with JavaBeans.

# Why EJB?

The EJB architecture allows enterprise applications to be portable by running on a J2EE-compliant application server. An EJB application can be partitioned in a more usable, flexible, and expandable fashion. For example, new clients to access legacy systems can be easily built to meet user requirements. Moreover, the EJB architecture helps create a service-based model in which services are location-transparent components that can be delivered to their target clients. EJBs are highly reusable components, and represent the next step in the progression of Java technology for the development of application platforms capable of supporting mission-critical, component-based, enterprise applications. EJB components allow the development of business logic to be used across enterprise applications and to be portable across different platforms.

The EJB model is based on Java Remote Method Invocation (RMI) technology, which supports the separation of executable components across multiple tiers. This separation permits maximum implementation flexibility and high scalability. RMI allows access to remote components to appear as if it were local to the invoking client. Moreover, the introduction of infrastructure services provided by the container help to manage and offer such services to the deployed EJBs. These runtime services make it possible for the EJB developer to focus on writing robust and reliable applications.

The following summarizes the benefits gained by the enterprise and developers from using EJB technology:

- Simplicity: The EJB architecture simplifies the development of complex enterprise applications by providing built-in common services. This allows an EJB application developer to access and utilize these services, and results in a reduction of the overall development effort.

- Application portability: Portability can be accomplished by deploying an EJB application on any J2EE-compliant application server. Many Java application servers today implement all the services provided by J2EE-standard specifications.

- Component reusability: An EJB is a highly reusable building block. J2EE applications can be composed of custom-based EJBs, off-the-shelf EJBs, or both. In addition, the application business logic of a certain EJB can be reused through Java subclassing of the EJB class.

- Application partitioning: The separation of an application's business logic from its presentation allows ease of development and helps business programmers to work independently from Web page designers. Again, the separation of the application's business logic from its data helps manage each team independently. Any change of a component hosted in one tier does not affect the other tiers.

- Distributed applications: The EJB architecture helps create distributed applications, which can span multiple environments. Each subsystem can work independently of the others, but still can interact with one another to deliver enterprise services to the target users. A user transaction, for example, can be executed across multiple servers within a single context, and will be perceived by the user as a single unit of work.

- Application interoperability: The EJB architecture helps EJB components to access other components written in other component-based models, such as CORBA and .NET.

- Application integration: One of the main objectives of the EJB architecture is to allow the integration of new applications with existing applications, such as legacy systems. Today, Enterprise Application Integration (EAI) is a hot topic for the corporate world. The related J2EE APIs, such as the J2EE Connector Architecture (JCA) and the Java Message Service (JMS) specification, make it possible to integrate enterprise bean applications with various non-Java applications, such as ERP systems or mainframe applications, in a standard way.

- Availability of Java application servers: An enterprise has many J2EE-compliant application servers to choose from. Each application server provides J2EE services at a minimum, with the addition of other value-added services. A J2EE-compliant server can be selected to meet the customer's needs, which prevents vendor lock-in.

The most significant value provided by the EJB architecture is the separation of business logic programming from the challenge of integrating business logic with the complexities of enterprise-class server-side runtime environments. If the containers in which EJB components are deployed assume responsibility for managing runtime services such as persistence, transactions, and concurrent database access, bean developers are free to focus on developing software components that encapsulate business logic.

The EJB architecture is flexible enough to implement components such as the following:

- An object that represents a stateless service, which is modeled using a stateless session bean.

- An object that represents a stateless service whose invocation is asynchronous and driven by the arrival of enterprise messages. This is modeled by EJB with a message-driven bean.

- An object that represents a conversational session with a particular client. Such session objects automatically maintain their conversational state across multiple client-invoked methods. This is modeled by EJB with a stateful session bean.

- An entity object that represents a business object that can be shared among multiple clients, which is modeled with an entity bean.

- An entity object that represents a fine-grained persistent object that embodies the persistent state of a coarse-grained business object. This is also modeled with an entity bean.

EJB introduces the following flavors of beans (see Figure 1.2):

- Session beans, which are divided into stateless session beans and stateful session beans

- Entity beans, which are divided into bean-managed persistence and container-managed persistence

- Message-driven beans

Later in this book, you'll be provided with a more detailed explanation of each bean type. But for now, as a general rule, a session bean represents a user session (stateful or stateless), and implements the workflow of an arbitrary business process. An entity bean, on the other hand, represents a data row (record), in a database that can be accessed to satisfy user requests. Although both session and entity beans are synchronous in nature, message-driven beans are used to receive asynchronous messages, and process them accordingly.

**FIGURE 1.2**

*Flavors of EJBs.*

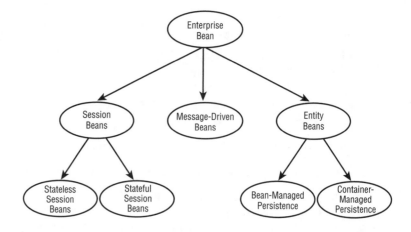

**EJB Types**

## EJB Design Goals

Since its inception by Sun Microsystems in 1997, the EJB architecture has had the following goals:

- To be the standard component-based architecture for building distributed object-oriented business applications in the Java programming language.

- To make it easy to write enterprise applications. Developers will not have to understand low-level transaction and state management details, multi-threading, connection pooling, and other complex low-level APIs.

- To enable an EJB to be developed once, and then deployed on multiple platforms without recompilation or source code modification.

- To address the development, deployment, and runtime aspects of an enterprise application's life cycle. Also, to define those contracts that enable tools from multiple vendors to develop and deploy components that can interoperate at runtime.

- To be compatible with existing server platforms and with other Java programming language APIs.

- To provide interoperability between EJBs and J2EE components as well as non-Java programming language applications.

- To be compatible with the CORBA protocols.

# Looking Inside an EJB

Generally, an EJB consists of two interfaces and one class. The interfaces are the home and component interfaces, and the class is the bean class. Figure 1.3 illustrates what's inside an EJB, and how a client interfaces with it.

The home interface lists the available methods for creating, removing, and finding EJBs in the container. The home object is the implementation of the home interface that's generated by the container at deployment time. At runtime, the home object will be used by the client in conjunction with a naming service to find the component and establish a connection to its component interface.

The component interface defines the business methods offered by a bean class. Note that the bean class does not directly implement this interface but, rather, uses an `EJBObject` class that mediates the client's calls to a bean object. The container provides the implementation of this interface, and the client (in conjunction with a naming service to find the component and establish a connection to its component interface) will use it. The component interface can be either remote or local, depending on the location of the EJB client with respect to the EJB. This distinction is made to avoid network traffic due to remote calls.

FIGURE 1.3

*Looking inside an EJB.*

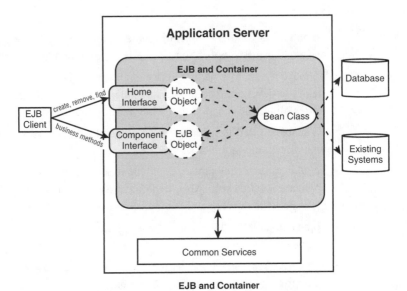

The bean class is the implementation of the business methods listed in the component interface. It's accessed by the client through the component interface; it's not accessed directly.

The primary key class (not shown in Figure 1.3) is used only for entity beans, and is provided only if the underlying data table has a segmented key.

The EJB client locates the EJB containers through the JNDI service, and it interfaces with the EJB through the objects generated by the container. After an EJB client finds a reference to an EJB home interface, it can retrieve the EJB component interface. It can then issue business methods on the EJB component interface, which the container in turn delegates to the bean itself. EJB clients can be servlets, JSPs, or Java application clients.

Additional interfaces defined in the EJB specification allow beans to interact with the transaction service and control persistence if they are designed to do so. For simplicity, these interfaces are not shown in Figure 1.3.

The EJB container hosts enterprise beans, providing life cycle management and services such as caching, persistence, and transaction management.

## EJB Server

The EJB server (also known as the J2EE application server) is the outermost container of the various elements that make up an EJB environment. The EJB server manages one or more EJB containers and provides required support services, such as transaction management, persistence, and client access. A JNDI-accessible naming space can be used by clients to locate the EJB. Figure 1.4 illustrates a J2EE application server.

The J2EE application server also provides operation resources, such as process and execution threads, memory, networking facilities, system resource management, connection pooling and caching, load balancing, fail-over, and so on to the containers and the elements within them. The EJB server can offer further vendor-specific features, such as optimized database access drivers, interfaces to backend systems, and CORBA accessibility.

**Note**

According to the current EJB specs, there's no clear distinction between an EJB container and an EJB server. An EJB server can run multiple containers of different types.

**FIGURE 1.4**

*J2EE application server.*

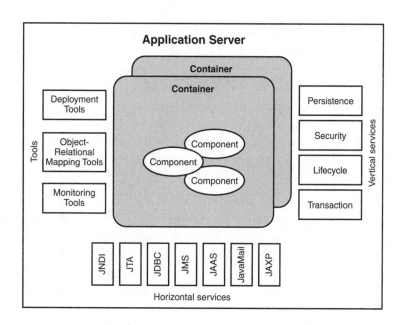

A number of J2EE application servers are available today, such as BEA's WebLogic Server, IBM's WebSphere, and the open source JBoss.

## EJB Containers

An EJB container is an abstract facility that manages instances of EJB components. The EJB specification defines the contractual agreement between the EJB and its container to provide both infrastructure and runtime services. Clients never access beans directly: Access is gained through container-generated methods, which in turn invoke the beans' methods. A container vendor may also provide additional services implemented in either the container or the server.

# Essential EJB Container Services

All EJB instances run within an EJB container. The container provides system-level services to its EJBs and controls their life cycle. Because the container handles most system-level issues, the EJB developer does not have to include this logic with the business methods of the enterprise bean. In general, J2EE containers provide three main types of services: common vertical services, common horizontal services, and common deployment tools (refer to Figure 1.4).

In the next few sections, we'll discuss the definition of these services. We'll discuss some of the services in detail in the following days.

## Common Vertical Services

The common vertical services are inherent services that are provided by the EJB container and are not specified explicitly by the J2EE architecture APIs. They contribute to the performance and runtime aspects of the EJBs and the services provided to them. EJB developers need not include any logic to manage these services. The following is a list of these common services:

- Life cycle management: The container creates and destroys enterprise bean instances based on client demand. This is done to maximize performance and minimize resource usage such as memory. In addition, a container may transparently multiplex a pool of instances to share among several clients.
- Security: The security services are designed to ensure that only authorized users access resources. J2EE specifies a simple role-based security model for enterprise beans and Web components. In addition, vendors typically provide integration with third-party security providers such as LDAP.

1

- Remote method invocation: The container transparently manages the communication between enterprise beans and other components. So, you do not have to worry about low-level communication issues such as initiating the connections, and marshalling/unmarshalling the method parameters. A bean developer simply writes the business methods as if they'll be invoked on a local platform.

- Transaction management: The transaction services relieve the enterprise bean developer from dealing with the complex issues of managing distributed transactions that span multiple enterprise beans and resources such as databases. The container ensures that updates to all the databases occur successfully; otherwise, it rolls back all aspects of the transaction.

- Persistence: Persistence services simplify the connection between the application and database tiers. Container-managed persistence of entity beans simplifies the coding effort for application developers.

- Passivation/activation: The mechanism that is used by the container to store an inactive enterprise bean to disk, and restore its state when the bean is invoked. The container uses this mechanism in support of both entity and stateful session beans. This allows the servicing of more active clients by dynamically freeing critical resources such as memory.

- Clustering: Supports replication of EJBs and services across multiple application server instances installed on the same machine or in different environments. Clustering involves load-balancing the requested services and EJBs among the replicated instances. It also supports fail-over—should one instance fail, the load will be picked up by another.

- Concurrency: Supports multithreading management. All components must be developed as single-threaded, and the container manages the concurrency and serialization access to the shared resources.

- Resource pooling: Supports the allocation of a pool of instances, and then assigns them to the requesting clients. When an instance is free, it goes back to the pool. This is applied for JDBC connections, stateless session beans, and entity beans.

## Common Horizontal Services

Common horizontal services are the services specified in the J2EE architecture. They're commonly known as J2EE APIs, and are provided by the EJB server to all the containers running on the server. Here's the standard list of the J2EE APIs:

- Java Naming and Directory Interface (JNDI): Provides Java-technology-enabled applications with a unified interface to multiple naming and directory services in the enterprise.

- Java Database Connectivity (JDBC): Provides access to virtually any tabular data source for J2EE applications.

- JavaServer Pages (JSP): Enables Web developers and designers to rapidly develop and easily maintain information-rich, dynamic Web pages that leverage existing business systems.

- Java Servlet: Provides Web developers with a simple, consistent mechanism for extending the functionality of a Web server and for accessing existing business systems.

- Java Transaction API (JTA): The standard Java interfaces between a transaction manager and the parties involved in a distributed transaction system: the resource manager, the application server, and the transactional applications.

- Java Message Service (JMS): A common API and provider framework that enables the development of portable, message-based enterprise applications.

- J2EE Connector Architecture (JCA): The key component for enterprise application integration in the Java platform. In addition to facilitating enterprise application integration, the JCA helps to integrate existing enterprise applications and information systems with Web services and applications.

- Java API for XML Processing (JAXP): Enables applications to parse and transform XML documents independent of a particular XML processing implementation.

- RMI over IIOP (RMI/IIOP): Delivers Common Object Request Broker Architecture (CORBA) distributed computing capabilities to the J2EE platform.

- Java Authentication and Authorization Security (JAAS): Enables services to authenticate and enforce access controls upon users.

- JavaMail: Provides a platform- and protocol-independent framework for building Java-technology-based mail and messaging applications.

- JavaBean Activation Framework (JAF): Standard services used by JavaMail to determine the type of an arbitrary piece of data, encapsulate access to it, discover the operations available on it, and instantiate the appropriate bean to perform said operation.

## Common Deployment Tools

These are the deployment services and tools provided by the EJB server; they are also available to the container. Here's a list of these services:

- Deployment tools: These are used to compile and deploy J2EE applications. They unpack the application package file and interpret all the runtime properties to install the EJB and other components of the applications.

- Object-relational mapping tools: A new generation of tools, such as TopLink, that map relational data in a database to its object counterpart properties in memory.

- Monitoring tools: These are used to monitor applications while they are running. Such tools are vital to checking the health of your application, and enable you to provide solutions when issues arise.

# Understanding EJB Roles

The EJB specification defines different roles in the development, assembly, and deployment of enterprise applications. The EJB architecture simplifies the development of complex business systems by dividing this process into six distinct roles, each with a specific task and objectives. These six roles address application development, infrastructure services, and deployment issues. Figure 1.5 illustrates the different roles involved in developing and deploying EJB components and applications.

**FIGURE 1.5**

*The EJB roles and their responsibilities.*

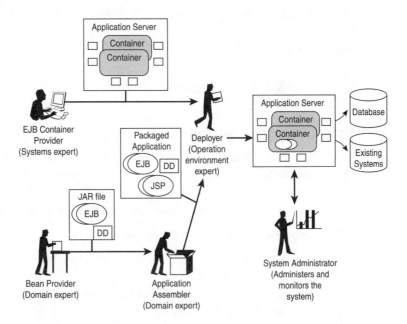

In the next few sections, we will discuss these roles in more detail.

## Application Development Roles

The task of building large component-based applications is typically divided into developing new components followed by the assembly of those components with existing reusable components. Some of the existing components could be components-off-the-shelf (COTS). The EJB architecture makes a clear distinction between the EJB developer (bean provider) and application assembler, even when, as in many cases, these two roles are combined and performed by one person or team.

### EJB Developer (Bean Provider)

The EJB developer is typically a domain expert with knowledge of the business rules, such as the financial or pharmaceutical industry. The EJB developer implements the business logic represented by the EJB's business methods, and defines the EJB's interfaces and deployment descriptor. The EJB developer defines a client view of an EJB. The client view is unaffected by the container and server in which the EJB is deployed. This ensures that both the EJBs and their clients can be deployed in multiple execution environments without code changes or recompilation.

### Application Assembler

The application assembler is a domain expert who assembles an application from many building blocks (such as EJBs, servlets, JSP, applets, and Java clients) to complete the application. An assembler is primarily concerned with the interfaces to EJBs (the home and remote interfaces) and with the EJB's deployment descriptor. The assembler is responsible for configuring both the security and transactional aspects of the EJBs in the deployment descriptor.

## Infrastructure Roles

The infrastructure roles address the container, application server, and deployment tools. These tasks are typically provided by a vendor with expertise in distributed infrastructures and services who implements a platform that facilitates the development of distributed applications and provides a runtime environment for these applications.

### EJB Container and Server Provider

This is an expert in distributed systems, transactions, and security who provides deployment tools for EJBs and runtime support for these deployed instances. A container is a runtime system for one or multiple EJBs that provide common services such as transaction, security, and lifecycle management. A container includes code and a tool that generates code particular to a particular enterprise bean. It also provides tools to deploy an EJB and a means for the container to monitor and manage the application.

## Deployment Roles

The EJB specification makes a clear distinction between the deployment roles because the cost of application deployment is much higher than application development.

## Deployer

The deployer (a new word for most dictionaries) adapts an application, composed of a number of EJBs, to a target operation environment by setting the properties and behaviors of the EJB. For example, the deployer sets properties in the deployment descriptor that determine transaction and security policies. The deployer also integrates the application with existing enterprise monitoring and management software. The deployer must be familiar with both the application operational requirements and the application server environment.

## System Administrator

The system administrator configures and administers the enterprise applications and infrastructure, including the application server, networking, databases, and Web servers. The administrator monitors the running application and takes appropriate actions in the event that the application behaves abnormally. Typically, an administrator uses enterprise monitoring and management tools that are connected to the application by the deployer through the hooks provided by the container.

**Note**

A traditional application programmer now becomes an EJB developer and, possibly, an application assembler. These tasks enable the programmer to focus on the business problem and business logic. The deployer defines and sets the deployment policies when installing the EJB. The complexity of implementing mechanisms for executing the deployment policies is delegated to the container provider. Although distributed applications remain complex, the application programmer's job becomes easier because much of the complexity is addressed by EJB server and container providers.

The various roles are not always performed by different people. In large applications, different individuals or teams might execute each of the roles. In some scenarios, such as small applications, a single person might perform multiple roles. During your 21-day journey of learning EJB, you'll execute multiple roles such as enterprise bean provider, application assembler, deployer, and system administrator. You'll use the EJB container and server provided by BEA's WebLogic Server or the JBoss organization's open source code application server, JBoss.

## Deployment Process

The efforts involved in developing and deploying an EJB require the following multi-step process:

1. Define all business methods in the component interface. This can be either a remote or local interface, depending on the design strategy you implement. A remote interface enables you to make your applications distributed in nature. A local interface allows access to the EJB from the same JVM.

2. Define the home interface of your EJB, which includes all the life-cycle management methods of the EJB, such as creation, location, and removal of the EJB.

3. Implement the business methods in the bean class. Other callback methods might be required for some types of EJB.

4. Create your EJB's deployment descriptor, which allows for the declaration of the EJB type, and transaction and security attributes.

5. Compile your EJB classes and interfaces.

6. Package the compiled EJB objects into a JAR file along with the deployment descriptor.

7. Deploy the EJB into the EJB container.

For all the examples in this book, we provide a script to carry out all the steps from 5–7. In addition, we provide a script to run the EJB client we develop in each day of our journey to learn EJB.

# The University Registration System

This book is based on a complete system that demonstrates the use of all EJBs and common services discussed during the 21 days of your study. The University Registration System (URS) is a hypothetical system (but it could be real), and will be our subject on Day 21. URS is a business-to-consumer (B2C) e-commerce application, which enables students to enroll and register in course offerings of a university. After a student is logged in, she is offered a catalog of the available courses to choose from. After she makes her decision, she's registered in her courses and an e-mail notification is sent to her.

Another part of the system is based on administering the university's Web site, where a JMS message will be sent to the registration office for enrollment approval. After the decision is made, a notification of acceptance in the courses will be sent to the student.

# Best Practices

You should consider using enterprise beans if you need to build business applications that are scalable, transactional, and secure. On the other hand, enterprise beans are not an appropriate choice for building systems applications, components on the client side of applications (such as GUI), and two-tier client/server systems.

# Summary

The EJB architecture simplifies enterprise applications by basing them on standardized, modular, reusable components. The EJB architecture provides a complete set of services to those components, and handles many details of application behavior automatically. By automating many of the time-consuming and difficult tasks of application development, J2EE technology enables enterprise developers to focus on adding value, which enhances business logic, rather than building infrastructure.

# Q&A

**Q  What is the EJB architecture and how is it related to the J2EE?**

**A**  The EJB architecture is a server-side component-based architecture that models business logic of enterprise architecture. EJB is at the heart of the J2EE architecture, which provides the big picture of enterprise applications. J2EE provides all infrastructure services to EJB, such as JDBC, JNDI, JMS, and JTA.

**Q  What are the main types of beans offered by EJB architecture?**

**A**  The EJB types are session beans, entity beans, and message-driven beans.

# Quiz

1. Which of the following is defined by EJB architecture?

    A. Transactional components

    B. Distributed object components

    C. Server-side components

    D. All of the above

2. What executes EJB components?

    A. An EJB container

    B. A Web server

    C. An application server

    D. A database server

3. The EJB's deployment descriptor is

    A. A format for accessing EJB at runtime

    B. An XML file used by EJB clients to learn about the EJB's settings, such as transaction, security, and access control

    C. An XML file for bundling EJBs for delivery to clients

    D. An XML file format used by the container to learn about the EJB's settings, such as transaction, security, and access control

## Quiz Answers

1. D
2. A
3. D

# Exercises

1. What are the goals of the EJB architecture?

3. What are the main differences between EJBs and JavaBeans?

4. What are the common services available to the EJB container?

5. What are all the roles and responsibilities in developing and deploying J2EE applications?

# DAY 2

# Understanding EJB Types and Interfaces

One challenge facing a new Enterprise JavaBeans (EJB) developer is to understand EJB types and interfaces, and how the EJB container performs its functionality behind the scenes.

Today, you'll learn all the different types of Enterprise JavaBeans and their interfaces. You'll look under the hood of the Enterprise JavaBean, which will help you get a better picture. You'll also learn the fundamentals of packaging and deploying Enterprise JavaBeans.

## Enterprise JavaBean Types

The EJB 2.0 specification defines three types of Enterprise JavaBeans: the session bean, the entity bean, and the message-driven bean. Figure 2.1 shows all three types of Enterprise JavaBeans.

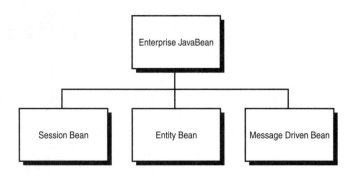

**FIGURE 2.1**

*Enterprise JavaBean types.*

Session beans contain business-processing logic. Entity beans contain data-processing logic. Message-driven beans allow clients to asynchronously invoke business logic. In the following sections, you'll learn about each type of Enterprise JavaBeans.

## Session Beans

As its name suggests, session beans implement a conversation between a client and the server side. Session beans execute a particular business task on behalf of a single client during a single session. They implement business logic such as workflow, algorithms, and business rules.

Session beans are analogous to interactive sessions. Just as an interactive session isn't shared among users, a session bean is not shared among clients. Like an interactive session, a session bean isn't persistent (that is, its data isn't saved to a database). Session beans are removed when the EJB container is shut down or crashes.

You can think of a session bean object as an extension of the client on the server side. It works for its client, sparing the client from complexity by executing business tasks inside the server.

Session beans typically contain business process logic and workflow, such as sending an email, looking up a stock price from a database, and implementing compression and encryption algorithms.

There are two types of session beans: stateless and stateful. A *stateless* session bean represents a conversation with the client without storing any state. On the other hand, a *stateful* session bean represents a conversational session with a particular client. Such a session object automatically maintains its conversational state, within its member variables, across multiple client-invoked methods.

In Day 3, "Understanding Session Beans," we'll scratch the surface of session beans and look into more details of both of their subtypes. In Day 5, "Developing Stateless Session

Beans," we'll take a hands-on approach to developing a stateless session bean. Day 6, "Developing Stateful Session Beans," is dedicated to stateful session beans with a practical example from our University Registration System.

## Entity Beans

If you've worked with databases, you're familiar with persistent data. The data in a database is persistent; that is, it exists even after the database server is shut down.

Entity beans are persistent objects. They typically represent business entities, such as customers, products, accounts, and orders. Typically, each entity bean has an underlying table in a relational database, and each instance of the bean corresponds to a row in that table.

The state of an entity bean is persistent, transactional, and shared among different clients. It hides complexity behind the bean and container common services. Because the clients might want to change the same data, it's important that entity beans work within transactions. Entity beans typically contain data-related logic, such as inserting, updating, and removing a customer record in the database.

Two types of entity beans are relevant to persistence: container-managed persistence (CMP) and bean-managed persistence (BMP). In a CMP entity bean, the EJB container manages the bean's persistence according to the data-object mapping in the deployment descriptor. Any change in the entity bean's state will be automatically saved to the database by the container. No code is required in the bean to reflect these changes or to manage the database connection. On the other hand, a BMP entity bean has to manage both the database connections and all the changes to the bean's state.

In Day 8, "Understanding Entity Beans," we'll scratch the surface of entity beans and look into more details of both of their subtypes. Day 10, "Developing Bean-Managed Persistence Entity Beans," is dedicated to developing a CMP entity bean. BMP is discussed with a hands-on example in Day 11, "Developing Container-Managed Persistence Entity Beans." We'll also look into the container-managed relationship of entity beans, a new enhancement to EJB 2.0.

## Message-Driven Beans

In synchronous communication, the client blocks until the server-side object completes processing. In asynchronous communication, the client sends its message and does not need to wait for the receiver to receive or process the message. Session and entity beans process messages synchronously.

Message-driven beans, on the other hand, are stateless components that are asynchronously invoked by the container as a result of the arrival of a Java Message Service (JMS) message. A message-driven bean receives a message from a JMS destination, such as a queue or topic, and performs business logic based on the message contents, such as logic to receive and process a client notification.

An example of a message-driven bean is when a shopper makes an online purchase order; an order bean could notify a credit verification bean. A credit verification bean could check the shopper's credit card in the background and send a notification message for approval. Because this notification is asynchronous, the shopper doesn't have to wait for the background processing to complete.

In Day 13, "Understanding JMS and Message-Driven Beans," we'll explore the JMS architecture and highlight the use of message-driven beans. Developing a message-driven bean will be the subject of Day 14, "Developing Messsage-Driven Beans," when we'll choose an example from our University Registration System.

# Enterprise JavaBean Under the Hood

Figure 2.2 shows the enterprise bean under the hood. The client looks up the EJB home object of the installed enterprise bean via Java Naming and Directory Interface (JNDI) services. The client then uses the home object to create an enterprise bean instance. However, the client isn't given a direct reference to the newly created enterprise bean instance. Instead the client receives reference to an EJB object, an object of the component interface. The client then calls the EJB object, which delegates calls to the enterprise bean instance.

**FIGURE 2.2**

*Enterprise JavaBean under the hood.*

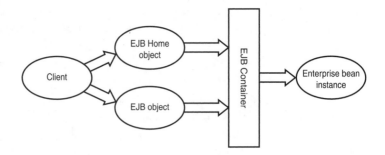

A client never directly creates or accesses instances of the Enterprise JavaBean instance. Only the container creates the Enterprise JavaBean instances, and registers its home interface into the JNDI service.

Because all method calls from a client to an Enterprise JavaBean are indirect (through the EJB home object or EJB object), the EJB container can control how and when calls to the Enterprise JavaBean class occur. This indirection allows the EJB container to provide functionality such as life cycle management, security, and transactions between Enterprise JavaBean class method calls.

**Caution** The material discussed in this section is applicable only to session and entity beans. Clients access session beans and entity beans through interfaces. However, clients don't access message-driven beans through interfaces. A message-driven bean contains only a bean class and doesn't have interfaces that define client access. The main access to a message-driven bean is through the JMS provider using a JMS destination (queue or topic).

2

# EJB Interfaces

Each session or entity bean has two interfaces (home and component) and a bean class. A message-driven bean has only a bean class and defines no interfaces.

In the following sections, you'll learn the fundamentals of the home interface, component interface, and bean class.

## The Home Interface

Clients use the home interface to create, remove, and find Enterprise JavaBean instances. You can think of the home object as the Enterprise JavaBean factory; you write the interface, the container tools generate the home class that corresponds to it, and the home interface defines the creation methods for the Enterprise JavaBean.

For example, the home interface EnrollmentCartHome is defined as follows:

```
public interface EnrollmentCartHome extends EJBHome {
  EnrollmentCart create() throws CreateException, RemoteException;
}
```

Therefore, to create an EnrollmentCart bean instance, you call the create() method with no parameters.

## The Component Interface

The component interface exposes an Enterprise JavaBean's business methods to a client. The client calls the methods defined in the component interface to invoke the business logic implemented by the bean. You can think of the component object as a proxy to the

Enterprise JavaBean instance. You write this interface. The container tools generate the component class corresponding to this interface.

The component interface `EnrollmentCart` is defined as follows:

```
public interface EnrollmentCart extends EJBObject {
   public void addCourses(String[] courseIds) throws RemoteException;
   public Collection getCourses() throws RemoteException;
   public void empty() throws RemoteException;
 }
```

Therefore, to add courses to the enrollment cart, you call the `addCourses` method on the component interface and pass the proper parameters.

**Note**

The component interface has only the methods that are callable by the client. The Enterprise JavaBean may have other methods in it, but if they aren't listed in the component interface, clients cannot call them.

When compiling both the home and component interfaces, a class may be generated for each interface by using a vendor-specific EJB compiler.

**Caution**

You cannot assume that any particular implementation of classes will be generated by the container tools. It is highly vendor-specific. The container might or might not generate a class corresponding to each interface.

## The Enterprise JavaBean Class

The Enterprise JavaBean class is where you implement the business logic defined in the component interface. Session beans implement the `javax.ejb.SessionBean` interface, whereas entity beans implement the `javax.ejb.EntityBean` interface, and message-driven beans implement the `javax.ejb.MessageDrivenBean` interface.

For example, the `EnrollmentCartEJB` session bean is implemented as follows:

```
public class EnrollmentCartEJB implements javax.ejb.SessionBean  {
     private SessionContext ctx;
     private HashSet cart;
     /*  callback methods  */
     public void setSessionContext(SessionContext ctx) {
        this.ctx = ctx;
     }
     public void ejbCreate() throws CreateException {
        cart = new HashSet();
     }
```

```
        public void ejbActivate() {}
        public void ejbPassivate() {}
        public void ejbRemove() {}

    /* Here you implement all business methods
        as defined in the component interface...
    */
    public void addCourses(String[] courseIds) {
        if (courseIds == null) {
            return;
        }
        for (int i = 0; i < courseIds.length ; i ++ ) {
            cart.add(courseIds[i]);
        }
    }
    public Collection getCourses() {
        return cart;
    }
    public void empty() {
        cart.clear();
    }
}
```

First, the EnrollmentCartBean implements all the business methods it advertised in its interfaces. Because it is a session bean, EnrollmentCartBean implements javax.ejb.SessionBean. The javax.ejb.SessionBean interface provides few *callback* methods to be implemented by any session bean. In the preceding example, the EnrollmentCartEJB implements the callback methods setSessionContext() and ejbCreate(). The EJB container calls these callback methods to perform some of its functionality and also to notify the instance of important events. Clients will never call such methods.

> **Note**
>
> The Enterprise JavaBean class implements neither the home interface nor the component interface. This is often a source of confusion for new developers.

> **Note**
>
> An Enterprise JavaBean may include other classes, or even other packages, but the classes listed earlier are the minimum.

# Java Remote Method Invocation over Internet Inter-ORB Protocol Technology

Java Remote Method Invocation (RMI) over CORBA's Internet Inter-Orb Protocol (IIOP) combines the best features of Java RMI technology with the best features of CORBA technology. The Enterprise JavaBeans architecture adopted RMI/IIOP as its standard communication protocol. Here we briefly discuss RMI and CORBA's IIOP and their benefits. This discussion will help you to better understand the next section, "Remote and Local Interfaces."

In the Java distributed object model, a *remote object* is one whose methods can be invoked from another Java Virtual Machine (JVM), potentially on a different host. An object of this type is described by one or more *remote interface*s, which are Java interfaces that declare the methods of the remote object. A remote interface must at least extend, either directly or indirectly, the interface `java.rmi.Remote`.

*Remote method invocation* is the action of invoking a method of a remote interface on a remote object. RMI uses a standard mechanism for communicating with remote objects: stubs and skeletons. A *stub* for a remote object acts as a client's local representative or proxy for the remote object. The caller invokes a method on the local stub, which is responsible for carrying out the method call on the remote object. In RMI, a stub for a remote object implements the same set of remote interfaces that the remote object implements.

When a stub's method is invoked, it does the following:

- Initiates a connection with the remote JVM containing the remote object.
- Marshals (writes and transmits) the parameters to the remote JVM.
- Waits for the result of the method invocation.
- Unmarshals (reads) the return value or exception returned.
- Returns the value to the caller.

The stub hides the serialization of parameters and the network-level communication in order to present a simple invocation mechanism to the caller.

In a remote JVM, each remote object may have a corresponding skeleton. A *skeleton* is responsible for dispatching the call to the actual remote object implementation. When a skeleton receives an incoming method invocation, it does the following:

- Unmarshals (reads) the parameters for the remote method.
- Invokes the method on the actual remote object implementation.
- Marshals (writes and transmits) the result (return value or exception) to the caller.

RMI provides the benefit of location transparency. Clients aren't aware of the location of the remote object. From the client's perspective, it makes no difference whether the remote object is in the same JVM as the client, in a different JVM but on the same machine as the client, or on a different machine from the client.

*CORBA (Common Object Request Broker Architecture)* is an industry-developed standard for communication among objects. It includes a communication protocol for interobject communication called *Internet inter-orb protocol*. A key feature of CORBA is its interoperability across platforms, languages, and vendors.

EJB adopted Java Remote Method Invocation (JRMI) over RMI/IIOP as the standard communication protocol. This allows maximum flexibility such as location transparency and interoperability. Other protocols are permitted, but IIOP is required for conformational EJB implementations to interoperate with one another.

You write the Enterprise JavaBean class itself, plus the bean's home and component interfaces. The client-side implementations of the home and component interfaces (the home class and component class) are generated by deployment tools, and handle the communication between the client and the EJB container. Clients can access an Enterprise JavaBean only through the bean's home and component interfaces.

# Remote and Local Interfaces

During design, you need to decide on the kind of interfaces you will provide to your enterprise bean. The interfaces you provide can be local or remote. Remote interfaces are RMI interfaces that are provided to allow the clients of a bean to be location-independent. EJB 2.0 introduced local interfaces to improve performance of client access to enterprise beans.

## Remote Interfaces

A remote client accesses a session bean or an entity bean through the bean's remote interface and remote home interface. The remote and remote home interfaces of the bean provide the *remote client view* of the EJB.

- The remote interface extends the `javax.ejb.EJBObject` interface. Container tools generate the corresponding EJB object implementing this interface.

- The remote home interface extends the `javax.ejb.EJBHome` interface. Container tools generate the corresponding EJB home object implementing this interface.

Figure 2.3 shows a remote client can run in the same or a different JVM as that of the Enterprise JavaBean. The remote client can be a Web component (such as a JSP or servlet) or another Enterprise JavaBean, or an application client.

**FIGURE 2.3**

*Remote clients.*

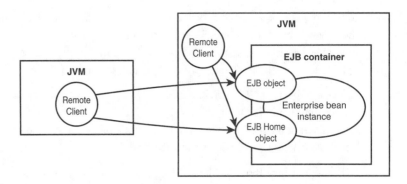

## Local Interfaces

Local interfaces were first introduced in the EJB 2.0 specification. Local interfaces improve the performance of client access to Enterprise JavaBeans that are located in the same JVM. This optimization is achieved by making a direct local process call instead of using remote invocation. Any RMI call is expensive compared to a local call. Local calls don't incur the communication overhead, such as connection initiation, and stubs and skeletons marshalling and unmarshalling the call parameters, that is associated with remote calls. Local calls are magnitude times faster compared to remote calls.

A local client accesses a session or entity bean through the bean's local interface and local home interface. A local client is located in the same JVM as the Enterprise JavaBean.

- The local interface extends the `javax.ejb.EJBLocalObject` interface. Container tools generate the corresponding EJB local object implementing this interface.

- The local home interface extends the `javax.ejb.EJBLocalHome` interface. Container tools generate the corresponding EJB local home object implementing this interface.

Figure 2.4 shows a local client must run in the same JVM as that of the Enterprise JavaBean. Unlike a remote client, a local client is not location-transparent. A local client can be a Web component (such as a JSP or servlet) or another Enterprise JavaBean.

**Note**

> If you provide remote interfaces, you get maximum flexibility through location transparency. Your clients can be located anywhere. If you provide local interfaces to your Enterprise JavaBean, you get maximum performance, but at the price of location transparency: Your clients must be located in the same JVM as the Enterprise JavaBean instance. On the other hand, with remote interfaces, you can improve the performance by distributing the components among different servers.

**Figure 2.4**

*Local clients.*

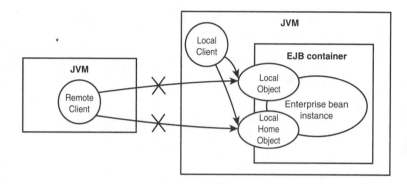

| Caution | The calling semantics of local interfaces are different from those of remote interfaces. Remote interfaces pass parameters using call-by-value semantics, whereas local interfaces use call-by-reference. For example, an Enterprise JavaBean could pass a large document to the client. With remote interfaces, the system would return a copy of the document to the client. On the other hand, with local interfaces, the client would get a reference to the bean's document. So, the client could potentially change the Enterprise JavaBean's state without the bean's knowledge. If this isn't acceptable, your Enterprise JavaBean must explicitly copy the data before returning to the client. |
|---|---|

# Deployment Descriptors

A *deployment descriptor* is an Extensible Markup Language (XML) document (with an .xml extension) that describes a component's deployment settings. Because deployment descriptor information is declarative, it can be changed without modifying the Enterprise JavaBean source code. For example, a deployment descriptor declares transaction attributes and security authorizations for an Enterprise JavaBean. You can create the deployment descriptors by hand or use vendor tools to generate them. At deployment time, the J2EE server reads the deployment descriptor and acts on the component accordingly. The following sections describe various deployment descriptors.

## Standard `ejb-jar.xml`

This file is the standard deployment descriptor as specified by Sun, and it must contain the Sun Microsystems–specific EJB document type definition (DTD).

The `ejb-jar.xml` describes the Enterprise JavaBean's deployment properties, such as its bean type and structure. The file also provides the EJB container with information about where it can find, and then load, the home interface, remote interface, and bean class. It declares its internal dependences and the application assembly information, which describes how the Enterprise JavaBean in the bundled ejb-jar file is assembled into an application deployment unit.

Here is a sample ejb-jar.xml file:

```
<?xml version="1.0"?>

<!DOCTYPE ejb-jar PUBLIC
'-//Sun Microsystems, Inc.//DTD Enterprise JavaBeans 2.0//EN'
'http://java.sun.com/dtd/ejb-jar_2_0.dtd'>

<ejb-jar>
  <enterprise-beans>
    <session>
      <ejb-name>EnrollmentCart</ejb-name>
      <home>EnrollmentCartHome</home>
      <remote>EnrollmentCart</remote>
      <ejb-class>EnrollmentCartEJB</ejb-class>
      <session-type>Stateful</session-type>
      ...
    </session>
  </enterprise-beans>
</ejb-jar>
```

The prolog contains the declaration and the DTD for the validation. The document root is the <ejb-jar> tag. The element <enterprise-beans> contains subelements to describe the bean deployment properties. The remote and home interfaces and the bean class name are described using their fully qualified names. The bean's subtype is declared as a stateful session bean.

**Note**  The Enterprise JavaBean type is differentiated by the interface implemented and by the subtype declaration in the deployment descriptor.

## Vendor-Specific Deployment Descriptor

In addition to standard ejb-jar.xml, an application typically requires a certain amount of additional environment-specific or vendor-specific binding information. In deploying an EJB to a specific application server, you might be required to have a vendor-specific deployment descriptor that provides information about how to map a package name to a JNDI name, and how to handle both security and persistence. For example, jboss.xml is specific to the JBoss server, and weblogic-ejb-jar.xml is specific to BEA WebLogic Server.

**Caution** | Vendor-specific deployment descriptors aren't standardized. They are different for different vendors. Also, they could potentially change for a given vendor.

# Packaging and Deploying Enterprise JavaBeans

The process of assembling components into modules, and modules into applications, is known as *packaging*. The Java ARchive (JAR) file format enables you to bundle multiple files into a single archive file. Enterprise beans use the JAR file format for packaging Enterprise JavaBeans in a generic and portable way.

The ejb-jar file is the standard format for packaging Enterprise JavaBeans. Figure 2.5 shows sample contents of an ejb-jar file. It contains deployment descriptor(s), one or more Enterprise bean classes, their home and component interfaces, and related files.

**FIGURE 2.5**

*Standard* ejb-jar *file.*

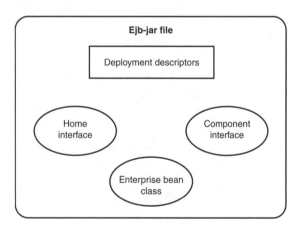

After you have packaged your Enterprise JavaBeans, you need to install and configure them in an EJB container for loading and execution. This is known as *deployment,* which makes the new functionality available as a service.

During deployment, you'll make several decisions, such as how clients find the components (naming, security, authorization), concurrency, data access (which component maps to which database objects, vendor/type of databases, JDBC drivers), which component lives where (partitioning), and which component participate in distributed transactions and which ones don't. Containers provide tools to help you with the deployment process.

# Enterprise JavaBean Restrictions

The EJB container provides functionality such as life cycle management, threading, security, and resource pooling. Enterprise bean instances may be distributed; that is, they may run in separate JVMs or on separate machines. To efficiently manage resources such as memory, the container can swap the instances from memory to disk.

To run properly, the container imposes certain restrictions on the components that live within. This ensures the proper functioning of the container and the Enterprise JavaBean's portability and scalability.

The following are some of the restrictions imposed on Enterprise JavaBeans:

- **Must not read/write static fields:** It's okay to use read-only static fields. It is better to declare the static fields as `final`. Static fields are shared among all instances of a particular class. Updating a static field works if all the instances are running in the same JVM, but it doesn't work if the instances are distributed in separate JVMs.

- **Must not use thread synchronization primitives to synchronize execution of multiple instances:** Thread synchronization works if all the instances are running in the same JVM, but doesn't work if the instances are distributed in separate JVMs.

- **Must not create or manage (start, stop, suspend, resume, change priority) threads:** The EJB container is responsible for creating and managing threads. Allowing the Enterprise JavaBean instances to create and manage threads interferes with the container functionality.

- **Must not read or write files and directories or access file descriptors:** Files, directories, and file descriptors are typically local resources to a machine, and can't be distributed across machines in a portable way. Also, access to the file system is a security hazard because the Enterprise JavaBean could potentially read and write the contents of sensitive files.

- **Must not listen or accept connections on a socket:** This isn't allowed because if an Enterprise JavaBean is listening on a socket, it can't be swapped to disk. It's okay for Enterprise JavaBeans to be network socket clients.

# Best Practices

You should consider using a session bean if only one client has access to the bean instance and the state of the bean is not persistent. An entity bean is best used if multiple clients can access the bean and the state of the bean is persistent. You should consider using a message-driven bean when you want to develop loosely coupled systems and process asynchronous messages.

Deciding on remote or local access depends on several factors. If your client runs on a different JVM or machine, you must provide remote access. For example, in large production systems, Web components might run on a different machine. On the other hand, entity beans with container-managed relationships (CMR) with other entity beans (discussed on Day 11) must provide local access. In other situations, when in doubt, prefer remote access. This gives you maximum flexibility to distribute the components across machines to meet a higher load.

**2**

# Summary

If today was your first exposure to EJB fundamentals, it probably seems theoretical and a bit overwhelming. Don't be alarmed. You'll be using these concepts for the rest of this book, and they will become familiar as you gain more experience using them.

Here is the summary of terms and concepts covered today.

A *session bean* executes a particular business task on behalf of a single client. An *entity bean* is a persistent business object. A *message-driven bean* allows clients to asynchronously invoke business logic.

Clients use the *home interface* to create, remove, and find Enterprise JavaBean instances. A client calls the methods defined in the *component interface* to invoke the business logic implemented by the Enterprise JavaBean.

The *remote home interface* is a location-transparent version of the home interface. Container tools generate the corresponding *EJB home object*. The *remote interface* is the location-transparent version of the component interface. Container tools generate the corresponding *EJB object* when implementing this interface.

The *local home interface* is a non-location-transparent, high-performance version of the home interface. Container tools generate the corresponding *EJB local home object* when implementing this interface. The *local interface* is a non-location-transparent, high-performance version of the component interface. Container tools generate the corresponding *EJB local object* when implementing this interface.

*Packaging* is the process of assembling components/modules into an application. *Deployment* is the process of installing and configuring the packaged components and applications in a container.

# Q&A

**Q  Can a client directly create an Enterprise JavaBean?**

**A**  No, a client never directly creates or accesses instances of the Enterprise JavaBean instance. Only the EJB container creates the Enterprise JavaBean instances. Remember that the container tools generate the home object. This allows the container to provide functionality such as life cycle management, security, transaction, concurrency, and other common services.

**Q  Can I write both local and remote interfaces for my Enterprise JavaBean?**

**A**  Yes, you can write both local and remote interfaces to your Enterprise JavaBean. This allows both remote and local clients to access your Enterprise JavaBean. Typically, only either local or remote interfaces are provided.

# Quiz

1. Which of the following Enterprise JavaBeans processes messages asynchronously?

    A. Stateless session bean

    B. Stateful session bean

    C. Entity bean

    D. Message-driven bean

2. Which one of the following can access the local client view of an Enterprise JavaBean?

    A. Servlet within the same JVM as the Enterprise JavaBean

    B. Servlet in a different JVM than the Enterprise JavaBean

    C. A non-EJB in a different JVM than the Enterprise JavaBean

    D. An EJB in a different JVM than the Enterprise JavaBean

3. Which one of the following isn't a programming restriction for an Enterprise JavaBean?

    A. Read/write static fields

    B. Start a new thread

    C. Open a socket client

    D. Listen on a socket

## Quiz Answers

1. D
2. A
3. C

# Exercises

1. Describe all the different types of Enterprise JavaBeans.
2. Describe the differences between a remote client and a local client.

2

# DAY 3

# Understanding Session Beans

Session beans were first introduced in March of 1998 when Sun Microsystems published the EJB 1.0 specification.

A session bean is one type of enterprise bean that resides in EJB container. Session beans model business processes. They provide a robust way for handling sessions in a J2EE application.

Today's road map:

- Learn the fundamentals of session beans, and their characteristics and types
- Learn how the concepts of instance pooling, activation, and passivation are applicable to session beans
- Learn session bean methods and examine their life cycle diagrams

# What Is Conversational State?

Client/server interaction typically involves multiple request/response roundtrips. A *session* is a single client's interaction with a server. The session state is client-specific data that is accumulated during the session. This session state is also known as *conversational state*.

The conversational state can be maintained in the client, the server, or split between them. For example, the contents of the temporary shopping cart can be maintained in the client side or in the server object's instance variables. The division of responsibility is based on factors such as performance, security, and so on.

The use of session beans to maintain client interactions is the standard method in any J2EE application. As their name implies, session beans were designed with this purpose in mind. Services such as security, concurrency, and transactions are provided to session beans by the container.

# What Are Session Beans?

A session bean implements a conversation between a client and the server side. Session beans execute a particular business task on behalf of a single client during a single session. They implement business logic such as workflow, algorithms, and business rules.

You can think of a session object as extension of client on the server side. It works for its client, sparing the client from complexity by executing business tasks inside the server.

For example, a session bean can send email, help in workflow management, and implement algorithms such as compression, encryption, and so on.

 **Note**

> Session bean clients can be from the EJB tier, as other session beans, from the Web tier, as servlets and taglibs, or they can be from the client tier as a J2EE client. The session bean by itself implements the business logic. The container provides functionality for remote access, security, concurrency, transactions, and so on.

# Session Bean Files

Like other enterprise beans, a session bean consists of the home interface, the component interface, the bean class, and the deployment descriptor.

- The home interface is either a remote home interface or local home interface. A remote home interface extends the `javax.ejb.EJBHome` interface, whereas a local home interface extends `javax.ejb.EJBLocalObject`. The home interface is used as the bean factory. The client uses the home interface to manage the life cycle of the session bean.

- The component interface is either a remote interface or a local interface. The remote interface extends the `javax.ejb.EJBObject` interface and the local interface extends the `javax.ejb.EJBLocalObject` interface. The component interface defines all the methods that are callable by the client.

- The bean class implements the `javax.ejb.SessionBean` interface. In addition, it implements all business methods listed in the remote interface.

- The deployment descriptors define the session bean type, transaction, security, and run-time properties.

# Characteristics of Session Beans

Session beans typically have the following characteristics:

- Represent a conversation between client and server.

- Execute on behalf of single client. They cannot be shared by more than one client at the same time. Also, they cannot be called by the same client using multiple threads.

- Can be both transaction-aware and use security.

- Do not directly represent data in a database. However, they can access and update data on behalf of the client.

- Are relatively short-lived. They are removed when the client removes them, or when the EJB container shuts down or crashes.

# Types of Session Beans

There are two types of session beans: stateless and stateful. Stateless session beans are business objects that hold conversations that span a single client-invoked method call. They do not maintain any conversational state associated with any client. Stateful session beans are business objects that hold conversations that span multiple client-invoked method calls. Stateful session beans provide an easy and robust way to handle conversational state.

## Stateless Session Beans

Stateless session beans do not maintain the conversational state associated with any client. The client is responsible for maintaining the conversational state, if any. The container could reuse the same instance to serve multiple clients. This makes perfect sense because the bean instance doesn't maintain any client specific state.

An example of stateless session bean is a stock quote component that returns the current price of a given stock symbol. Such a bean could look up the stock price from a database that is updated by a real-time feed. Another example is a stateless session bean that implements a compression algorithm. This bean accepts a plain text as a parameter and returns a compressed buffer.

The sample university registration application uses a stateless session bean to model a SignOn component to verify the user's login and password. It also allows new users to create a login and password in the system.

The remote interface SignOn is defined as follows:

```
public interface SignOn extends EJBObject {
  public void addUser(String username, String password)
    throws RemoteException;
  public boolean validateUser(String login, String password)
    throws InvalidLoginException, RemoteException;
}
```

This interface contains two business methods, addUser and validateUser, which are callable by the client.

The home interface SignOnHome is defined as follows:

```
public interface SignOnHome extends EJBHome {
  SignOn create()
    throws CreateException, RemoteException;
}
```

So, to create a bean instance, you call the create() method on the home interface. Notice that the create() method returns a remote interface instance (as opposed to the enterprise bean class).

The bean class SignOnEJB is defined as follows:

```
public class SignOnEJB implements SessionBean {
private SessionContext ctx;
/* --- callback methods --- */
/* container calls this method to set the associated session context */
public void setSessionContext(SessionContext c) {
    ctx = c;
}
```

```
/* container calls this method so that you can
   initialize your session bean instance
*/
public void ejbCreate() {}
/* container invokes this method before it
   ends the life of the session object.
*/
public void ejbRemove() {}
/* ejbActivate and ejbPassivate  are
   not used by stateless session beans
*/
public void ejbActivate() {}
public void ejbPassivate() {}
/* ---here you implement all business methods
  as defined in the component interface---
*/
public void addUser(String userName, String password)  {
  /* code to add a new user to the database */
}
public boolean validateUser(String userName, String password)
   throws InvalidLoginException {
  /* code to validate the user login and password from database */
}
}
```

**Caution**

> The create() method of a stateless session bean should not accept any parameters. Because a stateless session bean does not maintain any conversational state, you must make sure that none of the client-passed parameters are stored beyond the method call.

The deployment descriptor for the enterprise bean is specified as follows:

```
<session>
  <ejb-name>SignOnEJB</ejb-name>
  <home>SignOnHome</home>
  <remote>SignOn</remote>
  <ejb-class>SignOnEJB</ejb-class>
  <session-type>Stateless</session-type>
    ...
</session>
```

The session element declares a session bean and an ejb-name element within the session element, which defines the session bean's name (SignOnEJB). The session element also declares other things, such as the home interface (SignOnHome), remote interface (SignOn), and bean's class (SignOnEJB). The session-type element declares this is a stateless session bean (as opposed to a stateful session bean).

### Instance Pool

The creation and destruction of enterprise beans are expensive operations. To reduce this cost, the EJB container maintains an instance pool for each type of stateless session bean. At start up, the container creates instances as specified in the deployment descriptor of the stateless session bean. The EJB container may reuse the same instance to serve multiple client requests. This mechanism of multiplexing enhances the performance and response time of client interaction. Using a small number of instances in a predefined pool to satisfy a large number of clients has been proven to be a good practice for increasing performance and managing resources. The instance pool is also called the *caching policy*.

Instance pooling is applicable only to stateless session beans, not to stateful session beans.

Two or more different clients cannot share a stateless session bean instance concurrently. They can, however, reuse the same instance that comes from the instance pool.

## Stateful Session Beans

Stateful session beans maintain the state associated with a client. Stateful session bean fields contain a conversational state on behalf of the session object's client. This state describes the conversation represented by a specific client/session object pair. The conversational state is preserved across method invocations and transactions.

Unlike a stateless session bean, a stateful session object has a unique identity that is assigned by the EJB container at create time.

An example of a stateful session bean is a shopping cart that represents the collection of products selected by a particular customer for purchase during a session. The shopping cart should not be shared because it represents a particular interaction with a particular customer and is alive only for the customer's session. Also, the shopping cart is not saved into the database unless the customer is ready to place an order. Another example of a stateful session object is a trader session component that allows a trader to interactively add, remove, and place trades.

Stateful session beans are useful in workflow management that requires the bean to maintain client data over different method invocations. Behind the scenes, the bean manages the workflow of several enterprise beans. The bean mediates between the client and the other components of the application, presenting a simplified view to the client.

The sample university registration application uses stateful session beans to model enrollment cart component. An enrollment cart is similar to a shopping cart. It represents the collection of courses selected by a particular student for purchase during a session.

The remote interface `EnrollmentCart` is defined as follows:

```
public interface EnrollmentCart extends EJBObject {
   public void addCourses(String[] courseIds) throws RemoteException;
   public Collection getCourses() throws RemoteException;
   public void empty() throws RemoteException;
}
```

The business methods callable by clients are defined in this interface. For example, the `EnrollmentCart` interface defines three business methods: `addCourses` (to add courses to the cart), `getCourses` (to retrieve the courses in the cart), and `empty` (to empty the enrollment cart).

The home interface `EnrollmentCartHome` is defined as follows:

```
public interface EnrollmentCartHome extends EJBHome {
  EnrollmentCart create() throws CreateException, RemoteException;
}
```

So, to create a enrollment cart instance, the client calls the `create()` method on the home interface. The `create()` method returns a remote interface instance (as opposed to the enterprise bean class).

The bean class `EnrollmentCartEJB` is defined as follows:

```
public class EnrollmentCartEJB implements SessionBean  {
/* ctx and cart constitute the conversational state */
    private SessionContext ctx;
    private HashSet cart;
/* --- callback methods  */
/* container calls this method to set the associated session context */
    public void setSessionContext(SessionContext c) {
       ctx = c;
    }
    public void ejbCreate() throws CreateException {
       cart = new HashSet();
    }
    /* This method is called when the instance
```

```
        is activated from its "passive" state.
   */
   public void ejbActivate() {}
   /*
     This method is called when the container intends to
     passivate the bean instance.
   */
   public void ejbPassivate() {}
   /* Container invokes this method before it
      ends the life of the session object.
   */
   public void ejbRemove() {}
   /* ...here you implement all business methods
      as defined in the component interface...
   */
   public void addCourses(String[] courseIds) {
      if ( courseIds == null) {
         return;
      }
      for ( int i = 0; i < courseIds.length ; i ++ ) {
         cart.add(courseIds[i]);
      }
   }
   public Collection getCourses() {
      return cart;
   }
   public void empty() {
      cart.clear();
   }
}
```

The `EnrollmentCartEJB` implements all the methods it defined in the `EnrollmentCart` interface. In addition, it implements callback methods to be implemented by any session bean.

The deployment descriptor for the enrollment cart session bean is specified as follows:

```
<session>
  <ejb-name>EnrollmentCartEJB</ejb-name>
  <home>EnrollmentCartHome</home>
  <remote>EnrollmentCart</remote>
  <ejb-class>EnrollmentCartEJB</ejb-class>
  <session-type>Stateful</session-type>
  ...
</session>
```

The deployment descriptor for a stateful session bean is similar to that of a stateless session bean except for the element `session-type` (which is stateful in this case).

## Passivation and Activation

The EJB container creates a separate stateful bean instance for each new connected client. In large e-commerce applications, the number of clients connected concurrently to a web site can be in the thousands. This can have an adverse effect on performance when resources are used up. Passivation and activation are mechanisms that are provided by the EJB container to manage these valuable resources, such as memory, in order to reduce the number of stateful session bean instances required to service all concurrent clients.

Passivation is the mechanism by which the EJB container stores the bean's state into a back store, such as the file system or a database. The container starts passivation as soon as the number of allocated stateful session beans exceeds a certain threshold.

The passivation process serializes all non-transient member variables to a persistent store. After serializing the enterprise bean state, the EJB container calls the `ejbPassivate()` method on the instance. In this method, you would close any resources, such as sockets, JDBC connections that you are holding.

Activation, on the other hand, is the process of restoring the bean state from the back store. The EJB container activates a passivated instance when the bean's client decides to continue interactions with the bean instance. After restoring the bean's state, the EJB container calls the `ejbActivate()` method on the instance. In this method, you would open any resources you need to service the client, such as sockets, JDBC connections, and so on.

For example, you can specify the threshold (maximum number of beans in the cache) in the deployment descriptor for the WebLogic server as follows:

```
<stateful-session-cache>
   <max-beans-in-cache>1000</max-beans-in-cache>
</stateful-session-cache>
```

As new concurrent clients request the bean's services, WebLogic creates new instances of the bean. When the 1001st client requests the bean's services, the server passivates some of the idle beans (perhaps using an LRU [Least Recently Used] algorithm).

 **Caution**   Passivation and activation are applicable only to stateful session beans and not to stateless session beans.

# Session Bean Methods

Table 3.1 provides summary of session bean methods.

**TABLE 3.1**   Summary of Session Bean Methods

| Method | Purpose | What You Need to Do |
|---|---|---|
| `setSessionContext` `(SessionContext)` | The EJB container calls this method to set the associated session context. | You store the reference to the session context in an instance variable, if you need to query it later. The session context provides access to runtime session context such as identifying the caller, access or change current transaction state, and so on. |
| `ejbCreate<method>(...)` | The container calls this method so that you can initialize your session bean instance. A client creates a stateful instance using the create methods defined in the session bean's home interface. The container calls the corresponding `ejbCreate` method. | You initialize the bean here.<br><br>Each stateful session bean class must have at least one `ejbCreate<method>(...)` and each one can take different arguments.<br><br>A stateless session bean can have only one `ejbCreate` method, with no parameters. |
| Business Methods | The session bean's component interface defines the business methods callable by a client. The container delegates an invocation of a business method to the matching business method that is implemented in the session bean class. | You write business logic in these methods. |

| Method | Purpose | What You Need to Do |
|---|---|---|
| ejbActivate() | This method is called when the instance is activated from its passive state. | For stateful session bean, open resources, if any. For example, open sockets, JDBC connections, and so on. For a stateless session bean, this is empty because the container never activates the bean instance. |
| ejbPassivate() | This method is called when the container intends to passivate the bean instance. | For a stateful session bean, close resources, if any. For example, close sockets, JDBC connections, and so on. For a stateless session bean, this is empty because the container never passivates the bean instance. |
| ejbRemove() | A container invokes this method before it ends the life of the session object. This happens as a result of a client's invoking a remove operation, or when a container decides to terminate the session object after a timeout. | Close resources, if any, and assign corresponding instance fields to null. For example, close sockets, JDBC connections, and so on.For a stateless session bean, this is empty because the container never passivates the bean instance. |

**3**

# Life Cycle of Session Beans

Stateful and stateless session beans have different life cycles. The stages from the time they are instantiated, ready to be used, and then destroyed vary from one type to another. We will examine the life cycle of each stateless and stateful session bean in the following sections.

## Stateless Session Bean Life Cycle

Figure 3.1 shows the life cycle of a stateless session bean instance. If you are not familiar with state diagrams, we recommend that you read Appendix D, "Introduction to UML Notation," before you read this section.

**FIGURE 3.1**

*Stateless session bean
life cycle.*

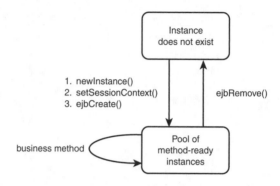

Life Cycle of a Stateless Bean instance

The following steps describe the life cycle of a stateless session bean instance:

- The bean instance's life cycle starts when the container decides to instantiate a bean instance. This decision is based on the caching policy and client demand. For example, if more clients want the session bean services, the container instantiates more beans. The container allows you to specify the caching policy in a vendor-specific deployment descriptor.

- The container instantiates the bean using the newInstance method and then calls the methods setSessionContext and ejbCreate. The container also sets the transaction context and security attributes (as set in the deployment descriptor). Now the bean is ready to serve any client.

- The container calls a business method on the instance, based on the client call. Note that container could use the same instance to serve multiple clients.

- The container decides to remove the bean instance. This could be because the container wants to reduce the number of instances in the method-ready pool. This is based on the caching policy and reduced demand.

- Container calls the ejbRemove() method of the bean instance.

## Life Cycle of a Stateful Session Bean

Figure 3.2 shows the life cycle of a stateful session bean instance.

The following steps describe the lifecycle of a stateful session bean instance:

- The bean instance's life cycle starts when a client invokes create<method>(...) on the session bean's home interface. The container instantiates a new session bean using newInstance() and then calls the setSessionContext method, followed by ejbCreate<method>(...).

**FIGURE 3.2**

*Stateful session bean life cycle.*

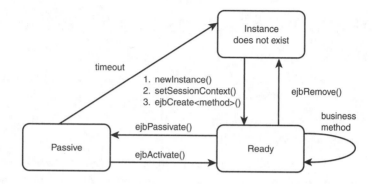

Life Cycle of a Stateful Session Bean

- The instance is now ready to serve the client's business methods.

- The container decides to evict your instance from memory. This decision is based on the container's caching policy and reduced demand. The container invokes the `ejbPassivate()` method on the instance and swaps it out to secondary storage.

- If a client invokes a session object whose session bean instance has been passivated, the container will activate the instance. To activate the session bean instance, the container restores the instance's state from secondary storage and issues `ejbActivate()` method on it. The session bean instance is again ready for client methods.

- When the client calls `remove` on the home or component interface to remove the session object, the container issues `ejbRemove()` on the bean instance. This ends the lives of the session bean instance and the associated session object. Note that a container can also invoke the `ejbRemove()` method on the instance without a client call to remove the session object after the lifetime of the EJB object has expired.

**Note**

You cannot rely on the container calling the `ejbRemove()` method. The container might not call `ejbRemove()` in the following scenarios: a) A timeout due to client inactivity while the instance is in the passive state; b) A shutdown or crash of the container; c) A system exception thrown from the instance's method. If your instance frees up resources in the `ejbRemove()` method, those resources are not freed in the preceding scenarios.

You should provide some mechanism to periodically clean up the unreleased resources. For example, if a shopping cart component is implemented as a session bean, and the session bean temporarily stores the shopping cart content in a database, the application should provide a program that runs periodically and removes abandoned shopping carts from the database.

# Comparing Stateless and Stateful Session Beans

Stateless session beans do not maintain state associated with any client. Each stateless session bean can server multiple clients.

Stateful session beans maintain the state associated with a client. Each stateful session bean serves exactly one client.

Stateless session beans are intended to be simple and lightweight; that is, they are easy to develop with low runtime resource requirements on the server. If required, any state is maintained by the client, and thereby makes the server highly scalable. Because no state is maintained in this enterprise bean type, stateless session beans aren't tied to any specific client. Therefore, any available instance of a stateless session bean can be used to service another client.

The container creates an implicit identity for a stateful session bean to manage its passivation and activation phases. On the other hand, the container doesn't create any identity for a stateless session bean.

The number of stateful session beans is equal to the number of active clients, whereas a small number of stateless session beans can be used to satisfy a large number of clients.

Stateful session beans provide easy and transparent state management on the server side. Because state is maintained in this enterprise bean type, the application server manages client-bean pairs. In other words, each instance of a given enterprise bean is created on behalf of a client, and is intended to be a private resource to that client (although it could be shared across clients using the enterprise bean instance's handle). In essence, a stateful session bean is a logical extension of the client, except that some of the client's load is distributed between itself and the enterprise bean on the server. Any conversational state-related data in the object's variables doesn't survive a server shutdown or crash, although a vendor could provide an enhanced implementation to make shutdowns and crashes transparent to the client by maintaining the enterprise bean's state.

# Best Practices

Stateless beans offer better performance than stateful beans. Activation and passivation are expensive operations. The EJB container might occasionally write a stateful session bean to secondary storage. However, stateless session beans are never written to secondary storage. To support the same number of clients, an application typically requires fewer stateless session beans than stateful session beans. Whenever possible, choose stateless session beans instead of stateful session beans.

A client should explicitly remove a stateful session bean by calling the `remove()` method of the component interface. Otherwise, the container keeps the stateful bean until it times out. This wastes resources such as memory, secondary storage, and so on.

A client should be prepared to re-create a new session object if it loses the one it is using. The client could lose the session bean because the container may terminate a session bean instance's life after a specified timeout or as a result of an EJB shutdown or crash.

Stateless session beans are ideal components for clustering because they do not maintain state. This provides high-availability to applications designed with stateless session beans. Stateful session beans can be clustered with more effort and design considerations.

**3**

## Summary

Today you learned the fundamentals of session beans. Session beans execute a particular business task on behalf of a single client during a single session. There are two types of session beans: stateless and stateful. Stateless session beans do not maintain the conversational state associated with any client. Stateful session beans maintain the conversational state associated with a client.

The EJB container maintains an instance pool for each type of stateless session bean. The EJB container may reuse the same instance to serve multiple client requests.

Passivation and activation are mechanisms that are provided by the EJB container to manage the valuable resources in order to reduce the number of stateful session bean instances required to service all concurrent clients. Passivation is the mechanism by which the EJB container stores the bean's state into a back store. Activation is the process of restoring the bean's state from the back store.

## Q&A

**Q Can a stateless session bean maintain state?**

**A** Yes. A stateless session beans can contain non-client specific state across client-invoked methods. For example, states such as socket connection, database connections, reference to an `EJBObject`, and so on can be maintained. However, they cannot have state specific to any client across client-invoked methods.

**Q** **In which tier should client state be maintained?**

**A** In a typical transactional J2EE application, client state should be maintained in the EJB tier. A stateful session bean is used to manage workflow and maintain state during client interactions.

**Q** **How does the container recognize the session bean type?**

**A** The EJB container recognizes the session bean type from the bean's deployment descriptor(`ejb-jar.xml`).

# Quiz

1. Which of the following is true for a session bean?

    A. It performs a task for a client

    B. It performs a task for multiple clients

    C. It represents shared data in a database

    D. It survives an EJB server crash

2. Which of the following methods is invalid for a stateless session bean?

    A. `ejbCreate()`

    B. `ejbCreate(...)`

    C. `ejbRemove()`

    D. `setSessionContext()`

3. Which of the following is first called by the container on a stateless session bean?

    A. `ejbCreate();`

    B. `newInstance();`

    C. `ejbActivate();`

    D. `setSessionContext()`

## Quiz Answers

1. A

2. B

3. B

# Exercises

1. What are the types of session beans?

2. Which type of session bean can use instance pooling? Why?

# DAY 4

# Using JNDI for Naming Services and Components

In today's lesson, you will learn about JNDI (Java Naming and Directory Interface), one of the commonly used services in any J2EE component-based application. JNDI is a standard interface to naming and directory services for enterprise applications. JNDI also can be used to access heterogeneous naming and directory services from the same application by using the same API. The following sections will explore the concepts of both naming and directory services. Then you will start to learn about the JNDI API and its interfaces and classes to access those services. We will also shed light on how JNDI can be used to look up resources and components as the foundation for other J2EE APIs.

Developers write J2EE components that use JNDI to locate both administrative and declarative objects. In the following days, JNDI will be used in detail with respect to each J2EE service. However, in today's lesson, an understanding of the concepts of JNDI is fundamental to Enterprise JavaBean (EJB) enterprise applications. Clients use the JNDI API to locate EJB components (Days 6, 8,

10, and 11), Java Message Service (JMS) queues and topics (Day 13), and Java Database Connectivity (JDBC) DataSources (Day 9).

- Learn the concepts of naming services
- Learn the concepts of directory services
- Explore the JNDI architecture
- Learn the JNDI API classes and interfaces
- Study the JNDI context and its operations
- Explore how to use the JNDI to support other J2EE services

Before you start, you must download and install an application server, either WebLogic Server or JBoss Server. Appendix A, "WebLogic Application Server 7.0," explains how to install WebLogic Server. Appendix B, "JBoss Application Server 3.0," contains the instructions for installing the JBoss Server.

# Naming Services

Generally, components in distributed systems must find one another to work together. Naming is one of the common services of any distributed system. The names of objects and components are added and stored in the naming service (also called the *namespace*), and can then be located later by the clients of the system.

It's easier for humans to remember the name www.samspublishing.com than the IP address 165.193.123.117. Naming also adds a level of indirection, where the associated IP can be changed without changing the name. The process of associating an object with a name is called *binding*. An example of a pervasive naming service is DNS (Domain Naming Service), which is used to refer to a host by its name instead of its numeric IP address. COS (Common Object Services) is another naming service used for CORBA (Common Object Request Broker Architecture) applications to register CORBA objects. NDS (Novell Directory Services) is another product used as a naming service to store user and group information for authentication purposes.

In each system, names are organized in a tree-like fashion, delimited with a special character, and follow a special syntax or naming convention (see Figure 4.1). As an example, a DNS name is read from right to left, and is delimited by a dot (.). Therefore, the fully qualified name www.samspublishing.com starts at the root com, followed by samspublishing, and then www.

In the Windows and DOS file systems file names are read from left to right, starting from the root directory and delimits its segments with a backslash "\". For example, the file myfile.doc, located in the directory c:\projects can be written as c:\projects\myfile.doc.

LDAP (Lightweight Directory Access Protocol) has a different naming convention, in which a name is read from right to left, and uses the comma "," as a delimiter. For example, the LDAP name cn=Lillian Ghaly, o=Diamond, c=US, starts with c=US, followed by o=Diamond, and ends with cn=Lillian Ghaly.

**FIGURE 4.1**

*Some naming conventions.*

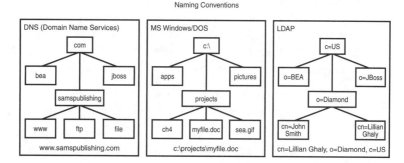

Naming Conventions

A name is used with a naming system to locate objects. A naming system is simply a collection of objects with unique names. To look up an object in a naming system, you provide a name to the naming system, and the naming system returns the stored object with that name.

A composite name is a sequence of names that spans multiple namespaces. An example of a composite name is www.samspublishing.com:\books\styejb.doc, which spans the DNS and the Windows file system namespaces. The name components of the composite name are host (www.samspublishing.com), directory (books), and file (styejb.doc).

# Directory Services

A directory service is a hierarchical database—a special type of database that stores objects for fast retrievals, and has infrequent insertions, deletions, and updates. The quick access of a directory service is achieved by different techniques of indexing, caching, and disk access. Most directory services include naming services as well. An example of a directory service is the yellow pages of your phone book. LDAP is the most popular directory protocol and is used as a standard network directory service. Active Directory is another directory service that is commonly used for Windows applications.

A directory service provides a way to manage the storage and distribution of shared information. Such information can range from usernames, passwords, email addresses, and phone numbers to the IP addresses, computers, and printers to the configuration information for a group of applications or servers. Each entry in the directory service has attributes associated with it. An attribute consists of a name as an identifier and one or more values. The attributes describe the entry, and the exact set of attributes depends on the type of the entry.

# What Is JNDI?

JNDI is a unified Java API designed to standardized access to a variety of naming and directory services. This abstract mechanism is what makes J2EE an attractive enterprise architecture for Internet and intranet applications. Applications are written in a standard way to use the JNDI API, which transparently calls the underlying naming or directory service. A JNDI-compliant service must implement part of the JNDI API. Here is a brief description of the two parts that make up the JNDI architecture:

- An application-level programming interface (API). APIs are used by the application components to access naming and directory services.
- A service provider interface (SPI). This part of the API is used to plug in a provider of a naming and directory service to the J2EE platform.

Figure 4.2 illustrates these APIs.

**FIGURE 4.2**

*JNDI architecture.*

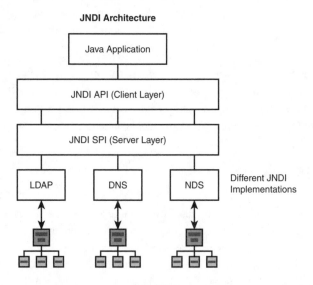

The JNDI model defines a hierarchical namespace in which you name objects. Each object in the namespace may have attributes that can be used to search for the object.

 **Note**    It's important to remember that JNDI is an interface or an API, and not an implementation, to abstract the access layer to naming and directory service providers.

Naming and directory services are intimate partners. In fact, most existing products provide both sets of functionality. Naming services provide name-to-object mapping, and directory services provide information about the objects and tools for searching for them.

As part of the common J2EE services, JNDI enables seamless connectivity to heterogeneous enterprise naming and directory services. Developers can build powerful and portable directory-enabled applications using the JNDI standard.

 **Note**

> JNDI naming and directory services are best used in maintaining small amounts of stable data that is accessible to all servers.

# JNDI API

The main JNDI API package is the `javax.naming` package, which contains one key class, `InitialContext`, and two key interfaces, `Context` and `Name`.

In using JNDI, a client first establishes a connection to the JNDI service (sometimes called the JNDI *tree*). After the client is connected, a context is created to facilitate the access to system components and resources. Context is a fundamental concept in the JNDI model. A *context* is a set of name-to-object bindings within a naming service that all share the same naming convention.

All naming operations in JNDI are performed within a context. Therefore, establishing a context is the initial step prior to any operation. The `javax.naming.InitialContext` class implements the `javax.naming.Context` interface. Clients use this class to establish a connection, and create a `Context` object as a result:

```
Context ctx = new InitialContext();
```

Some naming services provide a subcontext, which is similar to a subdirectory in a file system. The tree-like structure of JNDI is a natural to support subcontexts. The `Context` class also provides methods for creating and destroying subcontexts.

# Context Operations

After a client connects to the JNDI service and obtains a JNDI context using `InitialContext()`, it can apply any of the interface methods. The main operations of the `javax.naming.Context` interface are the use of `bind()` to add an entry, `rebind()` to replace an entry name, `lookup()` to find or locate an object, and `unbind()` to delete an entry. Figure 4.3 illustrates these operations. Logically, the server is the application that performs the binding, unbinding, and rebinding operations. Clients perform the lookup of objects by providing the name.

4

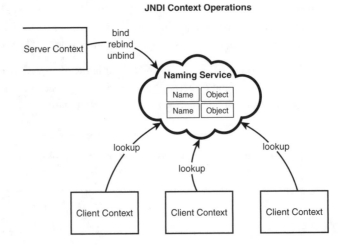

**FIGURE 4.3**

*JNDI context operations.*

The next sections give more details about the Context operations.

## Add an Entry—bind()

Servers add an object or a component into the JNDI tree by binding its name to its location or reference. Here is a scenario of binding a new object to its name. First, a Context object must be obtained by using

```
Context ctx = new InitialContext();
```

When InitialContext() is used with no parameters, the application is connected to the default JNDI service provider. This can be set in the configuration files as explained later today in the section "Selecting a JNDI Provider." Using no parameters also indicates the use of the default user or anonymous user. For a secure system, only certain components or resources must be authenticated first. The section "Using JNDI in User Authentication" later today gives an example of how to connect with a specific user.

Now, you can add a new name by using an example of binding a new object as implemented as follows:

```
String name = "mary";
String email = "mary@samspublishing.com"
ctx.bind(name, email);
```

If the name "mary" already exists, the exception NameAlreadyBoundException will be thrown.

Applications and services can use JNDI service in different ways to store and look up objects. For example, an application might store a copy of the object itself, a reference to an object, or the attributes of the object. Objects that must be remotely accessed (through the use of Remote Method Invocation or RMI) must be in a serialized form (that is, implement the `java.io.Serializable` interface) that contains the object's serializable objects that can be marshalled and unmarshalled between remote servers.

> **Note**
>
> RMI is a protocol that enables an object on one JVM (Java Virtual Machine) to invoke methods on another object in different JVM. Any object whose methods can be invoked in this way must implement the `java.rmi.Remote` interface.
>
> When such an object is invoked, its arguments are marshalled (converted to a bit stream) and sent from the local JVM to the remote one, where the arguments are unmarshalled and used. When the method terminates, the results are marshalled from the remote machine and sent to the caller's virtual machine.

## Delete an Entry—`unbind()`

Applications can also delete entries by using `unbind()` of an object from the JNDI service, provided that a context is already obtained. For example, the line

```
ctx.unbind("mary");
```

will remove the binding established in the previous section.

## Find an Entry—`lookup()`

One of the most common operations of JNDI is the `lookup()` method, which is used to locate or find an object. Provided that a context is already obtained, here is an example of looking up an object:

```
String str = (String) ctx.lookup("mary");
```

The `lookup()` operation returns an `java.lang.Object`, which must be cast to the required object's class. In the previous example, `lookup` is cast to `String`, and the value of `str` will be "mary@samspublishing.com". If the name is not found, the exception `javax.naming.NamingException` will be thrown.

To look up an object in the JNDI service, the name must be provided as a parameter to the `lookup()` operation. The returned object is cast to the known object class. Now any operation can be performed on that object. The following example illustrates the power of the naming services as a method of dynamically binding a name to the real object:

```
try {
    // Connect to JNDI and create the initial context
```

4

```
    Context ctx = new InitialContext();
    // Perform lookup and cast to target class
    File f = (File) ctx.lookup("myfile.txt");
    f.open();
    // ...do something with the file...
    f.close();
    // Close the context when we're done
    ctx.close();
} catch (NamingException e) {
    System.out.println("Lookup failed: " + e);
}
```

Table 4.1 summarizes the JNDI operations that can be applied to the context. These operations throw the javax.naming.NamingException that must be captured in a catch clause. A class hierarchy for exceptions is defined as part of the JNDI API. These exceptions can be thrown in the course of performing naming operations. The root of this class hierarchy is NamingException. Programs can catch generally the NamingException or, specifically, any other exception in the class hierarchy.

Each of these methods accepts a name of type java.lang.String as a parameter, and has an overloaded method with a name of type javax.naming.Name. For example, the lookup() method has the following signatures:

```
lookup(java.lang.String name)
```

```
lookup(javax.naming.Name name)
```

The javax.naming.Name interface represents a generic name as an ordered sequence of name components. It can be a composite name (one that spans multiple namespaces) or a compound name (one that is used within a namespace).

**TABLE 4.1**    Summary of Context Operations

| Method | Purpose |
| --- | --- |
| Context InitialContext() | Connects to the default JNDI service and establishes a new context |
| Context InitialContext(Properties p) | Connects to the a specific JNDI service and establishes a new context |
| void bind (Name name, Object obj) | Binds or adds a new name/object association |
| void bind (String name, Object obj) | Binds or adds a new string/object association |
| void rebind (String name, Object obj) | Rebinds or replaces an existing string/object association |
| void unbind (Name name) | Unbinds or removes the binding of an object to an associated name |

| Method | Purpose |
| --- | --- |
| `Object lookup(Name name)` | Looks up an object in the naming service using a name |
| `void rename` `(String oldName, String newName)` | Changes the name to which an object is bound |
| `NamingEnumeration listBindings` `(Name contextName)` | Enumerates all the names bound in the context name, along with the objects bound to them. |
| `NamingEnumeration listBindings` `(String contextName)` | Enumerates all the names bound in the context name, along with the objects bound to them. |
| `void close()` | Disconnects from the JNDI service, and is used to free resources used by a context |

## Example of Using JNDI Context Operations

The following program demonstrates some of the operations listed in Table 4.1. Listing 4.1 creates an initial context from the default JNDI provider, lists the environment, adds a new entry, and then finds it by looking up the entry. To query the existing environment, you can use the `getEnvironment()` method of the `Context` interface. The `CommunicationException` is thrown if the operation fails to connect to the JNDI service.

**LISTING 4.1** The Full Text of `day04/Client.java`

```
package day04;

import java.util.*;
import java.rmi.*;
import java.io.*;
import javax.naming.*;
import javax.ejb.*;

// This client demonstrates a sample usage of the JNDI tree

public class Client{
    public static InitialContext ctx;
 public static void main(String[] argv)  {
    print("Demonstration of the usage of JNDI...");
    if(argv.length < 1){
        print("Usage : Client <JNDI root name>\n");
        return;
    }
    try    {
      print("Connecting to a JNDI service...");
      ctx = new InitialContext();
      print("  Connected successfully. Initial context created.\n");
```

4

**LISTING 4.1**    continued

```
        print("Getting Environment Properties...");
        print("  Properties: " + ctx.getEnvironment().toString() + "\n");
        // Adding a binding
        String name = "mary";
        String email = "mary@hotmail.com";
        print("Binding a new name: " + name + " to an object: "+email+"...");
        ctx.bind(name, email);
        print("  Object: "+ email+ " is bound to name: " + name + "\n");
        // Lookup a binding
        print("Looking up the name...");
        String s = (String) ctx.lookup("mary");
        print("  Found Name= mary, with email= " + s + "\n");
        // Delete a binding
        print("Unbinding the name...");
        ctx.unbind("mary");
        print("  Name is unbound successfully!\n");
        print("Spanning JNDI context bindings...");
        spanJNDI(argv[0]);
        print("\n");
        // Lookup a "deleted" binding
        print("Lookup for the unbound name...error expected");
        s = (String) ctx.lookup("mary");
        print("  Found Name= mary, with email= " + s);

    }
     catch (CommunicationException e) {
        print("**ERROR: Failed to connect with the JNDI server." +
          "Startup the App Server, and run again.."+e);
     }
     catch (Exception e) {
        print("**ERROR: An unexpected exception occurred..."+e);
     }
     finally {
        if (ctx != null) {
          try {
            print("Unbinding the name...");
             ctx.unbind("mary");
            ctx.close();
            print("Connection to JNDI is closed successfully.");
          }
          catch (NamingException e) {
            print("**ERROR: Failed to close context due to: " + e);
          }
        }
     }
   }

   static void spanJNDI(String name){
     try{
```

LISTING 4.1 continued

```
        ctx = new InitialContext();
        NamingEnumeration bindList = ctx.listBindings(name);
        // Go through each item in list
        while (bindList !=null && bindList.hasMore()) {
            Binding bd = (Binding)bindList.next();
          print("   " + bd.getName() + ": " + bd.getClassName() + ": " +
➥bd.getObject());
            spanJNDI(bd.getName());
        }
    }catch (NamingException e) {

    }
  }
  static void print(String s)  {
    System.out.println(s);
  }
  }
 }
```

This example is made available to run on both the WebLogic and JBoss servers. To run this example on either of the servers, you must have the server installed and set up your environment to run the server and the example. The accompanying Readme.txt file will help you perform these steps.

When you run this example on the WebLogic server, the output should look like the following:

```
 > {java.naming.provider.url=t3://localhost:7001,
java.naming.factory.initial=weblogic.jndi.WLInitialContextFactory}
  > javax: weblogic.jndi.internal.WLContextImpl: WLContext (javax)
  > weblogic: weblogic.jndi.internal.WLContextImpl: WLContext (weblogic)
  > java:comp: weblogic.jndi.internal.WLContextImpl: WLContext (java:comp)
Binding name:maryto an object: mary@hotmail.com...
  > Object: mary@hotmail.com is bound to name: mary
  > Found Name= mary, with email= mary@hotmail.com
  > Name is unbound sucessfully!
*ERROR: An unexpected exception occurred...
   javax.naming.NameNotFoundException: Unable to resolve mary.
   Resolved: '' Unresolved:'mary' ; remaining name ''
*ERROR: Connection to JNDI is close successfully.
```

The output lists the environment of the JNDI service (in this case, WebLogic) and all the existing bindings. The error was produced when an exception was raised because we tried to look up an entry that was not found. The error was captured and an error message was displayed. For your convenience, the WebLogic Server environment provides a JNDI browser, which you can access using the WebLogic Console. This is accomplished by pointing with your Web browser to the URL http://localhost:7001/console,

4

(provided that WebLogic Server is running). From the left pane, click on myserver, and then on the right pane click on View JNDI Tree. A new window will pop up displaying a list similar to the listing of the example output.

Running the same example on JBoss should produce a similar output, except that the environment and the bindings will be specific to JBoss environment. You can also access the JBoss JNDI tree by pointing to the URL `http://localhost:8082` (if you are using JBoss 3.0.0), or `http://localhost:8080/jmx-console` (if you are using JBoss 3.0.1 or later). Click on the link `service=JNDIView`, and then invoke the `list()` operation.

## Specifying a JNDI Provider

For clients to access a JNDI service, programs must specify the provider name and the location of the JNDI service on the network. Programs can specify this environment setting in either a programmatic or a declarative method.

### Programmatic Method

Setting `Context.INITIAL_CONTEXT_FACTORY` specifies the JNDI provider, and setting `Context.PROVIDER_URL` specifies the URL location. The following sample code illustrates the access to a JNDI service from inside your code:

```
// Set JNDI environment in the properties
Properties prop = new Properties();
// Set the JNDI provider as WebLogic
prop.put(Context.INITIAL_CONTEXT_FACTORY,
         "weblogic.jndi.WLInitialContextFactory");
// set the JNDI URL (host name and port) to access the service
prop.put(Context.PROVIDER_URL, "t3://localhost:7001");
// Connect to the JNDI service as specified above
Context ctx = new InitialContext(prop);
```

**Caution**

The last call establishes a connection to the default JNDI service and creates an Enterprise Naming Context (ENC). Naming services usually reside on a remote server on the network. Clients remotely access these services using RMI protocol, which is more expensive than to access these services locally.

The Properties object specifies both the JNDI provider (in this case, WebLogic Server) and the location of the naming services on the network.

### Declarative Method

The programmatic method is not a good practice in developing large projects. The declarative method is convenient for setting these environment parameters, instead of hard-coding them in the client code itself. Using the declarative approach avoids recompilation, which results from changing the existing code, should you decide to switch from one JNDI provider to another.

The environment parameters can be specified in an application resource file, or can be passed as the `-D` command-line option to the Java interpreter. In the first case, the JNDI provider parameters can be set in a special application resource file `jndi.properties`. It contains a list of key/value pairs presented in the properties file format (which is typically mapped to `java.util.Properties` used inside the program). A sample of the content of `jndi.properties` file for the WebLogic server:

```
java.naming.factory.initial=weblogic.jndi.WLInitialContextFactory
java.naming.provider.url=t3://localhost:7001
```

In JBoss, environment properties are set in the following sample of `jndi.properties`:

```
java.naming.factory.initial=org.jnp.interfaces.NamingContextFactory
java.naming.provider.url=jnp://localhost:1099
java.naming.factory.url.pkgs=org.jboss.naming:org.jnp.interfaces
```

This simplifies the task of setting up the environment required by a JNDI application; you may distribute application resource files along with application components and service providers. The key is the name of the property (for example, `java.naming.factory.object`) and the value is a string in the format defined for that property.

The other option in setting these parameters is to pass them as system properties. These properties can be made available to a Java program via the `-D` command-line option to the Java interpreter. Here's an example of the WebLogic server command line:

```
java -Djava.naming.factory.initial=weblogic.jndi.WLInitialFactory \
    -Djava.naming.provider.url=t3://localhost:7001
```

When using JBoss, the command line looks like the following:

```
java -Djava.naming.factory.initial=org.jnp.interfaces.NamingContextFactory \
    -Djava.naming.provider.url=localhost:1099 \
    -Djava.naming.factory.url.pkgs=org.jboss.naming
```

If you use any of the declarative methods mentioned, the client application will use the default `InitialContext` constructor to create a context (without specifying any parameters). This makes your application more portable to any other application server.

```
Context ctx = new InitialContext();
```

Here, the JNDI automatically reads the application resource files from all defines in the applications' class paths and *JAVA_HOME*/lib/`jndi.properties`, where *JAVA_HOME* is the file directory that contains your JRE (Java Runtime Environment). The JNDI then makes the properties from these files available to the JNDI providers and other components that need to use them. Therefore, these files should be considered world-readable and should not contain sensitive information, such as clear text passwords.

## Using JNDI in User Authentication

In addition to using JNDI as a naming service, it is common to use it to provide a security mechanism for authenticating users to access system resources. User information and credentials (passwords) can be stored as entries in the directory service. It worth pointing out the fact that JNDI does not define a security model, but uses the security model that is defined in the underlying naming/directory service.

As you learned earlier today, the default InitialContext (with no parameters specified), creates a new Context used by an anonymous client.

```
// Connect to the default naming server as a default user
Context ctx = new InitialContext();
```

When authenticating a user, both user ID and password must be combined and passed as a parameter to the InitialContext. If the password is not matched, the exception javax.naming.NoPermission will be thrown to the client. Here is an example of authenticating a user with the WebLogic default JNDI server:

```
// Set up the environment properties for the user
Properties prop = new Properties();
// Login use both user id, and password passed as Strings
prop.put(Context. SECURITY_PRINCIPAL, "Laura");
prop.put(Context. SECURITY_CREDENTIALS, "whiskers");
Context ctx = new InitialContext(prop);
```

System resources and components can be protected by Access Control Lists (ACLs), which in turn can be accessed by the authorized user's Context. By creating a context for a particular user, the application server is responsible to verify the appropriate usage of these resources by the correct user.

In the preceding code sample, Context.SECURITY_PRINCIPAL is a constant that specifies the name of the user or program that is doing the authentication. Context.SECURITY_CREDENTIALS is a constant that specifies the credentials of the user or program doing the authentication.

A similar code can be established to authenticate users using the JBoss server. The only changes will be in setting both Context.INITIAL_CONTEXT_FACTORY and Context.PROVIDER_URL to the right values.

# Using JNDI in J2EE Applications

JNDI is a fundamental service to all J2EE applications. One key target is the isolation of the development of J2EE component code from the deployment environment. This allows an application component to be customized without the need to access or change its source code.

JNDI defines a logical namespace (directory) that application components (such as EJBs, servlets, JavaServer Pages [JSPs], and JDBC) can use to name resources, components, and other data. The namespace is provided to a component by its container, which executes the component. Typically, a component has a deployment descriptor that contains, among other data, information about the logical names and types of resources that the component references. Components of the Web tier are specified in the web.xml deployment descriptor, and those of the EJB tier are specified in the ejb-jar.xml deployment descriptor.

Starting with EJB 1.1, all beans have a default JNDI context called the *enterprise naming context*. The default context exists in the namespace called java:comp/env (based on a URL context for the java: URL scheme) and its subdirectories. When a bean is deployed, any beans it uses are mapped into the java:comp/env/ejb directory so that the bean references can be obtained at runtime through a simple and consistent use of the JNDI ENC. This eliminates network and implementation specific use of JNDI to obtain bean references. For example, you might use a name such as "java:comp/env/jdbc/myDB" from the initial context to name the myDB database. At the root context of the namespace is a binding with the name "comp", which is reserved for component-related bindings.

In addition, the name "env" is bound to a subtree that is reserved for the component's environment-related bindings, as defined by its deployment descriptor. The J2EE specifications recommend that EJBs be placed under the "ejb" subtree. For example, an EnrollmentCartHome EJB might be named "java:comp/env/ejb/EnrollmentCartHome".

Resource factory references are placed in subtrees differentiated by their resource manager type. Table 4.2 shows some examples.

**TABLE 4.2**    Resource Factory Subcontexts

| Subcontext | Purpose |
| --- | --- |
| jdbc: | JDBC DataSource references |
| jms: | JMS connection factories |
| mail: | JavaMail connection factories |
| ejb: | EJB component factories (home interface) |

Typical J2EE application clients that use the JNDI are Java applications, applets, servlets, JSPs, TagLibs, and EJBs. Such clients locate services or components that are either local on the same JVM or remote and reside on a different host. Clients can be calling from the Web tier to the business-tier, or from the client tier to either the Web tier or to the EJB tier.

Three main types of J2EE objects can be maintained in JNDI:

- Simple serializable JavaBeans (or Java objects)
- Distributed object references, such as EJB home and remote interfaces
- Common object services, such as transaction contexts

JNDI is used to declare a great deal of information to separate application code from its environment. The JNDI name that the application component uses to access the information is declared in the standard deployment descriptor. The following are the types of information that may be stored in the deployment descriptors by deployers and retrieved by developers using JNDI API:

- Environment entries as declared by the `env-entry` elements
- EJB references as declared by `ejb-ref` and `ejb-local-ref` elements
- Resource manager connection factory references as declared by the `resource-ref` elements
- Resource environment references as declared by the `resource-env-ref` elements

These XML elements of the deployment descriptors help you create portable applications across different environments. This is accomplished by specifying a logical name, to be used by the application, in the standard deployment descriptor. You then map this logical name to an environment-specific name. You specify this mapping in the server's specific deployment descriptor. Examples of this declarative concept will be illustrated in Day 9 and Day 16.

Each type of deployment descriptor element has a JNDI usage convention with regard to the name of the JNDI context under which the information is bound.

In addition to the standard deployment descriptors, there are deployment descriptors specific to each application server. For example, WebLogic Server uses `weblogic-ejb-jar.xml`, whereas JBoss uses `jboss.xml` as an additional EJB deployment descriptor that maps the JNDI name as used by each of the specific JNDI providers.

The following are sample codes to access some of the resources typically used in J2EE application. Details of these concepts will be covered in detail in the following days.

## Looking Up EJB Components

The container is responsible for binding the home interfaces of its deployed enterprise beans available to the client through JNDI. A client locates a session bean's home interface using JNDI. For example, the remote home interface for the `EnrollmentCart` session bean can be located using the following code segment:

```
// Connect to JNDI service provider, and obtain ENC context
Context ctx = new InitialContext();
// Perform JNDI lookup to obtain EJB Home interface factory
EnrollmentCartHome enrollmentCartHome =
    (EnrollmentCartHome) ctx.lookup("java:comp/env/ejb/EnrollmentCartHome");
```

The deployment descriptor of the EJB is an XML file that specifies information (among other things) such as the JNDI names of the application's enterprise beans. The following is the `<jndi-name>` tag:

```
<jndi-name>ejb/EnrollmentCartHome</jndi-name>
```

The client begins by obtaining the `InitialContext` for a bean's home object. The `InitialContext` remains valid while the client session is valid. The client provides the JNDI registered name for the required object to obtain a reference to an administered object. In the context of an EJB application, a typical administered object is an enterprise bean's home object. You'll see more detail coverage of JNDI access to EJB in Days 6, 8, 10, and 11.

## Looking Up JMS Factory and Destination

A client can locate the JMS `Destination` (`Queue` or `Topic`) to which it should send messages (that are to be delivered to a message-driven bean) by means of the standard JNDI API:

```
// Connect to JNDI service provider, and obtain ENC context
Context ctx = new InitialContext();
// Perform JNDI lookup to obtain queue connection factory
QueueConnectionFactory qcf = (QueueConnectionFactory)
        ctx.lookup("java:comp/env/jms/QueueCF");
// Perform JNDI lookup to obtain queue name
Queue  q = (Queue) ctx.lookup("java:comp/env/jms/StudentQueue");
```

For JMS applications, the administered object can be a JMS `ConnectionFactory` (for a `Topic` or a `Queue`) or a JMS `Destination` (a `Topic` or a `Queue`). A detailed explanation of these concepts is provided in Day 13, "Understanding JMS and Message-Driven Beans."

## Looking Up JDBC Connection Pool

Administrators or deployers of J2EE application can specify external resources such as JDBC pools. A resource file, such as a deployment descriptor, is used for this purpose:

```
// Connect to JNDI service provider, and obtain ENC context
Context ctx = new InitialContext();
// Perform JNDI lookup to obtain JDBC connection pool factory
DataSource ds = (DataSource) ctx.lookup ("java:/comp/env/jdbc/myDBPool");
```

The following is the associated deployment descriptor to specify the resource:

```
<resource-ref>
      <res-ref-name>jdbc/myDBPool</res-ref-name>
      <res-type>java.sql.DataSource</res-type>
</resource-ref>
```

More detailed coverage of JDBC can be found in Day 9, "Using JDBC to Connect to a Database."

## Looking Up JTA User Transaction

The JTA interface is used in distributed transactions to demarcate transaction boundaries within EJB applications. Clients use it to look up the `UserTransaction` as a resource factory:

```
// Connect to JNDI service provider, and obtain ENC context
Context ctx = new InitialContext();
// Perform JNDI lookup to obtain User Transaction resource factory
UserTransaction tx = (UserTransaction) ctx.lookup(
      "java:comp/UserTransaction");
tx.begin();
//...perform the distributed transaction...
tx.commit();
```

More detailed coverage of JTA can be found in Day 18, "Building Bean-Managed Transaction Beans."

## Looking Up JavaMail Session

The JavaMail interface is important in J2EE applications for sending mail from inside EJBs or other components. Clients use it to obtain a `Session` object in order to send email messages to the mail server:

```
// Connect to JNDI service provider, and obtain ENC context
InitialContext ctx = new InitialContext();
// Perform JNDI lookup to obtain Mail Session resource factory
Session session = (Session) ctx.lookup("java:comp/env/mail/MailSession");
```

More detailed coverage of JavaMail can be found in Day 20, "Putting It All Together."

# Best Practices

Every remote JNDI lookup is an expensive remote method call, and in order to perform JNDI lookup, it is optimum for applications to do it once (usually at the component initialization). Therefore, caching the home handles improves the performance in such situations. Establishing a connection to a JNDI service is also an expensive task, and caching such context references improves application performance.

Use one class to abstract all JNDI usage and to hide the complexities of initial context creation, EJB home object lookup, and EJB object re-creation. Multiple clients can reuse such objects to reduce code complexity, provide a single point of control, and improve performance by providing a caching facility.

An object stored in a JNDI tree must implement either the `java.io.Serializable` or `java.rmi.Remote` interface. Both WebLogic and JBoss use nonpersistent JNDI service. This in-memory caching technique increases the performance of retrievals. To increase the reliability of these services, vendors rely on replicating them across all the nodes of a cluster. This provides both fail-over and load balancing of the naming services. In a clustered JNDI service, each node propagates the JNDI changes that occurred due to binding, rebinding, and unbinding through IP multicast to other nodes of the cluster.

# Summary

JNDI is one of the J2EE common services that provides naming and directory functionality to enterprise components. It provides applications with methods for performing standard naming and directory operations, such as associating names with objects and looking up objects using their names. Using JNDI, a J2EE application can store and retrieve any type of named Java object. Because JNDI is independent of any specific implementation, applications can use JNDI to access multiple naming and directory services, including existing naming and directory services such as LDAP, NDS, DNS, and NIS. This allows J2EE applications to coexist with other enterprise applications and systems.

4

**Note**

For a thorough introduction and tutorial on JNDI, which covers both the client and service provider APIs, see the Sun tutorial at http://java.sun.com/products/jndi/tutorial/.

# Q&A

**Q What are the main class and interface used in accessing a JNDI service?**

**A** Clients access a JNDI service provider by establishing a `Context` using the `InitialContext` interface. Clients look up objects in the JNDI service by using an object name.

**Q** **What are the required parameter(s) to specify in order to connect to a JNDI service?**

**A** Clients must specify both the provider name (by `Context.INITIAL_CONTEXT_FAC-TORY`) and the JNDI URL (by `Context.PROVIDER_URL`) to connect to a JNDI service provider.

# Quiz

1. Which is the CORBA naming service equivalent of JNDI?

    A. Interface Definition Language (IDL)

    B. Common Object Services (COS) Naming

    C. Lightweight Directory Access Protocol (LDAP)

    D. Interoperable Inter-Orb Protocol (IIOP)

2. Which lookup service provides a unified interface to multiple naming and directory services in the enterprise so that application components can access those services?

    A. Domain Name Services (DNS)

    B. Common Object Services (COS)

    C. Lightweight Directory Access Protocol (LDAP)

    D. Java Naming and Directory Services (JNDI)

3. By default, what is returned from a JNDI `lookup()` method call when accessing an EJB?

    A. Home interface

    B. Remote interface

    C. Session bean

    D. Bean class

## Quiz Answers

1. B
2. D
3. A

# Exercises

Modify the sample `day04/Client.java` to bind more than one name. Try to use composite names such as the DNS name `www.samspublishing.com` and the Windows/DOS name `file://c:/projects/myfile.doc`.

# DAY 5

# Developing Stateless Session Beans

Today you'll work on a complete example of developing an enterprise bean. The sample university registration application enables an existing user to log in to the system by verifying his login name and password. It also enables a new user to register her login name and password. Such a component does not need to maintain client-specific state information across method invocations, so the same bean instance can be reused to service other client requests. This can be modeled as a stateless session bean.

The SignOn component verifies the user's login name and password. For the sake of simplicity, the user's login name and password are stored in the deployment descriptor, as environment entries. On Day 21, "Developing a Complete Enterprise Application," we'll integrate the SignOn component with an entity bean to store and retrieve the user's login name and password from the database.

The following is a summary of today's activities:

- Learn the interactions between the client, EJB container, and the stateless session bean by looking under the hood of the bean
- Define the home and component interfaces
- Implement the stateless session bean class
- Learn how to write the deployment descriptor for stateless session bean and declare environment entries in it
- Learn how to compile, package, and deploy the bean in a container
- Write the client that accesses the stateless session bean

# Looking Under the Hood of a Stateless Session Bean

Figure 5.1 shows the interactions between the client, the EJB container, and the stateless session bean.

**FIGURE 5.1**

*Under the hood of a stateless session bean.*

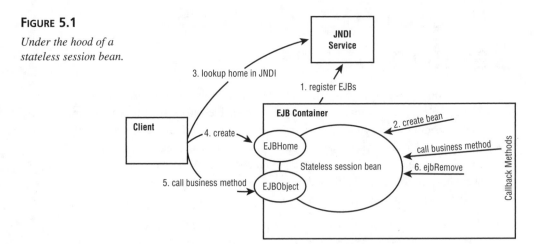

The following steps describe the sequence of interactions in detail:

1. At startup, the EJB container registers all the deployed enterprise beans, including stateless session beans, with the Java Naming and Directory Interface (JNDI) service, based on the JNDI name specified in the deployment descriptor.

2. The EJB container decides to instantiate a stateless session bean based on the caching policy. In this example, the EJB container instantiates the SignOn bean using the Class.newInstance("SignOnEJB.class") and then calls the methods

setSessionContext() and ejbCreate() on the instance. Now the bean is ready to serve any client.

3. The client looks up the home interface of the deployed enterprise bean via JNDI. For example, the remote home interface for the SignOn stateless bean can be located using the following code segment:

```
Context initialContext = new InitialContext();
Object obj = initialContext.lookup("day05/SignOn");
SignOnHome signOnHome = (SignOnHome)
javax.rmi.PortableRemoteObject.narrow(obj, SignOnHome.class);
```

4. The client uses the remote home interface to create a remote sign-on session object. For example:

```
SignOn signOn =  (SignOn)signOnHome.create();
```

5. The client calls a business method on the remote object. For example, the client verifies the login name and password as follows:

```
signOn.validateUser("student1", "password1");
```

The container assigns a stateless session bean from the instance pool to service the client request. The container calls the appropriate business method on the stateless session object instance. For example, the EJB container calls the validateUser() method on the stateless session bean instance. After the bean services the client method call, the container puts the session bean back into the instance pool.

6. The EJB container decides to terminate the session bean instance by calling the ejbRemove() method of the bean instance.

# Designing the Stateless Session Bean

Figure 5.2 shows the design of the SignOn component. The SignOn stateless session bean implements the SessionBean interface. It implements the methods setSessionContext(), ejbCreate(), ejbActivate(), ejbPassivate(), and ejbRemove() as defined in the javax.ejb.SessionBean interface. In addition, it implements the validateUser() method, which accepts the user's login name and password as parameters and returns true if they are valid.

We also provide remote interfaces to our stateless session bean. They include a remote home interface (SignOnHome) and a remote interface (SignOn). The SignOnHome home interface extends the javax.ejb.EJBHome interface and defines a single create() method. The SignOn remote interface extends the javax.ejb.EJBObject interface and defines the validateUser() method. As you learned on Day 2, "Understanding EJB Types and Interfaces," EJB container tools generate the classes that correspond to the home and remote interfaces.

5

FIGURE 5.2

SignOn *stateless bean design.*

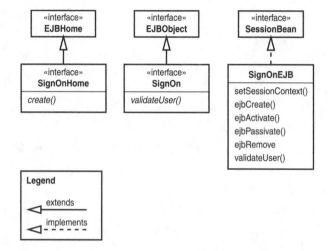

# Implementing the Stateless Session Bean

This section discusses the implementation of the remote home interface SignOnHome, remote interface SignOn and the stateless session bean class SignOnEJB.

## Defining the Home Interface

The home interface, SignOnHome, is defined in Listing 5.1.

**LISTING 5.1** The Full Text of day05/SignOnHome.java

```
package day05;

import java.rmi.RemoteException;
import javax.ejb.*;

public interface SignOnHome extends EJBHome {
  SignOn create()
      throws CreateException, RemoteException;
}
```

So, to create a bean instance, you call the create() method on the home interface, and receive a reference to the remote interface.

**Note**

For a stateless session bean, the return parameter of create() method of home interface must be remote interface instance. Also, a stateless session bean can define a single create() method with no parameters. The throws clause of the `create()` method must include `CreateException`. This exception is thrown to the client, when there is a problem in creating or initializing the bean instance.

**Note**

The remote home interface is a Java Remote Method Invocation (RMI) interface. All RMI interfaces conform to certain rules. The method arguments and return types of a remote method must be legal types for the RMI over Internet Inter-Orb Protocol (RMI/IIOP), such as primitives, serializable objects, and RMI/IIOP remote objects. Each method declared in the remote interface must include `java.rmi.RemoteException` in its `throws` clause. This exception is thrown when a remote invocation fails for some reason, such as network failure, protocol errors, and so on.

## Defining the Component Interface

The `SignOn` remote interface is defined in Listing 5.2.

**LISTING 5.2**    The Full Text of `day05/SignOn.java`

```
package day05;

import java.util.*;
import java.rmi.*;
import javax.ejb.*;

public interface SignOn extends EJBObject {
    public boolean validateUser(String login, String password)
        throws InvalidLoginException, RemoteException;
}
```

5

This interface contains the one business method—`validateUser`—that is callable by the client. The remote interface is a Java RMI interface. So, method arguments and return types of a remote method must be legal types for RMI/IIOP and the method must include `java.rmi.RemoteException` in its `throws` clause. `InvalidLoginException` is a customized application exception thrown by the `SignOn` enterprise bean to report an unsuccessful login attempt.

**Note**

Enterprise JavaBeans define two types of exceptions: application exceptions and system exceptions.

> Enterprise beans use *application exceptions* to signal an error in the business logic to the client. There are two types of application exceptions: predefined and customized. The `javax.ejb` package includes several predefined exceptions that are designed to handle common problems. For example, `javax.ejb.CreateException` is a predefined exception. You can code your own customized exceptions to indicate an error in business logic. For example, the `SignOn` enterprise bean throws `InvalidLoginException` to report an unsuccessful login attempt.
>
> A *system exception* indicates a problem with the services that support an application. Examples of these problems include remote invocation failure, failure to obtain database connection, JNDI exceptions, and so on. If your enterprise bean encounters a system-level problem, it should throw a `javax.ejb.EJBException`. The EJB container logs system exception and throws `java.rmi.RemoteException` if the client is a remote client, or `javax.ejb.EJBException` if the client is a local client. If a system exception is thrown, the EJB container might destroy the bean instance.

## Implementing the Enterprise Bean Class

Listing 5.3 shows the `SignOnEJB` enterprise bean class implementation. The stateless session bean implements the `javax.ejb.SessionBean` interface. It implements the methods `setSessionContext()`, `ejbCreate()`, `ejbActivate()`, `ejbPassivate()`, and `ejbRemove()`, as defined in the `SessionBean` interface. The `ejbCreate()` method creates an instance of `javax.naming.InitialContext` and looks up the environment naming context via the `InitialContext` under the name `"java:comp/env"`. In addition, it implements the `validateUser` method that accepts the user's login name and password as parameters and returns true if the login is successful. The method throws `InvalidLoginException` if the login name and password are invalid. For simplicity, this method uses environment entries to validate the user's login name and password. On Day 21, we'll integrate the `SignOn` bean with an entity bean to store and retrieve the user's login name and password from the database.

**LISTING 5.3**   The Full Text of day05/SignOnEJB.java

```
package day05;

import java.util.*;
import javax.ejb.*;
import javax.naming.*;

public class SignOnEJB implements SessionBean  {
    private SessionContext ctx;
    private Context environment;
```

**LISTING 5.3** continued

```java
public SignOnEJB() {
   print("The container created this instance.\n");
}
/* --- Callback methods --- */
public void setSessionContext(SessionContext c) {
   print("The container called the setSessionContext method ");
   print("to associate session bean instance with its context.\n");
   ctx = c;
}
public void ejbCreate() throws CreateException {
   print("The container called the ejbCreate method\n");
   print("so that we can initialize the bean instance.\n");
   try {
      InitialContext ic = new InitialContext();
      environment = (Context) ic.lookup("java:comp/env");
   } catch (NamingException ne) {
      throw new CreateException("Could not look up context");
   }
}
/* Methods ejbActivate and ejbPassivate  are
   not used by stateless session beans
*/
public void ejbActivate() {}
public void ejbPassivate() {}

public void ejbRemove() {
   print("This instance is in the process of being removed ");
   print("by the container.\n");
}

/* ---Here you implement all business methods
   as defined in the component interface---
*/
public boolean validateUser(String userName, String password)
 throws InvalidLoginException {
   try {
      String storedPassword = (String) environment.lookup(userName);
      if ( storedPassword.equals(password) ) {
         return true;
      }
      else {
         throw new InvalidLoginException("Invalid login/password");
      }
   } catch(NamingException ne) {
      throw new InvalidLoginException("Invalid login/password");
   }
}
void print(String s) {
   System.out.println(s);
}
}
```

5

> **Note** Because the concepts of activation and passivation are not applicable to stateless session beans, we provide empty implementations for the methods `ejbActivate()` and `ejbPassivate()`.

## Writing the Exception Class

Listing 5.4 shows the `InvalidLoginException` class. `InvalidLoginException` derives from `java.lang.Exception`.

**LISTING 5.4**   The Full Text of `day05/InvalidLoginException.java`

```
package day05;

public class InvalidLoginException extends Exception {
    public InvalidLoginException() {
        super();
    }
    public InvalidLoginException(Exception e) {
        super(e.toString());
    }
    public InvalidLoginException(String s) {
        super(s);
    }
}
```

As mentioned earlier, the `SignOn` enterprise bean throws `InvalidLoginException` if the login name and password are invalid.

## Declaring the Deployment Descriptors

As you learned on Day 2, the deployment descriptor describes a component's deployment settings. Listing 5.5 shows the `ejb-jar.xml` deployment descriptor for the `SignOn` enterprise bean. `ejb-jar.xml` describes the enterprise bean's deployment properties, such as its bean type and structure. The file also provides the EJB container with information about where it can find, and then load, the home interface, remote interface, and bean class.

**LISTING 5.5**   The Full Text of `day05/ejb-jar.xml`

```
<?xml version="1.0"?>

<!DOCTYPE ejb-jar PUBLIC
'-//Sun Microsystems, Inc.//DTD Enterprise JavaBeans 2.0//EN'
'http://java.sun.com/dtd/ejb-jar_2_0.dtd'>
```

---

**LISTING 5.5**    continued

```xml
<ejb-jar>
  <enterprise-beans>
    <session>
      <ejb-name>SignOnEJB</ejb-name>
      <home>day05.SignOnHome</home>
      <remote>day05.SignOn</remote>
      <ejb-class>day05.SignOnEJB</ejb-class>
      <session-type>Stateless</session-type>
      <transaction-type>Container</transaction-type>
      <env-entry>
        <env-entry-name>student</env-entry-name>
        <env-entry-type>java.lang.String</env-entry-type>
        <env-entry-value>password</env-entry-value>
      </env-entry>
      <env-entry>
        <env-entry-name>student1</env-entry-name>
        <env-entry-type>java.lang.String</env-entry-type>
        <env-entry-value>password1</env-entry-value>
      </env-entry>
    </session>
  </enterprise-beans>
</ejb-jar>
```

---

The `ejb-jar` element is the root element of the EJB deployment descriptor. It contains the structural information about all the included enterprise beans. The `enterprise-beans` element contains the declarations of one or more enterprise beans. The `session` element declares a session bean, and an `ejb-name` element within the `session` element defines the session bean's name (`SignOnEJB`). The `session` element also declares other things such as the home interface (`day05.SignOnHome`), the remote interface (`day05.SignOn`), and the bean's class (`day05.SignOnEJB`). The `session-type` element declares that this is a stateless session bean (as opposed to a stateful session bean).

The `env-entry` element defines an environment property that the enterprise bean can access via JNDI. Each `env-entry` element describes a single environment entry. The `env-entry` element consists of the environment entry name relative to the `java:comp/env` context, the Java type of the environment entry value, the environment entry value, and so on. For example, the value of the environment entry name `student` is `password`, and its type is `java.lang.String`. The `SignOn` enterprise bean uses environment entries to validate the user's login name and password.

As you learned on Day 2, in addition to the standard `ejb-jar.xml`, an application typically requires a certain amount of additional environment-specific or vendor-specific binding information. Listing 5.6 shows a `weblogic-ejb-jar.xml` deployment descriptor that is specific to WebLogic Server.

5

**LISTING 5.6**    The Full Text of `day05/weblogic-ejb-jar.xml`

```
<?xml version="1.0"?>

<!DOCTYPE weblogic-ejb-jar PUBLIC
'-//BEA Systems, Inc.//DTD WebLogic 7.0.0 EJB//EN'
'http://www.bea.com/servers/wls700/dtd/weblogic-ejb-jar.dtd'>

<weblogic-ejb-jar>
  <weblogic-enterprise-bean>
    <ejb-name>SignOnEJB</ejb-name>
    <jndi-name>day05/SignOn</jndi-name>
  </weblogic-enterprise-bean>
</weblogic-ejb-jar>
```

The `jndi-name` element declares the JNDI name of the enterprise bean. So, the JNDI name of the `SignOnEJB` is `day05/SignOn`.

Listing 5.7 shows a `jboss.xml` deployment descriptor that is specific to JBoss.

**LISTING 5.7**    The Full Text of `C:\styejb\examples\day05\jboss.xml`

```
<?xml version="1.0" encoding="UTF-8"?>
<jboss>
  <enterprise-beans>
    <session>
      <ejb-name>SignOnEJB</ejb-name>
      <jndi-name>day05/SignOn</jndi-name>
    </session>
  </enterprise-beans>
</jboss>
```

The preceding file declares the JNDI name of `SignOnEJB` as `day05/SignOn`.

# Packaging the Enterprise Bean

The next few sections show how to package and deploy the enterprise bean and run the sample client in WebLogic Server. The corresponding steps for JBoss are presented later today.

The following snippet shows the directory structure for the `SignOn` bean files for WebLogic Server:

```
C:\styejb\examples\
            day05\
                    SignOn.java
                    SignOnHome.java
                    SignOnEJB.java
```

```
InvalidLoginException.java
ejb-jar.xml
weblogic-ejb-jar.xml
```

For JBoss, replace the vendor-specific weblogic-ejb-jar.xml file with jboss.xml.

As you learned on Day 2, *packaging* is the process of assembling the enterprise bean files into an ejb-jar file. To package the SignOn component, you must perform the following steps:

1. Set up the environment for the build in a new command window using the following commands:

   **C:\>cd styejb\examples**

   C:\styejb\examples>**setEnvWebLogic.bat**

   C:\styejb\examples>**cd day05**

   C:\styejb\examples\day05>

---

**Caution**

Getting the proper environment is necessary to run the example correctly. You can verify the environment by using the env command as follows:

C:\styejb\examples\day05>**env**

APPLICATIONS=c:\bea\weblogic700\config\mydomain\applications

CLASSPATH=C:\bea\jdk131_03\lib\tools.jar;

c:\bea\weblogic700\server\lib\weblogic_sp.jar;

c:\bea\weblogic700\server\lib\weblogic.jar;

c:\bea\weblogic700\samples\server\eval\pointbase\lib\pbserver42ECF17
➥2.jar;

c:\bea\weblogic700\..;. . .

PATH=c:\bea\weblogic700\bin;C:\bea\jdk131_03\bin;. . .

Make sure that the environment variables PATH and CLASSPATH point to valid directories.

---

**5**

2. Create a stating area for the build using the following commands:

   C:\styejb\examples\day05>**mkdir build build\META-INF**

   C:\styejb\examples\day05>**copy %STYEJB_HOME%\day05\ejb-jar.xml build\**
   ➥**META-INF**

   C:\styejb\examples\day05>**copy %STYEJB_HOME%\day05\weblogic-ejb-jar.xml**
   ➥**build\META-INF**

   The preceding commands create a build directory in which the compiled files and deployment descriptors will be placed before they are packaged into an ejb-jar file. The .xml files are placed under META-INF within the build directory.

3. Compile the Java files using the following commands:

```
C:\styejb\examples\day05>javac -g -d build SignOn.java SignOnHome.java
➥SignOnEJB.java InvalidLoginException.java
```

4. Package the enterprise bean files into an `ejb-jar` file using the following commands:

```
C:\styejb\examples\day05>cd build
```
```
C:\styejb\examples\day05\build>jar cv0f tmp_day05_SignOn.jar META-INF day05
```
```
C:\styejb\examples\day05\build>cd ..
```

5. Generate the container classes using the WebLogic tool `ejbc` as follows:

```
C:\styejb\examples\day05>java weblogic.ejbc -keepgenerated -g
➥-deprecation build\tmp_day05_SignOn.jar build\day05_SignOn.jar
```
The `ejbc` tool generates and inserts the container classes into the `ejb-jar` file `day05_SignOn.jar`. The `ejbc` tool is specific to WebLogic.

The `day05_SignOn.jar` file is now ready for deployment into WebLogic Server.

## Deploying the Enterprise Bean

The process of installing and customizing the `ejb-jar` file in the EJB container is known as *deploying*. To deploy the `day05_SignOn.jar` file into WebLogic Server, you must perform the following steps:

1. Start WebLogic Server in a new command window as follows:

```
C:\>cd styejb\examples
```
```
C:\styejb>setEnvWebLogic.bat
```
```
C:\styejb>startWebLogic.bat
```

**Caution**

> You must wait for the application server to completely start before proceeding to the next step. For example, WebLogic Server displays the following message when it is completely started and ready to accept client requests:
>
> ```
> <Notice> <WebLogicServer> <Started WebLogic Admin Server "myserver"
> for domain "mydomain" running in Development Mode>
> ```

2. Deploy the component by copying the `ejb-jar` file into the WebLogic applications directory. You can deploy the bean in the same command window you used for packaging the bean by using the following command:

```
C:\styejb\examples\day05>copy build\day05_SignOn.jar
➥%APPLICATIONS%
```
We use the hot deployment feature of both WebLogic (version 6.1 and higher) and JBoss (version 2.4 and higher). Deployment is performed by simply copying the bean's JAR file into the application deployment directory.

**Note**

> You can verify the bean deployment by using the WebLogic administrative console (http://localhost:7001/console). When prompted, enter **system** as the username and **administrator** as the password. In the left panel, click mydomain->Deployments->EJB. If the day05_SignOn.jar is properly deployed, you should see it under the EJB node. Click on day05_SignOn to see more information about it. Figure 5.3 shows a corresponding screen shot.

**FIGURE 5.3**

*Enterprise bean deployment verification in WebLogic Server.*

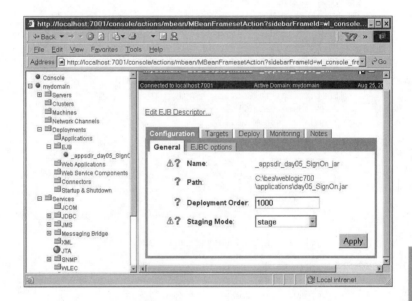

The following shows the contents of the ejb-jar file:

```
META-INF/
        ejb-jar.xml
        vendor-specific deployment files
day05/
    SignOn.class
    InvalidLoginException.class
    SignOnHome.class
    SignOnEJB.class
```

The ejb-jar file includes the standard deployment descriptor ejb-jar.xml, and other vendor-specific files such as weblogic-ejb-jar.xml, under the directory META-INF. In addition, it contains the class files for each enterprise bean, such as home and component interfaces, enterprise bean classes, and any dependent classes.

5

# Writing a Client

Listing 5.8 demonstrates how a client accesses a stateless session bean.

**LISTING 5.8**    The Full Text of day05/Client.java

```java
package day05;

import java.util.*;
import javax.naming.*;
import javax.ejb.*;

public class Client {

  public static void main(String[] args) {
    print("Starting Client . . .\n");
    Context initialContext = null;
    SignOnHome signOnHome = null;
    SignOn signOn = null;

    try {
      print("Looking up the sign on component via JNDI.\n");
      initialContext = new InitialContext();
      Object object = initialContext.lookup("day05/SignOn");
      signOnHome = (SignOnHome)
       javax.rmi.PortableRemoteObject.narrow(object,SignOnHome.class);

      print("Creating an signOn object.\n");
      signOn =  (SignOn) signOnHome.create();

      print("Testing a successful login/password\n");
      signOn.validateUser("student", "password");

      print("Testing an invalid login/password\n");
      try {
         signOn.validateUser("student", "invalidpassword");
      } catch(InvalidLoginException ile) {
         System.err.println(ile);
      }
      print("Removing the signOn object.\n");
      signOn.remove();
    } catch ( Exception e) {
      e.printStackTrace();
    }
  }
  static void print(String s) {
    System.out.println(s);
  }
}
```

The client locates the `SignOnHome` home interface of the deployed enterprise bean via JNDI, and then uses the remote home interface to create a remote `SignOn` session object. The client then calls the `validateUser()` business method with a valid login name and password on the remote object. It also demonstrates the application-specific exception by calling the `validateUser()` method with an invalid login name and password. Finally, the client calls the `remove()` method on the remote interface. The container will destroy the remote session object.

You can build the client in the same command window you used for packaging the enterprise bean by using the following command:

```
C:\styejb\examples\day05>javac -g -classpath %CLASSPATH%;.\build -d build
➥Client.java
```

For convenience, we provide a single script, `buildWebLogic.bat`, under the `c:\styejb\examples\day05` directory to package and deploy the enterprise bean. It also builds the client.

# Running the Example

You can run the client in the same window you used to build it by issuing the following command:

```
C:\styejb\examples\day05>java -Djava.naming.factory.initial=
➥weblogic.jndi.WLInitialContextFactory -Djava.naming.provider.url=
➥t3://localhost:7001  -classpath %CLASSPATH%;.\build day05.Client
```

Running the client produces the following output:

```
Starting Client . . .
Looking up the sign on component via JNDI.
Creating an signOn object.
Testing a successful login/password
Testing an invalid login/password
day05.InvalidLoginException: Invalid login/password
Start server side stack trace:
day05.InvalidLoginException: Invalid login/password
 at day05.SignOnEJB.validateUser(SignOnEJB.java:52)
 at day05.SignOnEJB_keukm7_EOImpl.validateUser(SignOnEJB_keukm7_EOImpl.java:37)
 at day05.SignOnEJB_keukm7_EOImpl_WLSkel.invoke(Unknown Source)
 at weblogic.rmi.internal.BasicServerRef.invoke(BasicServerRef.java:298)
 at weblogic.rmi.cluster.ReplicaAwareServerRef.invoke
➥(ReplicaAwareServerRef.java:93)
 at weblogic.rmi.internal.BasicServerRef.handleRequest(BasicServerRef.java:267)
 at weblogic.rmi.internal.BasicExecuteRequest.execute
➥(BasicExecuteRequest.java:22)
 at weblogic.kernel.ExecuteThread.execute(ExecuteThread.java:139)
 at weblogic.kernel.ExecuteThread.run(ExecuteThread.java:120)
End  server side stack trace
Removing the signOn object.
```

5

For convenience, we provide the script runClientJBoss.bat under the c:\styejb\exam-ples\day05 directory to run the sample client.

The following steps describe how to package, deploy the SignOn component and run the sample client for the JBoss server:

1. Package and deploy the component in a new command window using the following commands:

```
C:\>cd styejb\examples
C:\styejb\examples>setEnvJBoss.bat
C:\styejb\examples>cd day05
C:\styejb\examples\day05>buildJBoss.bat
```

The preceding steps package the enterprise bean files into an ejb-jar file day05_SignOn.jar. In addition, they copy this ejb-jar file into the deployment area of JBoss. They also build the sample client.

2. Start JBoss in a new command window using the following commands:

```
C:\>cd styejb\examples
C:\styejb\examples>setEnvJBoss.bat
C:\styejb\examples>startJBoss.bat
```

**Note**  You can verify the bean deployment by using the JBoss management con-sole (http://localhost:8080/jmx-console). Look for day05_SignOn.jar in the console. If the day05_SignOn.jar is properly deployed, you should see it under the jboss.j2ee section as shown in Figure 5.4.

**FIGURE 5.4**

*Enterprise bean deployment verifica-tion in JBoss.*

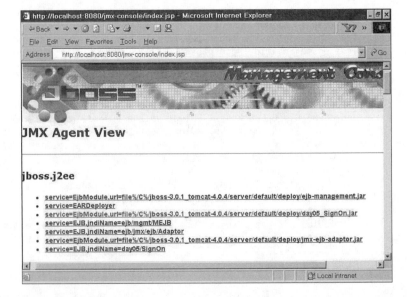

3. You can run the sample client in the same window you used to package the bean and build the client by using the following command:

```
C:\styejb\examples\day05>runClientJBoss.bat
```

# Best Practices

Some best practices are already mentioned on Day 3, "Understanding Session Beans." Stateless beans offer better performance than stateful beans because they require fewer resources. To support the same number of clients, an application typically requires fewer stateless session beans than stateful session beans. Whenever possible, choose stateless session beans instead of stateful session beans.

It's useful to follow a naming convention for enterprise bean class names. For example, use the suffix Home for a remote home interface (for example, SignOnHome); no suffix for remote interface (for example, SignOn); the suffix LocalHome for a local home interface (for example, SignOnLocalHome); the suffix Local for a local interface (for example, SignOnLocal); and the suffix EJB for enterprise bean class (for example, SignOnEJB).

# Summary

Today you wrote your first enterprise bean. You wrote the home interface, component interface, enterprise bean class, and application exception for a stateless session bean. The remote home interface extends the javax.ejb.EJBHome interface and contains a single create method. The remote interface extends javax.ejb.EJBObject and contains the business methods callable by the client. The enterprise bean class implements the javax.ejb.SessionBean interface. In addition, it implements the ejbCreate method and business methods defined in the remote interface. The deployment descriptor for a session bean includes information such as the bean's name, home interface, component interface, bean class, and its subtype. You learned how to package and deploy the enterprise bean. You also wrote and ran a client that accesses the enterprise bean.

You learned about the types of exceptions: application exceptions and system exceptions. Application exceptions, such as javax.ejb.CreateException, indicate an error in business logic to the client. System exceptions, such as java.rmi.RemoteException, indicate an error with the services that support an application and the EJB container may destroy the bean instance.

The process of writing, packaging, and deploying enterprise bean files is similar for other types of enterprise beans as well. You'll use this procedure in the following days.

5

# Q&A

**Q** **What files do I need to write for a stateless session bean?**

**A** Like other enterprise beans, stateless session beans consist of a home interface, component interface, enterprise bean class, and deployment descriptor. You must provide a session bean's remote home interface and remote interface, if the session bean provides a remote client view. If the session bean provides a local client view, you must provide a local interface and local home interface. Your session bean may provide both local and remote client views.

**Q** **How do I specify the JNDI name for a stateless session bean?**

**A** The JNDI name for a stateless session bean is specified in the vendor-specific deployment descriptor, such as `weblogic-ejb-jar.xml` or `jboss.xml`.

# Quiz

1. A stateless session bean implements which of the following interfaces?

   A. `javax.ejb.StatelessBean`

   B. `javax.ejb.SessionBean`

   C. `javax.ejb.EJBObject`

   D. `javax.ejb.SignOnHome`

2. Which of the following methods is not used by a stateless session bean?

   A. `ejbCreate()`

   B. `ejbRemove()`

   C. `setSessionContext()`

   D. `ejbActivate()`

3. Which of the following is true for a stateless session bean?

   A. Maintains conversational state on behalf of a client

   B. Activation and passivation are applicable

   C. Can be pooled

   D. Can't open database connections

## Quiz Answers

1. B

2. D

3. C

# Exercises

To extend your knowledge of the subjects covered today, try the following exercise:

Define an `addUser (String userName, String password)` method in the remote interface `SignOn`. Add a corresponding method in the enterprise bean class `SignOnEJB`.

For today, you can provide an empty implementation for the method. Later, you'll extend it to write to database using an entity bean.

5

# DAY 6

# Developing Stateful Session Beans

Today you'll learn how to develop applications that maintain the conversational state on behalf of the client. You'll work on a complete example of developing a stateful session bean.

The sample university registration application enables students to browse the online course catalog. While browsing the catalog, the student can select the course(s) she likes and place them in a temporary enrollment cart. The student can view or delete courses from the cart, and may later decide to place an order for the cart contents.

`EnrollmentCart` represents a collection of courses selected by a student in a particular session. The cart should not be shared, because it represents a particular interaction with a particular student and is alive only for the student's session. Also, the cart is not saved into the database unless the student is ready to place an order. The cart becomes a persistent order when the student decides to purchase it. A cart must be allocated by the system for each student concurrently connected to the Web site. All these characteristics make

`EnrollmentCart` an ideal candidate for a stateful session bean. You will undertake each of the following:

- Examine the interactions between the client, EJB container, and the stateful session bean by looking under the hood of the bean
- Define the home and component interfaces for the stateful session bean
- Implement the stateful session bean class
- Learn how to write the deployment descriptors, and package and deploy the enterprise bean
- Write a sample client that accesses the stateful session bean

# Looking Under the Hood of the Stateful Session Bean

Figure 6.1 shows the interactions between the client, the EJB container, and the stateful session bean.

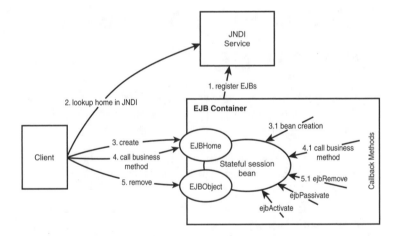

The following steps describe the sequence of interactions in detail:

1. At startup, the EJB container registers enterprise beans with the Java Naming and Directory Interface (JNDI) service.
2. The client looks up the home interface of the installed enterprise bean via JNDI. For example, the remote home interface for the enrollment cart session bean can be located using the following code segment:

```
Context initialContext = new InitialContext();
Object obj = initialContext.lookup("day06/EnrollmentCartHome");
```

```
EnrollmentCartHome eCartHome = (EnrollmentCartHome)
javax.rmi.PortableRemoteObject.narrow(obj, EnrollmentCartHome.class);
```

3. The client uses the remote home interface to create an enrollment cart session object. For example,

```
EnrollmentCart eCart =  (EnrollmentCart) eCartHome.create();
```

The container creates a session bean instance on behalf of the client. The creation process involves setting the context and calling the appropriate ejbCreate<method> method. For example, the container calls the setSessionContext and the ejbCreate methods of the session bean instance.

4. The client calls business methods on the remote object For example, the client adds courses to the enrollment cart as follows:

```
String[] courseIds = { "CS101", "CS102", "CS103"};
enrollmentCart.addCourses(courseIds);
```

The container calls the appropriate business method on the session bean. For example, it calls session bean's method:

```
addCourses(String[] courseIds).
```

5. The client calls the remove method of the remote object. For example, the client removes the enrollment cart object as follows:

```
enrollmentCart.remove();
```

The container calls the ejbRemove method on the session bean instance.

> **Note**
>
> A client never directly accesses instances of the session bean's class.

During the life cycle of the stateful session bean, the container can passivate and activate the session bean instance. This usually occurs when the number of instances reaches a certain limit specified by the developer in the deployment descriptor. During this process, the container calls the session bean's ejbPassivate and ejbActivate methods.

# Designing the Stateful Session Bean

Like other enterprise beans, stateful session beans consist of a home interface, component interface, enterprise bean class, and deployment descriptor. The home and component interfaces can be local, or remote, or both.

Figure 6.2 shows the design of the EnrollmentCart component. The EnrollmentCart stateful session bean implements the SessionBean interface. It implements the methods setSessionContext(), ejbCreate(), ejbActivate(), ejbPassivate(), and ejbRemove() as defined in the javax.ejb.SessionBean interface. In addition, it implements the addCourses(String[] courseIds) method, which accepts an array of course IDs and adds them to the cart. The getCourses() method returns a collection of course IDs in the cart and the empty() method clears the contents in the cart.

**FIGURE 6.2**

*EnrollmentCart sample class diagram.*

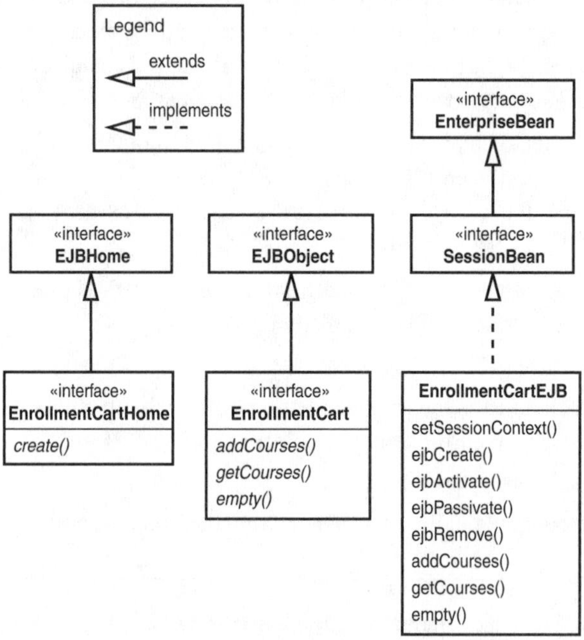

We provide remote interfaces to our stateful session bean. They include a remote home interface (EnrollmentCartHome) and a remote interface (EnrollmentCart). The EnrollmentCartHome home interface extends the javax.ejb.EJBHome interface and defines a single create() method. The EnrollmentCart remote interface extends the javax.ejb.EJBObject interface and defines the methods addCourses(), getCourses() and empty().

**Note**

Both stateful and stateless session beans provide the following class files: a) session bean class; b) session bean's remote home interface and remote interface, if the session bean provides a remote client view; c) session bean's local interface and local home interface, if the session bean provides a local client view.

Your session bean may provide both local and remote client views.

# Implementing the Stateful Session Bean

This section discusses the implementation of the remote home interface `EnrollmentCartHome`, the remote interface `EnrollmentCart`, and the stateful session bean class `EnrollmentCartEJB`.

## Defining the Home Interface

Clients use home interface to create and remove session bean instances. Within the home interface, we define one or more `create<method>(...)` methods. The container tools generate the class that corresponds to this interface.

 **Note**

> A stateful session bean may have more than one `create()` methods, and some of them may have arguments. This is different, though, from the case of a stateless session bean, which can only have one `create()` method with no arguments.

Listing 6.1 shows the home interface `EnrollmentCartHome`.

**LISTING 6.1** The Full Text of day06/EnrollmentCartHome.java

```
package day06;

import java.rmi.RemoteException;
import javax.ejb.*;

public interface EnrollmentCartHome extends EJBHome {
  EnrollmentCart create() throws CreateException, RemoteException;
}
```

The `EnrollmentCartHome` interface consists of a single `create()` method. To create the bean instance, a client calls the `create()` method of the home interface.

The `throws` clause of the `create()` method must include `CreateException`. This exception is thrown when there is a problem in creating or initializing the bean instance.

The remote home interface `EnrollmentCartHome` is a Java Remote Invocation Method (RMI) interface. So, the method arguments and return types of a remote method must be legal types for the RMI over Internet Inter-ORB Protocol (RMI/IIOP), such as primitives, serializable objects, and RMI/IIOP remote objects. Each method declared in the remote interface must include `java.rmi.RemoteException` in its `throws` clause. This exception is thrown when a remote invocation fails for some reason, such as network failure, protocol errors, and so on.

6

## Defining the Remote Interface

This interface exposes a session bean's business methods to the client. The client calls the methods defined in the remote interface to invoke the business logic implemented by the bean. The container tools generate the class corresponding to this interface.

As shown in Listing 6.2, our EnrollmentCart interface defines three business methods: addCourses() for adding courses to the cart, getCourses() to get the currently selected courses, and empty() to clear the enrollment cart.

**LISTING 6.2**    The Full Text of day06/EnrollmentCart.java

```
package day06;

import javax.ejb.*;
import java.rmi.RemoteException;
import java.util.Collection;

public interface EnrollmentCart extends EJBObject {
    public void addCourses(String[] courseIds) throws RemoteException;
    public Collection getCourses() throws RemoteException;
    public void empty() throws RemoteException;
}
```

The remote interface EnrollmentCart is a Java RMI interface. So, method arguments and return types of a remote method must be legal types for RMI/IIOP and the method must include java.rmi.RemoteException in its throws clause.

## Implementing the Enterprise Bean Class

Listing 6.3 shows the EnrollmentCartEJB enterprise bean class.

**LISTING 6.3**    The Full Text of day06/EnrollmentCartEJB.java

```
package day06;

import java.util.*;
import javax.ejb.*;
import javax.naming.*;

public class EnrollmentCartEJB implements SessionBean  {
    private SessionContext ctx;
    private HashSet cart;
    public EnrollmentCartEJB() {
        print("The container created this instance.\n");
```

**Listing 6.3**   continued

```
        }
        public void setSessionContext(SessionContext ctx) {
            print("The container called the setSessionContext method ");
            print("to associate session bean instance with its context.\n");
            this.ctx = ctx;
        }

        public void ejbCreate() throws CreateException {
            print("The container called the ejbCreate method.\n");
            cart = new HashSet();
        }
        public void ejbActivate() {
            print("This instance has just been reactivated.\n");
        }
        public void ejbPassivate() {
            print("The container intends to passivate the instance.\n");
        }
        public void ejbRemove() {
            print("This instance is in the process of being removed ");
            print("by the container.\n");
        }
        public void addCourses(String[] courseIds) {
            print("The container called addCourses method.\n");
            if ( courseIds == null) {
                return;
            }
            for ( int i = 0; i < courseIds.length ; i ++ ) {
                cart.add(courseIds[i]);
            }
        }
        public Collection getCourses() {
            print("The container called getCourses method.\n");
            return cart;
        }
        public void empty() {
            print("The container called empty method.\n");
            cart.clear();
        }
        void print(String s) {
            System.out.println(s);
        }
    }
}
```

6

The stateful session bean implements the `javax.ejb.SessionBean` interface. The member variable `cart` constitutes the enterprise bean's conversational state. The bean implements the methods `setSessionContext()`, `ejbCreate()`, `ejbActivate()`, ejbPassivate(), and ejbRemove(), as defined in the javax.ejb.SessionBean interface. The ejbCreate() method initializes the bean instance. The bean class implements the business methods addCourses(), getCourses() and empty() defined in its remote interface.

**Note**

> The EJB container serializes calls to each stateful session bean instance. This enables you to program a stateful bean as single-threaded, non-reentrant code. If two clients attempt to simultaneously access a session bean instance, the container throws an exception to the second client. The container throws java.rmi.RemoteException if the client is a remote client and javax.ejb.EJBException if the client is a local client.
>
> The container does not serialize calls to a stateless session bean instance because the container routes each client request to a different instance of the session bean class.

### Optional SessionSynchronization Interface

The SessionSynchronization interface, when implemented by the stateful session bean, allows the bean to be more transaction-aware. The container provides the bean with three callback methods: afterBegin(), beforeCompletion(), and afterCompletion(int). When the transaction begins, the container calls the afterBegin() method. The beforeCompletion() and afterCompletion(int) methods are used to manage resources before the transaction commits and aborts. We'll explore this interface on Day 16.

## Declaring the Deployment Descriptors

Now it's time to create the deployment descriptors. We need to create two deployment descriptors before creating the bean's JAR file (in our case, day06_EnrollmentCart.jar), which is required to deploy the enrollment cart's stateful session bean into the WebLogic EJB container. These deployment descriptors are

- Standard deployment descriptor ejb-jar.xml, as specified by Sun Microsystems, which is common to all EJBs
- Vendor-specific deployment descriptor; WebLogic uses weblogic-ejb-jar.xml and JBoss uses jboss.xml

### Declaring the Standard Deployment Descriptor ejb-jar.xml

This file is the standard descriptor as specified by Sun, and must contain the Sun Microsystems–specific EJB DTD.

The ejb-jar.xml describes the enterprise bean's deployment properties, such as its type and structure. As we learned on Day 2, this file provides the EJB container with information where it can find, and then load, the home interface, remote interface, and bean class. It declares its internal dependences and the application assembly information, which describes how the enterprise bean in the ejb-jar file (day06_EnrollmentCart.jar) is assembled into an application deployment unit.

Listing 6.4 shows the ejb-jar.xml file for the deployment descriptor of the EnrollmentCart EJB.

**LISTING 6.4**   The Full Text of day06/ejb-jar.xml

```
<?xml version="1.0"?>

<!DOCTYPE ejb-jar PUBLIC
'-//Sun Microsystems, Inc.//DTD Enterprise JavaBeans 2.0//EN'
'http://java.sun.com/dtd/ejb-jar_2_0.dtd'>

<ejb-jar>
  <enterprise-beans>
    <session>
      <ejb-name>EnrollmentCart</ejb-name>
      <home>day06.EnrollmentCartHome</home>
      <remote>day06.EnrollmentCart</remote>
      <ejb-class>day06.EnrollmentCartEJB</ejb-class>
      <session-type>Stateful</session-type>
      <transaction-type>Container</transaction-type>
    </session>
  </enterprise-beans>
</ejb-jar>
```

The prolog contains the declaration and the DTD for the validation. The document root is the <ejb-jar> tag. It contains the structural information about all the included enterprise beans. The enterprise-beans element contains the declarations of one or more enterprise beans. The session element declares a session bean, and an ejb-name element within the session element defines the session bean's name (EnrollmentCart). The session element also declares other things such as the home interface (day06.EnrollmentCartHome), the remote interface (day06.EnrollmentCart), and the bean's class (day06.EnrollmentCartEJB). The session-type element declares that this is a stateful session bean.

The transaction-type element specifies that this bean uses container-managed transactions. Container-managed transactions are discussed in detail on Day 18.

6

The deployment descriptor element session-type is where the EJB container recognizes a stateful or stateless session bean.

## Declaring the Vendor-Specific Deployment Descriptor

As you learned on Day 2, in addition to standard ejb-jar.xml, an application typically requires a certain amount of additional environment-specific or vendor-specific binding information, such as naming, security, and persistence. The following sections describe both the WebLogic and JBoss deployment descriptors.

### Declaring the WebLogic Deployment Descriptor: weblogic-ejb-jar.xml

The weblogic-ejb-jar.xml file contains the WebLogic Server–specific EJB DTD that defines the naming, caching, clustering, and performance behavior of the deployed EJBs.

Listing 6.5 shows the weblogic-ejb-jar.xml deployment descriptor.

**LISTING 6.5**   The Full Text of day06/weblogic-ejb-jar.xml

```
<?xml version="1.0"?>

<!DOCTYPE weblogic-ejb-jar PUBLIC
'-//BEA Systems, Inc.//DTD WebLogic 7.0.0 EJB//EN'
'http://www.bea.com/servers/wls700/dtd/weblogic-ejb-jar.dtd'>

<weblogic-ejb-jar>
  <weblogic-enterprise-bean>
    <ejb-name>EnrollmentCart</ejb-name>
        <stateful-session-descriptor>
          <stateful-session-cache>
              <max-beans-in-cache>5</max-beans-in-cache>
          </stateful-session-cache>
        </stateful-session-descriptor>
    <jndi-name>day06/EnrollmentCartHome</jndi-name>
  </weblogic-enterprise-bean>
</weblogic-ejb-jar>
```

The jndi-name element declares day06/EnrollmentCart as the JNDI name of the EnrollmentCart enterprise bean. The max-bean-in-cache element specifies the threshold at which WebLogic Server starts to passivate inactive instances in the instance cache to the back store. For demonstration purposes, we set the value to 5. As new concurrent clients request the bean's services, WebLogic Server creates new instances of the bean.

When the sixth client requests the bean's services, the server passivates some of the idle beans, perhaps using the LRU (Least Recently Used) algorithm.

### Declaring the JBoss Deployment Descriptor: `jboss.xml`

`jboss.xml`, the deployment descriptor that's specific to the JBoss server, defines the naming, caching, and other properties to control the behavior of the deployed EJBs. Listing 6.6 shows the `jboss.xml` file.

**LISTING 6.6**  The Full Text of `day06/jboss.xml`

```
<?xml version="1.0" encoding="UTF-8"?>

<jboss>
  <enterprise-beans>
    <session>
      <ejb-name>EnrollmentCart</ejb-name>
      <jndi-name>day06/EnrollmentCartHome</jndi-name>
    </session>
  </enterprise-beans>

 <container-configurations>
 <container-configuration>
   <container-name>Standard Stateful SessionBean</container-name>
   <container-cache-conf>
    <cache-policy>
<![CDATA[org.jboss.ejb.plugins.LRUStatefulContextCachePolicy]]>
     </cache-policy>
       <cache-policy-conf>
           <max-capacity>100</max-capacity>
           <max-bean-age>2</max-bean-age>
           <overager-period>2</overager-period>
       </cache-policy-conf>
   </container-cache-conf>
  </container-configuration>
 </container-configurations>
</jboss>
```

**6**

In this deployment descriptor, the `jndi-name` element declares `day06/EnrollmentCart` as the JNDI name of the `EnrollmentCart` enterprise bean. The `max-capacity` element specifies the maximum capacity of the cache as 100. The element `max-bean-age` element specifies the maximum period of inactivity in seconds that a bean can have before it will be passivated by the container. The `overager-period` element specifies the period in seconds at which the container scans the cache for inactive beans and passivates them.

For demonstration purposes, we specify the container look for inactive beans every two seconds and the bean is considered inactive if it is not accessed for two seconds.

# Writing the Client

Listing 6.7 demonstrates how a client accesses a stateful bean.

**LISTING 6.7**    The Full Text of day06/Client.java

```
package day06;

import java.util.*;
import javax.naming.*;
import javax.ejb.*;
public class Client {
  public static void main(String[] args) {
    print("Starting Client . . .\n");
    Context initialContext = null;
    EnrollmentCartHome enrollmentCartHome = null;
    EnrollmentCart enrollmentCart = null;
    print("Demonstration of a simple client . . . \n");
    try {
      // Looking up the enrollment cart home via JNDI
      initialContext = new InitialContext();
      Object object = initialContext.lookup("day06/EnrollmentCartHome");
      enrollmentCartHome = (EnrollmentCartHome)
       javax.rmi.PortableRemoteObject.narrow(object,
                                 EnrollmentCartHome.class);
      print("Creating an enrollment cart.\n");
      enrollmentCart =  (EnrollmentCart) enrollmentCartHome.create();
      String[] courseIds = { "CS101", "CS102", "CS103"};
      print("Adding some courses to our enrollment cart.\n");
      enrollmentCart.addCourses(courseIds);
      String[] moreCourseIds = { "CS201", "CS202", "CS203"};
      print("Adding some more courses to our enrollment cart.\n");
      enrollmentCart.addCourses(moreCourseIds);
      print("Getting the collection of courses in our enrollment cart.\n");
      Collection collection = enrollmentCart.getCourses();
      print("Removing our enrollment cart.\n");
      enrollmentCart.remove();

    } catch ( Exception e) {
      e.printStackTrace();
    }

    print("Demonstration of exceptions . . .\n");
```

**LISTING 6.7**   continued

```
        try {
           print("Now trying to access enrollment cart that was removed.\n");
           String[] courseIds = { "CS501" };
           enrollmentCart.addCourses(courseIds);
        } catch ( Exception e) {
          print("Exception caught while trying to access ");
          print(" enrollment cart that was removed.\n");
          print(e.toString());
        }
        print("Demonstration of Activation/Passivation . . .\n");
        try {
           EnrollmentCart carts[] = new EnrollmentCart[15];
           for ( int i = 0; i < 15 ; i++ ) {
              print("Creating cart " + i );
              carts[i] = enrollmentCartHome.create();
              String[] courseIds = { "CS601" };
              carts[i].addCourses(courseIds);
              Thread.sleep(1000);
           }
           for(int i = 0; i < 10; i++ ) {
              print("Removing cart" + i );
              carts[i].remove();
           }
        }
        catch(Exception e) {
           e.printStackTrace();
        }
     }
     static void print(String s) {
       System.out.println(s);
     }
}
```

The client locates the `EnrollmentCartHome` home interface of the deployed enterprise bean via JNDI, and then uses the remote home interface to create a remote `EnrollmentCart` session object. The client then calls the `addCourses()` business method, followed by the `getCourses()` business method, and removes the cart by calling `remove` method on the remote interface. Later, the client tries to access the session object that was removed earlier. This results in a `java.rmi.NoSuchObjectException` exception.

The client also demonstrates the activation and passivation by creating multiple instances of the bean. As you know, the container starts to passivate the instances when the number of instances in the cache reaches the threshold set in the vendor-specific deployment descriptor.

6

**Caution**

The EJB container may remove the session object in the following scenarios: a) A timeout due to client inactivity while the instance is in the passive state; b) A shutdown or crash of the container; c) A system exception thrown from the instance's method. All the object references and handles for the session object become invalid. If your client attempts to access the session object, the container will throw a `java.rmi.NoSuchObjectException` exception if the client is a remote client, or the `javax.ejb.NoSuchObjectLocalException` exception if the client is a local client.

# Packaging and Deploying the Enterprise Bean

The following shows the directory structure for the `EnrollmentCart` bean files and client for WebLogic Server:

```
C:\styejb\
        examples\
            day06\
                EnrollmentCart.java
                EnrollmentCartHome.java
                EnrollmentCartEJB.java
                ejb-jar.xml
                weblogic-ejb-jar.xml
                Client.java
```

For JBoss, replace the vendor-specific `weblogic-ejb-jar.xml` file with `jboss.xml`.

For JBoss, replace the vendor-specific `weblogic-ejb-jar.xml` file with `jboss.xml`.

To package and deploy the `EnrollmentCart` session bean for WebLogic Server, run the following commands:

```
C:>cd styejb\examples
```

```
C:\styejb\examples>setEnvWebLogic.bat
```

```
C:\styejb\examples>cd day06
```

```
C:\styejb\examples\day06>buildWebLogic.bat
```

You can run the script by entering the following commands:

```
C:>cd styejb\examples
```

```
C:\styejb\examples>setEnvWebLogic.bat
```

```
C:\styejb\examples>cd day06
```

```
C:\styejb\examples\day06>buildWebLogic.bat
```

The corresponding script for JBoss is `buildJBoss.bat`. Here are the steps to run the commands:

```
C:>cd styejb\examples
```

```
C:\styejb\examples>setEnvJBoss.bat
```

```
C:\styejb\examples>cd day06
```

```
C:\styejb\examples\day06>buildJBoss.bat
```

To deploy the `EnrollmentCart` bean, we used the hot deployment feature of both WebLogic (version 6.1 and higher) and JBoss (version 2.4 and higher). Deployment is performed simply by copying the bean's JAR file into the application deployment directory.

# Running the Example

The following steps describe how to run the example in either WebLogic Server or JBoss:

The following steps describe how to run the example in either WebLogic Server or JBoss:

1. Start the application server in a command window.

   In the case of WebLogic Server, use the following steps:

   ```
   C:>cd styejb\examples
   ```

   ```
   C:\styejb\examples>setEnvWebLogic.bat
   ```

   ```
   C:\styejb\examples>startWebLogic.bat
   ```

   In the case of JBoss, use the following steps:

   ```
   C:>cd styejb\examples
   ```

   ```
   C:\styejb\examples>setEnvJBoss.bat
   ```

   ```
   C:\styejb\examples>startJBoss.bat
   ```

2. Start the client program in another command window.

   In the case of WebLogic Server, use the following steps:

   ```
   C:>cd styejb\examples
   ```

   ```
   C:\styejb\examples>setEnvWebLogic.bat
   ```

   ```
   C:\styejb\examples>cd day06
   ```

   ```
   C:\styejb\examples\day06>runClientWebLogic.bat
   ```

6

In the case of JBoss, use the following steps:

```
C:>cd styejb\examples
C:\styejb\examples>setEnvWebLogic.bat
C:\styejb\examples>cd day06
C:\styejb\examples\day06>runClientJBoss.bat
```

The output of the `EnrollmentCart`, on both the client window, and the server window, should look like the following (see Figure 6.3). The correlation between both outputs is depicted in the figure.

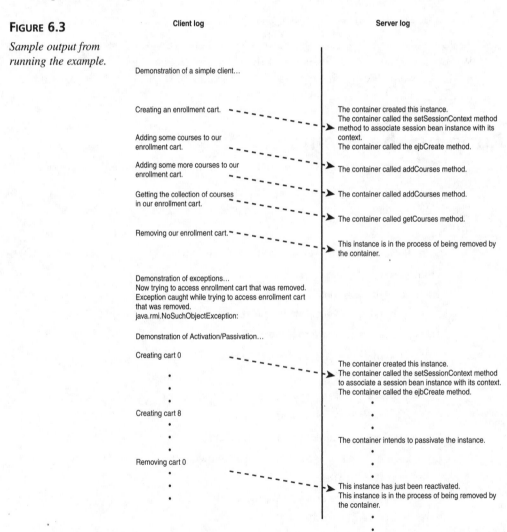

**FIGURE 6.3**

*Sample output from running the example.*

# Best Practices

A client should explicitly remove a stateful session bean by calling the `remove()` method of the component interface. Otherwise, the container keeps the stateful bean until it times out. This wastes resources such as memory, secondary storage, and so on.

Stateful session beans cannot be shared among different clients. A multithreaded client (such as a servlet or a Swing application) must serialize all its calls to the stateful session bean. Simultaneous access to a stateful session bean results in a `java.rmi.RemoteException` exception.

Consider tuning the stateful session bean's instance cache size. For best performance, the maximum number of beans in the cache should be equal to maximum number of concurrent clients. If the cache size is less than the number of concurrent clients, the container triggers activation and passivation, which degrades performance.

# Summary

Today you learned how to implement and deploy a stateful session bean. The home interface extends `javax.ejb.EJBHome` interface and contains `create` method(s). The remote interface extends `javax.ejb.EJBObject` and contains the business methods callable by the client. The enterprise bean class implements the `javax.ejb.SessionBean` interface. In addition, it implements the `ejbCreate` method(s) corresponding to the `create` methods defined in the home interface and business methods defined in the remote interface. The container recognizes the session bean type from the bean's deployment descriptor.

The EJB container serializes all calls to the stateful session bean instance and throws exception if clients attempt to simultaneously access the same bean instance. Also, the container throws an exception if the client attempts to access the session object that was removed earlier.

# Q&A

**Q What are the classes and interfaces that make a stateful session bean?**

**A** A stateful session bean is an EJB component, which extends two interfaces: a home interface (`EJBHome`) and a remote interface (`EJBObject`), and a bean class that implements the `SessionBean` interface.

**Q How can the EJB container recognize a bean as being a stateful session bean?**

**A** The EJB container distinguishes all types of beans from the standard deployment descriptor `ejb-jar.xml`. The tag `<session>` and the subtag `<session-type>` are used to set the stateful session bean in the deployment descriptor.

6

# Quiz

1. Which of the following are true about a stateful session bean:

    A. An instance is created for each client connected to the server.

    B. It can have a `create()` method that accepts arguments.

    C. It has a state or member fields that can be initialized and changed by the client with each business method invocation.

    D. It can never be passivated or activated by the container.

2. Which of the following are true when a stateful session bean is passivated by the container:

    A. The bean instance is stored for later reactivation.

    B. The bean instance is evicted from the application server memory.

    C. The bean instance is created and becomes ready.

    D. The bean state is serialized except for its transient member fields.

3. A stateful session bean is best used in which situation?

    A. More than one caller is concurrently connected to use the service.

    B. Persistence is a primary requirement.

    C. Instance is required to be thread-safe.

    D. You want to manage client state in a transactional and secure environment.

## Quiz Answers

1. A, B, and C
2. A, B, and D
3. C

# Exercises

To extend your knowledge of the subjects covered today, try the following exercises:

1. Define a `deleteCourses(String[] courseIds)` method in the remote interface `EnrollmentCart`. Add a corresponding `deleteCourses(String[] courseId)` method in the enterprise bean class `EnrollmentCartEJB`.

2. Modify the sample client to make use of the method in exercise 1 by deleting some of the courses in the `EnrollmentCartEJB`.

# DAY 7

# Designing Web Applications

Web applications consist of Web components that are responsible for processing Web client requests, invoking the business logic tier, and delivering data in response to client requests. Web components can be servlets, JavaServer Pages (JSPs), JavaBeans, or JSP tag libraries (taglibs). Web applications are packaged and deployed into the Web container using WAR (Web Archive) files. The Web tier handles all communications between Web clients (browsers) and business logic components in the EJB tier. The MVC (Model-View-Controller) architecture pattern is used mainly to design Web applications. The Web tier typically produces HTML (or XML) content in response to the client request, whereas business logic is often implemented as EJB components in the EJB tier, although it may also be implemented entirely within the Web tier using Web components.

In learning about the Web container and the Web components today, you'll

- Learn about Web applications, the Web container and its common services
- Learn about Java servlets as server-side components to process client requests
- Explore the JavaServer Pages technology to generate dynamic contents
- Learn how to develop a simple JSP tag library to hide application logic from its presentation
- Study the MVC architecture pattern that can be applied to the design of scalable Web applications
- Learn how to package and deploy a Web application using the Web tier deployment descriptor

# Understanding Web Applications

The Web tier manages the interactions between Web clients and the application business logic. Typically, the Web tier generates dynamic content including HTML, XML, images, sound, video, and Java applets as responses to a client's HTTP requests. These requests can be in the form of either HTTP PUT or GET actions that are processed by the Web components to generate results back to the client. Normally, the Web container can be configured to generate and serve any content type. Business logic, on the other hand, is often implemented as EJB, which is managed by the EJB container. Web components are not transactional by design; however, they might start the transactions, which can be executed by the EJBs.

The Web tier separates application business logic from direct interaction by the client. This allows more flexibility in designing enterprise applications with different types of clients. Presentation logic is captured by Web components such as servlets, JSPs, JSP tag libraries, and JavaBeans. These Web components are deployed to and managed by the Web container.

The presentation logic is usually encapsulated into Web components that are separated from the presentation itself (that is, the contents to be displayed). The presentation logic is responsible for processing client requests, validating user input, and determining the flow of the Web pages.

In designing Web applications, the Web container can be used to maintain the user sessions, the application state, and the component's life cycle. The Web container is part of the Java 2 Enterprise Edition (J2EE) application server, therefore all common services offered by the J2EE architecture are automatically available to the Web container. Examples of such services are Java Naming and Directory Interface (JNDI), Java

Database Connectivity (JDBC), Java Message Service (JMS), and JavaMail. Figure 7.1 depicts the Web container, Web components, and J2EE common services.

**Caution**

As you learned in Day 6, using stateful session beans to maintain session information is a better option in designing transactional and secure enterprise applications.

**FIGURE 7.1**

*The Web container and Web components.*

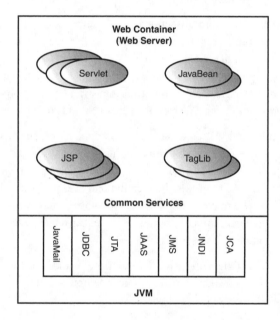

In the next few sections, you'll learn how to work with four types of Web components: servlets, JavaServer Pages, JSP tag libraries, and JavaBeans.

**Note**

Any of these components can access, in similar fashion, all the common services we discuss in this book. So far, we've covered JNDI on Day 4, "Using JNDI for Naming Services and Components." JDBC will be covered on Day 9, "Using JDBC to Connect to a Database," JMS on Day 13, "Understanding JMS and Message-Driven Beans," and "Implementing JavaMail in EJB Applications," on Day 20. Above all, these Web components act as clients to the EJB components. We'll discuss some of the design consideration of accessing EJB from the Web tier when we discuss the MVC pattern later today.

7

# Working with Servlets

A *servlet* is a server-side component (Java class) that is deployed, executed, and managed by a J2EE-compliant Web container (Web server). A servlet handles HTTP requests and provides HTTP responses, usually in the form of an HTML, XML, or text document.

Servlets are most effectively used for implementing presentation logic and generating binary content such as images. A servlet in the Web tier allows a Web client (browser) to indirectly interact with EJB business logic.

Servlets are portable and non-transactional Java components, which run in servlet engine (container) that can run on any operating system or hardware. They are analogous to the applets that are used on the client container (Web browser). Servlets are the backbone of any e-commerce application such as online shopping carts, financial services, and personalized content. They are mainly used to get and validate user input, authenticate user identity, and generate dynamic Web content that responds to the user's input.

Servlets are used to track a user session in Web applications, such as shopping carts. They also can be used to access directory and naming services, databases, JMS messaging services, and JavaMail. They can be used to build secure applications by using Access Control Lists (ACLs) for authentication and Secure Sockets Layer (SSL) to provide encryption for secure communications. The most important use of servlets is to act as controllers and delegates in accessing EJBs to encapsulate sessions, data from databases, and other functionality.

The following few sections will give brief descriptions of the servlet API, accompanied with few examples. Later today, we'll demonstrate how servlets work as controllers and are used to access EJBs as client delegates.

## Creating a Simple Servlet

Servlets are defined in the `javax.servlet` package. To write a servlet, you must extend the `javax.servlet.http.HttpServlet` class (which implements the `javax.servlet.Servlet` interface). The Web container instantiates the servlet by calling the `init()` method of the `Servlet` interface. All requests are dispatched by the container to the `service()` method, which is the heart of servlet operations. Based on the request type, the `service()` method dispatches calls to other specialized service methods. For example, the `service()` method dispatches HTTP GET requests to be handled by the service method `doGet()`, and HTTP POST requests to be handled by `doPost()` method, and so on. To implement a servlet, you must override any of the service methods. Each of the service methods runs on a separate thread of execution. Finally, the Web container removes the servlet from memory after calling the `destroy()` method. The following is the basic code to write a simple servlet:

```
import javax.servlet.*;
import javax.servlet.http.*;
import java.io.*;
public class SimpleServlet extends HttpServlet {
  // The service method handles HTTP requests and response
  public void service(HttpServletRequest request,
                      HttpServletResponse response)
                      throws IOException, ServletException {
    response.setContentType("text/html");
    PrintWriter out = response.getWriter();
    out.print("<html><head><title>" +
              "Hello from my first Servlet!</title></head><body>" +
              "<h3>Hello from my first Servlet!</h3></body></html>");
  }
  public void init(ServletConfig config)  throws ServletException{
      super.init(config);
  }
}
```

In the preceding example, the `SimpleServlet` extends the `HttpServlet` class and over-rides only the generic `service()` method.

**Note**

> If you choose to implement the `service()` method, you cannot implement the `doPost()` or `doGet()` method unless you call `super.service()` at the beginning of your `service()` method.

Any of the service methods accepts an HTTP request from the Web browser as input, and returns an HTTP response as output, as defined by the `HttpServletRequest` and `HttpServletResponse` classes, respectively.

**Note**

> HTTP request types can be GET, POST, PUT, HEAD, DELETE, OPTIONS, or TRACE. The corresponding service methods are `doGet()`, `doPost()`, `doPut()`, and so on. Each `doXXX()` method accepts the same parameters as the `service()` method.

In the response parameter, you first set the content type to `"text/html"`, get a reference to a `java.io.PrintWriter` object to use for output, and then create some HTML using the `print()` method of the `PrintWriter` object.

The `init()` method is called by the container before any service method. It accepts one parameter as an object of the `ServletConfig` class, which contains configuration data set

7

by the Web container. The `init()` method must call the `super.init()` method. In some Web applications, the `init()` method is used to establish a connection to external resources, which can be cleaned up in the `destroy()` method before the servlet ends its life cycle.

Our `SimpleServlet` can then be compiled and deployed to a J2EE-compliant Web container. To run the servlet, you simply call it by its URI from your browser. Servlets and other resources (such as JSPs and images) are packaged into a single unit (or module) called a *Web application*. A Web application utilizes a specific directory structure to contain its resources and a deployment descriptor `web.xml` file that defines how these resources interact and how the Web application is accessed by a Web client. A Web application may also be deployed as an archive file called a `.war` file. Figure 7.2 illustrates the directory structure of a sample Web application.

**FIGURE 7.2**

*Directory structure of a sample Web application.*

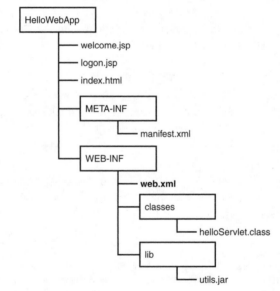

The servlet API has one exception, `ServletException`, which can be thrown when the servlet encounters difficulty.

**Note**

By default, the servlet architecture is multithreaded, which generally boosts the application's scalability. However, you can set your servlets to work in a single-threaded model by implementing the `SingleThreadModel` interface.

## Processing Client Requests

One of the major tasks of servlets is to process client requests to generate a result. Servlets use the `HttpServletRequest` method to retrieve data from the request object. Table 7.1 summarizes the methods of the `HttpServletRequest`.

**TABLE 7.1** Summary of Methods of `HttpServletRequest` Class

| Method | Description |
|---|---|
| getMethod() | Returns the name of the HTTP method; for example, GET, POST, or PUT. |
| getQueryString() | Enables you to access the query string (the remainder of the requested URL, following the ? character) of the HTTP GET method. |
| getParameter(String *name*) | Returns the value of a parameter as a `String`. |
| getParameterNames() | Returns an array of all the parameter names. |
| getParameterValues() | Returns an enumeration of values for all the parameter. |
| getInputStream() | Retrieves the body of the request as binary data. |

Here is an example to illustrate how to extract the request parameters and display them out on the screen. The following is the source of the FORM containing the login information of Figure 7.3:

```
<HTML>
<HEAD>
<TITLE>University Registration Page</TITLE>
</HEAD>
<BODY>
<FORM METHOD="POST" NAME="RegistrationPage"
        ACTION="/servlet/DisplayParameters">
<h3>Registration Form</h3>
 Login name<input type="text" size=20 name="loginname" value=""><br>
 Password : <input type="password" size=20 name="password" value="" ><br>
 First Name:<input type="text" size=20 name="firstname" value="" ><br>
 Last Name:<input type="text" size=20 name="lastname" value="" ><br>
 <input type="submit" value="Register" name="registerbutton"><br>
</FORM>
</BODY>
</HTML>
```

You'll notice that the preceding form uses the POST method and targets the `DisplayParameters` servlet, as displayed in the `Action` tag.

7

**Note**

There are two methods in submitting forms: POST and GET. The POST
method sends the action and the parameters as name/value pairs in the
body of the message. The GET method sends this data appended to the URL,
which is exposed to the user. Use GET if the length of your value strings is
not long (less than 8KB). POST is appropriate for long messages with more
private information.

**FIGURE 7.3**

*Logon form to the uni-
versity registration sys-
tem.*

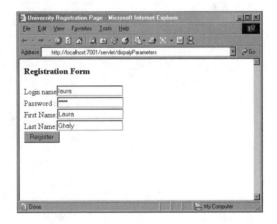

The following is the listing of the `DisplayParameters` servlet, which will display all the
parameters of the form and their values on the screen:

```
import javax.servlet.*;
import javax.servlet.http.*;
import java.io.*;
import java.util.*;

public class DisplayParameters extends HttpServlet{
  public void doPost(HttpServletRequest request,
                     HttpServletResponse response)
    throws ServletException, IOException {
    response.setContentType("text/html");
    PrintWriter out = response.getWriter();
    Enumeration params = request.getParameterNames();
    while(params.hasMoreElements()) {
      String param = (String)params.nextElement();
      out.println(param + " : ");
      String[] paramValues = request.getParameterValues(param);
      if (paramValues.length == 1)
          out.print(paramValues[0]);
      else
```

```
          for(int i=0; i< paramValues.length; i++)
            out.println(paramValues[i]);
      }
  }
```

When the preceding servlet is executed, the Web container directs the request to the
`service()` method, which in turn dispatches it to the `doPost()` method.

## Handling Both Static and Dynamic Content

Servlets generate both dynamic and static content to construct a Web page. When delivering content, a good practice is to cache all static content in the `init()` method, which
reduces the creation time for every request. The following listing shows a technique you
can use when you want to use servlets to deliver both static data and dynamic data to the
client:

```
import javax.servlet.*;
import javax.servlet.http.*;
import java.io.*;
import java.util.*;

public class CacheServlet extends HttpServlet{
  byte[] header, footer, navbar;
  byte[] staticContent;
  public void init(ServletConfig config) throws ServletException{
      super.init();
      // Cache all the static content
      StringBuffer tmp = new StringBuffer();
      // Cache the header
      tmp.append("<html><head><title>");
      tmp.append("University Registration</title></head><body>");
      header = tmp.toString().getBytes();
      // Cache the footer, and navbar here
  }
  public void service(HttpServletRequest req, HttpServletResponse res)
          throws ServletException, IOException {
      res.setContentType("text/html");
      PrintWriter out = res.getWriter();
      out.write(new String(header));
      out.write(new String(navbar));
      // write dynamic data here for the body
      out.write(new String(footer));
  }
}
```

This caching technique enhances your application performance because static data is
ready to be delivered in the response. Figure 7.4 depicts a site wire-frame in which
dynamic content is generated for the body part of the page outline.

7

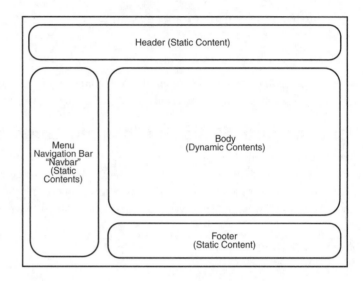

# Tracking User Session by Servlets

HTTP is a stateless protocol, and a Web application, such as a shopping cart, needs a mechanism of tracking user session over multiple HTML pages. A *session* is defined as a series of related browser requests that come from the same client during a certain period of time. Servlets provide the following mechanisms of tracking sessions. Notice that in all these techniques, some form of token is passed between the client and the server.

- Hidden fields
- HTTP cookies
- `HTTPSession` object
- URL rewriting

In the following section, we'll explore each technique.

## Tracking User Session Using Hidden Fields

This mechanism tracks user session in a hidden field of an HTML page and passes the data between the client and the server. The advantages of using this technique are its easy implementation, and that session state is not saved on the server side. Using a large amount of user data in the hidden fields will degrade application performance. Additionally, hidden fields are limited to storing only string values, which can be exposed in the generated HTML source unless encrypted to preserve user privacy. An example of an HTML page with hidden fields is as follows:

```
<FORM METHOD="POST" ACTION="/servlet/SignOnServlet">
...
```

```
<INPUT TYPE=hidden NAME="userid" VALUE="mary">
<INPUT TYPE=hidden NAME="type" VALUE="student">
...
</FORM>
```

In this technique, no data is stored on the client disk storage; only hidden fields are passed between the browser and the Web container.

## Tracking User Session Using Cookies

This mechanism of session tracking is used for storing limited amount of user data on the client side. A *cookie* is a piece of data that the server creates to store user information and asks the Web browser to save locally on the user's disk. A cookie is identified by the URL it originated from. Each time a browser visits the same server (URL), it sends all cookies relevant to that server with the HTTP request. Cookies are useful for identifying clients as they return to the server.

Each cookie has a name and a value. A browser that supports cookies generally allows each server domain to store up to 20 cookies of up to 4KB of ASCII data per cookie. Cookies cannot store Unicode or binary values. Users can disable or enable cookies from the browser.

The following listing creates a `SignOnCookie`, gives it the value `"mary"` as a user ID, and adds it to the `HttpServletResponse` object of the service method:

```
// Create a cookie
Cookie myCookie = new Cookie("SignOnCookie", "mary");
myCookie.setMaxAge(Integer.MAX_VALUE);
response.addCookie(myCookie);
```

When the Web browser receives the response, it stores all the cookies on the user's disk, provided that the user has enabled cookies. The following listing illustrates how a returning client can be recognized by the Web application:

```
public class CheckServlet extends HttpServlet{
 public void service(HttpServletRequest req, HttpServletResponse res){
   Cookie myCookie = null;
   HttpSession session = req.getSession(false);
    if (session==null) {
      // Try to retrieve the cookie from the request.
      Cookie[] cookies = req.getCookies();
      for(int i=0; i < cookies.length; i++) {
        myCookie = cookies[i];
        if (myCookie.getName().equals("SignOnCookie")) {
          isFound = true;
          break;
          }
        }
      if (isFound == true) {
```

7

```
        // Create a new session for this user.
        //session = request.getSession (true);
        session.setAttribute("mary", myCookie.getValue());
        // Refresh cookie to live indefinitely.
        myCookie.setMaxAge(Integer.MAX_VALUE);
        // Add the cookie to the response
        res.addCookie(myCookie);
      }
    }
  }
}
```

The cookie in the preceding example is set not to expire. Because cookies accept only string values, you should cast to and from the desired type that you want to store in the cookie.

## Tracking User Session Using `HttpSession`

This mechanism tracks the user session by storing all session information on the server side. Only a small piece of data (session ID) is stored on the client side and passed between the client and server for each request. According to the Servlet API, each servlet can access a server-side session by using its `HttpSession` object. You access the `HttpSession` object in the `service()` method of the servlet by using the `HttpServletRequest` object as follows:

```
HttpSession session = request.getSession(true);
```

A session is associated automatically with a particular client. An `HttpSession` object is created if one does not already exist for that client. Each client is matched with its particular session object by passing a session ID. The session object lives on the Web container for the lifetime of the session, during which the session object accumulates data related to that client. You can add or remove data from the session object as necessary, which will be maintained in the servlet context. In the following example, the `service()` method counts the number of hits that a client requests the servlet during one session:

```
public void service(HttpServletRequest req, HttpServletResponse res)
        throws ServletException, IOException {
  // Get the client session associated with this request
  PrintWriter out = res.getWriter();
  HttpSession session = req.getSession(true);
  Integer value = (Integer) session.getAttribute("mySession.hits");
  if (value == null)
     value = new Integer (1);
  else
     value = new Integer (value.intValue () + 1);
  // Set the new name/value pair
  session.setAttribute("mySession.hits", value);
  // Output the HTML page
  out.print("<HTML><head></head><body>");
```

```
   out.print("You have visited this page ");
   out.print(value + " times!");
   out.println("<br>Session ID: " + session.getId());
   out.println("<br>Session creation time: " +
                 session.getCreationTime());
   out.println("<br>Last accessed time: " +
                 session.getLastAccessedTime());
   out.print("</body></html>");
 }
```

The `HttpSession` mechanism gives better performance because it stores the session data in memory and reduces network overhead. Only the session ID will be passed between the client and the server. The `HttpSession` object can hold data such as shopping carts and visit history, but it is not used to hold user profiles.

## Tracking User Session Using URL Rewriting

This technique is used mainly if the users disable cookies from their browsers. URL rewriting allows servlets to append a user session ID at the end of any generated link (URL). URL rewriting resulted in moderate performance because the extra data must be passed between the client and the server for each request. Nonetheless, only a limited amount of user data can pass through URL rewriting. The Java servlet API provides two methods in the `HttpResponse` interface to encode the URLs. The `encodeURL()` method encodes the specified URL by appending the session ID to it. The following code shows an example of how URL rewriting may be used:

```
HttpSession session = req.getSession(true);
res.setContentType("text/html");
PrintWriter out = res.getWriter();
...
// URL Rewriting
String url = res.encodeURL("/servlet/SignOnServlet");
// Make a link to the URL rewritten
out.println("<A HREF=\"" + url + "\"> Login </A>");
...
```

The servlet will append the session ID to the URL. The new URL will look like this:

```
http://www.mysite.com/servlet/SignOnServlet;jsessionid=123456
```

All URLs generated by a servlet should be run through the `encodeURL()` method. URL rewriting is a useful technique when users have disabled cookies in their browsers.

# Working with Servlets as Delegates to EJBs

7

One of the primary tasks of servlets is to work as delegates for Web browsers to access an EJB indirectly. The following example illustrates how to access the `StudentFacade` EJB from our University Registration System (see Figure 7.5). Immediately after it creates the `SignOnServlet` instance, the Web container calls the instance's `init()` method. This method looks up the EJB home in the JNDI service, and then creates the bean:

```
public void init() throws ServletException {
    InitialContext ic = new InitialContext();
    StudentFacadeHome home = (StudentFacadeHome)
                        ctx.lookup("day21/StudentFacade");
    StudentFacade studentFacade = null;
    try {
        studentFacade = (StudentFacade) home.create();
        session.putValue("StudentFacade", studentFacade);
    catch(Exception e) {
        e.printStackTrace();
    }
  }
}
```

When the user clicks on the `Submit` button of the HTML form, the Web container calls the `doPost()` method of the `SignOnServlet`. The `doPost()` method fetches the value of the Login Name and Password fields (entered by the end user), and then invokes the `addUser()` business method of the `StudentFacade` EJB:

```
public void doPost (HttpServletRequest req, HttpServletResponse res)
        throws ServletException, IOException {
    String loginName = req.getParameter("Login name");
    String password = req.getParameter("Password");
    try{
      studentFacade.addUser(loginName, password);
      res.setContentType("text/html");
      PrintWriter out = res.getWriter();
      ...
    }catch{
      e.printStackTrace();
    }
}
```

**FIGURE 7.5**

*Servlets work as delegates of clients to EJBs.*

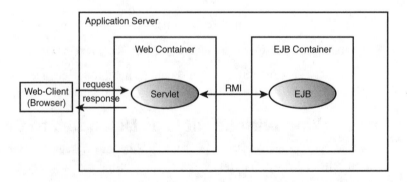

# Learning JavaServer Pages

Servlets provide an excellent mechanism for handling user requests for dynamic content, but they lack a useful way of displaying the response. Servlets rely on hard-coding of the presentation within the Java code. Any change in the look and feel of the presentation requires change to the code. This also mixes the roles of Web designers and Java programmers, which leads to chaos in the development process. JSP was developed to answer these concerns.

Servlets incorporate a tight coupling of content and logic, which reduces application flexibility. With JSP, you don't want to repeat the same issues. JSPs should be used with static content templates and generate dynamic content by calling presentation logic outside the JSP. Such presentation logic can be encapsulated in JSP tag libraries. This separation of the static content from the presentation logic makes the application more flexible to change. With JSP, Web designers can focus on developing only the system GUI with the required look and feel. On the other hand, Web developers can handle the presentation logic in taglibs, JavaBeans, or scriptlets. We'll talk more about these topics later today.

JSP is a cross-platform API, and it brings the power of server-side Java technology with static HTML pages. It provides an efficient method of delivering dynamic content through the Web. You can create and maintain JSP pages with conventional HTML/XML editors. A JSP page typically consists of the following elements:

- Static HTML/XML components
- Special JSP tags
- Scriptlets

## Writing a Simple JSP

The JSP API is defined on top of the Servlet API. Each JSP page inherently implements the HttpJspPage interface of the javax.servlet.jsp package. A JSP page is compiled into, and run as, a servlet (see Figure 7.6). Therefore, whatever experience you've gained about servlets thus far is applicable in developing JSPs. The main difference between servlets and JSPs is that servlet programming requires significant developer expertise, but JSP enjoys a much wider audience. JSP's primary owner is the page designer, who is responsible of proving contents to build the application's presentation. JSP is also used by the developer to provide the hooks and the references to the presentation logic. The main advantage of the concept of JSP is its inherent separation of presentation logic from content.

7

FIGURE 7.6

*A JSP is compiled and*
*run as a servlet.*

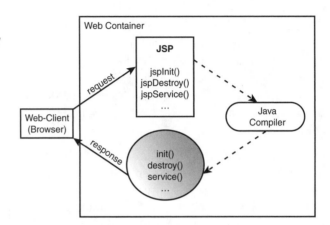

Here is an example of a JSP, which is stored in the file `simple.jsp`:

```
<!doctype html public "-//w3c/dtd HTML 4.0//en">
<html>
  <%@ page errorPage="error.jsp" %>
  <%@ page isThreadSafe="true" %>
  <!-- Standard HTML Comment-->
<head>
   <title>Hello World from a JSP</title>
</head>
<body>
  <font face="Arial"> <h2>Hello World from an HTML </h2></font>
  <!-- An expression to print Hello World From a JSP to the out object -->
  <% out.print("<h2>Hello World from a JSP!</h2>"); %>
</body>
</html>
```

In this example, JSP tags are embedded into the HTML code (shown in bold). You are already familiar with the comment symbols `<!-- comments -->` used in HTML markup. The `<%@ ... %>` tag is used as a directive to the JSP container, and the `<% exp %>` tag is used to execute the expression `exp`, which is also called a *scriptlet*.

When a JSP is compiled and translated into a Java servlet, all the implicit methods of the `HttpJspPage` interface, such as `_jspInt()`, `_jspDestroy()`, and `_jstService()` are translated into the underlying servlet methods `init()`, `destroy()`, and `service()`. You don't have to override any JSP methods unless you have to implement such logic, which is what we're trying to avoid.

Both JSPs and servlets typically run within multithreaded containers (see Figure 7.7).

**FIGURE 7.7**

*Multithreaded and single-threaded models of a servlet.*

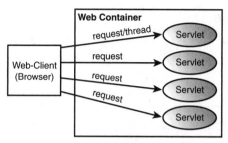

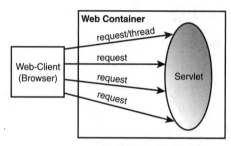

All running servlets and JSPs on the same container must handle concurrent requests, so you must be careful to synchronize access to any shared resources. Such shared resources include database connections and JMS destinations. By default, the service method of the JSP page is multithreaded. But if you need to change the default model and run using a `SingleThreadModel`, you can use the following directive:

```
<%@ page isThreadSafe="false" %>
```

This causes the JSP page implementation class to implement the `SingleThreadModel` interface, which results in the synchronization of the service method, and causes multiple instances of the servlet to be loaded in memory.

 **Tip**

Try to avoid the single-threaded approach because it is not scalable, and it has a negative impact on response time.

The next section summarizes the basic syntax of JSP.

7

## Learning JSP Basics

Learning JSP basic syntax is simple and can be classified into the following sections: comments, directives, scripting tags, and standard JSP actions.

### Comments

There are two types of comments in JSP. You can use the HTML comments `<!-- ...`
`-->`, as we did in the earlier example. This type of comment can be viewed in the page's source code. To avoid that, you can use the other type of JSP comments, the `<%-- ...`
`--%>` tag:

```
<%-- JSP comment. Only stays at the server side. Can't be viewed by user --%>
```

As usual, comments are very powerful constructs for all programming languages.

### Directives

JSP directives are messages to the Web container. They instruct the container what to do with the rest of the JSP page. All JSP directives are enclosed within the `<%@ ... %>` tag. The two main directives are `page` and `include`.

#### page Directive

The `page` directive is typically found at the top of almost all of your JSP pages. There can be any number of `page` directives within a JSP page. Two examples of `page` directives were included in the previous section, but here's another example:

```
<%@ page import="java.util.*, javax.naming.*" buffer="16k" %>
```

This imports the included packages for scripting and sets the page buffer to 16KB.

#### include Directive

The `include` directive performs a compile-time include. It enables you to separate your presentation into more manageable files, such as those for including a common page `header`, `navbar`, or `footer`. The included page can be any HTML, XML, or JSP page. An example of an `include` directive is as follows:

```
<%@ include file="header.html" %>
```

You can also use a fully qualified URL in the `include` directive.

### Scripting Tags

All JSP tags start with `<%` and end with `%>`. Each scripting tag is recognized by an extra special character. The following sections discuss these scripting tags.

### Declaring Variables and Methods

Like its Java parent, JSP is a strongly typed language. It requires all variables to be declared before they are used in your JSP code. This helps to create more robust code. When declaring a variable, you use the <%! ... %> tag. Remember to end your variable declarations with a semicolon. Here's an example of a declaration:

```
<%! float amount=0.0; %>
```

You can also declare methods using the same directive. For example, you can declare a method as follows:

```
<%! public float getCelsius(float f) {
  return (float) ((f - 32)/1.8);
}
%>
```

### Executing Expressions

An expression is the assignment statement in JSP. You basically evaluate the expression and assign the result to the page's output stream. Typically, expressions are used to display simple values of variables or return values by invoking JavaBean or taglib methods. JSP expressions use the <%= ... %> tags.

```
<H3><%= myJavaBean.getTitle() %></H3>
<p> The value of temperature in Celsius: <%= getCelsius(temp) %> </p>
<%= myTagLib.getWarning(temp) %>
```

The value of each expression is evaluated and printed to the output stream.

 **Caution**    JSP expressions do not end with a semicolon.

### Executing Java Code with Scriptlets

Scriptlets are Java code fragments that can be embedded within the <% ... %> tags. The Java code can be used to generate dynamic content. Any valid Java code snippet can be used within a scriptlet. The following is an example of displaying the string Hello from my JSP page! within different heading types:

```
<% for (int m=1; m<=4; m++) { %>
<H<%=m%>>Hello from my JSP page!</H<%=m%>>
<% } %>
```

This example combines both scriptlets and JSP expressions. Scriptlets are useful mechanisms for dealing with synchronization issues, as described later today.

7

### Summary of Scripting Tags

Each scripting element has a special type of tag syntax. All JSP tags start with <% and end with %>. An extra character is used to recognize the type of scripting element. The @ is used for directives, ! for declaration, and = for evaluating expressions. Table 7.2 summarizes the scripting tags used in authoring JSP pages and discussed in this section.

**TABLE 7.2**   Summary of Scripting Tags

| Tag | Purpose |
| --- | --- |
| <!-- ... --> | HTML or XML comments; can be viewed by the client |
| <%-- ... --%> | JSP comments; stays on the server side |
| <% ... %> | Scriptlets executing Java code fragments |
| <%@ ... %> | page and include directives |
| <%! ... %> | Declaration of variables and methods |
| <%= ... %> | Evaluation and output expressions |

## JSP Implicit Objects

Implicit objects are convenient tools that are automatically provided by the Web container. They can be used within scriptlets and JSP expressions. You don't have to instantiate any of these objects. They are defined within the Servlet API. Table 7.3 lists a summary of the JSP implicit objects.

**TABLE 7.3**   Summary of Implicit Objects

| Object | Purpose | Scope |
| --- | --- | --- |
| request | Represents the HttpServletRequest. | Request |
| response | Represents HttpServletResponse. Not intended for use by page authors. | Page |
| pageContext | Encapsulates implementation-dependent features in PageContext. | Page |
| application | Represents the ServletContext obtained from the ServletConfig object. | Application |
| out | JspWriter object that writes into the output stream. | Page |
| config | Represents the ServletConfig for the JSP. | Page |
| page | Represents HttpJspPage. Synonym to the this operator. Not intended for use by page authors. | Page |
| session | Represents HttpSession. | Session |
| exception | Represents Exception object. | Page |

## Standard JSP Actions (Taglibs)

Standard JSP actions are types of extension of tag libraries available by default and provided by the JSP API. In the next section, we'll introduce how to develop your own taglib. While the Web container is compiling a JSP into a servlet and encounters a taglib name, it generates all the classes required to perform such action. For example, the action

```
<jsp:forward page="register.jsp">
```

allows the response to be forwarded to another JSP.

Table 7.4 lists all the standard JSP actions provided by the JSP API. In the next section, you'll learn how to develop your own taglib.

**TABLE 7.4**   Summary of Standard JSP Actions (Taglibs)

| Standard Action | Action Description |
| --- | --- |
| `<jsp:useBean>` | Allows access to a JavaBean object, retrieved from a given scope or newly instantiated, through a named identifier. |
| `<jsp:setProperty>` | Sets the value of a JavaBean property. |
| `<jsp:getProperty>` | Outputs a JavaBean property, converted to a `String`. |
| `<jsp:include>` | Allows inclusion of static and dynamic content within the current JSP page. Any HTML, JSP, servlet, image, or text can be included. |
| `<jsp:forward>` | Forwards the responsibility for request handling to another static or dynamic resource. |
| `<jsp:plugin>` | Instructs the browser to enable use of the Java plug-in with applets or JavaBeans. |
| `<jsp:param>` | Used in connection with the `include`, `forward`, and `plugin` action tags to supply parameters in key/value pairs. Can be used as a subaction for `<jsp:include>`, `<jsp:forward>`, and `<jsp:plugin>`. |

We'll cover the `<jsp:useBean>` action in more detail in the "Understanding JavaBeans" section later today.

## Handling JSP Exceptions

The JSP architecture provides an elegant mechanism for handling runtime exceptions by making use of the `page` directive and the `errorPage` attribute. For example,

```
<%@ page isErrorPage="false" errorPage="errorPage.jsp" %>
```

7

instructs the Web container to forward any uncaught exception to the `errorPage.jsp`
page. It is then necessary for `errorPage.jsp` to flag itself as an error-processing page by
using the following directive:

```
<%@ page isErrorPage="true" %>
```

 **Note**

Handling exceptions with this built-in routine is much more appropriate
than providing your own exception handler, which would be required in all
your JSP pages, and might not anticipate all cases that could be encountered
at run-time.

# Using a JSP Tag Library

JSP is an efficient mechanism for providing presentation content, which is mainly the
look-and-feel view of the application. Putting too much logic in a JSP makes your application brittle and not easy to change. A custom tag library can be developed to provide a
clean separation of presentation logic (usually handled by Java developers) and presentation content (displaying the application's data, which is usually handled by page designers). To accomplish this goal, the JSP architecture provides a set of standard taglibs (refer
to the "Standard JSP Actions (Taglibs)" section earlier). In this section, you'll learn how
to develop your own taglib to customize your application.

A taglib, or tag handler, is a Java class that either extends the `TagSupport` (or
`BodyTagSupport`) class, or implements the `Tag` (or `BodyTag`) interface of the
`javax.servlet.jsp.tagext` package. The taglib class must react to the Web container
callback methods. Therefore, it must implement the `doStartTag()`, which is called when
the tag starts, and the `doEndTag()` method, which is called when the tag ends.

You use a tag to produce output or to define new objects that can be referenced and used
as scripting variables in the JSP page. The following is a simple example of a JSP that
uses a taglib to display a personalized greeting message to the student after she has
logged in to enroll for courses:

```
<%@ taglib uri="/welcome" prefix="student" %>
<HTML>
  <BODY>
    <student:welcome userId="remo"/>
  </BODY>
</HTML>
```

This JSP will display a personalized message:

```
Welcome back <Full student name>. It's <date and time>
```

In the example, the tag name is identified by the prefix student and the suffix welcome. No other attributes or scripting variables are used in this simple tag.

The following lists the supporting taglib class WelcomeTag.java, which extends the TagSupport class and implements the callback methods doStartTag() and doEndTag():

```java
import javax.servlet.jsp.*;
import javax.servlet.jsp.tagext.TagSupport;
import java.util.Date;
import java.io.IOException;
public class WelcomeTag extends TagSupport {
    public void setUserId (String userId) {
        id=userId;
    }
    public String getUserId () {
        return id;
    }
    public int doStartTag() throws JspException {
        try {
            JspWriter out = pageContext.getOut();
            String dateStr = new Date().toString();
            out.print("Welcome back "+ getName(id));
            out.println(". It's " + dateStr);
        } catch (Exception e) {
            e.printStackTrace();
            throw new JspException(e.getMessage());
        }
        return(EVAL_BODY_INCLUDE);
    }
    private String getName(String userId){
        // this can call a data source to get the real name
        return name;
    }
    private String id;
    private String name = "Raymond Ghaly";
}
```

The tag handler must implement setter and getter methods for each attribute, similar to those found in a JavaBean component (see the next section). The setUserId() and getUserId() methods are used to set and get the id attribute. The first letter of the attribute is capitalized after the get/set word in the method name. The Web container uses these methods to inform the tag handler instance of the attribute values before the doStartTag() or doAfterBody() method is invoked.

In the preceding example, the Web container calls the doStartTag() method, and returns a personalized welcome page for the userId "remo". The doStartTag() returns the EVAL_BODY_INCLUDE constant, meaning to evaluate the tag's body content, and any sub-tags. Other valid constants returned by the doStartTag() are SKIP_BODY (tag contents will be ignored) and EVAL_BODY_TAG (evaluate the tag contents). Similarly, SKIP_PAGE and EVAL_PAGE are valid constants for the doEndTag() callback.

In deploying a taglib, you need to write a Tag Library Descriptor (TLD) file (WEB-INF/tlds/welcome.tld). A TLD is an XML file that declares each attribute for the tag within the <tag> element using an <attribute> tag for each attribute. The tag attributes allow the JSP page to pass String values into the tag handler, which can be used to configure the tag behavior.

```
<?xml version="1.0" encoding="ISO-8859-1" ?>
<!DOCTYPE taglib PUBLIC
   "-//Sun Microsystems, Inc.//DTD JSP Tag Library 1.1//EN"
   "http://java.sun.com/j2ee/dtds/web-jsptaglibrary_1_1.dtd">
<taglib>
  <tlib-version>1.0</tlib-version>
  <jsp-version>1.2</jsp-version>
  <short-name>student</short_name>
  <description>Welcome Tag for Students. Author: Raymond Ghaly</description>
  <tag>
    <name>welcome</name>
      <tagclass>WelcomeTag</tagclass>
    <attribute>
        <name>userId</name>
        <required>true</required>
        <rtexprvalue>true</rtexprvalue>
    </attribute>
  </tag>
</taglib>
```

As a part of a Web application, a taglib must be included in the Web deployment descriptor file web.xml, as follows:

```
<web-app>
  ...
  <taglib>
    <taglib-uri>/welcome</taglib-uri>
    <taglib-location>/WEB-INF/tlds/welcome.tld</taglib-location>
  </taglib>
  ...
</web-app>
```

# Understanding the JavaBeans Java Class

A JavaBean is a Java class that uses setter and getter methods, as a means of introspection of the class attributes. *Introspection*, like reflection, is the ability to query class attributes by using get*XXX*(), where *XXX* is one of the class attributes. A JavaBean can save its state through persistence. Therefore, all of its persistent properties must be serializable. You use a JavaBean to encapsulate data mapping between a form's parameters and a database. It can be used as a data container (DataBean) to transfer information between the Web tier and the EJB tier. A JavaBean can encapsulate data for display purposes (ViewBean) and manage data flow between applets and applications. JavaBeans use events to interact with other beans. The most powerful use of a JavaBean is to automatically map and populate its properties from a form.

One example of a JavaBean is the `StudentDataBean` to transfer data between the `UserManager` EJB and the Web tier:

```
import java.io.Serializable;
public class StudentDataBean implements java.io.Serializable {
  private String userId;
  private String password;
  private String firstName;
  private String lastName;
  public StudentDataBean (String userId, String password,
                String firstName, String lastName) {
    this.userId = userId;
    this.password = password;
    this.firstName = firstName;
    this.lastName = lastName;
  }
  public void setFirstName(String n){ firstName = n;}
  public String getFirstName(){ return firstName;}
  public void setLastName(String n){ lastName = n;}
  public String getLastName(){ return lastName;}
  public void setUserId(String n){ userId = n;}
  public String getUserId(){ return userId;}
  public void setPassword(String n){ password = n;}
  public String getPassword (){ return password;}
}
```

JSP can use a JavaBean to automatically capture the form data of the client tier. Here, we use the standard tag `<jsp:useBean>` to process the form:

```
<%@ page import="day07.* %>
<jsp:useBean id="myBean" scope="session"
          class="day07.StudentDataBean" property="*" />
<html>
  <head>
    <title>Using Student Bean</title> </head>
  <body>
    <h1> Using Automatic Mapping of Student Bean</h1>
    <%
    String userName = request.getParameter( "Login Name" );
```

7

```
    out.print(userName + " : " + myBean.getUserId());
    %>
  </body>
</html>
```

In the preceding example, the `<jsp:useBean>` tag creates a JavaBean component by instantiating the `StudentDataBean` class, and automatically populates all its properties, as indicated by `"*"`.

Servlets can use JavaBeans as parameters passed to their method invocations when calling an EJB. The EJB populates the JavaBean properties with result data after processing the servlet's request from a database or other entity EJBs. For example, the following `doPost()` method displays all courses for which a student has enrolled:

```
public void doPost (HttpServletRequest req, HttpServletResponse res)
      throws ServletException, IOException {
    String studentId = req.getParameter("Login name");
    PrintWriter out = res.getWriter();
    try{
      Collection coll = userManager.getCourses(studentId);
      while (coll.hasNext){
        EnrollmentDataBean enroll = (EnrollmentDataBean) coll.getNext();
        out.write("Course id: " + enroll.getCourseId() + "<br>");
    }catch{
     e.printStackTrace();
    }
}
```

# Using MVC in Designing Web Applications

A good strategy when designing your enterprise application is to have separate layers, each of which is unaffected by changes done on the other layers. The Model-View-Controller is a design pattern that is used to partition your Web applications into the following components (see Figure 7.8):

- Model: A set of objects that represent the business logic of the application. This usually includes EJBs, JavaBeans, and other abstractions of real world entities.

- View: Represented by JSPs as the user interface, which is necessary to construct the presentation. You can have multiple views for the same model.

- Controller: Represented by servlets, which contain the necessary logic to process user events, manage screen flow, and select an appropriate response.

The main target here is that the model be kept separate from the details of how the application is structured (the controller) and how the information is presented to the user (the view).

**FIGURE 7.8**

*MVC design pattern for Web applications.*

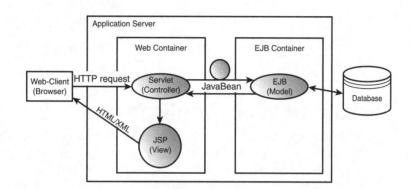

The advantage of the MVC strategy is that there is no application logic within the presentation component itself (JSPs). It is simply responsible for retrieving any objects or JavaBeans that might have been previously created by the controller, and for generating the dynamic content for insertion within its static templates. The separation of the presentation logic from its content helps divide the roles and responsibilities between page designers and Java developers. Moreover, using the servlet as a controller presents a central point of entry to the application, which makes the management of applications more consistent and easier to maintain.

## Working with a Servlet as a Controller

You learned earlier today how servlets work as delegates for the client tier to the business logic of the application. A primary role of a servlet is to act as a controller. A servlet is responsible for taking parameters from the client and then delegating those parameters to the appropriate components, which handle the business logic. Finally, the servlet takes the result back and uses it to provide a response to the user. The servlet usually forwards the response to a JSP to perform a presentation task (see Figure 7.9). Servlets are the link between the client request and the model (EJB and JavaBeans).

7

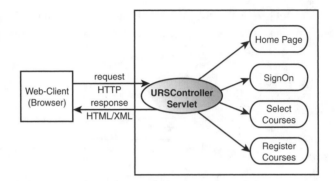

**FIGURE 7.9**

*Servlet as a controller.*

# Packaging Web Applications

All Web components are packaged together into a standard file, a Web Archive (WAR) file, which can be deployed into the Web container. A WAR file is a type of JAR file that can be created using the `jar` utility. It contains both server-side classes, such as servlets, JavaBeans, JSP, and taglibs, and client-side contents, such as applets, HTML, and images. The directory structure of a WAR file looks like Figure 7.2 illustrated earlier today.

When creating a WAR file, arrange the directory according to the structure in Figure 7.2, and then issue the `jar` command from the application's home directory:

```
jar -cvf  mywebapp.war *
```

The `web.xml` file is the standard Web deployment descriptor, and `weblogic.xml` is the vendor-specific deployment descriptor for the WebLogic Server. The subdirectory `classes` is used to store server-side Java classes such as servlets, whereas the `lib` subdirectory is used to store all the other JAR files, such as for JavaBeans.

The `web.xml` file describes each Web component used in the WAR file and the relationships between them. Here's an example of a `web.xml` that describes some of the components developed today:

```
<!DOCTYPE web-app PUBLIC "-//Sun Microsystems, Inc.//
DTD Web Application 1.2//EN" "http://java.sun.com/j2ee/dtds/web-app_2_2.dtd">
<web-app>
  <servlet>
    <servlet-name> URSControllerServlet</servlet-name>
    <servlet-class>myWebApp.URSControllerServlet</servlet-class>
  </servlet>
  <servlet-mapping>
    <servlet-name> URSControllerServlet </servlet-name>
    <url-pattern>/URSControllerServlet </url-pattern>
```

```
    </servlet-mapping>
    <welcome-file-list>
      <welcome-file>welcome.html</welcome-file>
    </welcome-file-list>
    <error-page>
      <error-code>404</error-code>
      <location>/errorPage.jsp</location>
    </error-page>
    <!-- Tag Library Descriptor -->
    <taglib>
      <taglib-uri>/welcome</taglib-uri>
      <taglib-location>/WEB-INF/tlds/welcome.tld</taglib-location>
    </taglib>
</web-app>
```

When the Web container start deploying the WAR file, it first reads the contents of the `web.xml` file and uses them as a road map to its target components.

In the preceding example of `web.xml`, each servlet must be defined by its name and full class name (includes the package). *Servlet mapping* is the concept of mapping a servlet name to a URL, which used by the container to translate requests to particular servlet. For instance, in WebLogic, the URL `http://localhost:7001/mywebapp/URSControllerServlet` will map the request to the URSControllerServlet servlet. In JBoss, the request `http://localhost:8080/mywebapp/URSControllerServlet` will have the same effect.

# Best Practices

There are many options and various situations that Web components can be used for. In general, the Web tier is used mainly for processing user input, server-side validation, and building dynamic content. It's not a good place to put application business logic, access the database, or perform transactions. All Web components are not transactional. Use EJBs to model your application business logic.

Don't put too much logic in JSPs. Use taglibs to capture presentation logic, and JavaBeans as data transfer objects between the Web tier and the EJB tier. Use servlets as controllers as well as delegates on behalf of the client to the EJB tier.

When tracking user sessions, try to activate URL rewriting to avoid disabled cookies by users. Use JSP error pages; they're an elegant mechanism provided by the JSP architecture.

Application servers provide persistence mechanisms for session data storage. You also can choose to maintain the session information in a database. Persistent sessions are slow

7

compared to replication of session information across cluster nodes. Here, only serializable objects can be replicated or persisted. Large data stored in collections, arrays, or tables should not be replicated because it's hard to detect changes to them.

One advantage of using servlets is that they can be used by different types of clients, such as Web clients, Java clients, and even Visual Basic clients. This is not the case, however, with JSPs, which are used only by Web clients. Another advantage of servlets is their ability to work with binary information, such as images.

When using EJBs, a common practice is to use the home handle of an EJB instance for the cookie value and to store the user's details in an EJB for later reference.

## Summary

Today we explored the Web tier, Web container, and Web components, and how each contributes to building Web applications. We briefly surveyed the four Web components: servlets, JSPs, taglibs, and JavaBeans, with an example to demonstrate each API. We scratched the surface of each Web component and its proper usage. Servlets were covered as delegates as well as controllers, in addition to handling user inputs. You learned JSP's main syntax and its scripting elements. JSP taglibs were explored as an extension to JSP. You learned also about the packaging and deployment of Web applications.

On Day 20, you'll learn how to create a complete Web application, and how to apply the MVC pattern as part of the JavaMail exercise.

## Q&A

**Q  What are the mechanisms used in tracking user session?**

**A**  You can use HttpSession and URL rewriting to track sessions on the server side, and you can use HTTP cookies and hidden fields in tracking sessions on the client side.

**Q  What role do servlets play in the J2EE architecture?**

**A**  Servlets are used mainly in processing user requests and delivering dynamic content. They also act as controllers in the MVC pattern. Moreover, they work as delegates for the session façade pattern. This makes an elegant separation between the Web tier for presentation logic and the EJB tier for business logic.

# Quiz

1. The main function of a servlet is to

    A. Read and write files to and from the server

    B. Provide graphical user interfaces

    C. Process HTTP requests and supply responses

    D. Act as delegate to access EJBs

2. An HTTP cookie can contain

    A. Any Unicode characters

    B. Only ASCII characters

    C. Any binary information about a user profile

    D. Any field/value pairs of a user session

3. After a JSP page is compiled, it turned into a(n)

    A. Applet

    B. EJB

    C. Servlet

    D. JavaBean

4. The best way to call an EJB from the Web tier is

    A. Call the EJB from a JavaBean embedded into a JSP

    B. Look up and use the EJBs directly from a JSP

    C. Look up the EJB in a taglib, which is called from JSP

    D. Look up the EJBs from within a servlet, and delegate usage from within a JSP

## Quiz Answers

1. C, D

2. B

3. C

4. D

7

# Exercises

1. Why and how should you avoid putting any logic in a JSP?

2. What mechanism of session tracking do you choose if you know that clients are disabling cookies on their browsers?

3. What are the benefits of using the MVC pattern?

4. Which common services of containers are you allowed to use for Web components?

# WEEK 2

# Entity Beans and Message-Driven Beans

8

9

10

11

12

13

14

# WEEK 2

# DAY 8

# Understanding Entity Beans

Today you'll learn about entity beans that were first introduced in the EJB 1.0 specification. They were made mandatory in the EJB 1.1 specification and later enhanced in EJB 2.0.

The EJB architecture greatly simplifies the connection between the application and the database tiers. The EJB 2.0 specification takes this benefit to the next level by enabling developers to develop portable applications that are database-independent and free of database access code.

Entity beans are persistent objects. We'll examine their characteristics and how they differ from session beans.

Next, you'll learn entity bean types bean-managed persistence and container-managed persistence and explore why container-managed persistent beans are portable and simpler to develop. Then we'll examine the methods that you need to implement for an entity bean class. Finally, we'll look at the life cycle of the entity bean instance.

# What Are Entity Beans?

If you've worked with databases, you're familiar with persistent data. Any change to the data will exist even after the database server is shut down. Entity beans are persistent objects. They typically represent business entities, such as customers, products, accounts, and orders. Normally, each entity bean has an underlying table in a relational database, and each instance of the bean corresponds to a row in that table. By *persistence*, we mean that the state of the entity bean in memory is synchronized with the data it represents in the database.

Multiple clients can share entity beans. Because those clients might want to change the same data, it's important that entity beans work within transactions.

Entity beans typically contain data-related logic that performs a task such as inserting, updating, or removing a customer record in the database.

 **Note**

> An entity bean is a server-side component that represents an object-oriented view of entities stored in persistent storage, such as a database, or entities that are implemented by an existing enterprise application.

# Characteristics of Entity Beans

Entity beans typically have the following characteristics:

- Provides an object view of data in the database. For example, as shown in Figure 8.1, the StudentEJB enterprise bean instance provides an object view of a record in the student table in the database. The EJB container transparently synchronizes the data between the server's memory and the database.

**FIGURE 8.1**

*An entity bean provides an object view of data in the database.*

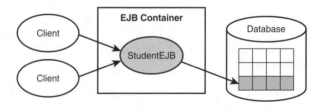

- Represents long-lived data. Its lifetime is the same as data in the database. The data of entity beans survives a crash of the EJB container.
- Allows shared access by multiple users.

- Just as a relational database has the concept of a primary key, its primary key identifies an entity bean. A student entity bean, for example, might be identified by a `student ID`.

- As with a table in a relational database, an entity bean may be related to other entity beans. For example, as shown in Figure 8.2, in a college enrollment application, `StudentEJB` and `CourseEJB` would be related because students enroll in classes. This is an example of many-to-many bidirectional relationship.

8

**FIGURE 8.2**

*An entity bean can be related to other entity beans.*

## Comparing Entity Beans and Session Beans

Entity beans differ from session beans in several ways. Entity beans are persistent, allow shared access, have primary keys, and may participate in relationships with other entity beans. Table 8.1 shows the differences between session and entity beans.

**TABLE 8.1**  Differences Between Session and Entity Beans

| Session Bean | Entity Bean |
| --- | --- |
| Typically contains business process logic, such as sending an e-mail, looking up the stock price from a database, implementing compression and encryption algorithms. They also implement business logic such as workflow, algorithms, and business rules. | Typically represents business entities, such as customers, products, accounts, and orders. |
| Executes a particular business task on behalf of a single client during a single session. | Can be shared by multiple clients. |
| The state is not persistent. | The state is persistent. |
| Usually does not correspond directly to data. | Usually corresponds directly to data. |

## Types of Entity Persistence

Entity beans have two types of persistence: bean-managed persistence (BMP) and container-managed persistence (CMP). These two types are based on who is responsible for entity bean persistence bean provider or EJB provider.

## Bean-Managed Persistence

With bean-managed persistence, the entity bean code that you write contains the calls that access the database. The data access can be coded into the entity bean class or encapsulated in a data access object that is part of the entity bean. Figure 8.3 depicts how bean-managed persistence works with database access.

**FIGURE 8.3**

*Bean-managed persis-tence contains the calls that access the database.*

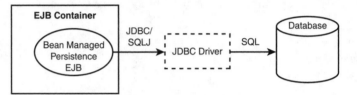

For example, as shown in the following snippet, the StudentEJB method ejbCreate con-tains the JBDC code to insert a student record into the students table:

```java
public class StudentEJB implements EntityBean {

  private String studentId; // also the primary Key
  private String firstName;
  private String lastName;
  private String address;

  public String ejbCreate(String studentId, String firstName,
    String lastName, String address) throws CreateException
  {
    this.studentId = studentId;
    this.firstName = firstName;
    this.lastName = lastName;
    this.address = address;

    Connection con = null;
    PreparedStatement ps = null;

    try {
      con = getConnection();
      ps = con.prepareStatement("insert into students (student_id, "+
        " first_name, last_name, address) values (?, ?, ?, ?) ");
      ps.setString(1, studentId);
      ps.setString(1, firstName);
      ps.setString(1, lastName);
      ps.setString(1, address);

      if (ps.executeUpdate() != 1) {
        String error = "JDBC did not create any row";
        log(error);
```

8

```
        throw new CreateException (error);
      }

      return studentId;
    } catch (SQLException sqe) {
    ...
    } finally {
      cleanup(con, ps);
    }
  }
  ...
}
```

Although writing this code is an additional responsibility, as an EJB developer, you'll have more control over how the entity bean accesses a database.

You'll learn more about bean-managed persistence on Day 10, "Developing Bean-Managed Persistence Entity Beans."

## Container-Managed Persistence

If your bean has container-managed persistence (CMP), the EJB container uses a persistence manager and automatically generates the necessary database access calls. The code that you write for the entity bean does not include these calls. The persistence manager is responsible for persistence of the entity bean, including creating, loading, and removing the entity bean instance in the database.

**FIGURE 8.4**

*The persistence manager is responsible for persistence of CMP.*

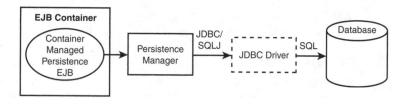

For example, as shown in the following listing, the OrderEJB method ejbCreate does not contain any JBDC code to insert order records into the orders table:

```
public abstract class OrderEJB implements EntityBean {

        /* get and set methods for cmp fields */
        public abstract String getOrderId();
        public abstract void setOrderId(String id);

        public abstract java.sql.Timestamp getOrderDate();
        public abstract void setOrderDate(java.sql.Timestamp timestamp);
```

```
      public abstract String getStatus();
      public abstract void setStatus(String status);

      public abstract double getAmount();
      public abstract void setAmount(double amount);

    /* get and set methods for relationship fields */
      public abstract Collection getLineItems();
      public abstract void setLineItems(Collection lineItems);

      public abstract StudentLocal getStudent();
      public abstract void setStudent(StudentLocal student);

      public String ejbCreate(String orderId, StudentLocal student,
        String status,double amount) throws CreateException {
       setOrderId(orderId);
       setOrderDate(new java.sql.Timestamp(System.currentTimeMillis()));
       setStatus(status);
       setAmount(amount);

       return null;
      }

  ...
}
```

You might question how the EJB container is able to generate the database access code.
The answer is that you specify the persistence fields, relationship fields, schema, and
queries in the deployment descriptor. Based on this information, the container tools generate data access calls corresponding to the underlying database, at deployment time.
We'll examine each of them in the following sections.

## Persistent Fields

A persistent field is designed to represent and store a single unit of data. Collectively,
these fields constitute the state of the bean. During deployment, the container typically
maps the entity bean to a database table and maps the persistent fields to the table's
columns. At runtime, the EJB container automatically synchronizes this state with the
database.

An OrderEJB entity bean, for example, might have persistent fields such as orderId,
orderDate, status, and amount. In container-managed persistence, these fields are virtual. You declare them in the abstract schema, but you do not code them as instance variables in the entity bean class. Instead, the persistent fields are identified in the code by
access methods (getters and setters).

## Relationship Fields

A relationship field is designed to represent and store a reference to another entity bean. This is analogous to a foreign key in a relational database table. Unlike a persistent field, a relationship field does not constitute the state of an entity bean.

An `OrderEJB` entity bean, for example, might have relationship fields such as `lineItems` and `student`.

## Abstract Persistent Schema

The CMP entity bean's deployment descriptor contains a description of the bean's abstract persistent schema. This schema is an abstract representation of an entity bean's persistent fields and relationship fields. The abstract schema is independent of the entity bean's implementation in a particular EJB container or particular database.

For example, the following snippet declares an abstract persistent schema named `Order` in the deployment descriptor:

```
. . .
<cmp-version>2.x</cmp-version>
<abstract-schema-name>Order</abstract-schema-name>
<cmp-field>
    <field-name>orderId</field-name>
</cmp-field>
 <cmp-field>
    <field-name>orderDate</field-name>
 </cmp-field>
 <cmp-field>
    <field-name>status</field-name>
 </cmp-field>
 <cmp-field>
    <field-name>amount</field-name>
 </cmp-field>
 . . .
```

The `cmp-version` must be 2.x if you want to take advantage of EJB 2.0 container-managed persistence. The schema declares four container-managed persistent fields (`cmp-field`): `orderId`, `orderDate`, `status`, and `amount`. The names of these fields must match the abstract get and set methods in your entity bean class. For example, your entity bean class's methods must be `getOrderId`, `setOrderId`, `getOrderDate`, `setOrderDate`, `getStatus`, `setStatus`, `getAmount`, and `setAmount`.

## The EJB Query Language

The EJB Query language (EJB QL) is new in EJB 2.0. EJB QL is similar to SQL. It enables you to specify queries of entity bean methods in a database-independent, portable way. For example, the following code line illustrates how the application uses an EJB QL query of the method `findOrdersByStatus(String status)` to find orders of a particular status, such as `COMPLETE`:

```
SELECT OBJECT(o) FROM Order AS o WHERE o.status = ?1
```

The preceding query returns `Order` objects, as indicated by the expression `OBJECT(o)`. The identifier o is analogous to an SQL correlation variable. The `WHERE` clause limits the orders to those whose status matches the value of the first parameter passed to the query, which is denoted by the expression `?1`.

The container tools will translate such queries into the target language of the underlying database. For example, in case of a relational database, the container translates an EJB QL query into an SQL query.

 **Note** Entity beans with container-managed persistence are portable. Their code is not tied to a specific database.

You will learn more about container-managed persistence on Day 11, "Developing Container-Managed Persistence Entity Beans," and on Day 12, "Developing Container-Managed Relationship Entity Beans."

# When to Use BMP or CMP

The choice between BMP and CMP is often decided by factors such as portability, availability of container tools, flexibility, and so on.

## Using BMP

Typically, you would use bean-managed persistence in the following situations:

- When you want complete control of managing persistence, such as writing optimized queries.
- When you're writing persistence logic to a very proprietary legacy database system for which container tools do not exist.
- When your persistent store is not a database, you might wrap an existing application using an entity bean.

## Using CMP

With container-managed persistence, the container takes responsibility for generating the data access code. This simplifies the task of writing entity beans.

The CMP entity bean's code is not tied to a specific persistent storage mechanism (database). Because of this flexibility, even if you redeploy the same entity bean on different J2EE servers that use different databases, you won't need to modify or recompile the bean's code. In short, your CMP entity beans are more portable than BMP entity beans.

> Whenever possible, you should use container-managed persistence beans because they are portable and easier to develop than bean-managed persistence beans.

## Instance Pool and Instance Cache

Just as with stateless session beans, an EJB container may maintain an instance pool of each type of entity bean. This saves the precious time of creating and destroying of objects. At startup, the container creates instances as specified in the deployment descriptor of the entity bean. While the instance is in the available pool, the instance is not associated with any particular entity object identity. All instances in the pool are considered equivalent; therefore, an instance can be assigned by the container to any entity object identity. You can control the instance pool size in the vendor-specific deployment descriptor.

For example, you can specify the pool size in the deployment descriptor `weblogic-ejb-jar.xml` for WebLogic Server as follows:

```
<pool>
  <max-beans-in-free-pool>100</max-beans-in-free-pool>
  <initial-beans-in-free-pool>50</initial-beans-in-free-pool>
</pool>
```

Similarly, you can specify the pool size in the deployment descriptor `jboss.xml` for the JBoss server as follows:

```
<instance-pool>org.jboss.ejb.plugins.EntityInstancePool</instance-pool>
<container-pool-conf>
  <MaximumSize>100</MaximumSize>
  <MinimumSize>10</MinimumSize>
</container-pool-conf>
```

Just as with stateful session beans, the EJB container can have an instance cache to manage all entity bean instances that are associated with an identity. In large applications, the number of clients connected concurrently to a Web site can be in the thousands. This can have an adverse effect on performance when resources are used up. Passivation and activation are mechanisms provided by the EJB container to manage valuable resources, such as memory, in order to reduce the number of entity bean instances needed to service all concurrent clients.

*Passivation* is the mechanism by which the EJB container stores the bean's state into the database. The container starts passivation as soon as the number of allocated entity beans exceeds a certain threshold. The EJB container provides the bean developer with `ejbPassivate()` as a callback method to release any allocated resources. *Activation*, on the other hand, is the process of restoring back the bean from the database. The EJB container activates a passivated instance when the bean's client references the bean instance. The EJB container provides the bean developer with `ejbActivate()` as a callback method to restore any connections and other resources.

For example, you can specify the instance cache size in deployment descriptor `weblogic-ejb-jar.xml` for WebLogic Server as follows:

```
<entity-cache>
 <max-beans-in-cache>1000</max-beans-in-cache>
</entity-cache>
```

Similarly, you can specify the instance cache size in deployment descriptor `jboss.xml` for JBoss server as follows:

```
<instance-cache>
<container-cache-conf>
 <cache-policy>
  <cache-policy-conf>
    <min-capacity>5</min-capacity>
    <max-capacity>10</max-capacity>
  </cache-policy-conf>
 </cache-policy>
</container-cache-conf>
</instance-cache>
```

 **Note**     Instance pooling is used to manage EJB instances that are not associated with any identity. Instance caching is used to manage EJB instances that are associated with an identity. Instance pooling is applicable to stateless session, entity, and message-driven beans, whereas instance caching is applicable to stateful session and entity beans.

# Entity Bean Files

Like other enterprise beans, an entity bean consists of a home interface, component interface, enterprise bean class, and deployment descriptor. In addition, an entity bean can have a primary key class.

**8**

In most cases, your primary key class will be a `String` or an `Integer`, which belong to J2SE standard libraries. For example, the primary key class for `StudentEJB` is `studentId`, which is a `String`.

For some entity beans, you must define your own primary key class. For example, if your primary key is composed of multiple fields (a composite primary key), you must define your own primary key class.

# Entity Bean Methods

The entity bean class implements the `javax.ejb.EntityBean` interface. Therefore, you need to implement the `setEntityContext`, `unsetEntityContext`, `ejbActivate`, `ejbPassivate`, `ejbLoad`, `ejbStore`, and `ejbRemove` methods defined in the `javax.ejb.EntityBean` interface. The bean may implement `ejbCreate<method>(...)` methods (and corresponding `ejbPostCreate<method>(...)` methods) used to initialize the bean instance. In addition, the bean class can implement business methods, home methods and remove methods. We'll discuss each of them in detail in the following sections.

## setEntityContext and unsetEntityContext Methods

The EJB container calls the `setEntityContext` method to set the associated entity context. The entity context provides access to the runtime entity context, such as identifying the caller, accessing or changing the current transaction state, or obtaining the primary key associated with the instance. You can store the reference to the entity context object in an instance variable, if you need it later. Also, it is here that you allocate any resources to be held by the instance for its lifetime.

The EJB container calls the `unsetEntityContext` method before removing the instance. This is the last method that the container invokes on the instance. The Java garbage collector will eventually invoke the `finalize()` method on the instance. Here you free any resources that are held by the instance.

## create Methods

The container calls this method so that you can initialize your entity bean instance. When a client invokes a `create<method>` method on the home interface, the EJB container invokes the corresponding `ejbCreate<method>` method.

The following local home interface illustrates the create method:

```
public interface StudentLocalHome extends EJBLocalHome {
 StudentLocal create(String studentId, String name, String password,
   String address) throws CreateException;
 ...
}
```

Typically, the ejbCreate<*method*> of a BMP validates the client-supplied parameters, inserts the entity state into the database, initializes the instance variables, and returns the primary key. In contrast, the ejbCreate<*method*> of CMP typically initializes the entity bean instance by assigning the input arguments to the persistent fields. After the ejbCreate<*method*> completes, the container inserts the row into the database.

> **Note**
>
> The ejbCreate<*method*> of a BMP returns the primary key, whereas the ejbCreate<*method*> of a CMP returns null.

The following example illustrates how a client creates a new entity object:

```
StudentLocalHome home =
Student student =
   home.create("1,", "Sam", "password", "123 Hollis Ave, Campbell, CA-95008");
```

## ejbPostCreate<*method*> Methods

This method enables you to complete any remaining initialization of entity bean instances. For example, you may obtain the component interface of the associated entity object and pass it to another enterprise bean as a method argument.

The container invokes the matching ejbPostCreate<*method*>(...) method on an entity instance after it invokes the ejbCreate<*method*>(...) method with the same arguments.

## ejbActivate and ejbPassivate Methods

The ejbActivate method enables you to acquire any resources (such as opening socket connections and so on) needed to service a particular client. The EJB container calls this method when it picks the entity instance from the instance pool and associates it to a specific entity object identity.

The ejbPassivate method enables you to release any resources you acquired in the ejbActivate method, such as closing socket connections. The EJB container calls this method when the container decides to disassociate the instance from an entity object identity and to put it back into the instance pool.

**Note** The instance should not use the `ejbActivate()` method to read the state of the entity from the database. The instance should load its state only in the `ejbLoad()` method. Also, the instance should not use the `ejbPassivate()` method to write its state to the database. An instance should store its state only in the `ejbStore()` method.

8

## Business Methods

The business methods contain business logic that you want to encapsulate within your entity bean. Typically, the business methods don't access the database, which enables you to separate the business logic from the database access code. You define the business methods in the component interface and implement them in the entity bean class.

For example, the `Account` bean's component interface defines the business methods `deposit()` and `withdraw()` as follows:

```
public interface Account extends EJBObject {
  public void deposit(double amount)
    throws RemoteException;
  public double withdraw(double amount)
    throws AccountException, RemoteException;
  ...
}
```

The `AccountEJB` bean implements the business methods as follows:

```
abstract public class AccountEJB implements EntityBean {
  /* container managed fields */
  abstract public double getBalance();
  abstract public void setBalance(double val);
  ...
  public double deposit(double amount) {
   setBalance(getBalance() + amount);
   return getBalance();
  }

  public double withdraw(double amount)
    throws ProcessingErrorException {
   if (amount > getBalance()) {
     throw new ProcessingErrorException(
       "Request to withdraw " + amount +
       "; is more than balance " + getBalance());
   }
   setBalance(getBalance() - amount);
   return getBalance();
  }
  ...
}
```

## `ejbLoad()` and `ejbStore()` Methods

The EJB container calls the `ejbLoad()` and `ejbStore()` methods when it needs to synchronize the state of the entity bean instance with the corresponding values in the database.

- `ejbLoad()`—The EJB container invokes this method to instruct the instance to synchronize its state by loading it from the underlying database.

  With BMP, the instance variables are refreshed by reading from the database. Also, you recalculate the values of any instance variables that depend on refreshed variables; for instance, calculate transient fields, decrypt a text field, or decompress a text field.

  With CMP, the container loads the bean's state from the database. You must recalculate the values of any instance variables that depend on persistent fields; for instance, calculate transient fields, decrypt a text field, or decompress a text field.

- `ejbStore()`—The EJB container invokes this method to instruct the instance to synchronize its state by storing it to the underlying database.

  With BMP, any updates cached in the instance variables are written to the database.

  With CMP, prepare the container-managed fields to be written to the database; for example, encrypt a text field, decompress a text field, and so on.

## `finder` Methods

Finder methods allow clients to locate entity beans. The arguments of a finder method are used by the entity bean implementation to locate the requested entity objects. The name of each finder method in the home interface starts with the prefix `find`.

In the following snippet, the client locates the student entity beans by using the finder methods `findByPrimaryKey` and `findByLastName`:

```
public interface StudentLocalHome extends EJBLocalHome {

    public StudentLocal findByPrimaryKey(String key) throws FinderException;
    public Collection findByLastName(String lastName) throws FinderException;
    ...
}
```

In BMP, for every finder method defined in the home interface, you must implement a corresponding method that begins with the prefix `ejbFind`. For example, `StudentEJB` implements the method `ejbFindByLastName`, which corresponds to the `findByLastName` method defined in the home interface.

In CMP, you do not write the `ejbFind` methods in your entity bean class. The finder methods are generated by the container provider tools.

The following example illustrates how a client uses the `findByPrimaryKey` method:

```
StudentLocalHome home= ...;
StudentLocal student = home.findByPrimaryKey("1");
```

8

**Note**

The remote home interface includes the `findByPrimaryKey(primaryKey)` method, which allows a client to locate an entity object by using a primary key. The name of the method is always `findByPrimaryKey`. The `findByPrimaryKey(primaryKey)` method is mandatory for all entity beans.

## Home Methods

Home methods contain business logic that that is not specific to an entity bean instance. These methods are analogous to static methods. Just as static methods can't access instance variables, home methods can't access the bean's state.

The following example shows the home method `getStudentCount`, which returns the total number of students in a table:

```
public interface StudentLocalHome extends EJBLocalHome {
    public int getStudentCount();
    ...
}
```

You write an `ejbHome<method>` method, in the entity bean class, for every home method defined in the home interface. For example, you would implement `ejbHomeGetStudentCount()` in the `StudentEJB` entity bean class.

**Note**

Because the home method isn't specific to an entity bean instance, the entity instance isn't associated with any unique identity during home method invocation. So, the home method implementation cannot access the entity bean's state (persistent fields).

## remove Method

The `javax.ejb.EJBHome` interface defines several methods that allow the client to remove an entity object:

```
public interface EJBHome extends Remote {
    void remove(Handle handle) throws RemoteException,
    RemoveException;
```

```
    void remove(Object primaryKey) throws RemoteException,
      RemoveException;
}
```

In BMP, the `ejbRemove()` method removes the entity state from the database and releases any resources that you acquired to service a particular client. In CMP, the `ejbRemove()` method releases any resources that you acquired to service a particular client. Table 8.2 summarizes the entity bean methods.

**TABLE 8.2**  Summary of Entity Bean Methods

| Method | Purpose | What You Need to Do |
| --- | --- | --- |
| `SetEntityContext (EntityContext)` | The EJB container calls this method to set the associated entity context. | Store the reference to the entity context object in an instance variable, if you need it later. You also allocate any resources that are to be held for the lifetime of the instance. |
| `unsetEntityContext()` | The container invokes this method before terminating the life of the instance. | Free any resources that are held by the instance. |
| `ejbCreate<method>(...)` | The EJB container invokes the corresponding `ejbCreate<method>` method when a client invokes a `create<method>` method on the home interface. | Each entity class can have zero or more `ejbCreate<method>(...)` methods and each one can take different arguments.<br><br>In BMP, validate the client-supplied parameters and insert a record into the database. The method also initializes the instance's variables.<br>In CMP, validate the client-supplied parameters and initialize the enterprise bean state. |
| `ejbPostCreate<method>(...)` | The container invokes the matching `ejbPostCreate<method>(...)` method on an entity instance after it invokes the `ejbCreate<method>(...)` method with the same arguments. | For each `ejbCreate<method>(...)` method, you must have a matching `ejbPostCreate<method>(...)` method.<br><br>This method enables you to complete any remaining initialization of entity bean instances. |

**TABLE 8.2** continued

| Method | Purpose | What You Need to Do |
|---|---|---|
| ejbActivate() | The EJB container calls this method when it picks the entity instance from the instance pools and associates it to a specific entity object identity. | Acquire any resources needed to service a particular client; for example, open socket connections. |
| ejbPassivate() | The EJB container calls this method when the container decides to disassociate the instance from an entity object identity and to put it back into the instance pool. | Release any resources that you acquired to service a particular client; for example, close socket connections. |
| Business methods | The business methods contain business logic that you want to encapsulate within your entity bean. | Write business logic in these methods. |
| ejbLoad() | The EJB container invokes this method to instruct the instance to synchronize its state by loading it from the underlying database. | In BMP, refresh the instance variables by reading from the database. Also recalculate any dependent values.<br><br>In CMP, recalculate the values of any instance variables that depend on the persistent fields; for example, transient fields. |
| ejbStore() | The EJB container invokes this method to instruct the instance to synchronize its state by storing it to the underlying database. | In BMP, write any updates cached in the instance variables to the data base.<br><br>In CMP, prepare the container-managed fields to be written to the database. |
| ejbFind<method>(...) | Finder methods allow clients to locate entity beans. | In BMP, for every finder method defined in the home interface, you must implement a corresponding method that begins with the ejbFind prefix.<br><br>With CMP, you do not write the ejbFind methods in your entity bean class. |

**TABLE 8.2**    continued

| Method | Purpose | What You Need to Do |
|---|---|---|
| ejbHome<*method*>(...) | Home methods contain business logic that that is not specific to an entity bean instance. | Implement the business logic using other methods or JDBC code. |
| ejbRemove() | The container calls this method as a result of the client's invocation of a remove method. | In BMP, remove the entity state from the database and release any resources that you acquired to service a particular client.

With CMP, release any resources that you acquired to service a particular client. |

# Life Cycle of an Entity Bean

Figure 8.5 shows a simplified state diagram of an entity bean instance.

The following paragraphs describe the life cycle of an entity bean instance.

Initially, the bean instance does not exist.

Your bean instance's life cycle starts when the container creates the instance using Class.newInstance() and then calls the setEntityContext method. Now the instance enters a pool of available instances. An instance in the pooled state is not associated with any particular entity object identity. All instances in the pooled state are identical. While the instance is in the pooled state, the EJB container may use the instance to execute any of the entity bean's finder methods or home methods.

Your bean instance moves from the pooled state to the ready state when the container selects that instance to service a client call to an entity object. There are two paths from the pooled stage to the ready stage. On the first path, the client invokes the create method, causing the EJB container to call the ejbCreate and ejbPostCreate methods. On the second path, the EJB container invokes the ejbActivate method.

While in the ready state, the instance is associated with a specific entity object identity. The container calls business methods on the instance, based on the client call. The EJB container also can synchronize the state of the instance with the database using methods ejbLoad and ejbStore.

Eventually, the EJB container will transition the instance to the pooled state. This happens when the client calls the remove method, which causes the EJB container to call the ejbRemove method. Second, the EJB container might call the ejbPassivate method.

**FIGURE 8.5**

*Simplified life cycle of an entity bean instance.*

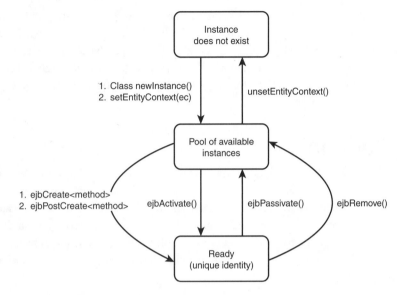

Life cycle of an entity bean instance

At the end of the instance's life cycle, the EJB container removes the instance from the pool and invokes the `unsetEntityContext` method.

**Note**

In bean-managed persistence, when the EJB container moves an instance from the pooled state to the ready state, it does not automatically set the primary key. Therefore, the `ejbCreate` and `ejbActivate` methods must set the primary key.

# Best Practices

Before the introduction of EJB 2.0 specification, developers often used BMP rather than CMP because the previous EJB spec did not support important features such as relationships. But the EJB 2.0 spec for CMP has good relationship support as well as performance improvements.

One of the CMP performance improvement techniques in EJB 2.0 is that the container can monitor a bean's data (in-memory buffer) change. If any change happens in that data, only the container will update the database. Because of this monitoring capability, CMP gives better performance than BMP.

Another performance-limiting technique is when you call a finder method in BMP. It initially retrieves the primary key with the first call to the database, and then retrieves the instance data by placing a second call to the database—it makes two calls to the database. But for finder methods, CMP gets the data with a single call to the database. Thus, CMP gives better performance techniques than BMP because the container has a good hold on CMP.

# Summary

Today you examined entity beans, and learned that they are server-side components that represent back-store data in the middle tier. By design, entity beans are persistent and survive any server crashes. They are transactional and share their state with multiple clients. You also learned about both types of persistence: bean-managed and container-managed persistence. You briefly explored the relationship between entity beans. Over the next three days, you will examine the last three topics in more detail with full examples.

# Q&A

**Q** **What are the main characterizes of entity beans?**

**A** Entity beans are persistent, transactional, and shared between multiple clients.

**Q** **What are the two main types of entity beans?**

**A** There are two main types of entity beans: bean-managed persistence and container-managed persistence.

# Quiz

1. An entity bean is identified by which of the following?

    A. Primary key.

    B. Persistent fields.

    C. Relationship fields.

    D. Home interface.

2. Which of the following statements is true of a bean-managed persistence entity bean?

    A. The container takes the responsibility of generating the data access code.

    B. The entity bean takes the responsibility of generating the data access code.

8

C. The entity bean is portable.

D. The entity bean is transactional.

## Quiz Answers

1. A

2. B, D

# Exercises

To extend your knowledge of the subjects covered today, try the following exercises.

1. Design a student bean-managed persistence bean. The bean consists of the persistent fields `studentId`, `firstName`, `lastName`, and `address`. Draw a class diagram that shows the entity bean class and its interfaces along with their methods. In addition, provide a method that calculates the total number of students.

2. Design an order container-managed persistence bean. The bean consists of persistent fields `orderId`, `studentId`, `orderDate`, and `amount`. Draw a class diagram that shows the entity bean class and its interfaces along with their methods. In addition, provide a method that calculates the total amount for all orders.

# DAY 9

# Using JDBC to Connect to a Database

Today, you'll learn how to use Java Database Connectivity (JDBC) to connect components of an enterprise application to any data source. JDBC is the standard and unified API to access any data in a tabular form, whether it is a relational database, spreadsheet, or flat file. We'll give a brief account of the JDBC architecture and the different clients and components across all the J2EE tiers that can use it. Using snippet of codes, the JDBC API will be explained. We'll wrap up with an example to highlight the main interfaces and classes of the JDBC. We'll emphasize the fact that JDBC is a vendor-neutral API by running an example in two different environments of application servers, without changes to the sample code.

We'll also discuss features of JDBC such as connection pooling, data sources, SQL queries and updates, and advanced concepts including prepared statements, local transactions, metadata, and batch updates. Finally, we'll explore the built-in features of the API to optimize your access to data sources.

- Learn the rationale behind JDBC
- Explore the JDBC architecture
- Learn the JDBC API's classes and interfaces
- Learn how to connect to a database using JDBC
- Learn how to perform local transactions using JDBC API
- Explore the data manipulation operations of databases using JDBC
- Study query optimization to databases
- Learn how to use batch updates for optimal operations
- Work with metadata for databases and query results
- Work with a practical example to apply what you learned today

# Why JDBC?

JDBC is a standard API that lets you access virtually any data source in tabular format from your J2EE applications. It provides cross-DBMS connectivity to a wide range of SQL databases, spreadsheets, and flat files. SQL is the *lingua franca* of the standard database language to separate application data from its logic.

JDBC enables developers to write enterprise applications that run on any J2EE-compliant application server that requires access to enterprise data. It provides separation of application logic from the underlying database operating environment. JDBC encapsulates the connecting method, database vendor, security, and multiuser access. With a JDBC technology–enabled driver, a developer can even connect all corporate data in a heterogeneous database environment.

JDBC is used by many components across all J2EE tiers. First, in the client tier, JDBC can be accessed by Java applets or Java applications. Second, in the Web tier, it can be accessed by JSP, servlet, or Taglib. Finally, all types of EJBs such as session, entity, and message-driven beans can use JDBC from the EJB tier.

Later in this book, on Day 11 "Developing Container-Managed Persistence Entity Beans," you'll learn about entity beans in a container-managed persistence (CMP) mode, where application logic is separated from its persistence. JDBC is still being used behind the scenes in the deployment descriptor and in a declarative manner, but is not used directly by the code. However, this is different from the case of bean-managed persistence (BMP) where entity beans use JDBC to manage database access, which will be addressed on Day 10, "Developing Bean-Managed Persistence Entity Beans."

# JDBC Architecture

JDBC is designed using a two-tier approach. It's a unified and standard API used by all J2EE applications and components to access databases through a provider-specific driver. Such clean separation of application logic and database-specific environment helps an enterprise application to be portable and reusable across multiple databases.

**Note**

JDBC is similar in concept to ODBC (Open Database Connectivity), a C-based standard to access databases. In fact, both JDBC and ODBC are interoperable; that is, both access each other through the JDBC-ODBC Bridge. JDBC provides enhanced services such as connection pooling, which will be covered later today.

Figure 9.1 illustrates the layered approach of the JDBC architecture. An application client uses a unified JDBC API to access one or many databases, even in a heterogeneous environment. Many of the database products provide JDBC drivers, including Oracle, SQLServer, DB2, Sybase, PointBase, Cloudscape, Hypersonic, Postgres, and mySQL.

**FIGURE 9.1**

*JDBC architecture.*

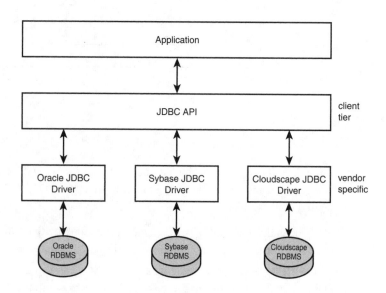

It's possible that clients and components across all the J2EE tiers can access the database through the JDBC API (see Figure 9.2). However, it's recommended in practice that JDBC connections should be *near* to the data source itself. This implies that components in the EJB-tier are encouraged to use the JDBC to connect to databases. This not only enhances the security aspect of your enterprise applications, but it also increases their portability. Moreover, EJBs provide built-in mechanisms for transaction control, and placing JDBC calls in well-designed EJBs frees you from programming local transactions using JDBC or distributed transactions. Transactions will be covered in detail in Day 16.

**FIGURE 9.2**

*JDBC clients.*

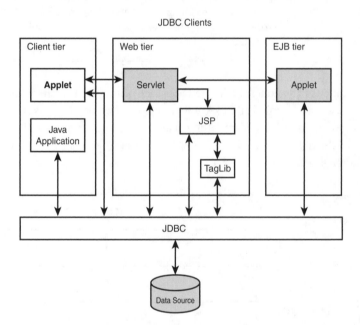

At a minimum, JDBC assumes that all underlying database vendors support the SQL-2 database access language. Since its original inception in 1997, the JDBC specification has focused on these issues:

- Offers vendor-neutral access to common functionality that most database server vendors must implement in order to be JDBC-compliant.
- Supports advanced SQL data types (part of SQL3), such as Blobs (Binary Large Object), Clobs (Character Large Object), and arrays and their mappings, to native Java objects.

- Provides implicit support for database reliability, availability, and scalability. The Standard Extension API describes advanced support features, such as enhancement of database performance and JNDI support.

# Choosing the Right JDBC Driver

Different types of JDBC drivers are available for a J2EE application's use. Two-tier drivers provide direct access to databases from a Java application. Two-tier drivers are vendor specific. Three-tier drivers provide access to databases through the middle tier, which enables you to manage database resources centrally through the application server. Three-tier JDBC drivers are vendor neutral, and make it easier to integrate off-the-shelf components to your DBMS environment and to write more portable code. Moreover, they help you to develop scalable, reliable, and available J2EE applications.

## JDBC Driver Types

JDBC drivers are commonly identified by type. The following list provides a brief description of each driver type, which will help you choose a JDBC driver type that fits your application requirements:

- **Type 1**: Uses ODBC as the primary interface to the database. The client makes JDBC calls that are converted to ODBC by the JDBC-ODBC Bridge, which is also required on the client tier.
- **Type 2**: Uses a native database library as an interface to the database. The client makes JDBC calls that are converted to the native code through a JDBC-native driver. The native library is a proprietary API, such as OCI (Oracle Client Interface). This driver type is normally used for high-performance and large transaction volume requirements.
- **Type 3**: This is a multitier, vendor-neutral driver. No driver is required at the client tier. Clients make JDBC calls through the network (RMI calls) to the JDBC driver that resides in the middle tier (application server tier).
- **Type 4**: This is an all-Java driver. Clients make JDBC calls directly to the database. Because it's a native Java driver, it performs according to the underlying Java Virtual Machine (JVM). It's the most frequently used JDBC driver type.

Figure 9.3 depicts these drivers in a multi-tier approach.

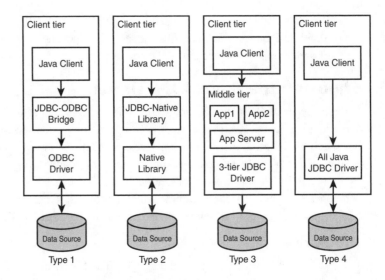

**FIGURE 9.3**

*Types of JDBC drivers.*

# Introducing the JDBC API

JDBC supports the development of both standard Java and enterprise Java applications. The JDBC API consists of the two main packages: the `java.sql` package, which is part of standard Java, and the `javax.sql` package, which is part of enterprise Java. The following two sections will briefly discuss these two main packages.

## The `java.sql` Package

This is a client-side API that allows making connection to a data source, handling database operations and queries, and providing security. The key interface to this package is the `Connection` interface, which encapsulates all the database operations in the application logic. Table 9.1 lists the JDBC interfaces and gives a brief description of each.

**TABLE 9.1**  Summary of JDBC Interfaces

| JDBC Interface | Description |
|---|---|
| DataSource | Represents a particular database or other data source and its connection pool. It's used as a factory to establish a `Connection` with a data source. |
| Connection | Represents a session to the database. It's used as a factory for other types of objects such as `Statement`. It handles all other database manipulation and operations. |
| Statement | Sends simple SQL statements, with no parameters, to a database. Created from a `Connection` object. |

**TABLE 9.1**    continued

| JDBC Interface | Description |
| --- | --- |
| PreparedStatement | Inherits from `Statement`. Used to execute a precompiled SQL statement with or without parameters. Used for more efficient data access. |
| CallableStatement | Inherits from `PreparedStatement`. Used to execute a call to a database stored procedure. |
| ResultSet | Contains the results of executing an SQL query. It contains the rows that satisfy the conditions of the query. |
| ResultSetMetaData | Provides information about the types and properties of the columns in a `ResultSet` object. |
| DataBaseMetaData | Provides information about database schema objects. |
| Clob | A built-in data type that stores a Character Large Object as a column value in a row of a database table. Part of SQL3 data types. |
| Blob | A built-in data type that stores a Binary Large Object as a column value in a row of a database table. Part of SQL3 data types. |

Figure 9.4 summarizes the main classes and interfaces of the JDBC API and the main methods used.

## The `javax.sql` Package

The `javax.sql` package extends the functionality of the JDBC API from a client-side API to a server-side API, and is an essential part of J2EE technology. The key interface to this package is the `DataSource` interface, which is the factory for creating connections. Other interfaces and classes of this package support distributed transactions, which are commonly used by EJB container providers. As application and bean developers, our main interface in this package is the `DataSource` interface.

## Using Connection Pooling

JDBC supports the concept of connection pooling. A *connection pool* is a collection of database connections maintained and managed by the application server. A J2EE application reuses database connections from the connection pool. An application server assigns a connection transparently to the application. A connection pool is represented as a `DataSource` object.

**Figure 9.4**

*JDBC API main classes and interfaces.*

JDBC Main Classes and Interfaces

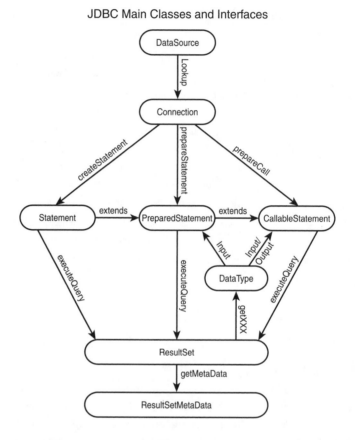

The main reason for using a connection pool is to enhance the performance of running applications. The task of establishing a connection to a database is usually slow because it requires considerable time for the initialization process. With connection pools, connections are established during application server startup and are available to be used by all components. Both database servers and application servers run more efficiently with dedicated connections than if they have to handle incoming connection attempts at runtime. Using connection pools increases the scalability of the system, which can therefore handle more number of users.

Another reason for using connection pools is to separate the application code from database configuration. In setting up a connection pool, we use a declarative approach to describe these configuration settings outside the application. Applications do not need to know of or transmit the database username, password, and location. This separation between application logic and database environment allows you to develop portable and reusable code, which is an important factor in designing enterprise applications. A connection pool, represented by a `DataSource` object, is created and registered by the system administrators into the JNDI service using a logical name. Hence it becomes available as a resource to be shared by all system components and users. Figure 9.5 illustrates how database connection pooling works.

**FIGURE 9.5**

*Database connection pool.*

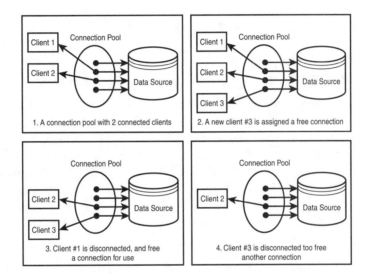

9

1. A connection pool with 2 connected clients

2. A new client #3 is assigned a free connection

3. Client #1 is disconnected, and free a connection for use

4. Client #3 is disconnected too free another connection

## Configuring the Connection Pool

Connection pools are set in the application server configuration files. Depending on the application, you can have more than one connection pool, with each being used by different components of the application. The following parameters are required to configure a connection pool:

- Connection pool name: Used to identify and register the `DataSource` with the JNDI service, and later used by the application to recognize the `DataSource`'s name.
- Initial number of connections: The number of connections to be created in the pool at startup.
- Maximum and minimum pool size.
- JDBC URL: Specifies the database location, database name, listening port, and the hostname.
- JDBC driver class name.
- JDBC driver properties: Any properties required to connect to the data source. They are name/value pairs, such as user ID and password.

Setting up both maximum and minimum pool size is of prime importance. The impact of setting your maximum below the expected peak load of system users will degrade performance at the time you need it most.

A full guide to the JDBC API and its extensions can be found at `http://java.sun.com/products/jdbc/`.

## Understanding `DataSource` Interface

A `DataSource` object is a factory for `Connection` objects. An object that implements the `DataSource` interface will typically be registered with a JNDI service provider. A `DataSource` is a representation of a database and its connection pool. An application uses the JNDI service provider to look up the connection pool name and creates a `DataSource` object factory. An application can be directed to a different data source simply by changing the `DataSource` object's properties; no change in the application code is needed. Likewise, a `DataSource` implementation can be changed without changing the application code that uses it, which enhances application portability.

To create a `Connection` object from a `DataSource` object, we can use either a declarative or a programmatic approach. In the following sections, we will discuss both these approaches.

## Declarative Approach

One of the objectives of the J2EE architecture is to enhance the deployment of enterprise applications. This is accomplished by separating the application code, from its deployment and configuration files. In the declarative approach, you set all configuration parameters of the databases and connection pools in a configuration file or deployment descriptor.

Using the declarative approach, a `Connection` object is created from a `DataSource` object by using the following method:

```
Connection Conn = datasource.getConnection()
```

This method has no parameters, and the container, behind the scenes, will use all the settings in the deployment and configuration files as the default settings.

If the database location or settings must be changed, you change only the configuration files without any modifications to the application code. This container-managed approach is one of the attractive features for many of the common services provided by the J2EE platform.

## Programmatic Approach

The programmatic approach, on the other hand, enables you to control and manage the database setting from inside the application code. The following method is used in making a connection to the database using this approach:

```
Connection conn =
    dataSource.getConnection
►(String username, String password);
```

This method creates a `Connection` to the database by overriding the default user and password. Both the `username` and `password` must be hard-coded in the application code, which has a negative affect on application portability.

| **Caution** | Another method of obtaining a database connection is the use of the `DriverManager`. The `DataSource` concept was introduced in the JDBC 2.0 Extension package. The JDBC specification recommends the cleaner `DataSource` method as the preferred method of obtaining a `Connection` for a J2EE application. The current use of obtaining a `Connection` through hard-coded parameters to the `DriverManager` method is deprecated. `DriverManager` is a shared object with synchronized methods and therefore it's single threaded. This technique establishes a bottleneck for the applications trying to access databases. On the other hand, the `DataSource` object is a multithreaded object than can handle the access of more than one concurrent user. |
|---|---|

## Learning the `Connection` Interface

A connection to a specific database represents a user session. Within the context of a `Connection`, SQL statements are executed and results are returned to the client for more processing. `Connections` are created from a `DataSource` object as described in the previous section. A connection is assigned transparently to the application by the JDBC driver. Table 9.2 summarizes the methods used for the `Connection` interface.

**TABLE 9.2**  Summary of `Connection` Methods

| Method | Purpose |
|---|---|
| `Statement createStatement()` | Creates a `Statement` object for sending SQL statements to the database |
| `PreparedStatement prepareStatement(String sql)` | Creates a `PreparedStatement` object for sending parameterized SQL statements to the database |
| `void commit()` | Makes all changes made since the previous `commit()`/`rollback()` permanent, and releases any database locks currently held by the `Connection` |

**TABLE 9.2**    continued

| Method | Purpose |
|---|---|
| `void rollback()` | Drops all changes made since the previous `commit()`/`rollback()`, and releases any database locks currently held by this `Connection` |
| `void setAutoCommit(boolean ac)` | Sets this connection's auto-commit mode |
| `DatabaseMetaObject getMetaData()` | Get all database schema information |
| `void close()` | Releases a `Connection`'s database and JDBC resources immediately instead of waiting for them to be released automatically |

A `Connection` object to the database is able to provide connection parameters and schema object information. This includes data tables, supported SQL grammar, stored procedures, and the capabilities of this connection. This information can be obtained with the `getMetaData()` method.

 **Note**

> A `Connection` object manages transaction behavior. By default, the `Connection` automatically commits changes after executing each statement. If `autoCommit` has been disabled, an explicit `commit()` must be done or database changes will not be saved.

## Exception Handling

A number of exceptions can be thrown as a result of connecting to a database or performing any of the operations mentioned earlier. The main exception is `SQLException`, which is thrown by most of the methods in the `java.sql` package. Other exceptions are summarized in Table 9.3.

**TABLE 9.3**    Summary of Exceptions

| Exception | Purpose |
|---|---|
| `SQLException` | Thrown by most methods when there is a problem accessing data and by some methods for other reasons. |
| `SQLWarning` | Queried from the `Statement` object to indicate a warning. It inherits from `SQLExecption`. |

**TABLE 9.3** continued

| Exception | Purpose |
|---|---|
| DataTruncation | Thrown to indicate that data might have been truncated. It inherits from SQLWarning. |
| BatchUpdateException | Thrown to indicate that not all commands in a batch update executed successfully. It inherits from SQLException. |

9

**Note**

> SQLWarning objects are not thrown as other exceptions—you have to query them. SQLWarning objects will build up due to multiple Statement method calls (such as execute() and executeUpdate()) until you ask for each Statement object with getWarning() and getNextWarning(). Statement objects automatically clear warnings on the next execution.

SQLExceptions must be handled in the catch clause. Information about errors can be obtained by the getErrorCode(), which prints a vendor-specific error. The getSQLState() method prints a standard SQL message. In addition, the method getMessage() prints a message that describes the error.

# Connecting to a Data Source

Applications must first be connected to a database before performing any database operation. As explained earlier, connections are made ready by the container, at startup, through the creation of a connection pool.

Connections are created using the DataSource object. Applications need to locate a DataSource object, before creating a Connection. Applications locate a DataSource through the JNDI service. The following is an example of these steps:

```
// Connect to the default JNDI service and establish a context
Context ctx = new InitialContext();
// Lookup the DataSource for the configured database
javax.sql.DataSource ds = (javax.sql.DataSource)
        ctx.lookup ("java:comp/env/jdbc/styejbDB");
// Make a connection to the database
java.sql.Connection conn = ds.getConnection();

// do some work

// Release the connection after you are done
conn.close();
```

> **Note**
>
> You must release the connection as soon as you have done work with it by closing the connection. When the client virtually closes the connection with `close()`, behind the scenes, the container returns the connection to the pool, and makes it available for use by other clients.

As recommended, JDBC `DataSource` references should always be declared in the `java:comp/env/jdbc` subcontext. This is established by the system administrator when the `DataSource` is being created.

Establishing a context to the JNDI service is an expensive operation, especially when using an RMI call. Always connect to the JNDI service to obtain a `DataSource` object in the initialization code of your application. This can be done once, and connection(s) can be assigned by the `DataSource` to other parts of the application during its lifetime.

Applications rely on the container to manage the connection pool, but when building scalable applications, releasing connections as soon as possible is the responsibility of the developer.

The traditional way of getting a connection is by using the `DriverManager`. As mentioned early today, this is a deprecated method, and we recommend using the `DataSource` method if possible. For the sake of completeness, the following snippet shows how to make a connection using the `DriverManager`:

```
String sourceURL = "jdbc:cloudscape:styejbPool";
String driverClass = "COM.cloudscape.core.JDBCDriver"
// Loading the JDBC driver
Class.forName(driverClass);
// Make a connection using the DriverManager
java.sql.Connection conn = DriverManager.getConnection(sourceURL);
```

# Data Manipulation

After a connection is made to the data source, the JDBC API is furnished with comprehensive operations. Both DDL (Data Definition Language) and DML (Data Manipulation Language) operations are available. Metadata (information about the database itself) or the result set can also be queried.

> **Note**
>
> We assume that the reader is familiar with SQL fundamentals. For more coverage of SQL, we recommend you to refer to the book, *Sams Teach Yourself SQL in 10 Minutes* (ISBN: 0672321289).

A Statement object represents a SQL statement, and must be created from the Connection object. A Statement sends simple SQL statements to the database:

```
// Create a Statement object
java.sql.Statement stmt = conn.createStatement();
```

One of the powerful methods of the Statement object is the execute() method. All DDL and DML database operations can be performed using the execute() method.

9

> **Caution**
>
> All DDL operations, such as creating and dropping objects, can be performed by the execute() method of the Statement object. However, creating a database instance is DBMS-specific, and is not available to all JDBC drivers.

```
// Using the execute method for some DDL operations
try {
    stmt.execute("DROP TABLE Student ");
} catch (SQLException e) {
    System.out.println("Table Student already exists.");
}
stmt.execute("CREATE TABLE Student
   (id integer, fname varchar(15), lname varchar(15), ssn varchar(12))");
System.out.println("Table Student is created...");
// Using the execute method for some DML operations
stmt.executeUpdate
("INSERT into Student values (1, 'Lillian', 'Ghaly' , '111-000-1111')");
stmt.executeUpdate
("INSERT into Student values (2, 'Raj', 'Talla' , '222-000-2222')");
stmt.executeUpdate
("INSERT into Student values (3, 'Tony', 'Hunter' , '333-000-3333')");
stmt.executeUpdate
("INSERT into Student values (4, 'John', 'Smith' , '444-000-4444')");
// close statements when done
stmt.close();
```

> **Note**
>
> When creating a Statement, resources will be allocated to the application in order to execute the SQL. It is vital to release these resources, by closing the Statement when execution is complete, using the close() method.

The execute() method returns a boolean: true if the next result is a ResultSet object, or false if it is an update count or there are no more results. The following code gets a ResultSet object, which holds the result of the last query:

```
stmt.execute("SELECT * from DAY09_STUDENTS");
// Obtain the result of the last query
ResultSet rs = stmt.getResultSet();
```

The ResultSet is initially positioned before the first row. Table 9.4 gives a summary of the ResultSet methods.

**TABLE 9.4**   Summary of ResultSet Methods

| Method | Purpose |
| --- | --- |
| Boolean next() | Scrolls the cursor to the next available row |
| String getString(int columnIndex) | Returns data at the current cursor, under a particular column number or index |
| String getString(String columnName) | Returns data at the current cursor, under a particular column name |
| Boolean isFirst() | Returns true if the cursor is at the first row |
| Boolean isLast() | Returns true if the cursor is at the last row |
| int getFetchSize() | Returns the default fetched number of rows |
| setFetchSize(int rows) | Set the required number of rows to be fetched |
| ResultSetMetaData getMetaData() | Returns data about the ResultSet, such as number of columns and the properties of data elements |

Now we can scroll through the ResultSet to display the retrieved data using getString() method. From the earlier example, the ResultSet contains four columns and four rows. Columns can be identified by column name or column number. This example uses the column name:

```
// Display the ResultSet data on the screen using column name
while (rs.next())
        System.out.println(rs.getString("student_id") + " ," +
                           rs.getString("first_name") + " ," +
                           rs.getString("last_name") + " ," +
                           rs.getString("address"));
```

When using the column number, you pass an integer value to getString() that starts with 1, which represents the first column:

```
// Display the ResultSet data using column number
while (rs.next())
        System.out.println(rs.getString(1) + " ," +
                           rs.getString(2) + " ," +
                           rs.getString(3) + " ," +
```

```
                                rs.getString(4));
// close the result set after done.
rs.close();
```

In both cases, the output of the last `println` should look like this:

```
1, LILLIAN, GHALY, 15 DIAMOND ST, BOSTON, MA
3, SAM, LE, 12 APPLEBEE RD, LOS ANGELES, CA
```

Much like the `Statement` object, the `ResultSet` object can be tuned to the optimum number of fetched rows. To do this, use the `getFetchSize()` and `setFetchSize()` methods of `ResultSet`. This increases the performance when a large number of rows is retrieved during search operations. Close the `ResultSet` object when you're done to release allocated resources.

9

# Optimized Queries to the Database

A shortcut method of querying the database is to use the `executeQuery()` method of the `Statement` object. This combines both `execute()` and `getResultSet()` in one method. The preceding example can be written as

```
// Obtain the ResultSet directly
ResultSet rs = stmt.executeQuery("SELECT * DAY09_STUDENTS");
```

Both simple queries, such as the one specified in the preceding example, and more sophisticated joins can be specified as a parameter `String` to the `executeQuery()` method.

Another variant used with the INSERT, UPDATE, and DELETE operations is the `executeUpdate()` method:

```
// Using the executeUpdate method instead of execute()
String sql = "INSERT into DAY09_STUDENTS values " +
   "('1', 'LILLIAN', 'GHALY', '15 DIAMOND ST, BOSTON, MA')");
stmt.executeUpdate(sql);
```

The `executeUpdate()` method specializes in DML operations. DDL operations, such as `drop table`, `create table`, and so on, are made available only through the `execute()` method as explained in the previous section.

## Using a `PreparedStatement`

In situations where the same statement is performed repeatedly, a more optimized way is to use a `PreparedStatement`. This divides the operation into a creation phase and an execution phase. When creating the statement, the database is instructed to be ready by pre-parsing and compiling the statement, and preparing its buffers to assign variables to the table elements. The execution phase requests the database to execute the operation after the required elements filled up. Let's illustrate this with the following code:

```
// Create a PreparedStatement
PreparedStatement pstmt =
    conn.preparedStatement("INSERT INTO DAY09_STUDENT values (?,?,?,?)")
```

The database is now instructed to prepare the buffers for the operation. Each data element is mapped to the wild card in sequence. We use `setString()` method to fill up the holes:

```
// Fill up the data elements and execute
pstmt.setInt(1, 2);
pstmt.setString(2, "DOUG");
pstmt.setString(3, "ZANDER");
pstmt.setString(4, "11 ORANGE AVE, SACRAMENTO, CA");
int rcount = pstmt.executeUpdate();
```

Other methods to pass these parameters depend on the parameter type, and take the pattern set*XXX*(). For example, `setInt()` to pass in an `int`, `setFloat()` to pass in a `float`, `setBoolean()` to pass in a `boolean`, and so on.

Using `PreparedStatement` saves time for a repeated statement, and hence enhances the performance of your application. The return value of the last `executeUpdate()` indicates the number of rows affected as a result of any `INSERT`, `UPDATE`, or `DELETE` operation. The `PreparedStatement` inherits all its properties and methods from the `Statement` object.

## Using a `CallableStatement` for Stored Procedures

The JDBC API provides support for calling a stored procedure. The `CallableStatement` inherits from `PreparedStatement`, and is used to call a stored procedure. A *stored procedure* is a group of SQL statements that can be called by name, and are stored in a file and managed by the underlying Relational Database Management System (RDBMS). Stored procedures, once written, can be compiled and then reused. They are executed on the database server, which relieves the application server of performing the task. The `CallableStatement` is created from the `Connection` method `prepareCall()`.

The following snippet demonstrates how the stored procedure `getStudentById` is created and sent to the RDBMS to compile and store under the name `getStudentById`:

```
// Create stored procedure
String storedPoc = "create procedure GetStudentById(Stid integer)" +
    "as begin" +
    "SELECT * FROM DAY09_STUDENT" +
    "WHERE student_id = 'Stid'" +
```

```
        "end";
Statement stmt = conn.createStatement();
stmt.executeUpdate(storedPoc);
```

The next code demonstrates the use of a `CallableStatement` that calls the previous stored procedure `getStudentById`:

```
CallableStatement cstmt = conn.prepareCall(
            "{call getStudentById(?)}");
cstmt.setInt(1,4);
ResultSet rs = cstmt.executeQuery();
```

9

The variable `cstmt` contains a call to the stored procedure `getStudentById`, which has one `IN` parameter, represented by the wildcard `?` placeholder. Normally, stored procedure parameter types can be one of type `IN`, `OUT`, or `INOUT`. Passing in any `IN` parameter values to a `CallableStatement` object is done using the `setXXX()` methods inherited from `PreparedStatement`. The JDBC type of each `OUT` parameter must be registered before the `CallableStatement` object can be executed. Registering the JDBC type is done with the method `registerOutParameter()` of the `CallableStatement`. After the statement has been executed, `CallableStatement`'s `getXXX()` methods can be used to retrieve `OUT` parameter values. An `INOUT` parameter requires both treatments of `IN` and `OUT` parameter.

 **Caution**
> Care should be taken when writing stored procedures. Because it belongs to the data layer, too much logic in a stored procedure violates the purpose of separating data from the application logic. Be aware also that stored procedures do not work the same way across all RDBMSes. In addition, all stored procedures must be compiled again if you have to change just one of them.

# Using Local Transactions

A *transaction* is a group of SQL statements that represents one unit of work. A transaction executes all of its statements or none at all. JDBC handles both local and distributed transactions. Today we're covering only local transactions; distributed transactions are deferred to Day 16, when you'll study the concepts of the JTA (Java Transaction API).

A local transaction belongs only to the current process, and deals with only a single resource manager that handles a `DataSource`. An RDBMS is an example of a resource manager., A distributed transaction, on the other hand, manages multiple `DataSources` across multiple processes. All database operations mentioned earlier today that use a `Statement` object are implicitly transactional with auto-commit. That means the DBMS commits the transaction as soon as any `execute()`, `executeUpdate()`, or `executeBatch()` is done.

Local transactions are managed by the Connection object, and not by the EJB container. To change this implicit behavior, JDBC provides the method setAutoCommit(false) to set the transaction mode on the Connection object. The commit() and rollback() methods also are used by the Connection object to control the transaction's behavior. An example of a local transaction is as follows:

```
// Create a Statement from Connection and its set transaction mode
conn.setAutoCommit(false);
Statement stmt = conn.createStatement();
try {
  stmt.executeUpdate("UPDATE DAY09_STUDENT set first_name='Laura' where
➥student_id ='5'");
  // assume something wrong happen here…..
  stmt.executeUpdate("UPDATE DAY09_STUDENT set last_name='Smith' where
student_id ='5'");
  conn.commit();
} catch (SQLException ex) {
  conn.rollback();
  stmt.close();
}
```

Disabling auto-commit using setAutoCommit(false) is required when a batch of SQL statements must execute together, or the EJB container is managing the transaction. Controlling transactions can increase performance because you commit a batch of SQL statements instead doing so one at a time. JDBC architects realized this fact and have built the concept of batch updates into the JDBC API. Batch updates will be covered in the next section.

Another concept related to local transactions is handling concurrency by setting the transaction isolation level, which will be covered during your study of transactions on Day 16.

# Using Batch Updates

Another aspect of enhancing performance of applications is the reduction of network traffic between J2EE tiers, or applications that partitioned to run on different servers. One way to reduce network traffic back and forth between components and enhance the performance of the running application is to use bulk updates, which are coarse-grain updates. This experience is reflected by the JDBC architects in the JDBC API, and is implemented by using the addBatch() method of the Statement object to prepare the batch before using the executeBatch() method. Batch updates use any of the INSERT, UPDATE, and DELETE operations. To use batch updates, you must disable the auto-commit mode.

```
try{
  // Disable auto-commit
```

```
    conn.setAutoCommit(false);
    // Create a Statement from Connection
    Statement stmt = conn.createStatement()
    stmt.addBatch("INSERT INTO DAY09_STUDENT " +
    "values('7', 'ERIC', 'CHRISTIAN', '1 MEMORIAL DRIVE, CAMBRIDGE, MA')";
    stmt.addBatch("UPDATE DAY09_STUDENT set first_name='Laura' where id='5'");
    int [] rc = stmt.executeBatch();
    conn.commit();
    conn.setAutoCommit(true);
} catch(BatchUpdateException sqlb) {
    System.err.println("SQL State: " + sqlb.getSQLState());
    System.err.println("Message: " + sqlb.getMessage());
    System.err.println("Vendor Error: " + sqlb.getErrorCode());
    System.err.print("Update counts:   ");
    int [] updateCounts = sqlb.getUpdateCounts();
    for (int i = 0; i < updateCounts.length; i++) {
      System.err.print(updateCounts[i] + "   ");
    }
    System.err.println("");
  }
```

The executeBatch() method returns an array of integers that specifies the row count of each operation in the batch.

Batch updates throw BatchUpdateException, which inherits from SQLException, and information can extracted about each update. Performance can be enhanced by tuning the number of rows to be fetched at a runtime from database. By default, you can get the default number of rows provided by the JDBC driver by using getFetchSize() on the Statement object. You can tune the size by using the setFetchSize(int rows) method of the Statement object.

# Working with Metadata

Metadata is data about data, and in the context of our study of JDBC, it's the information provided about the properties of data sources and result sets. Querying metadata is very powerful in creating tools for database manipulation and sophisticated database applications.

To find information about the connected database, we use the method getMetaData() of the Connection object to retrieve a DatabaseMetaData object. You can get information about schemas, tables, and properties of each table. The following sample queries database metadata to display all the table names and properties of each table in the schema "APP":

```
// Finding MetaData about database
```

```
DatabaseMetaData dbmd = conn.getMetaData();
String[] types = {"TABLE"};
System.out.println("Database Table Names for the Schema "APP")
rs = dbmd.getTables(null, "APP", null, types);
while (rs.next()){
    String tableName = rset.getString("TABLE_NAME");
    System.out.println("Table Name: " + tableName);
    ResultSet rsc = dbmd.getColumns(null,null,tableName,"%");
    System.out.println("Column Name" + "    Data Type" + " Width");
    while (rsc.next()){
      System.out.println(rsc.getString("COLUMN_NAME") + "..." +
                         rsc.getString("TYPE_NAME") + "..." +
                         rsc.getInt("COLUMN_SIZE"));
    }
}
```

When sending a SELECT statement to the database, you receive a ResultSet that holds the records to satisfy your criteria. To find metadata information about a ResultSet object, use the getMetaData() method of the ResultSet interface. This metadata will be captured and retrieved by getMetaData() into a ResultSetMetaData object. Such metadata of a ResultSet is the number of columns and the database properties of each column, such as its name, type, width, and precision. An example of retrieving a ResultSetMetaData object about a ResultSet is the following:

```
// Finding MetaData about result set
Statement stmt = conn.createStatement();
ResultSet rs = stmt.executeQuery("select * from student");
ResultSetMetaData rsmd = rs.getMetaData();
int cn = rsmd.getColumnCount();
// Printing column information
for (int i=1; i<= cn ; i++) {
    if (i > 1) { System.out.print(", "); }
    System.out.print(rsmd.getColumnLabel(i));
}
System.out.print("")
// Printing the data
while (rs.next ()) {
    for (int i=1; i<=cn; i++) {
      if (i > 1) { System.out.print(", "); }
        System.out.print(rs.getString(i));
    }
    System.out.println("");
}
```

By combining ResultSetMetaData and DatabaseMetaData, toolmakers can build very powerful database interactive tools to query and schema objects and data.

# Working with JDBC Through a Full Example

Now it's time for today's example. Listing 9.1 gives a skeleton of code that performs the following:

- Connects to a database
- Performs few of both DDL and DML statements
- Queries `ResultSet` metadata and database metadata
- Closes the statements and the connection
- Handles SQL exceptions

To demonstrate the strong aspect of JDBC as a vendor-neutral API, the same example runs on two different application servers, without changing any line of code. The `QueryDB` session bean is used to represent the client in query the database. Listings 9.1 to 9.3 are for the home interface, remote interface, and the bean class. Listings 9.4 to 9.7 are for the EJB client, standard deployment descriptor, WebLogic Server deployment descriptor, and the JBoss deployment descriptor.

**LISTING 9.1**    The Home Interface day09/QueryDBHome.java

```
package day09;
import java.rmi.RemoteException;
import javax.ejb.*;

/*
  QueryDBHome is the home interface for the stateless session bean.
 */
public interface QueryDBHome extends EJBHome{
  QueryDB create() throws CreateException, RemoteException;
}
```

**LISTING 9.2**    The Remote Interface day09/QueryDB.java

```
package day09;
import java.util.*;
import javax.ejb.*;
import java.rmi.RemoteException;

/*
  QueryDB is the remote interface for the stateless session bean.
 */
public interface QueryDB extends EJBObject{
    public void initDB() throws RemoteException;
    public void doDDL() throws RemoteException;
```

**LISTING 9.2** continued

```
    public void getMetaData() throws RemoteException;
}
```

**LISTING 9.3** The Bean Class day09/QueryDBBean.java

```java
package day09;

import java.util.*;
import javax.ejb.*;
import javax.naming.*;
import java.sql.*;

/**
 * QueryDBEJB is stateless session bean to query database properties
 */
public class QueryDBBean implements SessionBean
{
  public void initDB(){
    try {
      System.out.println("\nDay 9: Demonstrate the use of JDBC...\n");
      System.out.println("initDB: Get initial context from the JNDI service...");
      ctx = new InitialContext();
      System.out.println("Lookup the DataSource as configured by administra-
tor...");
      ds = (javax.sql.DataSource)ctx.lookup ("java:comp/env/jdbc/styejbDB");
      System.out.println("Getting a Connection from the pool...");
      conn = ds.getConnection();
      System.out.println("Connection is obtained...");
    } catch (Exception e) {
      System.out.println("Exception was thrown: " + e.getMessage());
    } finally {
        try {
          if (stmt != null)
                stmt.close();
          if (conn != null)
                conn.close();
        } catch (SQLException sqle) {
                System.out.println("SQLException during close(): " +
➡sqle.getMessage());
        }
    }
  }
  public void doDDL(){

   System.out.println("Run some DDL statements:");
   try{
     conn = ds.getConnection();
```

**LISTING 9.3**    continued

```
stmt = conn.createStatement();
try {
        System.out.println("Trying to drop table DAY09_STUDENTS...");
        stmt.execute("DROP TABLE DAY09_STUDENTS");
} catch (SQLException e) {
        System.out.println("Table DAY09_STUDENTS already exists.");
}
stmt.execute("CREATE TABLE DAY09_STUDENTS (student_id varchar(12),"+
                            "first_name varchar(15),"+
                            "last_name varchar(15),"+
                            "address varchar(64))");
System.out.println("Table DAY09_STUDENTS is created...");

System.out.println("Run some DML statements:");
stmt.executeUpdate("INSERT into DAY09_STUDENTS values " +
                "('1', 'LILLIAN', 'GHALY', '15 DIAMOND ST, BOSTON, MA')");
stmt.executeUpdate("INSERT into DAY09_STUDENTS values " +
                "('2', 'DOUG','ZANDER','11 ORANGE AVE, SACRAMENTO, CA' )");
stmt.executeUpdate("INSERT into DAY09_STUDENTS values " +
                "('3', 'SAM','LE', '12 APPLEBEE RD, LOS ANGELES, CA' )");
stmt.executeUpdate("DELETE from DAY09_STUDENTS where student_id = '2'");
rs = stmt.executeQuery("SELECT * from DAY09_STUDENTS");
// Get some Metadata about result set
System.out.println("Query ResultSet Metadata:");
rsmd = rs.getMetaData();
cn = rsmd.getColumnCount();
for (i=1; i<= cn ; i++) {
        if (i>1) System.out.print(", ");
        System.out.print(rsmd.getColumnLabel(i));
}
System.out.println("");
while (rs.next()) {
        for (i=1; i<= cn ; i++) {
                if (i>1) System.out.print(", ");
                System.out.print(rs.getString(i));
        }
        System.out.println("");
}
} catch (Exception e) {
        System.out.println("Exception was thrown: " + e.getMessage());
} finally {
        try {
        if (stmt != null)
                stmt.close();
        if (conn != null)
                conn.close();
        } catch (SQLException sqle) {
            System.out.println("SQLException during close(): " +
➥sqle.getMessage());
```

9

**LISTING 9.3**    continued

```java
            }
    }
}
public void getMetaData() {
 // Get some Metadata about database
 System.out.println("Query Database Metadata:");
 try{
   conn = ds.getConnection();
   dbmd = conn.getMetaData();
   System.out.println("  Product Name: " + dbmd.getDatabaseProductName());
   System.out.println("  Driver Name: " + dbmd.getDriverName());
   rs = dbmd.getSchemas();
   System.out.println("Database Schemas:");
   rsmd = rs.getMetaData();
   cn = rsmd.getColumnCount();
   for (i=1; i<= cn ; i++) {
         if (i>1) System.out.print(", ");
         System.out.print(rsmd.getColumnLabel(i));
   }
   System.out.println("");
   while (rs.next()) {
         for (i=1; i<= cn ; i++) {
               if (i>1) System.out.print(", ");
               System.out.print(rs.getString(i));
               if (schema == null)
                   schema = new StringBuffer(rs.getString(i));
         }
         System.out.println("");
   }
   String[] types = {"TABLE"};
   System.out.println("Printing All Data Tables for Schema: " + schema);
   rs = dbmd.getTables(null, schema.toString(), null, types);
   while (rs.next()){
         String tableName = rs.getString("TABLE_NAME");
         System.out.println("Table Name: " + tableName);

         ResultSet rsc = dbmd.getColumns(null,null,tableName,"%");
         rsmd = rsc.getMetaData();
         cn = rsmd.getColumnCount();
         for (i=1; i<= cn ; i++) {
               if (i>1) System.out.print(", ");
               System.out.print(rsmd.getColumnLabel(i));
         }
         System.out.println("");
         while (rsc.next()) {
               for (i=1; i<= cn ; i++) {
                   if (i>1) System.out.print(", ");
                   System.out.print(rsc.getString(i));
               }
```

**LISTING 9.3**   continued

```
                            System.out.println("");
                }
        }
    } catch (Exception e) {
        System.out.println("Exception was thrown: " + e.getMessage());
    } finally {
        try {
                if (stmt != null)
                        stmt.close();
                if (conn != null)
                        conn.close();
        } catch (SQLException sqle) {
            System.out.println("SQLException during close(): " + sqle.getMessage());
        }
    }
}
 public void setSessionContext(SessionContext ctx) {this.bctx = ctx;}
 public void ejbCreate() throws CreateException {}
 public void ejbRemove() {}
 public void ejbActivate() {}
 public void ejbPassivate() {}

 private SessionContext bctx;
 private Context ctx                       = null;
 private StringBuffer schema     = null;
 private javax.sql.DataSource ds           = null;
 private java.sql.Connection conn = null;
 private java.sql.Statement stmt    = null;
 private java.sql.ResultSet rs             = null;
 private java.sql.ResultSetMetaData rsmd     = null;
 private int cn, i;
 private java.sql.DatabaseMetaData dbmd     = null;
```

**LISTING 9.4**   The EJB Client `Client.java`

```
package day09;
import java.util.*;
import java.rmi.*;
import java.io.*;
import javax.naming.*;
import javax.ejb.*;

public class Client {
    public static void main(String argv[]) {
        Context initialContext = null;
        QueryDBHome qdbHome = null;
        QueryDB qdb = null;
```

**LISTING 9.4**    continued

```
        System.out.print("\nDay 9: Demonstration the use of JDBC...\n ");
         try
         {
            System.out.print("Looking up the QueryDB home via JNDI.\n");
            initialContext = new InitialContext();
            Object object = initialContext.lookup("day09/QueryDBHome");
            qdbHome = (QueryDBHome)
               javax.rmi.PortableRemoteObject.narrow(object, QueryDBHome.class);
            System.out.print("Creating an Query DB.\n");
            qdb =  (QueryDB) qdbHome.create();
            qdb.initDB();
            qdb.doDDL();
            qdb.getMetaData();
         }catch ( Exception e){
         e.printStackTrace();
         }
      }
   }
```

**LISTING 9.5**    The Standard Deployment Descriptor `ejb-jar.xml`

```
    <?xml version="1.0"?>
    <!DOCTYPE ejb-jar PUBLIC
    '-//Sun Microsystems, Inc.//DTD Enterprise JavaBeans 2.0//EN'
    'http://java.sun.com/dtd/ejb-jar_2_0.dtd'>

    <ejb-jar>
      <enterprise-beans>
        <session>
          <ejb-name>QueryDB</ejb-name>
          <home>day09.QueryDBHome</home>
          <remote>day09.QueryDB</remote>
          <ejb-class>day09.QueryDBBean</ejb-class>
          <session-type>Stateless</session-type>
          <transaction-type>Container</transaction-type>
          <resource-ref>
           <res-ref-name>jdbc/styejbDB</res-ref-name>
           <res-type>javax.sql.DataSource</res-type>
           <res-auth>Application</res-auth>
          </resource-ref>
          <resource-env-ref>
           <resource-env-ref-name>jdbc/styejbDB</resource-env-ref-name>
           <resource-env-ref-type>javax.sql.DataSource</resource-env-ref-type>
          </resource-env-ref>
        </session>
      </enterprise-beans>
    </ejb-jar>
```

**LISTING 9.6**  The WebLogic Deployment Descriptor `weblogic-ejb-jar.xml`

```xml
<?xml version="1.0"?>

<!DOCTYPE weblogic-ejb-jar PUBLIC
'-//BEA Systems, Inc.//DTD WebLogic 6.0.0 EJB//EN'
'http://www.bea.com/servers/wls600/dtd/weblogic-ejb-jar.dtd'>

<weblogic-ejb-jar>
  <weblogic-enterprise-bean>
    <ejb-name>QueryDB</ejb-name>
    <reference-descriptor>
      <resource-description>
        <res-ref-name>jdbc/styejbDB</res-ref-name>
        <jndi-name>jdbc.styejbDB</jndi-name>
      </resource-description>
      <resource-env-description>
        <res-env-ref-name>jdbc/styejbDB</res-env-ref-name>
        <jndi-name>jdbc.styejbDB</jndi-name>
      </resource-env-description>
    </reference-descriptor>
    <jndi-name>day09/QueryDBHome</jndi-name>
  </weblogic-enterprise-bean>
</weblogic-ejb-jar>
```

**LISTING 9.7**  The JBoss Deployment Descriptor `jboss.xml`

```xml
<?xml version="1.0" encoding="UTF-8"?>

<jboss>
  <enterprise-beans>
    <session>
      <ejb-name>QueryDB</ejb-name>
      <jndi-name>day09/QueryDBHome</jndi-name>
      <resource-ref>
        <res-ref-name>jdbc/styejbDB</res-ref-name>
        <jndi-name>java:/DefaultDS</jndi-name>
      </resource-ref>
      <resource-env-ref>
        <resource-env-ref-name>jdbc/styejbDB</resource-env-ref-name>
        <jndi-name>java:/DefaultDS</jndi-name>
      </resource-env-ref>
    </session>
  </enterprise-beans>
</jboss>
```

Because each application server has its own way of referencing its own resources in the JNDI services, your application needs to be written to avoid such dependency. In order to make your application portable, you need to use the `<resource-env-ref>` element in the standard deployment descriptor (`ejb-jar.xml`) to define a logical name, which is used by the application. Then you need to map this logical name to a `<reference-descriptor>` in your server-specific deployment descriptor, which is the physical reference to the JNDI name. The lines of code (shown in bold) in the preceding example demonstrate the use of such technique.

## Configuring the `DataSource` and the Connection Pool

Before you run the example, you need first to create and configure the connection pool `styejbPool`. You also need to create the `DataSource` `styejbDB` for the connection pool and register it in the JNDI service. The accompanying `day09/Readme.txt` file explains this process for both WebLogic and JBoss servers.

## Compile and Run the Example

This section describes the steps to comoile and run the example for both WebLogic Server and JBoss application servers.

To run the example in WebLogic Server, you must follow these steps:

1.  Open a new command window.

    Set up the environment for the appropriate application server, and then start the server. Run the accompanying script, found at the root of the sample directory, to set up an environment for either WebLogic Server or JBoss. The following are the scripts for WebLogic Server, (follow Figures 9.6, 9.7, and 9.8 to assist you in setting up the JDBC connection pool in the WebLogic Server environment):

2.  Set up and start the PointBase database using the following steps:

    ```
    c:\>cd c:\styejb\examples

    c:\styejb\examples>startPointbase.bat

    c:\styejb\examples>setEnvWebLogic.bat

    c:\styejb\examples>setupPointbase.bat
    ```

    The above steps start PointBase Server and  create the tables in a PointBase server named `styejbPool`.

3.  Start WebLogic Server using the following steps:

    ```
    c:\>cd c:\styejb\examples

    c:\styejb\examples>setEnvWebLogic.bat

    c:\styejb\examples>startWebLogic.bat
    ```

4.  Open the WebLogic Administration Console using a Web browser such as Internet Explorer, and point to the URL `http://localhost:7001/console`. When

prompted, enter the user name (**system**) and password you chose when you installed WebLogic Server (see Appendix A, "WebLogic Application Server 7.0").

5. Create a connection pool for the Pointbase Database by doing the following:

In the left pane, expand Services > JDBC.

Click Connection Pools.

In the right pane, click Configure a New JDBC Connection Pool.

Enter these values:

Name: **styejbPool**

URL: **jdbc:pointbase:server://localhost:9092/styejbPool**

Driver: **com.pointbase.jdbc.jdbcUniversalDriver**

Properties: **user=PBPUBLIC**

Password: **PBPUBLIC**

Leave both the fields ACLName and Open String Password blank.

Click Create.

Figure 9.6 shows the corresponding screen shot.

Click the Connections tab and change the Maximum Capacity to 10 and click the Apply button.

Click the Targets tab.

Move myserver to the Chosen (right) column.

Figure 9.7 shows the corresponding screen shot.

Click Apply.

6. Create the JDBC data source.

Click the Home icon in the upper-right corner of the Administration Console.

In the left pane, expand Services > JDBC.

Click Tx Data Sources.

In the right pane, click Configure a New JDBC Data Source.

For Name, enter **styejbDB**

For JNDI Name, enter **jdbc.styejbDB**

For Pool Name, enter **styejbPool**

Figure 9.8 shows the corresponding screen shot.

Click Create.

Click the Targets tab.

**FIGURE 9.6**

*Configuring the connection pool* styejbPool *in WebLogic Server.*

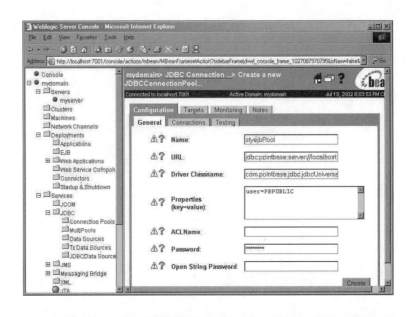

**FIGURE 9.7**

*Configuring a JDBC connection pool.*

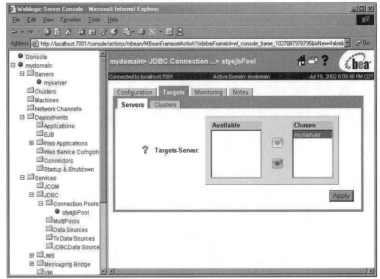

Move myserver to the Chosen (right) column.

Click Apply.

To check the current list of data sources, click Home, and then click JDBC > TXData Sources.

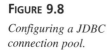

**FIGURE 9.8**

*Configuring a JDBC connection pool.*

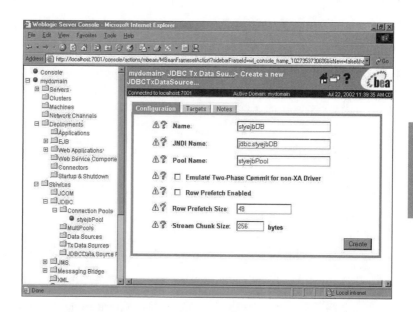

9

7. Build the example for the appropriate application server. From the directory `Day09`, run the build script. This creates a subdirectory with the name `build`, which contains all the compiled code.

```
c:\>cd c:\styejb\examples
```

```
c:\styejb\examples>setEnvWebLogic.bat
```

```
c:\styejb\examples>cd day09
```

```
c:\styejb\examples\day09>buildWebLogic.bat
```

8. To run the example, use the appropriate script for each server. Set up the environment for the client in a new command window, and then use the run script in the `Day09` directory:

```
c:\styejb\examples>setEnvWebLogic.bat
```

```
c:\styejb\examples>cd day09
```

```
c:\styejb\examples\day09> runClientWebLogic.bat
```

Refer to the README.TXT file in the day09 directory to information to configure your JBoss datasource. The following is the server-side output of the example:

```
Day 9: Demonstrate the use of JDBC...

initDB: Get initial context from the JNDI service...
Lookup the DataSource as configured by administrator...
Getting a Connection from the pool...
Connection is obtained...
Run some DDL statements:
Trying to drop table STUDENTS...
```

```
Table STUDENTS is created...
Run some DML statements:
Query ResultSet Metadata:
STUDENT_ID, FIRST_NAME, LAST_NAME, ADDRESS
1, LILLIAN, GHALY, 15 DIAMOND ST, BOSTON, MA
3, SAM, LE, 12 APPLEBEE RD, LOS ANGELES, CA
Query Database Metadata:
  Product Name: PointBase
  Driver Name: PointBase JDBC Driver
Database Schemas:
TABLE_SCHEM
PBPUBLIC
POINTBASE
Printing All Data Tables for Schema: PBPUBLIC
Table Name: COURSES
...
```

**Note** If your output contains an exception such as `Exception was thrown: Unable to resolve jdbc.styejbDB. Resolved: 'jdbc' Unresolved:'styejbDB'`, your connection pool and data source configuration are incorrect. You must correct the values as specified in the previous section, "Configuring the DataSource and Connection Pool."

The following steps describe how to start JBoss server, run the sample client, and set up the database tables required for the remaining days:

1. Start JBoss server in a new command window as follows:

```
C:\>cd styejb\examples
C:\styejb\examples>setEnvJBoss.bat
C:\styejb\examples>startJBoss.bat
```

The JBoss server automatically starts the default HyperSonic database.

2. Build and run the example as follows:

```
c:\>cd c:\styejb\examples

c:\styejb\examples>setEnvJBoss.bat

c:\styejb\examples>cd day09

c:\styejb\examples\day09>buildJBoss.bat

C:\styejb\examples\day09>runClientJBoss.bat
```

3. Set up the database tables required for the remaining days by doing the following:

In the command window that you used to build and run the example, run the following command:

```
c:\styejb\examples>setupHypersonic.bat
```

This opens the HSQL Database Manager Connect window. Enter the value **jdbc:hsqldb:hsql://localhost:1476** for the URL field. Leave default values for other fields. Figure 9.9 shows the corresponding screen shot. Click the Ok button.

**FIGURE 9.9**

*Connecting to the HyperSonic Database Manager.*

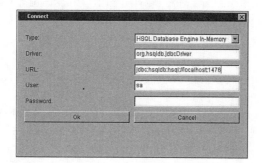

9

Click the File\Open Script… menu item. When prompted, enter the filename
`c:\styejb\examples\styejbhs.sql`.

Click the Execute button on the right. Figure 9.10 shows the corresponding screen shot.

**FIGURE 9.10**

*Setting up the database tables in HyperSonic database.*

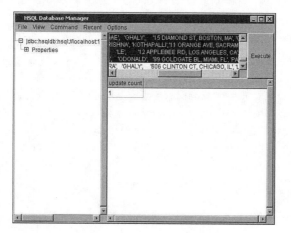

# Best Practices

Some of the best practices are already built-in the JDBC API itself, such as connection pooling, PreparedStatement, and batch updates. Still some of the widely known practices help when developing large and enterprise J2EE applications.

Some factors affecting the performance of your application with respect to database are independent of JDBC or any other access method. Examples of such factors are writing optimized queries, and tuning the database using caching of often-used resources. Both database tuning and query optimization are beyond the scope of this book. A simple example such as using the query `"SELECT * from Student"` rather than `"SELECT id from Student"` when you need only the student IDs, increases network traffic and the allocated resources to handle such `ResultSet`. Performing an `UPDATE` row operation rather than a `DELETE` on the row followed by an `INSERT` of new row, is another type of good practice.

With respect to JDBC, performance gain can be established by obtaining a `Context` to the `DataSource` in the initialization code. Use `PreparedStatement` to performing the same query repeatedly. `CallableStatement` also gives better performance than `PreparedStatement` and `Statement` when there is a requirement for single request to process multiple complex statements. It parses and stores the stored procedures in the database and optimizes the work at the database itself to improve its performance. Use stored procedure and triggers for large operations, but use them with care. Stored procedures are handled differently by database products. This has a negative affect on application portability and makes you rely on vendor-specific stored procedures.

Use batch updates to perform batches of SQL statements. Release all resources appropriately; that is, in the reverse order of how they were allocated. If possible, avoid transaction auto-commit, and control your transaction behavior.

Tuning your connection pool is a prime factor in the overall system performance. Both minimum and maximum size should be selected based on the expected user load. Another factor is that the `Connection` must be returned to the pool as soon as you are done working with it. Delaying the release of the connection has negative impact on an application's scalability. Disabling auto-commit to control batch operations through a single transaction also helps improve application performance.

# Summary

Today we covered JDBC as a standard and unified API to access many data sources in tabular forms, such as relational tables, flat files, and spreadsheets. J2EE applications and components use JDBC across all tiers. We examined the methods of connecting to a data source, and showed how to construct and implement SQL statements, and the optimized ways of handling them. We looked briefly at local transactions and stored procedures. Metadata of both the DBMS and the `ResultSet` was discussed, and we ended by giving a brief account of the best practices in dealing with database objects and queries using JDBC.

Tomorrow, you will learn how to develop a stateless session bean. You will see a full life cycle example by writing, compiling, deploying, and running the bean.

# Q&A

**Q  Which JDBC driver is best for my J2EE applications?**

**A**  Each JDBC driver has its usage environment and depends on the availability of the driver. Type 2 is best used when high transaction rate is required because itís optimized for the native DBMS API. Type 4 is all Java, and is attractive for most J2EE applications because itís optimized with the underlying JVM technology.

**Q  What is the appropriate sequence to access a `DataSource` through JDBC?**

**A**  There are two important group of tasks to be performed: one by the administrator and the other by the application developer.

The administrative tasks are

- Configure a `DataSource` and registered it in into the JNDI service provider.
- Configure a connection pool and map it to the defined `DataSource`.

The developer writes code in the following sequence:

- Connect to a JNDI service, and establish a `Context` by looking up a named `DataSource`.
- Create a `Connection` object from the `DataSource` factory. A `Connection` is assigned from the connection pool. A `Connection` represents a database session.
- Create a `Statement` object from `Connection` (can be `PreparedStatement` or `CallableStatment`).
- Perform SQL statements (both DDL and DML database operations) on the `Statement` object, such as `execute()`, `executeQuery()`, `updateQuery()`, and `executeBatch()`.
- Retrieve output in a `ResultSet` object, and process it according to the application's needs.
- Close all allocated resources in proper sequence: First, close all `Statement` objects in the reverse order of how they were allocated, then close the `Connection` objects, and finally the `Context` object.

## Quiz

1. Which of the following statement type should be used to call a stored procedure?

   A. `Statement`

   B. `PreparedStatement`

   C. `CallableStatement`

   D. `Connection`

2. From which object do you ask for `DatabaseMetaData`?

   A. `Connection`

   B. `ResultSet`

   C. `DriverManager`

   D. `DataSource`

3. Which of the following statements will get return the data from the first column of `ResultSet rs`, returned by from executing the following SQL statement: `"SELECT student_id, first_name, last_name, address FROM DAY09_STUDENT"`?.

   A. `.rs.getString(0)`

   B. `.rs.getString("student_id")`

   C. `.rs.getString(1)`

   D. `.rs.getInt(1)`

### Quiz Answers

1. C
2. A
3. B and C

## Exercises

Modify the day's example to perform few batch updates on the `Student` table. Batch updates include only `INSERT`, `UPDATE`, or `DELETE` SQL statements.

# DAY 10

# Developing Bean-Managed Persistence Entity Beans

Today, you'll work on a complete example of developing a bean-managed persistence (BMP) entity bean. You might question why you need to learn bean-managed persistence when container-managed persistence (CMP) is simpler to write and is the preferred approach. The answer is that you should use bean-managed persistence if you want complete control of managing persistence, if you're writing persistence logic to a very proprietary legacy database system, or when your persistent store is not a database.

The concept of the student is central to the sample university registration application. Multiple clients must share behavior, such as creating a student account, verifying an existing account, and updating account information. Updates to the state of a student object must be written to the persistent store. The student object must live even when the client's session with the server is over. Therefore, in the sample application, a student object is modeled as an entity bean. Today, we'll model a student entity bean as bean-managed persistence entity bean.

A BMP is responsible for managing its persistence. It consists of a home interface, a component interface, and a bean class. First, we'll examine the interaction between the client, EJB container and the entity bean by looking under the bean's hood. Next, we'll write each of the interfaces and implement the bean class.

Typically, a BMP contains calls to access the database. The data access calls can be embedded in the entity bean class or encapsulated in a helper object, known as a Data Access Object (DAO), that's part of the entity bean. Today, we'll learn about DAOs and use them to encapsulate data access calls.

The BMP deployment descriptor specifies the bean's name, the home and component interfaces, and the bean class. In addition, it specifies the bean's primary key. We'll write the BMP deployment descriptor. Finally, we'll package and deploy the bean and also write a client that accesses the BMP.

# Looking Under the Hood of a BMP Entity Bean

Figure 10.1 shows the interactions between the client, EJB container, bean-managed persistence bean, and the database.

The following steps describe the sequence of interactions in detail:

1. At startup, the EJB container registers all the deployed enterprise beans, including entity beans, with the JNDI service.

2. The client looks up the home interface of the deployed enterprise bean via the Java Naming and Directory Interface (JNDI). For example, the remote home interface for the Student bean can be located using the following code segment:
```
Context initialContext = new InitialContext();
Object obj = initialContext.lookup("day10/Student");
StudentHome studentHome = (StudentHome)
 javax.rmi.PortableRemoteObject.narrow(obj, StudentHome.class);
```

3. The client uses the remote home interface to create a remote Student object. For example, the client creates a new student as follows:
```
Student student=(Student)studentHome.create("1",  "Raghava",
            "Kothapalli", "1234, People Dr. Pleasonton, CA");
```

   When a client invokes a create<*method*> method on the home interface, the EJB container invokes the corresponding ejbCreate<*method*> method, followed by the ejbPostCreate<*method*> method on the bean instance.

4. The client calls a method on the remote object. For example, the client calls the getStudentId() method on the remote object as follows:
```
String studentId = student.getStudentId();
```

**FIGURE 10.1**

*Under the hood of a bean-managed persistence bean.*

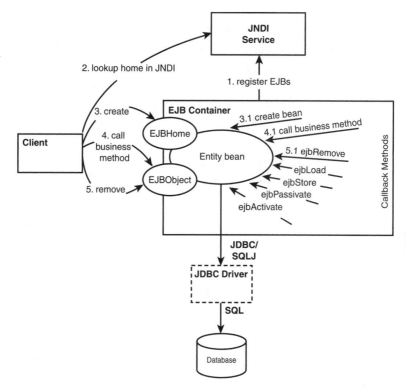

The container calls the appropriate method on the entity bean instance. For example, the EJB container calls the getStudentId() method on the entity bean instance.

5. The client calls the remove() method of the remote object. For example, the client removes the order object as follows:

```
student.remove();
```

The container then calls the ejbRemove() method on the entity bean instance.

The EJB container synchronizes the state of the instance with the database using the ejbLoad() and ejbStore() methods. For example, to passivate the entity bean instance, the container first calls ejbStore() to allow the instance to synchronize the database state with the instance's state, and then calls the ejbPassivate() method.

The bean-managed persistence bean contains calls to access the database. The data access can be coded into the entity bean class or encapsulated in a data access object that is part of the entity bean.

# Designing the BMP Entity Bean

Figure 10.2 shows the design of the Student component. The StudentEJB bean-managed entity bean implements the javax.ejb.EntityBean interface. It implements the methods setEntityContext(), unsetEntityContext(), ejbActivate(), ejbPassivate(), ejbLoad(), ejbStore(), and ejbRemove() as defined in the javax.ejb.EntityBean interface. It also implements the ejbCreate() and ejbPostCreate() methods.

A StudentEJB entity bean class consists of the persistent fields studentId, firstName, lastName, and address. You code them as instance variables in the entity bean class. A Student entity bean is identified by its primary key, studentId.

The StudentEJB bean class also implements the home method ejbHomeGetTotalNumberOfStudents().

**FIGURE 10.2**

*Student entity bean design.*

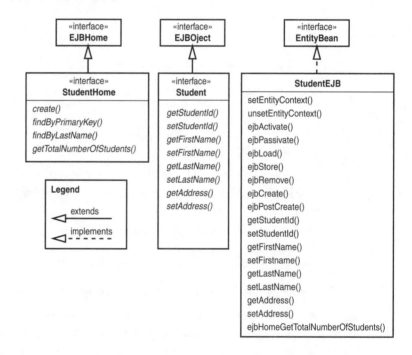

We provide remote interfaces to our entity bean. They include a remote home interface (StudentHome) and a remote interface (Student). The StudentHome home interface extends the javax.ejb.EJBHome interface and defines a single create method, two finder methods(findByPrimaryKey, findByLastName) and one getTotalNumberOfStudents home method. The Student remote interface extends the javax.ejb.EJBObject interface and defines the getters and setters for persistent fields. As you learned on Day 2,

"Understanding EJB Types and Interfaces," container tools generate the classes that correspond to the home and remote interfaces.

The state of StudentEJB is stored in the students table of the relational database. The Data Definition Language (DDL) to create the students table is as follows:

```
create table students (student_id varchar(64),
                        first_name varchar(64),
                        last_name varchar(64),
                        address varchar(64));
```

Today's example uses the PointBase database server with WebLogic Server. In the case of the JBoss server, we'll use the HyperSonic database.

The StudentEJB bean class uses database access objects (DAOs) to access the database. Data access objects are discussed in the following section.

## Data Access Objects

A data access object is a helper object used to encapsulate access to databases. Data access objects can encapsulate access to more than one database, more than one table within one database, and different types of databases. By encapsulating data access calls, DAOs allow the adaptation of data access to different schemas or even to different database types. Both session beans and entity beans with bean-managed persistence can use DAOs.

When an entity bean with bean-managed persistence or a session bean needs to access a database within a method implementation, a corresponding method in the DAO implements the actual logic of fetching or updating data in the database. This removes the data access logic from the enterprise bean class. The bean's business logic is not cluttered with data access calls, such as JDBC calls, which makes it much cleaner and readable.

As shown in Figure 10.3, the application uses the interface StudentDAO to access the students table. The sample application contains the subclass StudentDAOPB, which is used to access a PointBase database.

**Note**

Many database vendors provide proprietary extensions to SQL to provide additional functionality and to achieve higher performance. If the enterprise bean contains data access logic in addition to business logic, it would be difficult to modify it to use a different type of database. The DAO design pattern is used to separate business logic from data access logic. The DAO interface provides a well-defined API for accessing and manipulating the data. The enterprise bean is coded to use this DAO interface. Typically, you would write one DAO class for each database that you want to support. At

> deployment time, the deployer would choose the DAO corresponding to the database. This ensures the enterprise bean class is not modified to use a different database type.

**FIGURE 10.3**

*Student data access object.*

# Implementing the BMP Entity Bean

This section discusses the implementation of the remote home interface `StudentHome`, remote interface `Student`, and the BMP bean class `StudentEJB`. We'll also discuss how to write the DAO and deployment descriptors in detail.

## Defining the Home Interface

The home interface provides methods for creating and removing enterprise beans. In addition, for entity beans, the home interface of an entity bean contains methods to find the instances of a bean based on certain search criteria. The home interface for an entity bean may also contain home business methods. Listing 10.1 shows the `StudentHome` remote home interface.

**LISTING 10.1**    The Full Text of `day10/StudentHome.java`

```
package day10;

import javax.ejb.*;
import java.util.Collection;
import java.rmi.RemoteException;

public interface StudentHome extends EJBHome
{
    /* Create methods */
    Student create(String studentId, String firstName, String lastName,
```

LISTING **10.1**   continued

```
                      String address) throws CreateException, RemoteException;
    /* Finder methods */
    public Student findByPrimaryKey(String studentId)
        throws FinderException, RemoteException;
    public Collection findByLastName(String lastName)
        throws FinderException, RemoteException;
    /* Home methods */
    public int getTotalNumberOfStudents() throws RemoteException;
}
```

To create the bean instance, a client calls the create() method of the home interface and passes appropriate values for studentId, firstName, lastName, and address.

The StudentHome home interface provides two finder methods: findByPrimaryKey() and findByLastName(). The findByPrimaryKey() method allows clients to locate a student bean using the primary key. The single-object finder method findByPrimaryKey() returns the Student remote interface. The findByLastName() method allows clients to locate students with a given last name. The multi-object finder method findByLastName() returns java.util.Collection. The container throws a FinderException from the implementation of finder methods to indicate an application-level error.

The remote home interface is a Java Remote Invocation Method (RMI) interface. So, the method arguments and return types of a remote method must be legal types for RMI/IIOP (RMI over Internet Inter-Orb Protocol) and the method must include java.rmi.RemoteException in its throws clause.

**Note**

Single-object finder methods (such as findByPrimaryKey()) are designed to return one entity object at most. For single-object finders, the result type of the method in the entity bean's remote home interface is the entity bean's remote interface. Similarly, the result type of the method in the entity bean's local home interface is the entity bean's local interface.

Multi-object finder methods (such as findByLastName()) are designed to return multiple entity objects. For multi-object finders, the result type of the method in the entity bean's remote home interface is a collection of objects implementing the entity bean's remote interface. Similarly, the result type of the method in the entity bean's local home interface is a collection of objects implementing the entity bean's local interface. You use the java.util.Collection interface to define the collection type for the result type of a container-managed persistence entity bean.

**10**

## Predefined Exceptions for Entity Beans

Figure 10.4 shows the application exceptions for entity beans as defined in the Enterprise JavaBeans 2.0 specification.

**FIGURE 10.4**

*Predefined exceptions
for entity beans.*

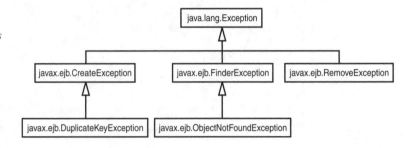

The enterprise bean throws `CreateException` from the `ejbCreate<method>(...)` and `ejbPostCreate<method>(...)` methods to indicate an application-level error from the create or initialization operation.

The enterprise bean throws `DuplicateKeyException` from the `ejbCreate<method>(...)` to indicate to the client that an entity object with the same key already exists. `DuplicateKeyException` is a subclass of `CreateException`.

The enterprise bean throws `FinderException` from the `ejbFind<method>(...)` to indicate to the client that an application-level error occurred in the finder method.

The enterprise bean throws `ObjectNotFoundException` from the `ejbFind<method>(...)` to indicate to the client that the requested entity object does not exist.

The enterprise bean throws `RemoveException` from the `ejbRemove()` method to indicate to the client that an application-level error occurred in the entity bean removal operation.

**Caution**

> Only single-object finders should throw the `ObjectNotFoundException` exception. Multi-object finders should return an empty collection as an indication that no matching objects were found.

## Defining the Component Interface

The remote interface `Student` is defined as follows:

**LISTING 10.2**   The Full Text of day10/Student.java

```java
package day10;

import javax.ejb.EJBObject;
import java.rmi.RemoteException;

public interface Student extends EJBObject
{
    public String getStudentId() throws RemoteException;
    public String getFirstName() throws RemoteException;
    public void setFirstName(String firstName) throws RemoteException;
    public String getLastName() throws RemoteException;
    public void setLastName(String lastName) throws RemoteException;
    public String getAddress() throws RemoteException;
    public void setAddress(String address) throws RemoteException;
}
```

The remote interface contains business methods callable by the client. Note that the Student interface does not contain setStudentId() method because we don't allow clients to modify the student ID after a student object is created.

The remote interface is a Java RMI interface. So, method arguments and return types of a remote method must be legal types for RMI/IIOP and the method must include java.rmi.RemoteException in its throws clause.

## Implementing the Enterprise Bean Class

Using bean-managed persistence, the entity bean provider writes database access calls (for example, using JDBC) directly in the entity bean component. The data access calls can be coded directly into the entity bean class, or they can be encapsulated in a data access component that is part of the entity bean.

**Caution**

> Directly coding data access calls in the entity bean class might make it more difficult to adapt the entity bean to work with a database that has a different schema or a different type of database.

Listing 10.3 shows the StudentEJB entity bean class.

**LISTING 10.3**   The Full Text of day10/StudentEJB.java

```java
package day10;

import java.sql.*;
```

**LISTING 10.3**    continued

```java
import javax.naming.*;
import javax.ejb.*;
import java.util.*;

public class StudentEJB implements EntityBean {
    protected EntityContext ctx;
    /* persistent state */
    private String studentId;
    private String firstName;
    private String lastName;
    private String address;
    /* Accessor methods for entity bean fields */
    public  String getStudentId() {
        return studentId;
    }
    public  void setStudentId(String id) {
        studentId = id;
    }
    public  String getFirstName() {
        return firstName;
    }
    public  void setFirstName(String firstName) {
        this.firstName = firstName;
    }
    public  String getLastName() {
        return lastName;
    }
    public  void setLastName(String lastName) {
        this.lastName = lastName;
    }
    public  String getAddress() {
        return address;
    }
    public  void setAddress(String address) {
        this.address = address;
    }
    /* Callback methods */
    public void setEntityContext(EntityContext ctx) {
        System.out.println("Student.setEntityContext called");
        this.ctx = ctx;
    }
    public void unsetEntityContext() {
        System.out.println("Student.unsetEntityContext called");
        this.ctx = null;
    }
    public void ejbActivate() {
        System.out.println("Student.ejbActivate() called.");
        studentId = (String) ctx.getPrimaryKey();
    }
```

**LISTING 10.3** continued

```
public void ejbPassivate() {
   System.out.println("Student.ejbPassivate () called.");
   studentId = null;
}
public void ejbLoad() {
  try {
   System.out.println("Student.ejbLoad() called.");
   StudentDAO dao = getDAO();
   StudentDetails student = dao.load(studentId);
   firstName = student.getFirstName();
   lastName = student.getLastName();
   address = student.getAddress();
  } catch(Exception ex) {
    throw new EJBException("ejbLoad: Unable to load Student "
        + studentId + " from database", ex);
  }
}
public void ejbStore() {
  try {
   System.out.println("Student.ejbStore() called.");
   StudentDAO dao = getDAO();
   dao.store(studentId,firstName, lastName,address);
  } catch(Exception ex) {
                   throw new EJBException("Student " + studentId +
                   " failed to save to database", ex);
  }
}
public String ejbCreate(String studentId, String firstName,
  String lastName, String address)
   throws CreateException {
  try {
   System.out.println("Student.ejbCreate() called.");
   StudentDAO dao = getDAO();
   dao.create(studentId, firstName, lastName, address);
   setStudentId(studentId);
   setFirstName(firstName);
   setLastName(lastName);
   setAddress(address);
   return studentId;
  } catch(Exception ex) {
     throw new CreateException("Failed to create student "
        + studentId + ex.getMessage());
  }
}
public void ejbPostCreate(String studentId, String firstName,
  String lastName, String address) throws CreateException {
   System.out.println("Student.ejbPostCreate() called.");
}
```

10

LISTING **10.3**    continued

```java
public void ejbRemove() throws RemoveException {
  try {
   System.out.println("Student.ejbRemove() called.");
   StudentDAO dao = getDAO();
   dao.remove(studentId);
  } catch(Exception ex) {
    throw new RemoveException("Failed to remove student "
      + studentId + ex.getMessage());
  }
}
/* Finder methods */
public String ejbFindByPrimaryKey(String studentId)
   throws FinderException  {
   try {
     StudentDAO dao = getDAO();
     boolean result = dao.findByPrimaryKey(studentId);
     if(!result) throw new ObjectNotFoundException
       ("Student id "+ studentId+ " not found");
     return studentId;
   } catch(Exception ex) {
     throw new ObjectNotFoundException
       ("Student id "+ studentId+ " not found");
   }
}
public Collection ejbFindByLastName(String lastName)
   throws FinderException  {
   try {
     StudentDAO dao = getDAO();
     return dao.findByLastName(lastName);
   } catch(Exception ex) {
     throw new FinderException
       ("FinderException:"+ lastName+ ex.getMessage());
   }
}
/* Home methods */
public int ejbHomeGetTotalNumberOfStudents() {
   try {
     StudentDAO dao = getDAO();
     return dao.findTotalNumberOfStudents();
   } catch(Exception ex) {
     throw new EJBException
       ("ejbHomeGetTotalNumberOfStudents:" + ex.getMessage());
   }
}
/* Helper methods */
private StudentDAO getDAO()  {
```

LISTING 10.3    continued

```
    try{
        StudentDAO dao = null;
        Context context = new InitialContext();
        dao = (StudentDAO) Class.forName
         ((String)context.lookup("java:comp/env/param/StudentDAOClass"))
            .newInstance();
        return dao;
    } catch(Exception ex) {
        throw new EJBException ("getDAO:" + ex.getMessage());
    }
  }
}
```

The StudentEJB entity bean implements the javax.ejb.EntityBean interface and is a
concrete class. The instance variables studentId, firstName, lastName, and address
constitute the bean's persistent state. The bean class uses StudentDAO class to access the
database. It implements the methods setEntityContext(), unsetEntityContext(),
ejbActivate(), ejbPassivate(), ejbLoad(), ejbStore(), and ejbRemove() as defined
in the javax.ejb.EntityBean interface. In the ejbLoad() method, you refresh the
instance variables by reading from the database. The ejbStore() method updates the
instance variables to the database. The ejbCreate() method inserts the entity state into
the database, initializes the instance variables, and returns the primary key. The bean
implements the ejbPostCreate method that corresponds to the ejbCreate method. The
bean class implements the finder methods ejbFindByPrimaryKey() and
ejbFindByLastName(). The single-object finder method ejbFindByPrimaryKey() verifies that the object exists in the database and returns the primary key. The multi-object
finder method ejbFindByLastName() returns a collection of primary keys that match the
search criteria.

In addition, the StudentEJB bean class implements the
ejbHomeGetTotalAmountOfAllOrders() home business method. This home business
method is independent of any particular student instance. It returns the total number of
students in the system.

**Note**

The entity bean instance can discover its primary key by calling the
getPrimaryKey() method on its entity context object. This method can be
called when the entity object is associated with an identity in operations
such as ejbPostCreate, ejbRemove, ejbActivate, ejbPassivate, ejbLoad,

10

ejbStore, and business methods from the component interface. The following code snippet illustrates the getPrimaryKey method call:

```
EntityContext   ctx;
String studentId;
...
public void ejbActivate() {
    studentId = (String) ctx.getPrimaryKey();
    }
```

The client can retrieve the primary key for an entity object by invoking the getPrimaryKey() method on the EJBObject as follows:

```
Student student = ...  ;
String studentId = (String)student.getPrimaryKey();
```

**Note**

The data access calls are performed in ejbCreate<method>(...), ejbRemove(), ejbFind<method>(...), ejbLoad(), and ejbStore() methods, and/or in the business methods. Table 10.1 shows the summary of SQL statements for the StudentEJB bean class.

**TABLE 10.1**   Summary of the SQL Statements in Entity Bean Methods

| Entity Bean Method | SQL Statement |
| --- | --- |
| ejbCreate() | insert |
| ejbLoad() | select |
| ejbStore() | update |
| ejbFindByPrimaryKey() | select |
| ejbFindByLastName() | select |
| ejbHomeGetTotalNumberOfStudents() | select |
| ejbRemove() | delete |

Listing 10.4 shows the StudentDAO interface. The StudentEJB class uses this interface to access the database.

**LISTING 10.4**   The Full Text of day10/StudentDAO.java

```
package day10;
import java.util.Collection;
```

**LISTING 10.4**   continued

```
public interface StudentDAO
{
   public void create(String id, String firstName,
                      String lastName, String address)
      throws StudentDAOSysException;
   public void remove(String studentId)
      throws StudentDAOSysException;
   public boolean findByPrimaryKey(String studentId)
      throws StudentDAOSysException;
   public Collection findByLastName(String lastName)
      throws StudentDAOSysException;
   public int findTotalNumberOfStudents()
      throws StudentDAOSysException;
   public void store(String id, String firstName,
                     String lastName, String address)
      throws StudentDAOSysException;
   public StudentDetails load(String studentId)
      throws StudentDAOSysException;
}
```

Listing 10.5 shows the implementation of the StudentDAOPB class. This class implements
the StudentDAO interface and is used to access a PointBase database. Methods in the
StudentDAOPB class implement the actual logic of inserting, fetching, or updating data in
the database. Note that, in each data access method, we acquire a connection, perform
data access, and release the connection. When the client virtually releases the connection
with close(), behind the scenes, the container returns the connection to the pool and
makes it available for use by other clients. The class throws StudentDAOSysException to
indicate a data access error.

**LISTING 10.5**   The Full Text of day10/StudentDAOPB.java

```
package day10;

import java.util.*;
import javax.naming.*;
import java.sql.*;
import javax.sql.*;

public class StudentDAOPB implements StudentDAO {
   private Connection con;
   public StudentDAOPB() {}
   public void create(String id, String firstName,
     String lastName, String address) throws StudentDAOSysException {
     PreparedStatement stmt = null;
     try {
```

**LISTING 10.5**  continued

```java
            getDBConnection();
            stmt = con.prepareStatement
               ("insert into students(student_id, first_name, last_name, "+
                 " address) values (?, ?, ?, ?)");
            stmt.setString(1, id);
            stmt.setString(2, firstName);
            stmt.setString(3, lastName);
            stmt.setString(4, address);
            stmt.executeUpdate();
         }
         catch(SQLException ex) {
            throw new StudentDAOSysException("SQLException:"+ ex.getMessage());
         }
         finally {
            closeStatement(stmt);
            closeDBConnection();
         }
      }
      public void remove(String studentId)
         throws StudentDAOSysException {
         PreparedStatement stmt = null;
         try {
            getDBConnection();
            stmt = con.prepareStatement
               ("delete from students where student_id = ?");
            stmt.setString(1,studentId);
            stmt.executeUpdate();
            stmt.close();
         }
         catch(SQLException ex) {
            throw new StudentDAOSysException("SQLException:"+ ex.getMessage());
         }
         finally {
            closeStatement(stmt);
            closeDBConnection();
         }
      }
      public boolean findByPrimaryKey(String studentId)
         throws StudentDAOSysException {
         boolean result = false;
         PreparedStatement stmt = null;
         try {
            getDBConnection();
            stmt  = con.prepareStatement
               ("select student_id from students where student_id = ?");
            stmt.setString(1, studentId);
            ResultSet rs = stmt.executeQuery();
            result = rs.next();
```

**LISTING 10.5**    continued

```
            rs.close();
        }
        catch(SQLException ex) {
            throw new StudentDAOSysException("SQLException: "+ ex.getMessage());
        }
        finally {
            closeStatement(stmt);
            closeDBConnection();
        }
        return result;
    }
    public Collection findByLastName(String lastName)
        throws StudentDAOSysException {
        Collection students = new ArrayList();
        PreparedStatement stmt = null;
        try {
            getDBConnection();
            stmt = con.prepareStatement
                ("select student_id from students where last_name = ?");
            stmt.setString(1, lastName);
            ResultSet rs = stmt.executeQuery();
            while(rs.next()){
                String studentId = rs.getString(1);
                students.add(studentId);
            }
            rs.close();
        }
        catch(SQLException ex) {
            throw new StudentDAOSysException("SQLException: "+ ex.getMessage());
        }
        finally {
            closeStatement(stmt);
            closeDBConnection();
        }
        return students;
    }
    public int findTotalNumberOfStudents()
        throws StudentDAOSysException {
        int total = 0;
        PreparedStatement stmt = null;
        try {
            getDBConnection();
            stmt = con.prepareStatement
                ("select count(student_id) from students");
            ResultSet rs = stmt.executeQuery();
            rs.next();
            total = rs.getInt(1);
        }
```

10

**LISTING 10.5**    continued

```
        catch(SQLException ex) {
           throw new StudentDAOSysException("SQLException:"+ ex.getMessage());
        }
        finally {
           closeStatement(stmt);
           closeDBConnection();
        }
        return total;
    }
    public StudentDetails load(String studentId)
        throws StudentDAOSysException {
        StudentDetails student = null;
        PreparedStatement stmt = null;
        try{
           getDBConnection();
           stmt = con.prepareStatement ("select first_name, last_name, " +
             " address from students where student_id=?");
           stmt.setString(1, studentId);
           ResultSet rs = stmt.executeQuery();
           rs.next();
           student = new StudentDetails(studentId,
                                   rs.getString(1),
                                   rs.getString(2),
                                   rs.getString(3));
           rs.close();
        }
        catch(SQLException ex) {
           throw new StudentDAOSysException("SQLException:"+ ex.getMessage());
        }
        finally {
           closeStatement(stmt);
           closeDBConnection();
        }
        return student;
    }
    public void store(String id, String firstName, String lastName,
      String address)  throws StudentDAOSysException {
        PreparedStatement stmt = null;
        try{
           getDBConnection();
           stmt = con.prepareStatement ("update  students set "+
             "first_name=?,last_name = ?,address = ? where student_id=?");
           stmt.setString(1, firstName);
           stmt.setString(2,lastName);
           stmt.setString(3, address);
           stmt.setString(4, id);
           stmt.executeUpdate();
```

LISTING 10.5 continued

```
            stmt.close();
         }
         catch(SQLException ex) {
            throw new StudentDAOSysException("SQLException:"+ ex.getMessage());
         }
         finally {
            closeStatement(stmt);
            closeDBConnection();
         }
      }
      private void getDBConnection()
         throws StudentDAOSysException {
         try {
            Context context = new InitialContext();
            DataSource ds = (DataSource) context.lookup("jdbc/styejbDB");
            con = ds.getConnection();
            if(con==null)
               System.err.println("Database Connection is null");
         }
         catch(SQLException ex) {
            throw new StudentDAOSysException("SQLException:"+ ex.getMessage());
         }
         catch(NamingException ex) {
            throw new StudentDAOSysException("NamingException:"+ex.getMessage());
         }
      }
      private void closeDBConnection()
         throws StudentDAOSysException {
         try {
            con.close();
         }
         catch(SQLException ex) {
            throw new StudentDAOSysException("SQLException:"+ ex.getMessage());
         }
      }
      private void closeStatement(PreparedStatement stmt)
         throws StudentDAOSysException {
         try {
            stmt.close();
         }
         catch(SQLException ex) {
            throw new StudentDAOSysException("SQLException:"+ ex.getMessage());
         }
      }
   }
}
```

Listing 10.6 shows the StudentDetails value object.

**LISTING 10.6**   The Full Text of `day10/StudentDetails.java`

```java
package day10;

public class StudentDetails
{
    String id;
    String firstName;
    String lastName;
    String address;
    StudentDetails(String id, String firstName,
                   String lastName, String address)
    {
        this.id = id;
        this.firstName = firstName;
        this.lastName = lastName;
        this.address = address;
    }
    public String getFirstName() {return firstName; }
    public String getLastName() {return lastName;}
    public String getAddress() {return  address; }
}
```

Listing 10.7 shows the `StudentDAOSysException` class. The `StudentDAO` interface throws this exception to indicate a data access error.

**LISTING 10.7**   The Full Text of `day10/StudentDAOSysException.java`

```java
package day10;

public class StudentDAOSysException extends RuntimeException {
    public StudentDAOSysException (String str) {
        super(str);
    }
    public StudentDAOSysException () {
        super();
    }
}
```

# Declaring the Deployment Descriptor

The deployment descriptor describes a component's deployment settings. Listing 10.8 shows the `ejb-jar.xml` deployment descriptor for the `Student` enterprise bean. `ejb-jar.xml` describes the enterprise bean's deployment properties, such as its bean type and structure. The file also provides the EJB container with information about where it can find and then load the home interface, remote interface, and bean class. In addition, the entity bean's deployment descriptor declares the persistent type and its primary key.

**LISTING 10.8** The Full Text of day10/ejb-jar.xml

```xml
<?xml version="1.0"?>
<!DOCTYPE ejb-jar PUBLIC
'-//Sun Microsystems, Inc.//DTD Enterprise JavaBeans 2.0//EN'
'http://java.sun.com/dtd/ejb-jar_2_0.dtd'>
<ejb-jar>
  <enterprise-beans>
    <entity>
      <ejb-name>StudentEJB</ejb-name>
      <home>day10.StudentHome</home>
      <remote>day10.Student</remote>
      <ejb-class>day10.StudentEJB</ejb-class>
      <persistence-type>Bean</persistence-type>
      <prim-key-class>java.lang.String</prim-key-class>
      <reentrant>False</reentrant>
      <env-entry>
        <env-entry-name>param/StudentDAOClass</env-entry-name>
        <env-entry-type>java.lang.String</env-entry-type>
        <env-entry-value>day10.StudentDAOPB</env-entry-value>
      </env-entry>
       <resource-env-ref>
         <resource-env-ref-name>jdbc/styejbDB</resource-env-ref-name>
        <resource-env-ref-type>javax.sql.DataSource</resource-env-ref-type>
        </resource-env-ref>
     </entity>
  </enterprise-beans>
  <assembly-descriptor>
      <container-transaction>
        <method>
        <ejb-name>StudentEJB</ejb-name>
        <method-name>*</method-name>
        </method>
        <trans-attribute>Required</trans-attribute>
      </container-transaction>
    </assembly-descriptor>
  </ejb-jar>
```

The ejb-jar.xml file declares StudentEJB as the name of the entity bean and specifies the home interface, remote interface, and bean class. The persistence-type element declares this as a bean-managed entity bean (as opposed to a container-managed persistence bean). The primary-key-class element specifies the type of our primary key. The reentrant element specifies whether an entity bean is reentrant. If an instance of a

nonreentrant entity bean executes a client request in a given transaction context, and
another request with the same transaction context arrives for the same entity object, the
container will throw an exception to the second request. This rule allows the bean
provider to program the entity bean as single-threaded, nonreentrant code. The Student
enterprise bean uses environment entries to find the implementation class for student data
access object.

Resource environment references are declared by the resource-env-ref elements. The
resource-env-ref-name element specifies the JNDI name of the reference relative to
java:comp/env. The resource-env-ref-type element specifies the fully qualified class
name of the referenced object. For example, we specified the class name of
jdbc/styejbDB data source as javax.sql.DataSource. In the vendor-specific deployment descriptor such as weblogic-ejb-jar.xml or jboss.xml we bind the resource environment references to the actual administered object location. The assembly-descriptor
element contains application assembly information, and also includes specifying the
transaction attributes. The method-name element is assigned the value * (asterisk) to indicate that all methods have the transaction attribute Required. The Required transaction
attribute specifies the bean will always be part of a transaction. On Day 16, we'll learn
more about transactions.

Listing 10.9 shows the weblogic-ejb-jar.xml deployment descriptor that is specific to
WebLogic Server. The jndi-name element declares the JNDI name of the enterprise
bean. So, the JNDI name of the StudentEJB is day10/Student.

**LISTING 10.9**    The Full Text of day10/weblogic-ejb-jar.xml

```
<?xml version="1.0"?>

<!DOCTYPE weblogic-ejb-jar PUBLIC
'-//BEA Systems, Inc.//DTD WebLogic 7.0.0 EJB//EN'
'http://www.bea.com/servers/wls700/dtd/weblogic-ejb-jar.dtd'>

<weblogic-ejb-jar>
  <weblogic-enterprise-bean>
    <ejb-name>StudentEJB</ejb-name>
    <reference-descriptor>
        <resource-env-description>
          <res-env-ref-name>jdbc/styejbDB</res-env-ref-name>
          <jndi-name>jdbc.styejbDB</jndi-name>
      </resource-env-description>
       </reference-descriptor>
     <jndi-name>day10/Student</jndi-name>
  </weblogic-enterprise-bean>
</weblogic-ejb-jar>
```

Listing 10.10 shows the `jboss.xml` deployment descriptor that's specific to the JBoss server. Also, the `jndi-name` element declares the JNDI name of the `StudentEJB` as `day10/Student`.

**LISTING 10.10**   The Full Text of `day10/jboss.xml`

```xml
<?xml version="1.0" encoding="UTF-8"?>

<jboss>
  <enterprise-beans>
    <entity>
      <ejb-name>StudentEJB</ejb-name>
      <jndi-name>day10/Student</jndi-name>
       <resource-env-ref>
         <resource-env-ref-name>jdbc/styejbDB</resource-env-ref-name>
         <jndi-name>java:/DefaultDS</jndi-name>
       </resource-env-ref>
    </entity>
  </enterprise-beans>
</jboss>
```

# Writing a Client

Listing 10.11 demonstrates how a client accesses an entity bean.

**LISTING 10.11**   The Full Text of `day10/Client.java`

```java
package day10;

import java.util.*;
import javax.naming.*;
import javax.ejb.*;

public class Client {
   public static void main(String[] args) {
      print("Starting Client . . .");
      Context initialContext = null;
      StudentHome studentHome = null;
      Student student = null;
      try {
         print("Looking up the student home via JNDI.");
         initialContext = new InitialContext();
         Object object = initialContext.lookup("day10/Student");
         studentHome = (StudentHome)
            javax.rmi.PortableRemoteObject.narrow(object,StudentHome.class);
```

**LISTING 10.11** continued

```
                    String studentId = "raghava";
                    print("Creating a new student id:" + studentId + ".");
                    object=(Student)studentHome.create(studentId,  "Raghava",
                        "Kothapalli", "1234, People Dr. Pleasonton, CA");
                    student=(Student)javax.rmi.PortableRemoteObject.narrow
                            (object, Student.class);
                    print("Locating the student id " + studentId
                            + " using findByPrimaryKey method");
                    student=studentHome.findByPrimaryKey(studentId);

                    print("Locating all students with last name Kothapalli "
                            + " using findByLastName method.");
                    Collection col=studentHome.findByLastName("Kothapalli");
                    Enumeration students=Collections.enumeration(col);
                    while( students.hasMoreElements() ) {
                        student=(Student)javax.rmi.PortableRemoteObject.narrow
                            (students.nextElement(), Student.class);
                        print("id:" + student.getStudentId() +
                            " First name:"+ student.getFirstName());
                    }
                    print("Finding the total number of students using "
                            + " getTotalNumberOfStudents method");
                    int count = studentHome.getTotalNumberOfStudents();
                    print("Count:"+ count );
                }
                catch(Exception ex) {
                    ex.printStackTrace();
                }
            }
            static void print(String s) {
                System.out.println(s);
            }
        }
```

In this code, the client locates the StudentHome home interface of the deployed enterprise bean via JNDI. The client uses the remote home interface to create a remote Student entity object, and then demonstrates the usage of finder and home methods.

**Caution**

A client program that is portable to all EJB containers must use javax.rmi.PortableRemoteObject.narrow(...) method to perform type-narrowing of the remote and remote home interfaces. For example, the following code snippet is not portable:

Student student = ... ;

```
Enumeration students=Collections.enumeration(col);
while( students.hasMoreElements() ) {
    student=(Student)students.nextElement();
}
```

The following code snippet is portable:

```
Student student = ... ;
Enumeration students=Collections.enumeration(col);
while( students.hasMoreElements() ) {
            student= (Student)javax.rmi.PortableRemoteObject.narrow
                        (students.nextElement(),Student.class);
        . . .
}
```

# Packaging and Deploying the Enterprise Bean

This section describes the steps to package, deploy the Student entity bean and also build the client for both the WebLogic Server and JBoss application servers.

The following are the steps for WebLogic Server:

C:\>cd **styejb\examples**

C:\styejb\examples>**setEnvWebLogic.bat**

C:\styejb\examples>cd **day10**

C:\styejb\examples\day10>**buildWebLogic.bat**

The following are the steps for JBoss:

C:\>cd **styejb\examples**

C:\styejb\examples>**setEnvJboss.bat**

C:\styejb\examples>cd **day10**

C:\styejb\examples\day10>**buildJboss.bat**

# Running the Example

The following steps describe how to start the PointBase database server, the WebLogic Server, and run the sample client:

1. Start the PointBase server in a new command window as follows:

```
C:\>cd styejb\examples
C:\styejb\examples>setEnvWebLogic.bat
C:\styejb\examples>startPointBase.bat
```

2. Start WebLogic Server in a new command window as follows:

```
C:\>cd styejb\examples
C:\styejb\examples>setEnvWebLogic.bat
C:\styejb\examples>startWebLogic.bat
```

3. You can run the client in the same window you used to package the bean and build the client by using the following command:

```
C:\styejb\examples\day10>runClientWebLogic.bat
```

Running the client produces the following output:

```
Starting Client . . .
Looking up the student home via JNDI.
Creating a new student id:raghava.
Locating the student id raghava using findByPrimaryKey method
Locating all students with last name Kothapalli  using findByLastName method.
id:krishna First name:Krishna
id:raghava First name:Raghava
Finding the total number of students using  getTotalNumberOfStudents method
Count:2
```

The following steps describe how to start JBoss server and run the sample client:

1. Start JBoss Server in a new command window as follows:

```
C:\>cd styejb\examples
C:\styejb\examples>setEnvJBoss.bat
C:\styejb\examples>startJBoss.bat
```

2. You can run the client in the same window you used to package the bean and build the client by using the following command:

```
C:\styejb\examples\day10>runClientJBoss.bat
```

# Best Practices

Typically, you use bean-managed persistence if you want complete control of managing persistence, you're writing persistence logic to a very proprietary legacy database system, or your persistent store is not a database.

Extra effort is required to achieve portability for an enterprise bean that uses bean-managed persistence because the bean needs to ensure portability across all database as well as JDBC drivers. The foremost factor affecting portability relates to the SQL language. Many database vendors provide proprietary extensions to SQL to provide additional functionality and to achieve higher performance. Consider using only standard SQL constructs to achieve portability. If you do need to use proprietary extensions, consider using the data access object design pattern to encapsulate vendor-specific code.

# Summary

Today you wrote a bean-managed persistence enterprise bean. The home interface contains create, finder, and home methods, and the remote interface contains the business methods callable by the client. The bean class contains the instance variables representing its persistent state. It implements the callback, finder, and home methods. The bean delegated the data access calls to a data access object. You also learned how to package and deploy the enterprise bean. Finally, you wrote and ran a client that accesses the enterprise bean.

**10**

# Q&A

**Q What are the differences between a business method and a home method?**

**A** The component interface defines the business methods. For entity beans, the home interface defines home methods. Home methods contain business logic that is not specific to an entity bean instance. These methods are analogous to static methods.

In contrast, the logic in a business method applies to a single entity bean, an instance with a unique identity. Because a home method is not specific to an entity bean instance, the entity instance is not associated with any unique identity during home method invocation. So, a home method implementation cannot access an entity bean's persistence state (instance variables).

# Quiz

1. An `ejbCreate()` method of an entity bean class returns which of the following objects?

    A. Primary key

    B. `null`

    C. `EJBObject`

    D. `EJBHome`

2. Which one of the following statements is false for data access objects?

    A. DAOs encapsulate data access calls.

    B. Session beans can't use DAOs.

C. Entity beans can use DAOs.

D. DAOs can be used to encapsulate database vendor-specific code.

3. A bean-managed persistence bean performs which of the following SQL statements in `ejbCreate<method>(...)`?

A. `select`

B. `update`

C. `insert`

D. `delete`

## Quiz Answers

1. A

2. B

3. C

# Exercises

To extend your knowledge of the subjects covered today, try the following exercise:

1. Add the `findAllStudents()` method in `StudentHome` interface, and implement the corresponding `ejbFindAllStudents()` method in the `StudentEJB` entity bean class. In addition, package and deploy the entity bean.

# DAY 11

# Developing Container-Managed Persistence Entity Beans

Today you'll learn how to develop portable applications that are database independent and free of database access code. You'll work on a complete example of developing a container-managed persistence (CMP) entity bean.

In our sample University Registration System, a student selects items from the course catalog, places them in an enrollment cart, and, when ready, places an order for the cart contents. The order must live even when the student's session with the application is over. Therefore, in the sample application, the Order component is modeled as an entity bean. The Order component provides data-related logic, such as inserting, updating, and removing an order record in the database.

Today, we'll write the Order component as a container-managed persistence entity bean. Tomorrow, on Day 12, "Developing Container-Managed Relationship Entity Beans," we'll integrate the Order component with other entity beans.

The EJB container is responsible for the persistence of a container-managed persistence bean. We'll examine how the container achieves this goal by looking under the hood of a CMP bean. Just like BMP, a CMP bean consists of a home interface, a component interface, and a bean class. We'll write these interfaces and the bean class.

The CMP deployment descriptor is the interesting part of any CMP component. The deployment descriptor has been significantly changed in EJB 2.0 to improve its portability. The bean provider designs the abstract persistence schema and specifies queries with respect to the entity bean's abstract schema. At deployment time the deployer, using container tools, maps the abstract persistent schema to a physical schema of the target database. The container tools generate the necessary additional classes that enable the container to manage the entity bean's persistence. We'll write the CMP deployment descriptor. Finally, we'll package and deploy the bean, and write a client that accesses the CMP.

# Looking Under the Hood of a CMP Entity Bean

Figure 11.1 shows the interactions between the client, the EJB container, and the container-managed persistence bean.

The following steps describe the sequence of interactions in detail:

1. At startup, the EJB container registers all deployed enterprise beans, including entity beans, with the JNDI service.

2. The client looks up the home interface of the deployed enterprise bean via the Java Naming and Directory Interface (JNDI). In this example, the remote home interface for the Order bean can be located by using the following code segment:

```
Context initialContext = new InitialContext();
Object obj = initialContext.lookup("day11/Order");
OrderHome orderHome = (OrderHome)
 javax.rmi.PortableRemoteObject.narrow(obj, OrderHome.class);
```

3. The client uses the remote home interface to create a remote Order object. In this example, the client creates a new order as follows:

```
Order order =  (Order)orderHome.create("1", "Submitted", 200.00);
```

When a client invokes a create<*method*> method on the home interface, the EJB container invokes the corresponding ejbCreate<*method*> method, followed by ejbPostCreate<*method*> method on the bean instance.

4. The client calls a business method on the remote object. In this example, the client calls the getOrderId() method on the remote object as follows:

```
String orderId = order.getOrderId();
```

FIGURE 11.1

*Under the hood of a*
*container-managed*
*persistence bean.*

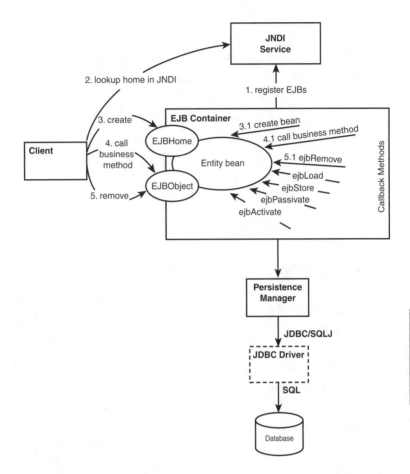

The container calls the appropriate method on the entity bean instance. For example, the EJB container calls getOrderId() method on the entity bean instance.

5. The client calls the remove() method of the remote object. For example, the client removes the order object as follows:

```
order.remove();
```

The container calls the ejbRemove() method on the entity bean instance.

The EJB container synchronizes the state of the instance with the database by using the methods ejbLoad() and ejbStore(). For example, to passivate an entity bean instance, the container first calls ejbStore() to allow the instance to prepare itself for the synchronization of the database state with the instance's state, and then calls the ejbPassivate() method.

Unlike a bean-managed persistence entity bean, a container-managed persistence bean does not contain calls to access the database. The EJB container is responsible for persistence of a CMP entity bean. The container may use a persistence manager for persistence of entity beans. The persistence manager is responsible for performing the following tasks:

- Creating an instance in a database
- Loading the state of an instance in a database
- Storing the state of an instance in a database
- Activating the state of an instance
- Passivating the state of an instance
- Removing an instance from a database

# Designing a CMP Entity Bean

Figure 11.2 shows the design of the `Order` component. The `OrderEJB` container-managed entity bean implements the `javax.ejb.EntityBean` interface. It implements the methods `setEntityContext()`, `unsetEntityContext()`, `ejbActivate()`, `ejbPassivate()`, `ejbLoad()`, `ejbStore()`, and `ejbRemove()` as defined in the `javax.ejb.EntityBean` interface. It also implements the `ejbCreate()` and `ejbPostCreate()` methods.

An `OrderEJB` entity bean class consists of the persistent fields `orderId`, `studentId`, `orderDate`, `status`, and `amount`. You do not code them as instance variables in the entity bean class. Instead, the persistent fields are identified in the code by access methods (getters and setters). An `Order` entity bean is identified by its primary key, `orderId`.

The `OrderEJB` bean class also implements the `ejbHomeGetTotalAmountOfAllOrders()` method and defines the select method `ejbSelectAllOrderAmounts()` method. We'll discuss select methods later today.

We also provide remote interfaces to our entity bean. These include a remote home interface (`OrderHome`) and a remote interface (`Order`). The `OrderHome` home interface extends the `javax.ejb.EJBHome` interface and defines a single `create()` method, two finder methods, and one `getTotalAmountOfAllOrders()` home method. The `Order` remote interface extends the `javax.ejb.EJBObject` interface and defines the getters and setters for persistent fields. As you learned on Day 2, "Understanding EJB Types and Interfaces," container tools generate the classes that correspond to the home and remote interfaces.

FIGURE 11.2

*Order entity bean design.*

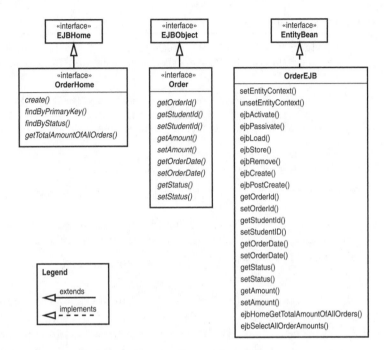

11

# Implementing the CMP Entity Bean

This section discusses the implementation of the remote home interface OrderHome, remote interface Order, and the CMP bean class OrderEJB. We'll also discuss how to write the deployment descriptors in detail.

## Defining the Home Interface

The home interface provides methods for creating and removing enterprise beans. In addition, for entity beans, the home interface also contains methods to find the instances of bean based on certain search criteria. The home interface for an entity bean may contain home business methods. Listing 11.1 shows the OrderHome remote home interface.

LISTING 11.1    The Full Text of day11/OrderHome.java

```
package day11;

import java.util.*;
import java.rmi.*;
import javax.ejb.*;

public interface OrderHome extends EJBHome {
   /* Create methods */
```

LISTING 11.1    continued

```
public Order create(String studentId,
 String status, double amount) throws CreateException, RemoteException;
/* Finder methods */
public Order findByPrimaryKey(String key)
   throws FinderException, RemoteException;
public Collection findByStatus(String status)
   throws FinderException, RemoteException;
/* Home methods */
public double getTotalAmountOfAllOrders()
   throws FinderException, RemoteException;
}
```

To create the bean instance, a client calls the create() method of that home interface and passes appropriate values for studentId, status, and amount. The bean internally generates the orderId primary key.

The OrderHome home interface provides two finder methods: findByPrimaryKey() and findByStatus(). The findByPrimaryKey() method allows clients to locate an order bean by using the primary key. The single-object finder method findByPrimaryKey() returns the Order remote interface. The findByStatus() method allows clients to locate orders that are of a particular status, such as SUBMITTED. The multi-object finder method findByStatus()returns java.util.Collection. The container throws a FinderException from the implementation of a finder method to indicate an application-level error.

**Note**

> With CMP beans, you do not write the ejbFind methods in your entity bean class. The finder methods are generated by the container provider tools.

The home interface also provides the home method getTotalAmountOfAllOrders(). This is a home method because it contains business logic that is not specific to an entity bean instance.

The remote home interface is a Java Remote Method Invocation (RMI) interface. So, method arguments and return types of a remote method must be legal types for the RMI over Internet Inter-ORB Protocol (RMI/IIOP), and the method must include java.rmi.RemoteException in its throws clause.

## Defining the Component Interface

The remote interface Order is defined as shown in Listing 11.2.

**LISTING 11.2**    The Full Text of day11/Order.java

```
package day11;

import java.rmi.*;
import javax.ejb.*;

public interface Order extends EJBObject {
    public String getOrderId()
        throws RemoteException;
    public String getStudentId()
        throws RemoteException;
    public void setStudentId(String studentId)
        throws RemoteException;
    public double getAmount()
        throws RemoteException;
    public void setAmount(double amount)
        throws RemoteException;
    public java.sql.Timestamp getOrderDate()
        throws RemoteException;
    public void setOrderDate(java.sql.Timestamp date)
        throws RemoteException;
    public String getStatus()
        throws RemoteException;
    public void setStatus(String status)
        throws RemoteException;
}
```

**11**

The remote interface contains business methods callable by the client. The Order interface contains access methods to the bean's persistent fields. Note that the Order interface does not contain the setOrderId() method because we don't allow clients to modify the order ID after an order is created.

The remote interface is a Java RMI interface. So, method arguments and return types of a remote method must be legal types for RMI/IIOP, and the method must include java.rmi.RemoteException in its throws clause.

## Implementing the Enterprise Bean Class

Listing 11.3 shows the OrderEJB bean class.

**LISTING 11.3**    The Full Text of day11/OrderEJB.java

```
package day11;

import java.util.*;
import java.io.*;
import java.rmi.*;
```

**LISTING 11.3**   continued

```
import javax.naming.*;
import javax.ejb.*;

public abstract class OrderEJB implements EntityBean
{
    protected EntityContext ctx;
    public abstract String getOrderId();
    public abstract void setOrderId(String orderId);
    public abstract String getStudentId();
    public abstract void setStudentId(String studentid);
    public abstract java.sql.Timestamp getOrderDate();
    public abstract void setOrderDate(java.sql.Timestamp timestamp);
    public abstract String getStatus();
    public abstract void setStatus(String status);
    public abstract double getAmount();
    public abstract void setAmount(double amount);
    /* Callback methods */
    public void setEntityContext(EntityContext ctx) {
        print("setEntityContext called");
        this.ctx = ctx;
    }
    public void unsetEntityContext() {
        print("unsetEntityContext called.\n");
        this.ctx = null;
    }
    public void ejbActivate() {
        print("ejbActivate() called.\n");
    }
    public void ejbPassivate() {
        print("ejbPassivate() called.\n");
    }
    public void ejbStore() {
        print("ejbStore() called.\n");
    }
    public void ejbLoad() {
        print("ejbLoad() called.\n");
    }
    public void ejbRemove() throws RemoveException {
        print("ejbRemove() called.\n");
    }
    public String ejbCreate( String studentId,
        String status, double amount) throws CreateException {
        print("ejbCreate() called.\n");
        String orderId = getUniqueId();
        setOrderId(orderId);
        setStudentId(studentId);
        setStatus(status);
        setAmount(amount);
        setOrderDate(new java.sql.Timestamp(System.currentTimeMillis()));
```

**LISTING 11.3**   continued

```
      return null;
   }
   public void ejbPostCreate(String studentId,
      String courseId, double amount) throws CreateException {
      print("ejbPostCreate() called.\n");
   }
   /* Home methods */
   public double ejbHomeGetTotalAmountOfAllOrders()
      throws FinderException {
      double totalAmount = 0.0;
      Collection col = ejbSelectAllOrderAmounts();
      Enumeration amounts=Collections.enumeration(col);
      while( amounts.hasMoreElements() ) {
         Double amount= (Double)amounts.nextElement();
         totalAmount += amount.doubleValue();
      }
      return totalAmount;
   }
   /* select methods. */
   public abstract Collection ejbSelectAllOrderAmounts()
      throws FinderException ;

   void print(String s) {
      System.out.println(s);      ·
   }
   String getUniqueId(){
      return new Long(System.currentTimeMillis()).toString();
   }
}
```

The OrderEJB entity bean implements the javax.ejb.EntityBean interface and is defined as an abstract class. It consists of abstract accessor methods for the persistent fields orderId, studentId, orderDate, status, and amount. It implements the methods setEntityContext(), unsetEntityContext(), ejbActivate(), ejbPassivate(), ejbLoad(), ejbStore(), and ejbRemove(), as defined in the javax.ejb.EntityBean interface. The ejbCreate() method initializes the entity bean instance by assigning the input arguments to the persistent fields and generates a unique order ID. Note that the ejbCreate() method returns NULL. The bean implements the ejbPostCreate() method that corresponds to the ejbCreate() method.

The OrderEJB bean class uses the ejbSelectAllOrderAmounts() select method as a helper method to compute the total order amount in the ejbHomeGetTotalAmountOfAllOrders() home method. ejbSelectAllOrderAmounts() is defined as an abstract method, and the corresponding EJB QL (Enterprise JavaBeans Query Language) query is specified in the deployment descriptor.

Note

Select methods are query methods used within an entity bean instance. You may define zero or more select methods in your bean class. Each select method name starts with the prefix ejbSelect and is defined as an abstract method in an entity bean class. Every select method must have a corresponding EJB QL query string in the deployment descriptor. Select methods are not exposed to the client via the bean's home or component interface.

A select method is similar to a finder method. But unlike a finder method, a select method can return values that correspond to any persistent field or relationship field. Typically, select methods are used as helper methods within a business method.

Caution

Select methods are applicable only to container-managed persistence beans, and not to bean-managed persistence entity beans.

## Declaring the Deployment Descriptor

Prior to EJB 2.0, queries for finder methods were written in a container-specific, proprietary way in the deployment descriptor. EJB 2.0 introduced a portable query language, based on the abstract schema, not on the more complex database schema. This portable query language provides a database- and vendor-independent way to specify queries in the deployment descriptor. In the following sections, we'll discuss the abstract persistent schema and EJB Query Language, and then we'll present the full listing of order deployment descriptors.

### Abstract Persistent Schema

The abstract persistent schema defines an entity bean's persistent fields and relationship fields and determines the method for accessing them. The abstract schema is independent of the entity bean's implementation in a particular EJB container or particular database.

The following listing shows the abstract persistent schema for an Order entity bean:

```
<entity>
  <ejb-name>OrderEJB</ejb-name>
  . . .
  <cmp-version>2.x</cmp-version>
  <abstract-schema-name>Order</abstract-schema-name>
  <cmp-field>
    <field-name>orderId</field-name>
  </cmp-field>
  <cmp-field>
```

```
      <field-name>studentId</field-name>
    </cmp-field>
    <cmp-field>
      <field-name>orderDate</field-name>
    </cmp-field>
    <cmp-field>
      <field-name>status</field-name>
    </cmp-field>
     <cmp-field>
      <field-name>amount</field-name>
    </cmp-field>
    . . .
</entity>
```

The `entity` element declares an entity bean, and an `ejb-name` element within the `entity` element defines the entity bean's name (`OrderEJB`). The `cmp-version` element must be 2.*x* to take advantage of EJB 2.0 container-managed persistence. The `abstract-schema-name` declares the name of this abstract schema (`Order`). You'll later use this abstract schema name to specify EJB QL queries. The schema declares five container-managed persistent fields (`cmp-field`): `orderId`, `studentId`, `orderDate`, `status`, and `amount`. The names of these fields must match the abstract get and set methods in your entity bean class. For example, your entity bean class's methods must be `getOrderId`, `setOrderId`, `getStudentId`, `setStudentId`, `getOrderDate`, `setOrderDate`, `getStatus`, `setStatus`, `getAmount`, and `setAmount`.

## Enterprise JavaBeans Query Language

EJB QL enables you to specify queries for entity beans with container-managed persistence in a database-independent, portable way. EJB QL uses an object-oriented, SQL-like syntax to specify queries for finder and select methods of a container-managed persistence entity bean. EJB QL queries are written with respect to entity bean's abstract schema. For example, the following line illustrates how the application uses an EJB QL query for the `findOrdersByStatus(String status)` method to find orders of a particular status, such as `COMPLETE`:

```
SELECT OBJECT(o) FROM Order AS o WHERE o.status = ?1
```

The preceding query returns `Order` objects, as indicated by the expression `OBJECT(o)` in the `SELECT` clause. In the `FROM` clause, the identifier `o` is analogous to an SQL correlation variable. The `WHERE` clause limits the orders to those whose status matches the value of the first parameter passed to the query, denoted by the expression `?1`.

The container tools will translate such queries into the target language of the underlying database. For example, in case of a relational database, the container translates an EJB QL query to an SQL query. This allows the execution of queries to be shifted to the native language facilities provided by the database, instead of requiring queries to be executed on the runtime representation of the entity bean's state. As a result, query methods can be optimized as well as portable.

An EJB QL query consists of the following three clauses:

- The SELECT clause determines the type of objects or values to be selected.
- The FROM clause defines the scope of the query by declaring one or more identification variables. These identification variables may be referenced in the SELECT and WHERE clauses.
- The optional WHERE is a conditional expression that restricts the objects or values retrieved by the query.

This section explains the details of EJB QL syntax. On Day 12, you'll learn more about EJB QL.

**The FROM Clause**    The FROM clause declares identification variable(s), based on the abstract schema, for navigating through the schema. These identification variables may be referenced in the SELECT and WHERE clauses.

For example, the following query restricts the domain of the query to Order entity beans only:

```
SELECT OBJECT(o) FROM Order AS o WHERE o.status = ?1
```

This query also declares an identification variable, o, whose type is the abstract schema type, Order. This variable is used in the SELECT and WHERE clauses.

**The WHERE Clause**    The WHERE clause consists of a conditional expression that is used to select or values that satisfy the expression. Therefore, the WHERE clause restricts the results of the query.

## Input Parameters

You can use input parameters to base a query on the parameters supplied by the client. An input parameter is designated by a question mark (?) followed by an integer. For example, the first input parameter is ?1, the second is ?2, and so forth.

For example, the following query is used for the finder method findByStudent(String studentId):

```
SELECT OBJECT(o) FROM Order AS o WHERE o.student = ?1
```

The preceding query retrieves the orders that belong a particular student identified by studentId.

Note that the query specifies studentId as a java.lang.String as follows:

```
<query>
 <query-method>
```

```
  <method-name>findByStudent</method-name>
  <method-params>
  <method-param>java.lang.String</method-param>
  </method-params>
</query-method>
<ejb-ql>
<![CDATA[ SELECT OBJECT(o) FROM Order AS o WHERE o.student = ?1
]]>
</ejb-ql>
</query>
```

 **Caution** If an input parameter is NULL, comparison operations or arithmetic operations involving input parameter will return an unknown value.

## Conditional Expressions

A WHERE clause consists of a conditional expression, which is evaluated from left to right within a precedence level.

**Note** You may change the order of evaluation with parentheses.

### BETWEEN Expressions

A BETWEEN expression determines whether an arithmetic expression falls within a range of values. For example, o.amount BETWEEN 100 and 200 is equivalent to o.amount >= 100 and o.amount <= 200. Similarly, o.amount NOT BETWEEN 100 and 200 is equivalent to o.amount < 100 OR o.amount > 200.

**Caution** If the value of an arithmetic expression used in a BETWEEN expression is null, the value of the BETWEEN expression will be unknown.

### IN Expressions

An IN expression determines whether a string belongs to a set of string literals. In the following example, if the status is Submitted, the expression is TRUE. If the status is Complete, it is FALSE.

```
o.status IN ('Submitted', 'Verified')
```

## LIKE Expressions

A LIKE expression determines whether a wildcard pattern matches a string.

Some examples are

- address.phone LIKE '12%3' is true for 12993 and false for 1234
- asentence.word LIKE l_se is true for lose and false for loose

## NULL Comparison Expressions

A NULL comparison expression tests whether a single-valued expression has a NULL value.

In the following example, if the status is NULL, the expression is TRUE. Otherwise, the expression is FALSE.

```
o.status is NULL
```

## Functional Expressions

EJB QL includes the following built-in functions:

### String Functions

- CONCAT(String, String) concatenates the two given Strings and returns a String.
- SUBSTRING(String, *start*, *length*) returns the substring of the given String beginning at position *start* and of *length* long.
- LOCATE(String, String [, *start*]) returns the index of the first occurrence of a String within another String as an int. You can optionally specify the *start* index of the search.
- LENGTH(String) returns an int indicating the length of the String.

### Arithmetic Functions

- ABS(number) returns the absolute value of a number.
- SQRT(double) returns the square root of a number as a double.

**The SELECT Clause**    The SELECT clause denotes the query result. The SELECT clause determines the type of objects or values to be selected. The SELECT clause of an EJB QL query defined for a finder method always corresponds to the abstract schema type of the entity bean for which the finder method is defined.

For example, because Order bean defines the findAllOrders() method in the OrderHome interface, the objects returned by the following query have the Order remote interface type:

```
SELECT OBJECT(o) FROM Order AS o
```

**Filter for Duplicates**    The DISTINCT keyword eliminates duplicate return values. For example, to receive a unique order list, you would specify the query as follows:

```
SELECT DISTINCT OBJECT(o) FROM Order AS o
```

**Note**

> If the method of the query returns a java.util.Collection, which allows duplicates, you must specify the DISTINCT keyword to eliminate duplicates. However, if the method returns a java.util.Set, the DISTINCT keyword is redundant because a java.util.Set may not contain duplicates.

**Note**

> EJB 2.1, which is currently work in progress at the time of writing the book, provides enhancements to EJB QL. For CMP entity beans it supports new features namely order by and aggregate operations.
>
> For ordering of results returned by a query, you can use ORDER BY clause in the SELECT statement. For example, the following query returns the list of orders in the ascending order of order date.
>
> ```
> SELECT OBJECT(o) FROM Order o ORDER BY o.orderDate ASC
> ```
>
> Query statements can use aggregate operators to return the aggregate values of the results. The five aggregate operators available in EJB 2.1 are AVG, SUM, COUNT, MIN, and MAX. These operators can be used in the SELECT clause of the query statement. For example, the following query returns the amount of all orders:
>
> ```
> SELECT SUM(o.amount) FROM Order o
> ```
>
> If DISTINCT keyword is used before an aggregate operator then the duplicate values are removed first before aggregate operator is applied.

11

Now that you have learned the fundamentals of the abstract persistent schema and EJB QL, let's examine the ejb-jar.xml deployment descriptor of our Order bean.

As shown in Listing 11.4, ejb-jar.xml declares OrderEJB as the name of the entity bean and specifies the home interface, remote interface, and bean class. It also declares the Order abstract persistent schema, and that orderId is the primary key using the primkey-field element. In addition, ejb-jar.xml specifies the EJB QL queries for all the finder and select methods (except the findByPrimaryKey() method). For example, the EJB QL for the findByStatus(String status) method is <![CDATA[SELECT OBJECT(o) FROM Order AS o WHERE o.status = ?1]]>.

**LISTING 11.4**    The Full Text of day11/ejb-jar.xml

```xml
<?xml version="1.0"?>
<!DOCTYPE ejb-jar PUBLIC
'-//Sun Microsystems, Inc.//DTD Enterprise JavaBeans 2.0//EN'
'http://java.sun.com/dtd/ejb-jar_2_0.dtd'>

<ejb-jar>
  <enterprise-beans>
    <entity>
      <ejb-name>OrderEJB</ejb-name>
      <home>day11.OrderHome</home>
      <remote>day11.Order</remote>
      <ejb-class>day11.OrderEJB</ejb-class>
      <persistence-type>Container</persistence-type>
      <prim-key-class>java.lang.String</prim-key-class>
      <reentrant>False</reentrant>
      <cmp-version>2.x</cmp-version>
      <abstract-schema-name>Order</abstract-schema-name>
      <cmp-field>
        <field-name>orderId</field-name>
      </cmp-field>
      <cmp-field>
        <field-name>studentId</field-name>
      </cmp-field>
      <cmp-field>
        <field-name>orderDate</field-name>
      </cmp-field>
      <cmp-field>
        <field-name>status</field-name>
      </cmp-field>
      <cmp-field>
        <field-name>amount</field-name>
      </cmp-field>
      <primkey-field>orderId</primkey-field>
      <query>
        <query-method>
          <method-name>findByStatus</method-name>
          <method-params>
            <method-param>java.lang.String</method-param>
          </method-params>
        </query-method>
        <ejb-ql>
          <![CDATA[SELECT OBJECT(o) FROM Order AS o
          WHERE o.status = ?1]]>
        </ejb-ql>
      </query>
      <query>
        <query-method>
          <method-name>ejbSelectAllOrderAmounts</method-name>
```

**LISTING 11.4**    continued

```
            <method-params>
            </method-params>
         </query-method>
         <ejb-ql>
           <![CDATA[SELECT o.amount FROM Order AS o
           WHERE o.orderId IS NOT NULL]]>
         </ejb-ql>
       </query>
     </entity>
   </enterprise-beans>
</ejb-jar>
```

Listing 11.5 shows a `weblogic-ejb-jar.xml` deployment descriptor that is specific to WebLogic Server. The `jndi-name` element declares the JNDI name of the enterprise bean. So, the JNDI name of the `OrderEJB` is `day11/Order`.

**LISTING 11.5**    The Full Text of `day11/weblogic-ejb-jar.xml`

```
<?xml version="1.0"?>
<!DOCTYPE weblogic-ejb-jar PUBLIC
'-//BEA Systems, Inc.//DTD WebLogic 7.0.0 EJB//EN'
'http://www.bea.com/servers/wls700/dtd/weblogic-ejb-jar.dtd'>

<weblogic-ejb-jar>
  <weblogic-enterprise-bean>
    <ejb-name>OrderEJB</ejb-name>
    <entity-descriptor>

      <persistence>
        <persistence-use>
          <type-identifier>WebLogic_CMP_RDBMS</type-identifier>
          <type-version>6.0</type-version>
          <type-storage>META-INF/weblogic-cmp-rdbms-jar.xml</type-storage>
        </persistence-use>
      </persistence>

    </entity-descriptor>
    <jndi-name>day11/Order</jndi-name>
  </weblogic-enterprise-bean>
</weblogic-ejb-jar>
```

Listing 11.6 shows the `weblogic-cmp-rdbms.xml`. It contains the WebLogic Server–specific deployment descriptors that define the container-managed persistence services. For example, you can define abstract schema to database element mapping. Typically the container tools allow you to map abstract schema to database schema at deployment time.

LISTING 11.6    The Full Text of day11/weblogic-cmp-rdbms-jar.xml

```
<!DOCTYPE weblogic-rdbms-jar PUBLIC
'-//BEA Systems, Inc.//DTD WebLogic 7.0.0 EJB RDBMS Persistence//EN'
'http://www.bea.com/servers/wls700/dtd/weblogic-rdbms20-persistence-700.dtd'>
<weblogic-rdbms-jar>
 <weblogic-rdbms-bean>
  <ejb-name>OrderEJB</ejb-name>
  <data-source-name>jdbc.styejbDB</data-source-name>
  <table-map>
  <table-name>orders</table-name>
  <field-map>
   <cmp-field>orderId</cmp-field>
   <dbms-column>order_id</dbms-column>
  </field-map>
  <field-map>
   <cmp-field>studentId</cmp-field>
   <dbms-column>student_id</dbms-column>
  </field-map>
  <field-map>
   <cmp-field>orderDate</cmp-field>
   <dbms-column>order_date</dbms-column>
  </field-map>
  <field-map>
   <cmp-field>status</cmp-field>
   <dbms-column>status</dbms-column>
  </field-map>
  <field-map>
   <cmp-field>amount</cmp-field>
   <dbms-column>amount</dbms-column>
  </field-map>
  </table-map>
 </weblogic-rdbms-bean>
</weblogic-rdbms-jar>
```

In the case of JBoss, you need to write the deployment descriptors jboss.xml and jbosscmp-jdbc.xml. Listing 11.7 shows the deployment descriptor jboss.xml. It declares the JNDI name of OrderEJB entity bean as day11/Order.

LISTING 11.7    The Full Text of day11/jboss.xml

```
<?xml version="1.0" encoding="UTF-8"?>
<jboss>
  <enterprise-beans>
```

**LISTING 11.7**   continued

```
    <entity>
      <ejb-name>OrderEJB</ejb-name>
      <jndi-name>day11/Order</jndi-name>
    </entity>
  </enterprise-beans>
</jboss>
```

Listing 11.8 shows the `jbosscmp-jdbc.xml`. It contains the abstract-schema-to-database-element mapping. In each `cmp-field` element, you specify the name of the `cmp-field` using the `field-name` element and the corresponding database column name using the `column-name` element.

**LISTING 11.8**   The Full Text of `day11/jbosscmp-jdbc.xml`

```
<?xml version="1.0" encoding="UTF-8"?>
<!DOCTYPE jbosscmp-jdbc PUBLIC
    "-//JBoss//DTD JBOSSCMP-JDBC 3.0//EN"
    "http://www.jboss.org/j2ee/dtd/jbosscmp-jdbc_3_0.dtd">
<jbosscmp-jdbc>
  <defaults>
    <datasource>java:/DefaultDS</datasource>
    <datasource-mapping>Hypersonic SQL</datasource-mapping>
    <create-table>false</create-table>
    <remove-table>false</remove-table>
    <pk-constraint>true</pk-constraint>
    <preferred-relation-mapping>foreign-key</preferred-relation-mapping>
  </defaults>
  <enterprise-beans>
    <entity>
      <ejb-name>OrderEJB</ejb-name>
      <table-name>orders</table-name>
      <cmp-field>
        <field-name>orderId</field-name>
        <column-name>order_id</column-name>
      </cmp-field>
      <cmp-field>
        <field-name>studentId</field-name>
        <column-name>student_id</column-name>
      </cmp-field>
      <cmp-field>
        <field-name>orderDate</field-name>
        <column-name>order_date</column-name>
      </cmp-field>
      <cmp-field>
        <field-name>status</field-name>
        <column-name>status</column-name>
```

11

**LISTING 11.8** continued

```
        </cmp-field>
        <cmp-field>
            <field-name>order</field-name>
            <column-name>amount</column-name>
        </cmp-field>
    </entity>
</jbosscmp-jdbc>
```

# Writing a Client

Listing 11.9 demonstrates how a client accesses an entity bean.

**LISTING 11.9** The Full Text of day11\Client.java

```
package day11;

import java.util.*;
import javax.naming.*;
import javax.ejb.*;

public class Client {
    public static void main(String[] args) {
        print("Starting Client . . .\n");
        Context initialContext = null;
        OrderHome orderHome = null;
        Order order = null;

        try {
            print("Looking up the order home via JNDI.\n");
            initialContext = new InitialContext();
            Object object = initialContext.lookup("day11/Order");
            orderHome = (OrderHome)
                javax.rmi.PortableRemoteObject.narrow(object,OrderHome.class);

            order = (Order)orderHome.create("1", "Submitted", 100);
            String orderId = order.getOrderId();
            print("Created a new order:" + orderId + " .\n");

            print("Locating the order " + orderId
                    + " using findByPrimaryKey method.\n");
            order=orderHome.findByPrimaryKey(orderId);

            print("Locating all orders with status Submitted "
                    + " using findByStatus method.\n");
            Collection col=orderHome.findByStatus("Submitted");
            Enumeration orders=Collections.enumeration(col);
```

**LISTING 11.9**   continued

```
         while( orders.hasMoreElements() ) {
            order=(Order)orders.nextElement();
            print("Order id:"+ order.getOrderId());
         }

         print("Finding the total amount of all orders using \n"
               + " getTotalAmountOfAllOrders home method.\n");
         double totalAmount = orderHome.getTotalAmountOfAllOrders();
         print("Total amount:"+ totalAmount );

      } catch ( Exception e) {
         e.printStackTrace();
      }
   }
   static void print(String s) {
      System.out.println(s);
   }
}
```

The client locates the OrderHome home interface of the deployed enterprise bean via JNDI and then uses the remote home interface to create a remote Order entity object. The client then demonstrates the use of the finder and home methods.

# Packaging and Deploying the Enterprise Bean

This section describes the steps to package and deploy the Order entity bean, and build the client for both WebLogic Server and JBoss application servers.

You can run the following commands for WebLogic:

C:\>**cd styejb\examples**

C:\styejb\examples>**setEnvWebLogic.bat**

C:\styejb\examples>**cd day11**

C:\styejb\examples\day11>**buildWebLogic.bat**

You can run the following commands for JBoss:

C:\>**cd styejb\examples**

C:\styejb\examples>**setEnvJboss.bat**

C:\styejb\examples>**cd day11**

C:\styejb\examples\day11>**buildJboss.bat**

11

# Running the Example

The following steps describe how to start PointBase database server and WebLogic Server, and run the sample client:

1. Start the PointBase server in a new command window as follows:

```
C:\>cd styejb\examples
C:\styejb\examples>setEnvWebLogic.bat
C:\styejb\examples>startPointBase.bat
```

2. Start WebLogic Server in a new command window as follows:

```
C:\>cd styejb\examples
C:\styejb\examples>setEnvWebLogic.bat
C:\styejb\examples>startWebLogic.bat
```

3. You can run the client in the same window you used to package the bean and build the client by using the following command:

```
C:\styejb\examples\day11>runClientWebLogic.bat
```

Running the client produces the following output:

```
Starting Client . . .
Looking up the order home via JNDI.
Created a new order:1027793589262 .
Locating the order 1027793589262 using findByPrimaryKey method.
Locating all orders with status Submitted  using findByStatus method.
Order id:1027793589262
Finding the total amount of all orders using
 getTotalAmountOfAllOrders home method.
Total amount:100.0
```

The following steps describe how to start the JBoss server and run the sample client:

1. Start JBoss in a new command window as follows:

```
C:\>cd styejb\examples
C:\styejb\examples>setEnvJBoss.bat
C:\styejb\examples>startJBoss.bat
```

2. You can run the client in the same window you used to package the bean and build the client by using the following command:

```
C:\styejb\examples\day11>runClientWebLogic.bat
```

Note that the JBoss server automatically starts the default HyperSonic database.

# Best Practices

Whenever possible, you should use container-managed persistence as rather than bean-managed persistence. A CMP entity bean is portable and easier to develop.

Use input parameters to write general EJB QL queries. For example, the query `SELECT OBJECT(o) FROM Order AS o WHERE o.status = ?1` is preferable to the query `SELECT OBJECT(o) FROM Order AS o WHERE o.status = 'SUBMITTED'`.

# Summary

Today you wrote a container-managed persistence enterprise bean. The container is responsible for generating the database access code. Similar to BMP, the CMP contains the home interface, the component interface, the bean class, and the deployment descriptor. The bean class contains the abstract accessor methods for persistent fields and implements the callback methods and home methods. The bean class may contain select methods, which are query methods used within an entity bean instance.

The CMP deployment descriptor contains the abstract persistence schema and EJB QL queries for finder and select methods. At deployment time, the abstract schema is mapped to the database schema allowing the container to generate the required data access code. You learned how to package and deploy the enterprise bean, and then wrote and ran a client that accesses it.

# Q&A

**Q What are the coding differences between a bean-managed persistence bean and a container-managed persistence bean?**

**A** The following are the coding differences between the two types of entity beans:

- With BMP, the developer is responsible for writing the database access calls. With CMP, the container is responsible for database access.

- The BMP bean class is not defined as abstract class. The CMP bean class is defined as an abstract class.

- The persistent state in a BMP is defined as instance variables. In CMP, you write public abstract accessor methods for persistent and relationship fields.

- A BMP implements all the finder methods in the bean class. A CMP bean class does not implement the finder methods. The queries for the finder methods are specified in the deployment descriptor.

- A CMP bean class can define select methods, whereas a BMP bean class cannot define select methods.

11

**Q** **What are the similarities and differences between the finder and select methods of a container-managed persistence entity bean?**

**A** Both finder and select methods use EJB QL to define the semantics of the method. Finder methods are exposed to the clients in the home interface, whereas select methods are used as internal helper methods of a bean class and are not exposed to the clients. Finder methods can return only `EJBObjects` or `EJBLocalObjects` of the same type as the entity bean. Select methods can return `EJBObjects`, `EJBLocalObjects`, or persistent field types.

# Quiz

1. An `OrderEJB` container-managed persistence entity bean implements which one of the following interfaces?

    A. `javax.ejb.EntityBean`

    B. `javax.ejb.ContainerManagedBean`

    C. `javax.ejb.OrderHome`

    D. `javax.ejb.Order`

2. The container invokes the `ejbPostCreate<method>(...)` method on an entity instance after it invokes which one of the following methods?

    A. `ejbCreate<method>(...)`

    B. `ejbLoad()`

    C. `ejbActivate()`

    D. `ejbRemove()`

3. Which one of the following is true for a select method?

    A. A select method is specified in the entity bean's home interface.

    B. Every select method must have an EJB QL query in the deployment descriptor.

    C. A client invokes a select method via a component interface.

# Quiz Answers

1. A

2. A

3. B

# Exercises

To extend your knowledge of the subjects covered today, try the following exercises:

1. Add the `findAllOrders()` method to the `OrderHome` interface, and specify the corresponding EJB QL query `SELECT OBJECT(o) FROM Order AS o` in the `ejb-jar.xml` deployment descriptor. In addition, package and deploy the entity bean.

2. Define local interfaces for the `OrderEJB` bean. Define an `OrderLocalHome` local home interface and `OrderLocal` local interface. We will use these local interfaces on Day 21.

11

# DAY 12

# Developing Container-Managed Relationships

Today, you'll learn how to develop relationships among container-managed persistence entity beans by using the advanced feature of container-managed relationships.

In our sample university registration system, a student's order consists of one or more line items. Each line item represents a single course item the student has ordered. So, there exists a one-to-many relationship between order and line items. Another example is a student can enroll in many courses, and each course can have many students enrolled in it. So, there exists a many-to-many relationship between students and courses. These are good candidates for container-managed relationships.

Today, we'll write a complete code example of the order-line item relationship.

Today's road map:

- Examine the concepts of cardinality and directionality that are applicable to container-managed relationships. You'll also learn how to implement different kinds of relationships using code snippets.

- Learn how to define the home and component interfaces for entity beans that are part of a relationship.
- Learn how to specify the container-managed persistent fields in the bean class and deployment descriptor.
- Learn how to compile, package, and deploy the beans in a container, and write a client that tests the container-managed relationships.

# Examining Container-Managed Relationships

As with a table in a relational database, an entity bean may be related to other entity beans. With BMP entity beans, you need to write code to manage the relationships. With CMP, you declare the relationships in the deployment descriptor and the container generates the code to manage the relationships. An entity bean relationship field represents a relationship to another entity bean. The EJB container provides automatic management of both the persistent state of an entity bean and its relationships to other entity beans.

Local interfaces provide the foundation for container-managed relationships. An entity bean uses its local interface to maintain its relationships to other entity beans. Also, the bean provider creates a single ejb-jar file that contains a deployment descriptor describing the entity beans and their relationships.

**Caution**

> Container-managed relationships are applicable only to container-managed persistence beans and not to bean-managed persistence entity beans. An entity bean that is the target of a container-managed relationship must provide local interfaces.

## Cardinality

*Cardinality* indicates how many instances of one class may be associated with a single instance of another class. Cardinality is also known as *multiplicity*. Container-managed relationships may be one-to-one, one-to-many, or many-to-many as described in the following list:

- **One-to-one**—Each entity bean is associated with a single instance of another entity bean. For example, each student has a corresponding mailing address.
- **One-to-many**—Each entity bean is associated with many instances of another entity bean. For example, each order is composed of many line items.

- **Many-to-many**—The entity bean instances may be related to multiple instances of each other. For example, a student can enroll in many courses and each course can have many students enrolled in it.

## Directionality

Relationships may be either unidirectional or bidirectional as follows:

- **Bidirectional**—If a relationship is bidirectional, it can be navigated in both directions. For example, the one-to-many relationship between order and line items is bidirectional because given an order, you need to find the associated line items; given a line item, you need to find the corresponding order.

- **Unidirectional**—A unidirectional relationship can be navigated in only one direction. For example, a line item bean would have a relationship field that identifies the associated course bean, but a course bean would not have a relationship field for the line item bean. In other words, the line item bean knows about the course bean, but the course bean doesn't know which line item bean instances refer to it.

# Implementing Container-Manager Relationships

In this section, we examine the sample implementations of different kinds of relationships. Later today, we'll design and implement a complete example of one-to-many bidirectional relationship between order and line items.

## Implementing One-to-One Relationships

Figure 12.1 shows a `StudentEJB` entity bean with a one-to-one unidirectional relationship to an `AddressEJB` entity bean. `Student-Address` is the name of the relationship. `Student-has-address` is the role name of the `StudentEJB`, and `Address-belongs-to-student` is the role name of the `AddressEJB` in this relationship.

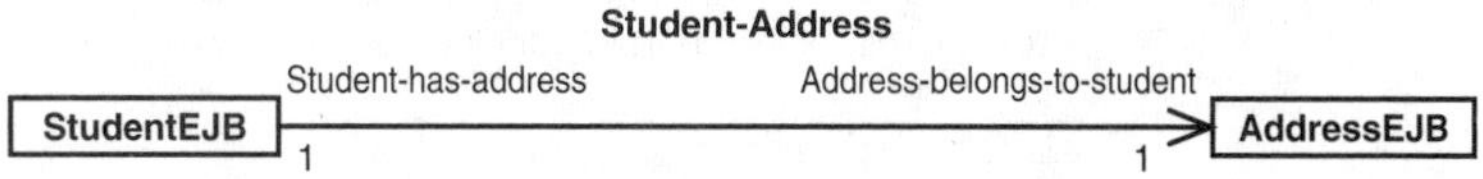

**FIGURE 12.1**

*One-to-one unidirectional relationship.*

The following code snippet shows the implementation of the relationship in Figure 12.1 using container-managed relationships:

```
public abstract class StudentEJB implements EntityBean{
...
public abstract AddressLocal getAddress();
```

```
public abstract void setAddress(AddressLocal address);
...
}
```

StudentEJB declares a public abstract get method, and sets the accessor methods for the address relationship field. Also notice that the methods use the AddressLocal local interface.

AddressEJB, as follows, contains no relationship fields:

```
public abstract class AddressEJB implements EntityBean{
...
/* no cmr-fields */
}
```

Because AddressEJB does not know about StudentEJB, there are no accessor methods in AddressEJB for accessing StudentEJB.

> **Note**
>
> The accessor method for a container-managed relationship field must be public and abstract. The get method of a single-valued container-managed relationship field must return the local interface of the entity bean. The set method for the relationship must take the entity bean's local interface as an argument.

The relationship fields must be declared in the deployment descriptor. A single deployment descriptor describes both the entity beans and their relationships. The deployment descriptor corresponding to the Student-Address relationship is written as follows:

```
<ejb-jar>
  ...
  <enterprise-beans>
  ...
  </enterprise-beans>
  <relationships>
    <ejb-relation>
    <!--ONE-TO-ONE uni-directional : Student Address -->
     <ejb-relation-name>Student-Address</ejb-relation-name>

      <ejb-relationship-role>
        <ejb-relationship-role-name>
          Student-has-address
        </ejb-relationship-role-name>
        <multiplicity>One</multiplicity>
        <relationship-role-source>
          <ejb-name>StudentEJB</ejb-name>
        </relationship-role-source>
```

```
    <cmr-field>
      <cmr-field-name>address</cmr-field-name>
    </cmr-field>
  </ejb-relationship-role>

  <ejb-relationship-role>
    <ejb-relationship-role-name>
      Address-belongs-to-student
    </ejb-relationship-role-name>
    <multiplicity>One</multiplicity>
    <relationship-role-source>
      <ejb-name>AddressEJB</ejb-name>
    </relationship-role-source>
  </ejb-relationship-role>

  </ejb-relation>
</relationships>
...
</ejb-jar>
```

The `ejb-relation` element declares a relationship. The name of the relation `Student-Address` is declared using the `ejb-relation-name` element. Each `ejb-relation` element contains a pair of `ejb-relationship-role` elements to describe the two roles in the relationship. Each `ejb-relationship-role` element describes a relationship role: its name, its multiplicity, and its navigability within a relation. Each relationship role refers to an entity bean by means of an `ejb-name` element contained in the `relationship-role-source` element. For example, the student side of the relationship declares the `Student-has-address` role name using the `ejb-relationship-role-name` element, cardinality of `One` using the `multiplicity` element, and `StudentEJB` as the EJB name using the `ejb-name` element in the `relationship-role-source` element. In addition, the student side of the relationship also specifies the container-managed relationship field `address` using the `cmp-field-name` element in the `cmp-field` element. Similarly, the deployment descriptor contains the address side of the relationship. Because the address does not know about the student, there is no `cmr-field` in `address` for accessing a student.

**Note**  A unidirectional relationship is implemented with a `cmr-field` on the entity bean instance from which navigation can take place, and no related `cmr-field` on the entity bean instance that is the target of the relationship.

## Implementing One-to-Many Relationships

Figure 12.2 shows an `OrderEJB` entity bean with a one-to-many bidirectional relationship to `LineItemEJB` entity beans. `OrderEJB` is composed of many `LineItemEJBs`.

`Order-LineItems` is the name of this relationship. `Order-has-lineitems` is the role name of `OrderEJB`, and `Lineitems-belongs-to-order` is the role name of `LineItemEJB` in this relationship.

**FIGURE 12.2**

*One-to-many bidirec-tional relationship.*

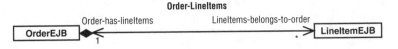

The following shows the code template for the `OrderEJB` class:

```
public abstract class OrderEJB implements EntityBean{
...
public abstract Collection getLineItems();
public abstract void setLineItems(Collection lineItems);
...
}
```

`OrderEJB` declares abstract get and set accessor methods for the line items relationship field. You need to use a collection of local interfaces for a collection-valued container-managed relationship field. The `getLineItems()` method returns a collection of `java.util.Collection` of `LineItemLocal` local interfaces. The `setLineItems()` method takes a collection of entity beans' `LineItemLocal` local interfaces as an argument.

 **Note**

> The get method of a collection-valued container-managed relationship field must return a collection (either `java.util.Collection` or `java.util.Set`) of local interfaces. The set method for the relationship must take a collection of entity beans' local interfaces as an argument.

The following snippet shows the code template for the `LineItemEJB` class:

```
public abstract class LineItemEJB implements EntityBean{
...
public abstract OrderLocal getOrder();
public abstract void setOrder(OrderLocal order);
...
}
```

`LineItemEJB` declares abstract get and set accessor methods for the order relationship field.

The deployment descriptor corresponding `Order-LineItems` relationship is written as follows:

```
<ejb-jar>
  ...
  <enterprise-beans>
  ...
  </enterprise-beans>
  <relationships>
    <!--ONE-TO-MANY bi-directional : Order LineItem -->
    <ejb-relation>
      <ejb-relation-name>Order-LineItems</ejb-relation-name>
      <ejb-relationship-role>
        <ejb-relationship-role-name>
          Order-has-lineitems
        </ejb-relationship-role-name>
        <multiplicity>one</multiplicity>
        <relationship-role-source>
          <ejb-name>OrderEJB</ejb-name>
        </relationship-role-source>
        <cmr-field>
          <cmr-field-name>lineItems</cmr-field-name>
          <cmr-field-type>java.util.Collection</cmr-field-type>
        </cmr-field>
      </ejb-relationship-role>

      <ejb-relationship-role>
        <ejb-relationship-role-name>
          LineItems-belongs-to-order
        </ejb-relationship-role-name>
        <multiplicity>many</multiplicity>
        <relationship-role-source>
          <ejb-name>LineItemEJB</ejb-name>
        </relationship-role-source>
        <cmr-field>
          <cmr-field-name>order</cmr-field-name>
        </cmr-field>
      </ejb-relationship-role>
    </ejb-relation>
  </relationships>
  ...
</ejb-jar>
```

**12**

The deployment descriptor declares the `Order-LineItems` relation using `ejb-relation-name`. The order side of the relationship declares the `Order-has-lineitems` role name with cardinality of `One`. It also declares `StudentEJB` as the EJB name using the `ejb-name` element in the `relationship-role-source` element. It specifies the container-managed relationship field `lineItems` using the `cmp-field-name` element in the `cmp-field` element. Similarly, the deployment descriptor contains the line items' side of the relationship.

## Implementing Many-to-Many Relationships

Figure 12.3 shows a StudentEJB entity bean with a many-to-many bidirectional relationship to a CourseEJB entity bean.

**FIGURE 12.3**

*Many-to-many bidirectional relationship.*

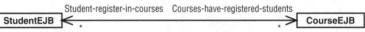

StudentEJB defines the abstract accessor methods for the course relationship field as follows:

```
public abstract class StudentEJB implements EntityBean{
...
public abstract Collection getCourses();
public abstract void setCourses(Collection courses);
...
}
```

CourseEJB defines the abstract accessor methods for the student relationship field as follows:

```
public abstract class CourseEJB implements EntityBean{
...
public abstract Collection getStudents();
public abstract void setStudents(Collection students);
...
}
```

The deployment descriptor is written as follows:

```
<ejb-jar>
  ...
  <enterprise-beans>
  ...
  </enterprise-beans>
  <relationships>
    <!--MANY-TO-MANY bi-directional: Student Course  -->
    <ejb-relation>
      <ejb-relation-name>Student-Course</ejb-relation-name>
      <ejb-relationship-role>
        <ejb-relationship-role-name>
          Students-register-in-courses
        </ejb-relationship-role-name>
        <multiplicity>many</multiplicity>
        <relationship-role-source>
          <ejb-name>StudentEJB</ejb-name>
        </relationship-role-source>
        <cmr-field>
          <cmr-field-name>courses</cmr-field-name>
```

```
        <cmr-field-type>java.util.Collection</cmr-field-type>
      </cmr-field>
    </ejb-relationship-role>

    <ejb-relationship-role>
      <ejb-relationship-role-name>
        Courses-have-registered-students
      </ejb-relationship-role-name>
      <multiplicity>many</multiplicity>
      <relationship-role-source>
        <ejb-name>CourseEJB</ejb-name>
      </relationship-role-source>
      <cmr-field>
        <cmr-field-name>students</cmr-field-name>
        <cmr-field-type>java.util.Collection</cmr-field-type>
      </cmr-field>
    </ejb-relationship-role>
  </ejb-relation>
</relationships>
...
</ejb-jar>
```

The student side of the Student-Course relationship declares Students-register-in-courses role name with cardinality of many. It also specifies the container-managed relationship field courses. Similarly, the deployment descriptor also contains the course side of the relationship.

**Note**

> You can model a many-to-many relationship into two one-to-many relationships using a new entity bean. For example, as shown in Figure 12.4, an enrollment entity bean models the join relationship between students and courses. This is a preferable design approach because it reduces the dependency between entity beans.

**12**

**FIGURE 12.4**

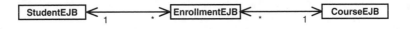

*Many-to-many bidirectional relationship.*

# Designing Container-Managed Relationships

Now that you understand the basics of container-manager relationships, let's examine the design of the order-line item relationship in detail and implement it. Figure 12.5 shows an order entity bean with a relationship to line items. Each order is composed of multiple line items. A composition relationship is shown as a solid line with a filled diamond at one end. The order is composed of many line items, and the name of the composition relationship is `Order-LineItems`. `Order-has-lineitems` is the role name of the `OrderEJB` and `Lineitems-belongs-to-order` is the role name of the `LineItemEJB` in this relationship.

An `OrderEJB` entity bean class consists of the persistent fields `orderId`, `studentId`, `orderDate`, `status`, and `amount`, and of the container-managed persistent field, `lineItems`. It also implements two business methods: `addLineItem()` and `getOrderLineItems()`. It implements the methods `setEntityContext()`, `unsetEntityContext()`, `ejbActivate()`, `ejbPassivate()`, `ejbLoad()`, `ejbStore()`, and `ejbRemove()` as defined in the `javax.ejb.EntityBean` interface. It also implements the `ejbCreate()` and `ejbPostCreate()` methods. An order entity bean is identified by its primary key, `orderId`.

An `OrderLineItemEJB` entity bean class consists of the persistent fields `orderLineItemId`, `courseId`, and `fee`, and of the container-managed persistent field, `order`. It implements the methods `setEntityContext()`, `unsetEntityContext()`, `ejbActivate()`, `ejbPassivate()`, `ejbLoad()`, `ejbStore()`, `ejbRemove()` as defined in the `javax.ejb.EntityBean` interface. It also implements the `ejbCreate()` and `ejbPostCreate()` methods. An `OrderLineItem` entity bean is identified by its primary key, `orderLineItemId`.

**FIGURE 12.5**

*Order-line item relationship.*

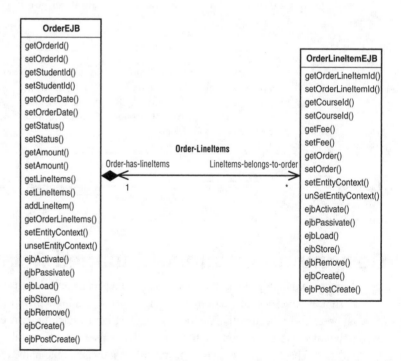

In addition (but not shown in Figure 12.5), the order entity bean uses the line item internally, but does not expose it to remote clients. This is achieved as follows: The order entity bean defines both a remote and a local component interface. The local interface is presented only to the line item entity bean and the remote interface is presented to the remote clients. Note that this satisfies the requirement that an entity bean that is the target of a container-managed relationship must provide local interfaces.

Also, the lifetime of the line items is coincident with the lifetime of the order. Because a line item object should exist only when the parent order exists, you want to ensure that when you delete an order, you also delete all the line items that belong to the order. This is known as a *cascade delete*. We'll discuss the cascade delete facility later today.

# Defining the Home Interfaces

We define both local and remote home interfaces for the order entity bean, but only a local home interface for the line item entity bean.

## Defining the Order Home Interfaces

Both the local and remote home interfaces of the order provide methods for creating and finding the instances of the bean based on the primary key.

Listing 12.1 shows the OrderHome remote home interface.

**LISTING 12.1**  The Full Text of day12/OrderHome.java

```
package day12;
import java.util.*;
import java.rmi.*;
import javax.ejb.*;
public interface OrderHome extends EJBHome {
    /* Create methods */
    public Order create(String studentId,
      String status, double amount) throws CreateException, RemoteException;
    /* Finder methods */
    public Order findByPrimaryKey(String key)
       throws FinderException, RemoteException;
}
```

Listing 12.2 shows the OrderLocalHome local home interface.

**LISTING 12.2**  The Full Text of day12/OrderLocalHome.java

```
package day12;
import java.util.*;
```

LISTING 12.2    continued

```
import java.rmi.*;
import javax.ejb.*;
public interface OrderLocalHome extends EJBLocalHome {
    /* Create methods */
    public OrderLocal create(String studentId,
        String status, double amount) throws CreateException;
    /* Finder methods */
    public OrderLocal findByPrimaryKey(String key)
        throws FinderException;
}
```

### Defining the `OrderLineItemLocalHome` Home Interface

The local home interfaces of the line items provide methods for creating and finding the instances of the bean based on the primary key. Listing 12.3 shows the `OrderLineItemLocalHome` local home interface.

**LISTING 12.3**    The Full Text of `day12/OrderLineItemLocalHome.java`

```
package day12;
import javax.ejb.*;
import java.util.*;
public interface OrderLineItemLocalHome extends EJBLocalHome {
    public OrderLineItemLocal create(String orderLineItemId,
        String courseId, double fee) throws CreateException;
    public OrderLineItemLocal findByPrimaryKey(String key)
        throws FinderException;
}
```

# Defining the Remote Interfaces

We define both local and remote interfaces for the order entity bean, but only the local interface for the line item entity bean.

## Defining the Order Interfaces

Both the local and remote home interfaces of the order entity bean provide methods for accessing the bean's persistent fields. In addition, they contain the business methods `addLineItem()` and `getOrderLineItems()`. The `addLineItem()` method is used to add a line item to the order. The `getOrderLineItems()` returns a collection of `ClientLineItem` objects (as opposed to `OrderLineItemLocal` objects).

Listing 12.4 shows the Order remote interface.

**LISTING 12.4**    The Full Text of day12/Order.java

```
package day12;
import java.util.*;
import java.rmi.*;
import javax.ejb.*;
public interface Order extends EJBObject{
    public String getOrderId()
        throws RemoteException;
    public String getStudentId()
        throws RemoteException;
    public void setStudentId(String studentId)
        throws RemoteException;
    public double getAmount()
        throws RemoteException;
    public void setAmount(double amount)
        throws RemoteException;
    public java.sql.Timestamp getOrderDate()
        throws RemoteException;
    public void setOrderDate(java.sql.Timestamp date)
        throws RemoteException;
    public String getStatus()
        throws RemoteException;
    public void setStatus(String status)
        throws RemoteException;
    public void addLineItem(String courseId, double fee)
        throws RemoteException;
    public Collection getOrderLineItems()
        throws RemoteException;
}
```

**12**

The Order remote interface does not provide accessor methods for the container-managed persistent field line items.

The accessor methods for container-managed relationship fields must not be exposed in the remote interface of the entity bean.

Listing 12.5 shows the OrderLocal local interface.

**LISTING 12.5**   The Full Text of day12/OrderLocal.java

```
package day12;
import java.util.*;
import java.rmi.*;
import javax.ejb.*;
public interface OrderLocal extends EJBLocalObject {
    public String getOrderId();
    public String getStudentId();
    public void setStudentId(String studentId);
    public double getAmount();
    public void setAmount(double amount);
    public java.sql.Timestamp getOrderDate();
    public void setOrderDate(java.sql.Timestamp date);
    public String getStatus();
    public void setStatus(String status);
    public void addLineItem(String courseId, double fee);
    public Collection getOrderLineItems();
}
```

## Defining the `OrderLineItemLocal` Local Interface

The local interface of the order line item entity bean provides methods for accessing the bean's persistent fields. In addition, it contains the accessor methods for the container-managed persistent field order.

Listing 12.6 shows the `OrderLineItemLocal` local interface.

**LISTING 12.6**   The Full Text of day12/OrderLineItemLocal.java

```
package day12;
import javax.ejb.*;
public interface OrderLineItemLocal extends EJBLocalObject {
    public String getOrderLineItemId();
    public String getCourseId();
    public void setCourseId(String courseId);
    public double getFee();
    public void setFee(double fee);
    public OrderLocal getOrder();
    public void setOrder(OrderLocal o);
}
```

# Implementing the Enterprise Bean Classes

Listing 12.7 shows the `OrderEJB` bean class.

**LISTING 12.7**    The Full Text of `day12/OrderEJB.java`

```java
package day12;
import java.util.*;
import java.io.*;
import java.rmi.*;
import javax.naming.*;
import javax.ejb.*;
public abstract class OrderEJB implements EntityBean {
protected EntityContext ctx;
/* get and set methods for cmp fields */
public abstract String getOrderId();
public abstract void setOrderId(String orderId);
public abstract String getStudentId();
public abstract void setStudentId(String studentid);
public abstract java.sql.Timestamp getOrderDate();
public abstract void setOrderDate(java.sql.Timestamp timestamp);
public abstract String getStatus();
public abstract void setStatus(String status);
public abstract double getAmount();
public abstract void setAmount(double amount);
/* get and set methods for relationship fields */
public abstract Collection getLineItems();
public abstract void setLineItems(Collection lineItems);
/* business methods */
public void addLineItem(String courseId, double fee) {
    try {
        Context ctx = new InitialContext();
        OrderLineItemLocalHome home = (OrderLineItemLocalHome)
            ctx.lookup("day12/OrderLineItemLocal");
        String lineItemId = getUniqueId();
        OrderLineItemLocal item =
            home.create(lineItemId, courseId, fee) ;
        getLineItems().add(item);
    } catch(Exception e) {
        throw new EJBException("Error adding line item:", e);
    }
}
public Collection getOrderLineItems() {
    Vector clientLineItems = new Vector();
    Collection lineitems = getLineItems();
    java.util.Iterator iterator = lineitems.iterator();
    ClientLineItem item;
    while (iterator.hasNext()) {
        OrderLineItemLocal litem = (OrderLineItemLocal)iterator.next();
        item = new ClientLineItem(litem.getOrderLineItemId(),
                            litem.getCourseId(), litem.getFee());
        clientLineItems.add(item);
    }
    return clientLineItems;
```

12

**LISTING 12.7**   continued

```
    }
/* Callback methods */
public void setEntityContext(EntityContext ctx) {
    this.ctx = ctx;
}
public void unsetEntityContext() {
    this.ctx = null;
}
 public void ejbActivate() {}
 public void ejbPassivate() {}
 public void ejbStore() {}
 public void ejbLoad() {}
 public void ejbRemove() throws RemoveException {
    print("Removing Order id:" + (String)ctx.getPrimaryKey() );
}
 public String ejbCreate(String studentId,
    String status, double amount) throws CreateException {
    String orderId = getUniqueId();
    setOrderId(orderId);
    setStudentId(studentId);
    setStatus(status);
    setAmount(amount);
    setOrderDate(new java.sql.Timestamp(System.currentTimeMillis()));
    print("Creating Order id:" + orderId );
    return null;
}
 public void ejbPostCreate(String studentId,
   String courseId, double amount) throws CreateException {}
 String getUniqueId(){
    return new Long(System.currentTimeMillis()).toString();
}
 void print(String s) {
    System.out.println(s);
}
}
```

The OrderEJB entity bean implements the javax.ejb.EntityBean interface and is
defined as an abstract class. It consists of abstract accessor methods for the persistent
fields orderId, studentId, orderDate, status, and amount, and the container-managed
persistent field, lineItems. The addLineItem() business method creates a new line item
and adds it to the persistent managed relationship. The getOrderLineItems() business
method retrieves the line items in this order using getLineItems() method, and creates a
collection of ClientLineItem objects. This method makes a view of the line items that
are in this order available to the client. It implements the methods setEntityContext(),
unsetEntityContext(), ejbActivate(), ejbPassivate(), ejbLoad(), ejbStore(), and

`ejbRemove()` as defined in the `javax.ejb.EntityBean` interface. The `ejbCreate()` method initializes the entity bean instance by assigning the input arguments to the persistent fields. The `ejbCreate()` method returns `null`. The bean implements the `ejbPostCreate()` method that corresponds to the `ejbCreate()` method.

Listing 12.8 shows the `OrderLineItemEJB` bean class.

**LISTING 12.8** The Full Text of `day12/OrderLineItemEJB.java`

```
package day12;
import javax.naming.*;
import javax.ejb.*;
import java.util.*;
public abstract class OrderLineItemEJB implements EntityBean {
 protected EntityContext ctx;
 /* get and set methods for cmp fields */
 public OrderLineItemEJB() {}
 public abstract String getOrderLineItemId();
 public abstract void setOrderLineItemId(String id);
 public abstract String getCourseId();
 public abstract void setCourseId(String courseId);
 public abstract double getFee();
 public abstract void setFee(double fee);
 /* get and set methods for relationship fields */
 public abstract OrderLocal getOrder();
 public abstract void setOrder(OrderLocal order);
 /* Callback methods */
 public void setEntityContext(EntityContext ctx) {
    this.ctx = ctx;
 }
 public void unsetEntityContext() {
    this.ctx = null;
 }
 public void ejbActivate() {}
 public void ejbPassivate() {}
 public void ejbStore() {}
 public void ejbLoad() {}
 public String ejbCreate(String orderLineItemId, String courseId,
              double fee) throws CreateException {
    setOrderLineItemId(orderLineItemId);
    setCourseId(courseId);
    setFee(fee);
    print("Creating OrderLineItem id:" + orderLineItemId );
    return null;
 }
 public void ejbPostCreate(String orderLineItemId, String  courseId,
                    double fee) throws CreateException {}
 public void ejbRemove() {
    print("Removing OrderLineItem id:" + (String)ctx.getPrimaryKey() );
```

12

LISTING **12.8**    continued

```
  }
  void print(String s) {
    System.out.println(s);
  }
}
```

The `OrderLineItemEJB` entity bean implements the `javax.ejb.EntityBean` interface and is defined as an abstract class. It consists of abstract accessor methods for the persistent fields `orderLineItemId`, `courseId`, and `fee`, and the container-managed persistent field, `order`. It implements the methods `setEntityContext()`, `unsetEntityContext()`, `ejbActivate()`, `ejbPassivate()`, `ejbLoad()`, `ejbStore()`, and `ejbRemove()` as defined in the `javax.ejb.EntityBean` interface. The `ejbCreate()` method initializes the entity bean instance by assigning the input arguments to the persistent fields. The `ejbCreate()` method returns `null`. The bean implements the `ejbPostCreate()` method that corresponds to the `ejbCreate()` method.

`ClientLineItem` is a value class that is used in the client view. Listing 12.9 shows the `ClientLineItem` class.

LISTING **12.9**    The Full Text of `day12/ClientLineItem.java`

```
package day12;
public class ClientLineItem implements java.io.Serializable {
   private String orderLineItemId;
   private String courseId;
   private double fee;
   public ClientLineItem(String orderLineItemId,
                    String courseId, double fee) {
     this.orderLineItemId = orderLineItemId;
     this.courseId = courseId;
     this.fee = fee;
   }
   public String getOrderLineItemId() {
     return orderLineItemId ;
   }
   public double getFee() {
     return fee;
   }
   public String getCourseId() {
     return courseId;
   }
}
```

# Declaring the Deployment Descriptors

EJB QL enables you to traverse entity bean relationships. In this section, we discuss how to declare collection members in EJB QL and then present the full listing of the deployment descriptors.

## Collection Member Declarations

In a one-to-many or a many-to-many relationship, the many side of the relationship consists of a collection of entity beans. You can declare a collection of values, in the FROM clause, using a collection member declaration. An identification variable of a collection member declaration is declared using the IN operator. For example, a finder method query to find all orders with pending line items can be written as follows:

```
SELECT DISTINCT OBJECT(o)
FROM Order AS o, IN(o.lineItems) as l
WHERE l.shipped = FALSE
```

In the preceding example, lineItems represents a collection of instances. In the FROM clause declaration IN(o.lineItems) l, the identification variable l evaluates to any LineItem value directly reachable from Order. This query navigates over the cmr-field lineItems (of the abstract schema type Order) to find line items, and uses the cmp-field shipped (of lineItem) to select those orders that have at least one line item that has not yet shipped. Note that this query does not select orders that have no line items. To find all orders with no associated line items, you can use the following query:

```
SELECT DISTINCT OBJECT(o)
FROM Order AS o
WHERE o.lineItems IS EMPTY
```

You can test whether a particular value is a member of the collection by using the MEMBER OF comparison operator as follows:

```
SELECT OBJECT(l)
FROM ORDER o, LineItem l
WHERE l MEMBER of o.lineItems
```

The preceding query finds all the line items that are attached to orders. In other words, it does not select line items that are not attached to any order.

## Declaring the Standard Deployment Descriptor
### ejb-jar.xml

Now let's examine the ejb-jar.xml deployment descriptor shown in Listing 12.10. The ejb-jar.xml declares OrderEJB as the name of the order entity bean and specifies the home interface, remote interface, local home interface, local interface, and bean class. It

**12**

declares the Order abstract persistent schema and declares that orderId is the primary
key using the primkey-field element. Similarly, the deployment descriptor declares
OrderLineItemEJB as the name of the order line item entity bean and specifies the home
interface, remote interface, local home interface, local interface, and bean class. It
declares the Order abstract persistent schema and declares that orderId is the primary
key using the primkey-field element.

**LISTING 12.10**    The Full Text of day12/ejb-jar.xml

```xml
<?xml version="1.0"?>
<!DOCTYPE ejb-jar PUBLIC
'-//Sun Microsystems, Inc.//DTD Enterprise JavaBeans 2.0//EN'
'http://java.sun.com/dtd/ejb-jar_2_0.dtd'>
<ejb-jar>
  <enterprise-beans>
    <entity>
      <ejb-name>OrderEJB</ejb-name>
      <home>day12.OrderHome</home>
      <remote>day12.Order</remote>
      <local-home>day12.OrderLocalHome</local-home>
      <local>day12.OrderLocal</local>
      <ejb-class>day12.OrderEJB</ejb-class>
      <persistence-type>Container</persistence-type>
      <prim-key-class>java.lang.String</prim-key-class>
      <reentrant>False</reentrant>
      <cmp-version>2.x</cmp-version>
      <abstract-schema-name>Order</abstract-schema-name>
      <cmp-field>
        <field-name>orderId</field-name>
      </cmp-field>
      <cmp-field>
        <field-name>studentId</field-name>
      </cmp-field>
      <cmp-field>
        <field-name>orderDate</field-name>
      </cmp-field>
      <cmp-field>
        <field-name>status</field-name>
      </cmp-field>
      <cmp-field>
        <field-name>amount</field-name>
      </cmp-field>
      <primkey-field>orderId</primkey-field>
    </entity>
    <entity>
      <ejb-name>OrderLineItemEJB</ejb-name>
      <local-home>day12.OrderLineItemLocalHome</local-home>
```

**LISTING 12.10**   continued

```
        <local>day12.OrderLineItemLocal</local>
        <ejb-class>day12.OrderLineItemEJB</ejb-class>
        <persistence-type>Container</persistence-type>
        <prim-key-class>java.lang.String</prim-key-class>
        <reentrant>False</reentrant>
        <cmp-version>2.x</cmp-version>
        <abstract-schema-name>OrderLineitem</abstract-schema-name>
        <cmp-field>
          <field-name>orderLineItemId</field-name>
        </cmp-field>
        <cmp-field>
          <field-name>courseId</field-name>
        </cmp-field>
        <cmp-field>
          <field-name>fee</field-name>
        </cmp-field>
        <primkey-field>orderLineItemId</primkey-field>
      </entity>
    </enterprise-beans>
    <relationships>
      <ejb-relation>
        <ejb-relation-name>Order-LineItems</ejb-relation-name>
          <ejb-relationship-role>
<ejb-relationship-role-name>Order-has-lineitems</ejb-relationship-role-name>
            <multiplicity>One</multiplicity>
            <relationship-role-source>
              <ejb-name>OrderEJB</ejb-name>
            </relationship-role-source>
            <cmr-field>
              <cmr-field-name>lineItems</cmr-field-name>
              <cmr-field-type>java.util.Collection</cmr-field-type>
            </cmr-field>
          </ejb-relationship-role>
          <ejb-relationship-role>
<ejb-relationship-role-name>lineItem-belongsto-Order
➥</ejb-relationship-role-name>
            <multiplicity>Many</multiplicity>
            <cascade-delete/>
            <relationship-role-source>
              <ejb-name>OrderLineItemEJB</ejb-name>
            </relationship-role-source>
            <cmr-field>
              <cmr-field-name>order</cmr-field-name>
            </cmr-field>
          </ejb-relationship-role>
        </ejb-relation>
    </relationships>
  </ejb-jar>
```

12

The deployment descriptor also declares a relationship using ejb-relation. The deployment descriptor declares the Order-LineItems relation using ejb-relation-name. The order side of the relationship declares the Order-has-lineitems role name with cardinality of One. It also declares OrderEJB as the EJB name using the ejb-name element in the relationship-role-source element. It specifies the container-managed relationship field lineItems using the cmp-field-name element in the cmp-field element. Similarly, the deployment descriptor also contains the line items' side of the relationship.

Because a line item object should exist only when the parent order exists, you want to ensure that when you delete an order, you also cascade delete all the line items that belong to the order. This is declared using the cascade-delete element on the line item side of the relationship.

**Note**

The cascade-delete element is used within a particular relationship to specify that the lifetime of one or more entity beans is dependent on the lifetime of another entity object. cascade-delete can be specified only for one-to-one and one-to-many relationships.

Let's examine how this works with an example. As shown in Figure 12.6, entity instances a and b are related. Instance b is composed of instance c and instance d is composed of c. Assume that the cascade-delete option was specified for composition relationships. When the remove method is called on an entity bean instance b, the EJB container performs the following:

1. Calls the ejbRemove() method on instance b.

2. Removes entity object b from all relationships, with instance a and instance c, in which it participates.

3. Removes entity object b from the persistent store.

4. If the cascade-delete element is specified for a related entity bean, removal is cascaded and any related entity bean instances are also removed. So, the container removes instance c, which in turn triggers the removal of instance d.

**FIGURE 12.6**

*Example of* cascade-delete.

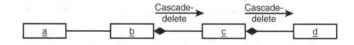

## Declaring the Vendor-Specific Deployment Descriptors

In this section, we'll examine the additional deployment descriptors that are specific to WebLogic Server and JBoss. Each server needs a couple of deployment descriptors.

In the case of WebLogic Server, you need to write the deployment descriptors `weblogic-ejb-jar.xml` and `weblogic-cmp-rdbms-jar.xml`. Listing 12.11 shows the `weblogic-ejb-jar.xml` deployment. It specifies the JNDI names of the `OrderEJB` entity bean's remote home interface using the `jndi-name` element and local home interface using `local-jndi-name`. The `type-storage` element specifies the full path (`META-INF/weblogic-cmp-rdbms-jar.xml`) of the file that stores the data of this persistence type. This file is stored in the `META-INF` subdirectory of the JAR file. Similarly, the elements `local-jndi-name` and so on are specified for the `OrderLineItemEJB` entity bean.

**LISTING 12.11**   The Full Text of `day12/weblogic-ejb-jar.xml`

```xml
<?xml version="1.0"?>
<!DOCTYPE weblogic-ejb-jar PUBLIC
'-//BEA Systems, Inc.//DTD WebLogic 7.0.0 EJB//EN'
'http://www.bea.com/servers/wls700/dtd/weblogic-ejb-jar.dtd'>
<weblogic-ejb-jar>
  <weblogic-enterprise-bean>
    <ejb-name>OrderEJB</ejb-name>
    <entity-descriptor>
      <persistence>
        <persistence-use>
          <type-identifier>WebLogic_CMP_RDBMS</type-identifier>
          <type-version>6.0</type-version>
          <type-storage>META-INF/weblogic-cmp-rdbms-jar.xml</type-storage>
        </persistence-use>
      </persistence>
    </entity-descriptor>
    <jndi-name>day12/Order</jndi-name>
    <local-jndi-name>day12/OrderLocal</local-jndi-name>
  </weblogic-enterprise-bean>
  <weblogic-enterprise-bean>
    <ejb-name>OrderLineItemEJB</ejb-name>
    <entity-descriptor>
      <persistence>
        <persistence-use>
          <type-identifier>WebLogic_CMP_RDBMS</type-identifier>
          <type-version>6.0</type-version>
          <type-storage>META-INF/weblogic-cmp-rdbms-jar.xml</type-storage>
        </persistence-use>
      </persistence>
    </entity-descriptor>
    <local-jndi-name>day12/OrderLineItemLocal</local-jndi-name>
  </weblogic-enterprise-bean>
</weblogic-ejb-jar>
```

**12**

Listing 12.12 shows the `weblogic-cmp-rdbms-jar.xml`. It contains the WebLogic Server–specific deployment descriptors that define container-managed persistence services. It specifies the abstract-schema-to-database-element mapping for both `OrderEJB` and `OrderLineItemEJB` (the mapping for `OrderLineItemEJB` is not shown in the listing). This file also specifies the relationship that is managed by WebLogic using the `weblogic-rdbms-relation` element. This element specifies the mapping from the `order_id` foreign key column in `OrderLineItemEJB` to the `order_id` primary key column of `OrderEJB`.

**LISTING 12.12**    The Text of `day12/weblogic-cmp-rdbms-jar.xml`

```
<!DOCTYPE weblogic-rdbms-jar PUBLIC
 '-//BEA Systems, Inc.//DTD WebLogic 7.0.0 EJB RDBMS Persistence//EN'
 'http://www.bea.com/servers/wls700/dtd/weblogic-rdbms20-persistence-700.dtd'>
<weblogic-rdbms-jar>
  <weblogic-rdbms-bean>
    <ejb-name>OrderEJB</ejb-name>
    <data-source-name>jdbc/styejbDB</data-source-name>
    <table-map>
    <table-name>orders</table-name>
    <field-map>
      <cmp-field>orderId</cmp-field>
      <dbms-column>order_id</dbms-column>
    </field-map>
    <field-map>
      <cmp-field>studentId</cmp-field>
      <dbms-column>student_id</dbms-column>
    </field-map>
    <field-map>
      <cmp-field>orderDate</cmp-field>
      <dbms-column>order_date</dbms-column>
    </field-map>
    <field-map>
      <cmp-field>status</cmp-field>
      <dbms-column>status</dbms-column>
    </field-map>
    <field-map>
      <cmp-field>amount</cmp-field>
      <dbms-column>amount</dbms-column>
    </field-map>
   </table-map>
  </weblogic-rdbms-bean>
  <weblogic-rdbms-bean>
    <ejb-name>OrderLineItemEJB</ejb-name>
    . . .
  </weblogic-rdbms-bean>
  <weblogic-rdbms-relation>
    <relation-name>Order-LineItems</relation-name>
      <weblogic-relationship-role>
        <relationship-role-name>
```

**LISTING 12.12**   continued

```
            lineItem-belongsto-Order
        </relationship-role-name>
        <relationship-role-map>
        <column-map>
            <foreign-key-column>order_id</foreign-key-column>
            <key-column> order_id </key-column>
        </column-map>
        </relationship-role-map>
        <db-cascade-delete/>
    </weblogic-relationship-role>
  </weblogic-rdbms-relation>
</weblogic-rdbms-jar>
```

In the case of JBoss, you need to write the deployment descriptors jboss.xml and jbosscmp-jdbc.xml. Listing 12.13 shows the deployment descriptor jboss.xml. It specifies the JNDI names of the OrderEJB entity beanís remote home interface using jndi-name element, and local home interface using local-jndi-name. Also, it specifies the JNDI names of the OrderLineItemEJB entity bean's remote home interface using jndi-name.

**LISTING 12.13**   The Full Text of day12/jboss.xml

```
<?xml version="1.0" encoding="UTF-8"?>
 <jboss>
  <enterprise-beans>
    <entity>
      <ejb-name>OrderEJB</ejb-name>
      <jndi-name>day12/Order</jndi-name>
      <local-jndi-name>day12/OrderLocal</local-jndi-name>
    </entity>
    <entity>
      <ejb-name>OrderLineItemEJB</ejb-name>
      <local-jndi-name>day12/OrderLineItemLocal</local-jndi-name>
    </entity>
  </enterprise-beans>
</jboss>
```

**12**

Listing 12.14 shows the jbosscmp-jdbc.xml file. It contains the abstract-schema-to-database-element mapping for both OrderEJB and OrderLineItemEJB (the mapping for OrderLineItemEJB is not shown in the listing). This file also specifies the relationship that is managed by JBoss using the ejb-relation element. This element specifies the mapping from the order_id foreign key column in OrderLineItemEJB to the order_id primary key column of OrderEJB.

**LISTING 12.14**   The Full Text of day12/jbosscmp-jdbc.xml

```xml
<?xml version="1.0" encoding="UTF-8"?>
<!DOCTYPE jbosscmp-jdbc PUBLIC
    "-//JBoss//DTD JBOSSCMP-JDBC 3.0//EN"
    "http://www.jboss.org/j2ee/dtd/jbosscmp-jdbc_3_0.dtd">
<jbosscmp-jdbc>
    <defaults>
        <datasource>java:/DefaultDS</datasource>
        <datasource-mapping>Hypersonic SQL</datasource-mapping>
        <create-table>false</create-table>
        <remove-table>false</remove-table>
        <pk-constraint>true</pk-constraint>
        <preferred-relation-mapping>foreign-key</preferred-relation-mapping>
    </defaults>
    <enterprise-beans>
        <entity>
            <ejb-name>OrderEJB</ejb-name>
            <table-name>orders</table-name>
            <cmp-field>
                <field-name>orderId</field-name>
                <column-name>order_id</column-name>
            </cmp-field>
            <cmp-field>
                <field-name>studentId</field-name>
                <column-name>student_id</column-name>
            </cmp-field>
            <cmp-field>
                <field-name>orderDate</field-name>
                <column-name>order_date</column-name>
            </cmp-field>
            <cmp-field>
                <field-name>status</field-name>
                <column-name>status</column-name>
            </cmp-field>
            <cmp-field>
                <field-name>amount</field-name>
                <column-name>amount</column-name>
            </cmp-field>
        </entity>
        <entity>
            <ejb-name>OrderLineItemEJB</ejb-name>
            . . .
    </enterprise-beans>
    <relationships>
        <ejb-relation>
            <ejb-relation-name>Order-LineItems</ejb-relation-name>
            <foreign-key-mapping/>
            <ejb-relationship-role>
```

**LISTING 12.14** continued

```
<ejb-relationship-role-name>Order-has-lineitems</ejb-relationship-role-name>
        <key-fields>
          <key-field>
            <field-name>orderId</field-name>
            <column-name>order_id</column-name>
          </key-field>
        </key-fields>
      </ejb-relationship-role>
      <ejb-relationship-role>
<ejb-relationship-role-name>lineItem-belongsto-Order
➥</ejb-relationship-role-name>
        <key-fields/>
      </ejb-relationship-role>
    </ejb-relation>
  </relationships>
</jbosscmp-jdbc>
```

# Writing a Client

Listing 12.15 shows a client that is used to test the order-line item relationship.

**LISTING 12.15** The Full Text of day12/Client.java

```
package day12;
import java.util.*;
import javax.naming.*;
import javax.ejb.*;
public class Client {
public static void main(String[] args) {
    print("Starting Client . . .\n");
    Context initialContext = null;
    OrderHome orderHome = null;
    Order order = null;
    try {
        print("Looking up the order home via JNDI.\n");
        initialContext = new InitialContext();
        Object object = initialContext.lookup("day12/Order");
        orderHome = (OrderHome)
         javax.rmi.PortableRemoteObject.narrow(object,OrderHome.class);
        object = (Order)orderHome.create("1", "Submitted", 100);
        order = (Order)
         javax.rmi.PortableRemoteObject.narrow(object,Order.class);
        String orderId = order.getOrderId();
        print("Created a new order:" + orderId + " .\n");
```

12

LISTING 12.15   continued

```
        print("Adding some line items to the order.\n");
        order.addLineItem("1", 200);
        order.addLineItem("2", 300);
        order.addLineItem("3", 300);
        print("Retrieving line items of the order.\n");
        Collection collection = order.getOrderLineItems();
        Iterator it = collection.iterator();
        while (it.hasNext()) {
      ClientLineItem item =(ClientLineItem)javax.rmi.PortableRemoteObject.narrow
                  (it.next(), ClientLineItem.class);
          print("Item id:" + item.getOrderLineItemId() +
                " Course id:" + item.getCourseId() +
                " Fee:" + item.getFee()
            );
        }
        print("Removing order:" + orderId + " .\n");
        order.remove();
      } catch ( Exception e) {
        e.printStackTrace();
      }
    }
    static void print(String s) {
      System.out.println(s);
    }
  }
```

The client locates the OrderHome home interface of the deployed enterprise bean via
JNDI. The client uses the remote home interface to create an Order entity object. The
client adds three line items to the order using the addLineItem() method and then
retrieves the orders using the getOrderLineItems() method of the Order interface. The
client finally removes the order. Because the cascade-delete element is specified on the
line items' side of the Order-LineItems relationship, this should trigger the removal of
line items that are attached to the order.

# Packaging and Deploying the Enterprise Beans

This section describes the steps to package and deploy the entity beans and also build the
client for both WebLogic Server and JBoss application servers.

You can run the following commands for WebLogic Server:

```
C:\>cd styejb\examples
```

```
C:\styejb\examples>setEnvWebLogic.bat
```

```
C:\styejb\examples>cd day12
```

```
C:\styejb\examples\day12>buildWebLogic.bat
```

You can run the following commands for JBoss:

```
C:\>cd styejb\examples
```

```
C:\styejb\examples>setEnvJboss.bat
```

```
C:\styejb\examples>cd day12
```

```
C:\styejb\examples\day11>buildJboss.bat
```

# Running the Example

The following steps describe how to start the PointBase database server and WebLogic Server, and run the sample client:

1. Start PointBase server in a new command window as follows:
   ```
   C:\>cd styejb\examples
   C:\styejb\examples>setEnvWebLogic.bat
   C:\styejb\examples>startPointBase.bat
   ```

2. Start WebLogic Server in a new command window as follows:
   ```
   C:\>cd styejb\examples
   C:\styejb\examples>setEnvWebLogic.bat
   C:\styejb\examples>startWebLogic.bat
   ```

3. You can run the client in the same window you used to package the beans and build the client, using the following command:

   ```
   C:\styejb\examples\day12> runClientWebLogic.bat
   ```

The following steps describe how to start the JBoss server and run the sample client:

1. Start the JBoss server in a new command window as follows:
   ```
   C:\>cd styejb\examples
   C:\styejb\examples>setEnvJBoss.bat
   C:\styejb\examples>startJBoss.bat
   ```

   The JBoss server automatically starts the default HyperSonic database. So, there is no separate step for it.

**12**

2.  You can run the client in the same window you used to package the beans and
    build the client by using the following command:

    ```
    C:\styejb\examples\day12>runClientJBoss.bat
    ```

Running the client produces the following client-side output similar to the following:

```
Starting Client . . .
Looking up the order home via JNDI.
Created a new order:1028476929797 .
Adding some line items to the order.
Retrieving line items of the order.
Item id:1028476929918 Course id:1 Fee:200.0
Item id:1028476929958 Course id:2 Fee:300.0
Item id:1028476929988 Course id:3 Fee:300.0
Removing order:1028476929797 .
```

The corresponding output on the server side is as follows:

```
09:02:09,797 INFO   [STDOUT] Creating Order id:1028476929797
09:02:09,918 INFO   [STDOUT] Creating OrderLineItem id:1028476929918
09:02:09,958 INFO   [STDOUT] Creating OrderLineItem id:1028476929958
09:02:09,988 INFO   [STDOUT] Creating OrderLineItem id:1028476929988
09:02:10,068 INFO   [STDOUT] Removing Order id:1028476929797
09:02:10,088 INFO   [STDOUT] Removing OrderLineItem id:1028476929958
09:02:10,098 INFO   [STDOUT] Removing OrderLineItem id:1028476929918
09:02:10,098 INFO   [STDOUT] Removing OrderLineItem id:1028476929988
```

Notice the cascade removal of line items corresponding to the removal of their parent
order.

# Best Practices

It is preferable to implement relationships between entity beans using container-managed
persistence as opposed to bean-managed persistence for the following reasons:

- The code is simpler to write. With BMP, you need to write code to manage relationships. With CMP, you need to declare how the relationships are managed in the
  deployment descriptor. The container generates all the relationship code.

- The container automatically handles referential integrity. For example, in a one-to-
  one relationship, if you change one side of the relationship, the container automatically drops the old relationship and replaces it with the newly formed one-to-one
  relationship.

- Containers typically provide performance optimizations, such as optimizing the
  SQL to load the entity bean and its relationships.

# Summary

The EJB container provides automatic management of both the persistent state of an entity bean and its relationships to other entity beans. An entity bean that is the target of a container-managed relationship must provide local interfaces. Container-managed relationships may be one-to-one, one-to-many, or many-to-many, and may be bidirectional or unidirectional.

Relationships are implemented as container-managed relationship fields. Similar to persistent fields, container-managed relationship fields are virtual fields that are defined and accessed by public abstract get and set accessor methods in the CMP entity bean class. The relationship fields are also declared in the deployment descriptor.

Container-managed relationships provide a cascade-delete facility that automatically enables the lifetime of the dependent object to be dependent on the lifetime of its parent.

# Q&A

**Q  What's the difference between a container-managed persistent field and container-managed relationship field?**

**A**  A persistent field is designed to represent or store a single unit of data. A relationship field is designed to represent or store a reference to another entity bean. Unlike a persistent field, a relationship field does not constitute the state of an entity bean.

**Q  How do I implement a container-managed relationship field in the entity bean class?**

**A**  Similar to container-managed persistent fields, container-managed relationship fields are not defined in the entity bean class and are virtual fields only. The entity bean class declares the public abstract get and set methods for each relationship field. The implementation of these methods is provided by the EJB container at deployment time.

12

# Quiz

1. A CMP entity bean that is the target of a container-managed relationship must implement which one of the following interfaces?

    A. Local interfaces

    B. Remote interfaces

    C.  Both local and remote interfaces

    D.  None of the above

2. Which of the following is a valid return type for a get method of a collection-valued container-managed relationship field?

    A.  Collection of entity bean's local interfaces

    B.  Collection of entity bean's remote interfaces

    C.  Collection of entity bean's home interfaces

    D.  Collection of entity bean's local home interfaces

3. Which of the following statements is true for container-managed relationship fields?

    A.  Container-managed relationship fields are virtual only.

    B.  The bean provider writes the implementation of container-managed persistent fields.

    C.  The accessor methods for container-managed persistent fields are exposed in the remote interface of the entity bean.

    D.  The accessor methods for container-managed persistent fields are exposed in the home interface of the entity bean.

## Quiz Answers

1. A

2. A

3. A

# Exercises

To extend your knowledge of the subjects covered today, try the following exercise:

Add the `deleteLineItem(String lineItemId)` method to the `OrderEJB` class and its remote and local interfaces. Also modify the client to use the newly added method. Finally, package and deploy the entity bean.

# WEEK 2

DAY **13**

# Understanding JMS and Message-Driven Beans

Today we'll explore the Java Message Service (JMS) and give a brief account of message-driven beans. JMS is the standard API used by J2EE applications to access Message-Oriented Middleware (MOM) services. *Messaging* is the ability of applications to interact and communicate with each other asynchronously. This is different from e-mail messaging, which takes place between humans. Message-driven applications are designed to accomplish loose coupling and portability. Each part of these enterprise applications can be developed as self-contained business components, and then can be integrated into a reliable yet flexible system. In general, messaging plays an important role in any large enterprise, and is usually a major part in integrating legacy systems with B2B and B2C applications.

Today's road map is to learn the main concepts and models of JMS, and to give an overview of message-driven beans, in particular:

- Learn about JMS architecture and its main objectives
- Study the API of both messaging models: point-to-point and publish/subscribe, and know when to use them

- Learn how to write a JMS client—either a message consumer or a message producer—in both messaging models
- Scratch the surface of message-driven beans, and learn how to use them as JMS consumers

# Learning the JMS Fundamentals

JMS provides a unified API for J2EE enterprise applications to create, send, receive, and process messages using any MOM products. These MOM products, also known as *JMS providers*, implement JMS API so that Java applications can use the JMS API (interfaces and classes) in a vendor-neutral manner. This allows applications to communicate with each other using messages through any JMS provider. Communications between applications occur in an *asynchronous* manner, which means that a sender sends a message and does not wait for the response, but continues the flow of execution. This is similar to sending an e-mail message, and you don't have to wait for a reply. The difference between JMS messages and e-mail messages is that JMS is used between applications, whereas e-mail is between users or humans.

 **Note**

> The term *messaging* is broadly defined in computing. It's used for describing various concepts in operating systems, e-mail systems, and fax systems. With JMS, it is used to describe asynchronous communication between enterprise applications.

Because messaging is peer-to-peer, all users of JMS are referred to as *JMS clients*. A JMS application consists of a set of application-defined messages and a set of JMS clients that exchange them. Each message consists of a header, which is used for routing purposes, and a body that holds the message content. Messages contain formatted data that describes specific business actions, and through the exchange of these messages, each application tracks the progress of the enterprise.

A *destination* is a logical channel that encapsulates the addresses of both the sending and receiving endpoints, like a queue or a topic. JMS providers either broadcast a message from a destination to many clients, or send a message to a single client. Similar to our local post office, a JMS provider optionally supports the guaranteed delivery of messages, but does not guarantee the order in which they are received. In many systems, such as financial applications, messages are required to be delivered once and only once. Messages can be delivered based on priority, expiration time, or whether acknowledgment is required.

# Understanding JMS Architecture

The JMS API is an abstraction of the interfaces and classes that JMS clients use to handle messages when in communication with a JMS provider. This is analogous to the use of JDBC as a unified API to access data sources, as you learned on Day 9, "Using JDBC to Connect to a Database," or JNDI to access naming and directory services, as you learned on Day 4, "Using JNDI for Naming Services and Components." JMS is not a messaging system by itself; it's an API to access an existing messaging system. The JMS architecture is best illustrated by Figure 13.1.

**FIGURE 13.1**

*JMS architecture.*

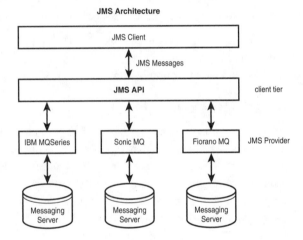

Figure 13.1 depicts all the layers that constitute JMS architecture, and the relationships between them. The following is a brief description of each layer, and the function it performs:

- JMS clients: Send and receive messages through a JMS provider.
- JMS messages: Applications define a set of messages that are used to communicate information between its clients.
- JMS API: Unified interfaces and classes to be used by all JMS clients.
- JMS provider: The messaging system (MOM) that implements JMS in addition to other administrative and control functionality required of a full-featured messaging product.
- Administered objects: Administered objects are pre-configured JMS objects created by the JMS provider's administrator for the use of clients. Administered objects are not shown in Figure 13.1.

13

JMS specification defines these architecture components to facilitate writing portable enterprise applications. It does not address certain operational functionality such as

- Clustering. JMS does not address load balancing or fail-over; support is left to the JMS provider.

- Security and administration. The JMS API does not provide control privacy and integrity of JMS messages. Security is considered to be a JMS provider-specific aspect.

- Error notification. MOM vendors (JMS providers) send proprietary notification messages to clients. JMS does not attempt to standardize these messages. Developers should be aware of these messages to avoid any portability issues.

A number of JMS providers offer products of varying JMS support. Some of these products are SonicMQ from Progress, FioranoMQ from Fiorano, WebLogic from BEA, MQSeries from IBM, and the open source JBossMQ from JBoss.

## Administered Objects

One of the objectives of the JMS architecture is writing portable and configurable applications. For JMS clients to be portable, they must be isolated from any proprietary aspects of JMS providers. This is done by defining JMS-administered objects. These objects are created and configured by a JMS provider's administrator and then registered in a JNDI namespace. Later, they are accessed by JMS clients through looking them up in the JNDI service. Administrators create these objects using a JMS provider-specific administrative tool.

There are two main two types of JMS administered objects:

- `ConnectionFactory`: The object a client uses to create a connection with a JMS provider.

- `Destination`: The object a client uses to specify the destination of messages it sends and the source of messages it receives.

Administered objects not only hide JMS provider-specific configuration details from JMS clients, but they also abstract JMS administrative information into Java objects that are easily organized and administered from a common management console.

**Tip**

As you learned in Day 4, it is recommended that you use the `java:comp/env/jms` environment as the standard context for JNDI namespace lookups of the JMS administered objects `ConnectionFactory` and `Destination`.

# Exploring Messaging Models

In general, there are two main types of messaging models: point-to-point (PTP) and publish-and-subscribe (Pub/Sub). JMS refers to these models as messaging *domains*. A single JMS application can use both models; however, JMS focuses on applications that use one or the other.

A JMS client that sends (or publishes) a message is called a *producer*, whereas a JMS client that receives (or subscribes) to a message is called a *consumer*.

## Point-to-Point Messaging Model

The PTP messaging model is intended for one-to-one delivery of messages, and is built around the concept of a message *queue*. Each message is sent to a specific queue; clients receive messages from the queue(s) established to hold their messages. They are point-to-point in the sense that a client sends a message to a specific queue. Receivers must either poll a queue periodically or listen to incoming events in order to extract their messages. Each message is consumed once and only once by a receiver. A message is automatically removed from the queue when it's consumed by a receiver. In PTP, a producer is called a *sender*, and a consumer is called a *receiver*. Figure 13.2 illustrates a few scenarios of PTP messaging.

As you can see in Figure 13.2, a queue might have more than one sender and more than one receiver, but only one receiver may consume each message. In the PTP model, a JMS client can choose to be a message *browser* that is allowed to peek into a message without consuming it.

## Publish-and-Subscribe Messaging Model

The Pub/Sub messaging model is intended for one-to-many broadcast of messages and is built around the concept of a message *topic*. Each message published to a topic is broadcast to all the clients that subscribe to this topic. A *Topic* object encapsulates a provider-specific topic name. It is the way a client specifies the identity of a topic to JMS methods. Many Pub/Sub providers group topics into hierarchies and provide various options for subscribing to parts of the hierarchy. This is similar to the concept of newsgroups, in which a user subscribes to the newsgroup topic of interest. Each consumer receives a copy of each message, which is pushed to the clients subscribed to it. In the Pub/Sub model, a producer is called a *publisher*, and a consumer is called a *subscriber*. Figure 13.3 illustrates a few scenarios of Pub/Sub messaging.

In the Pub/Sub model, a JMS client can choose to be a *durable subscriber* that can disconnect and later connect to get its messages that it subscribed to.

13

**FIGURE 13.2**

*Point-to-point messaging model.*

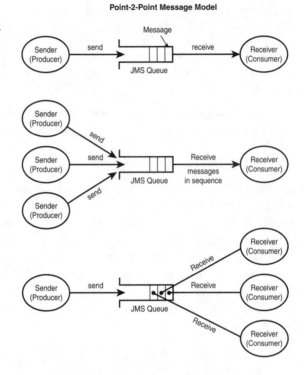

**FIGURE 13.3**

*Publish-and-subscribe messaging model.*

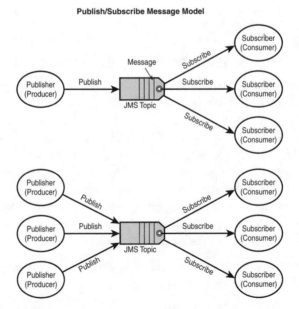

# Understanding JMS Interfaces and Classes

The main concepts of the JMS API (interfaces and classes) are included in the javax.jms package. JMS interfaces are based on a set of common messaging concepts. Both the PTP and the Pub/Sub JMS messaging models define a customized set of interfaces for these common (patent) concepts. Table 13.1 summarizes the JMS common interfaces for both the PTP model and Pub/Sub model interfaces.

**TABLE 13.1** Summary of PTP and Pub/Sub Interfaces

| JMS Parent Interface | PTP Specific | Pub/Sub Specific |
| --- | --- | --- |
| ConnectionFactory | QueueConnectionFactory | TopicConnectionFactory |
| Connection | QueueConnection | TopicConnection |
| Destination | Queue | Topic |
| Session | QueueSession | TopicSession |
| MessageProducer | QueueSender | TopicPublisher |
| MessageConsumer | QueueReceiver, QueueBrowser | TopicSubscriber |

Table 13.2 provides a brief definition of these JMS interfaces, and whether they support concurrent use.

**TABLE 13.2** Summary of Common Interfaces

| Interface | Description | Concurrent Use? |
| --- | --- | --- |
| ConnectionFactory | An administered object used by a client to create a Connection | Yes |
| Connection | An active connection to a JMS provider | Yes |
| Destination | An administered object that encapsulates the identity of a message destination | Yes |
| Session | A single-threaded context for sending and receiving messages | No |
| MessageProducer | An object created by a Session that is used for sending messages to a destination | No |
| MessageConsumer | An object created by a Session that is used for receiving messages sent to a destination | No |

13

To write a JMS client, you must first import the javax.jms package and then, depending on the JMS model you are using, work through the following outline of the basic steps

involved in developing a JMS client. The following steps replace the JMS parent interface with the appropriate interface of the messaging model you chose from those listed in
Table 13.1:

1. Import the `javax.jms` package

2. Look up the `ConnectionFactory` using the JNDI `Context`

3. Create a `Connection` from the `ConnectionFactory`

4. Create a `Session` from the `Connection` object

5. Look up the `Destination` using the same JNDI `Context`

6. Create a `MessageProducer` or a `MessageConsumer` using the `Session` object

7. Create a `Message` by choosing an appropriate JMS message type

8. Send/receive the `Message` after starting the `Connection`

 **Note**

> Remember that the administered objects `ConnectionFactory` and
> `Destination` are already created and registered into a JNDI namespace, as
> discussed earlier in the "Administered Objects" section.

The preceding steps are a generalized layout of the client code developed for any of the
JMS models. We stated the parent object, rather than the specific interface or class used
by a particular model. In the next section, you'll learn how to apply these steps for both
the PTP and Pub/Sub models.

**Caution**

> Not all JMS objects are multi-threaded. JMS imposes restrictions on the
> `Session` object to be single-threaded. This means that a JMS provider must
> serialize messages delivered to all consumers created from the `Session`
> object. A `Connection` object can be shared by many `Sessions` because it's
> multi-threaded.

Figure 13.4 summarizes the main interfaces of the JMS API. Developing a JMS client
depends on which JMS model you are using (either PTP or Pub/Sub), and on the client
type (either producer or consumer).

**Figure 13.4**

*JMS main interfaces.*

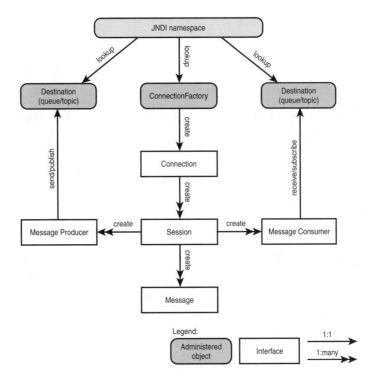

## Point-to-Point Concepts

Point-to-point concepts are about working with queues of messages. The main objects of the PTP API are the administered objects: the `QueueConnectionFactory` and `Queue` interfaces, which act as factories for creating other objects. The JMS PTP model defines how a client works with queues: how it finds them, how it sends messages to them, and how it receives messages from them. The following are the main steps in developing JMS PTP messaging clients:

1. Look up a `QueueConnectionFactory` in the JNDI namespace.

2. Create a `QueueConnection`.

3. Look up a message queue.

4. Create a `QueueSession`.

**13**

5. Create a QueueSender, QueueReceiver, or QueueBrowser.

6. Start sending, receiving, or browsing messages.

7. Close the connection.

We discuss these steps in more detail in the following sections.

## Step 1: Look Up a `QueueConnectionFactory` in the JNDI Namespace

A connection factory contains information about the JMS provider, the host, and the port that the server is listening to. It is created and configured by an administrator, and the client looks it up in the JNDI namespace. *We assume that a QueueConnectionFactory named qcFactory has been created for our use.*

**Note** You will learn how to configure these JMS administered objects on Day 14, "Developing Message-Driven Beans," for both WebLogic and JBoss, when you study message-driven beans.

```
import javax.naming.*;
import javax.jms.*;
// Establish a JNDI context
Context ctx = new InitialContext();
// Lookup the administered object qcFactory in the JNDI service
QueueConnectionFactory qcf = (QueueConnectionFactory)
        ctx.lookup("java:comp/env/jms/qcFactory");
```

## Step 2: Create a `QueueConnection`

After obtaining a QueueConnectionFactory, use it to create a QueueConnection. This creates an active connection to the JMS provider with the default security credentials for the JMS client.

```
QueueConnection qConn = qcf.createQueueConnection();
```

Alternatively, you can also create a connection using a user with a password:

```
String user = "john";
String password = "1234";
QueueConnection qConn = qcf.createQueueConnection(user, password);
```

## Step 3: Look Up a Message Queue

An administrator has created, configured, and registered a queue named myQueue in the JNDI for your use. Again, use JNDI to look it up:

```
Queue q = (Queue) ctx.lookup("java:comp/env/jms/myQueue");
```

### Step 4: Create a `QueueSession`

Use the `QueueConnection` to create one or more `QueueSession` objects, which will be used to create a `QueueSender` (if you want to `send()` messages) or a `QueueReceiver` (if you want to `receive()` messages):

```
QueueSession qSession = qConn.createQueueSession(false,
          Session.AUTO_ACKNOWLEDGE);
```

The first parameter of the `createQueueSession()` method is a `Boolean` that indicates whether this session will begin a local transaction (called a *transacted session*). In this example, no transaction started. The second parameter indicates the mode of acknowledging message receipt. Message acknowledgement is discussed later today.

**Note**

> A `QueueConnection` can be used to create more than one `QueueSession`. Each of these sessions is used in producing or consuming messages, and it can be transacted or not.

### Step 5: Create a `QueueSender`, `QueueReceiver`, or `QueueBrowser`

Three options are available to a JMS client: to become a sender, a receiver, or a browser for a queue.

**Step 5.1: Create a `QueueSender`**  If you will be sending messages to the `Queue`, use the `QueueSession` to create a `QueueSender`:

```
QueueSender sender = qSession.createSender(q);
```

**Step 5.2: Create a `QueueReceiver`**  Similarly, if you will be receiving messages from the queue, use the `QueueSession` to create a `QueueReceiver`. After a message is received and acknowledged, it will be removed automatically from the queue.

```
QueueReceiver receiver = qSession.createReceiver(q);
```

**Note**

> If messages have been received but not acknowledged when a `QueueSession` terminates, they are retained and redelivered by the JMS provider when a consumer next accesses the queue.

**13**

### Step 5.3: Create a `QueueBrowser`

If you need to look at pending messages in the queue without consuming them, use the
`QueueSession` to create a `QueueBrowser`. Queue browsing is useful for looking into
queue messages from monitoring tools.

```
QueueBrowser qBrowser = qSession.createBrowser(q);
```

 **Note**    The `QueueBrowser` feature is unique to the PTP model.

## Step 6: Start Delivering Messages

All previous steps are just to set up the connection to the appropriate queues.

**Step 6.1: Sending Messages**    Before sending a message, a `Message` object must be
created and populated with its content:

```
TextMessage msg = qSession.createTextMessage();
msg.setText("Hello World");
sender.send(msg);
```

**Step 6.2: Receiving Messages**    You must start the connection before receiving messages. It is implicitly started for either sending or browsing a queue.

```
qConn.start()
```

Receiving messages can be synchronous or asynchronous. In receiving synchronous messages, a JMS consumer uses the `receive()` method, which will be blocked indefinitely
until a message arrives on the destination. On the other hand, asynchronous messages are
received by using the `onMessage()` method of the `MessageListener`, where messages are
pushed by the container and processed by the consumer.

The `receive()` method is used in synchronous receivers. JMS offers two more variants:
`receiveNoWait()`, which is used for polling messages, and `receive(long timeout)`,
which will wait for the timeout period before returning.

```
TextMessage msg = (TextMessage)receiver.receive();
System.out.println(msg.getText());
```

To receive messages asynchronously, you can use either message-driven beans or
`MessageListener`. First, you need to register your message listener with the receiver by
using the `setMessageListener()` method:

```
receiver.setMessageListener(this);
```

We assume that our current JMS receiver implements the `MessageListener` interface. Now, implement the `onMessage()` method to listen to the incoming messages:

```
public void onMessage(Message message) {
 // unpack and process the messages received
}
```

**Note**

Some clients are designed with a message-based application triggering mechanism. The trigger is typically a threshold of waiting messages. JMS does not provide a mechanism for triggering the execution of a client. Some providers might support such a triggering mechanism via their administrative facilities.

A `Connection` also can be stopped using the `stop()` method and closed using the `close()` method.

**Step 6.3: Browsing Messages**    Browsing messages returns a `java.util.Enumeration` that is used to scan the queue's messages. It may be an enumeration of the entire content of a queue, or it may contain only the messages matching a message selector.

```
for (Enumeration msgList = qBrowser.getEnumeration();
        msgList.hasMoreElements(); ) {
        System.out.println(mmsList.nextElement());
}
```

## Step 7: Close the Connection

After all sending or receiving activities are finished, remember to close the `Connection` object before ending the client:

```
QConn.close();
```

## Publish-and-Subscribe Concepts

13

Publish-and-subscribe systems are about working with topics of messages. The main object of the Pub/Sub API is the `Topic` interface. It is common for a client to have all its messages broadcast to a single topic. Topics are created administratively and are treated as named objects by their clients. The JMS Pub/Sub model defines how a client works with topics: how it finds them, how it publishes messages to them, and how it subscribes to them to extract their messages. JMS also supports durable subscribers that remember the existence of topics while they are inactive.

The steps in developing a JMS Pub/Sub messaging client are similar to those in developing a JMS PTP client.

## Step 1: Look Up a `TopicConnectionFactory` in the JNDI Namespace

A `TopicConnectionFactory` named `tcFactory` has been registered in the JNDI namespace. Both publisher and subscriber programs must access a `tcFactory` in order to create a `Connection`.

```
import javax.naming.*;
import javax.jms.*;

// Establish a JNDI context
Context ctx = new InitialContext();
TopicConnectionFactory tcf = (TopicConnectionFactory)
        ctx.lookup("java:comp/env/jms/tcFactory");
```

## Step 2: Create a `TopicConnection` from `TopicConnectionFactory`

```
TopicConnection tConn = tcf.createTopicConnection();
```

You also can create a connection using a user and password:

```
String user = "john";
String password = "1234";
TopicConnection tConn = tcf.createTopicConnection(user, password);
```

## Step 3: Look Up a Message Topic

An administered object `myTopic` has been created, configured, and registered in the JNDI namespace:

```
Topic t = (Topic) ctx.lookup("java:comp/env/jms/myTopic");
```

## Step 4: Create a `TopicSession`

Use the `TopicConnection` to create one or more `TopicSession` objects, which will be used to create a `TopicPublisher` (if you want to `publish()` messages) or a `TopicSubscriber` (if you want to `subscribe()` to messages):

```
TopicSession tSession = tConn.createTopicSession(false,
            Session.CLIENT_ACKNOWLEDGE);
```

## Step 5: Create a `TopicPublisher` or `TopicSubscriber`

Three types of options are available to a JMS client: to become a `TopicPublisher`, a `TopicSubscriber`, or a durable subscriber.

**Step 5.1: Create a `TopicPublisher`**   `TopicPublisher publisher =`
`➥qSession.createPublisher (t);`

**Step 5.2: Create a `TopicSubscriber`**   `TopicSubscriber subscriber =`
➥`tSession.createSubscriber(t);`

**Step 5.3: Create a Durable Subscriber**   An ordinary subscriber is not durable, and its session lasts for its lifetime. A *durable subscriber* registers with a unique identity that is retained by the JMS provider. A subsequent subscriber with the same identity resumes the subscription in the state it was left before. If there is no active subscriber for a durable subscription, JMS retains the subscription's messages until they are received by the subscription or until they expire. Use the following to create a durable subscriber:

```
String durSubID = "Sub300";
TopicSubscriber dSubscriber = tSession.createDurableSubscriber(t, durSubID);
```

The preceding statement is used as many times as the durable subscribers need to connect to the JMS system to get their messages.

## Step 6: Start Delivering Messages

All previous steps are just to set up the connection to the appropriate topic.

**Step 6.1: Publishing a Message**   Before publishing a message, a `Message` object must be created and populated with its content:

```
TextMessage msg = tSession.createTextMessage();
msg.setText("Hello World");
publisher.publish(msg);
```

**Step 6.2: Subscribing to a Message**   You must start the `TopicConnection` before subscribing to messages. This is implicitly started when publishing to a topic. A durable subscriber becomes active when the connection is started.

```
tConn.start()
```

The `receive()` method is used in synchronous receivers:

```
TextMessage msg = (TextMessage)receiver.receive();
System.out.printline(msg.getText());
```

To receive messages asynchronously, use the following:

```
subscriber.setMessageListener(this);

  public void onMessage(Message message) {
  // unpack and process the messages received
  }
```

13

A more convenient way of implementing a JMS consumer to handle asynchronous messages is to use a message-driven bean, which will be discussed later today, and is the subject of Day 14.

**Step 6.3: Durable Subscription to a Message**   Durable subscribers are treated the same way as non-durable subscribers. You might want to close the durable subscriber:

```
dSubscriber.close();
```

To delete a durable subscription, first you close the subscriber, and then use the unsubscribe() method with the subscription name as the argument:

```
dSubscriber.close();
tSession.unsubscribe(durSubID);
```

## Step 7: Close the Connection

When all sending and receiving activities are complete, remember to close the connection before ending the client:

```
try {
   // do some stuff with JMS connection, and send/receive messages
     } catch (JMSException e) {
           System.out.println("Exception occurred: " +
               e.toString());
        } finally {
           if (tConn != null) {
               try {
                   tCon.close();
               } catch (JMSException e) {}
           }
        }
```

# Exception Handling

JMS defines JMSException as the root class for exceptions thrown by JMS methods. JMSException must be handled in the catch clause of your JMS client. Information about errors can be obtained by the getErrorCode(), which returns a vendor-specific error. The method getMessage() returns a message that describes the error. The method setLinkedException() references another exception that is a result of a lower-level problem. If appropriate, this lower-level exception can be linked to the JMS exception.

## Synchronous and Asynchronous Message Receivers

In both JMS models, as discussed in the previous sections, receiving messages can be synchronous or asynchronous. In receiving synchronous messages, a JMS consumer uses the `receive()` method, which will be blocked indefinitely until a message arrives at the destination. On the other hand, asynchronous messages are received by using the `onMessage()` method of the `MessageListener`, where messages are pushed by the container and processed by the consumer.

# Designing Reliable Messaging Clients

JMS applications are loosely coupled components and modules that work together in a flexible manner. There are some design considerations that can enhance the reliability and the integrity of your JMS applications. The following sections discuss some of these:

- Message persistence to guarantee message delivery
- Acknowledgment, priority, and time-to-live
- Transaction support
- Temporary destination

## Specifying Message Persistence

JMS supports two delivery modes for messages: persistent and non-persistent. The persistent delivery mode, which is the default, is based on guaranteed delivery. The JMS provider will take extra care to ensure that a message is not lost in case of a JMS provider failure. A message sent with this delivery mode is logged to stable storage before it is sent.

On the other hand, the non-persistent delivery mode does not require the JMS provider to store the message to guarantee its delivery in case the provider fails.

You can specify the delivery mode in either of two ways:

- Using the `setDeliveryMode()` method of the `QueueSender` or the `TopicPublisher` object to set a delivery mode for all messages sent by that producer:

  `sender.setDeliveryMode(DeliveryMode.NON_PERSISTENT);`
- Using an argument to the `send()` or `publish()` method to set the delivery mode for a specific message. Here's an example that sets the delivery mode for published messages to NON_PERSISTENT:

  `publisher.publish(msg, DeliveryMode.NON_PERSISTENT);`

**13**

**Caution**

Using the NON_PERSISTENT delivery mode might improve performance and reduce storage overhead by the provider, but it provides no guarantee of delivering the messages.

Figure 13.5 illustrates persistent and non-persistent messages.

**FIGURE 13.5**

*Persistent and non-persistent messaging.*

JMS Message Structure

**Header**
- JMSDestination
- JMSDeliveryMode
- JMSExpiration
- JMSPriority
- JMSMessageID
- JMSTimestamp
- JMSCorrelationID
- JMSReplyTo
- JMSType
- JMSRedelivered

**Properties**
- Application-specific
- JMS-specific: JMSX???
- Provider-specific: JMS_???

**Body (Payload)**

## Message Acknowledgment, Priority, and Expiration

Another factor in designing a reliable JMS application is to control the acknowledgment, priority, and expiration date of messages.

Acknowledgment is initiated either by the JMS provider or by the JMS client, depending on the session acknowledgment mode. Establishing message acknowledgments enhances application reliability. When a JMS client receives a message, it processes the message and then acknowledges receiving it.

In transacted sessions, acknowledgment occurs automatically when a transaction is committed. In non-transacted sessions, message acknowledgment depends on the value specified as the second argument of the createQueueSession() or createTopicConnection() method. Here's an example of a non-transacted PTP session:

```
QueueSession qSession = qConn.createQueueSession(false,
        Session.AUTO_ACKNOWLEDGE, 3, 5000);
```

In the preceding example, the first parameter specifies a non-transacted session, and the second parameter specifies `Session.AUTO_ACKNOWLEDGE` to indicate the consumer's receipt of a message when the client has successfully returned from either the `receive()` or `onMessage()` method.

The other possible settings are

- `Session.CLIENT_ACKNOWLEDGE`: When a client acknowledges a consumed message, it automatically acknowledges the receipt of all messages that have been consumed by its session.

- `Session.DUPS_OK_ACKNOWLEDGE`: This type is known as *lazy acknowledgment*, and is performed by consumers that use duplicate messages. If the JMS provider redelivers a message, it must set the value of the `JMSRedelivered` message header to true.

Message priority level is specified by the third parameter of the same method. You also can set priority by using the `setPriority()` method of `QueueSender` or `TopicPublisher`. Message priority levels values are 0–9 (where 0 is the lowest priority). The default priority level for JMS is 4. A JMS provider tries to deliver higher-priority messages first, but does not have to deliver messages in the exact order of priority.

Message expiration time (also called *time to live* or *TTL*) is specified by the fourth parameter, and is set to five seconds. By default, a message never expires. You also can set the expiration time by using the `setTimeToLive()` method of `QueueSender` or `TopicPublisher`. A JMS provider will delete undelivered messages after its expiration time. This helps in optimizing storage and computing resources.

## Using Local Transactions

As you learned in Day 9, a local transaction belongs only to the current process, and deals with only a single resource manager. JMS handles both local and distributed transactions. Today we'll cover local transactions, but we defer JMS distributed transactions to Day 16, "Understanding Transactions," when you'll study the concepts of Java Transaction API (JTA).

JMS local transactions are managed by the `Session` object, and not by the EJB container. To change this implicit behavior, JMS provides the concept of the transacted session. A transacted session is created by setting the flag to true for the method `createQueueSession(true)` in PTP or `createTopicSession(true)` in Pub/Sub. The `commit()` and `rollback()` methods also are used by the `Session` object to control the transaction's behavior. An example of a local transaction in PTP is as follows:

```
QueueSession qSession = qConn.createQueueSession(true);
QueueSender sender = qSession.createSender(q);
```

**13**

```
TextMessage msg1 = qSession.createTextMessage();
msg.setText("Enrollment is successful.");
TextMessage msg2 = qSession.createTextMessage();
msg.setText("Regsiteration is approved.");
try{
   sender.send(msg1);
   sender.send(msg2);
   qSession.commit();
}catch (JMSException e){
    qSession.rollback();
}
```

Here both messages are sent to the JMS provider, but they will be delivered as a unit of work to the queue only when the commit() method is issued. Also, acknowledgment happens automatically when a transaction is committed.

 **Caution**    JMS local transactions have no explicit begin() method to start a transaction. Therefore, transactions are chained and depend upon commit() or
rollback() method calls. Transactional messages are accumulated at the
JMS server until the transaction is committed or rolled back, which has negative impact on the JMS server's performance.

## Working with Temporary Destinations

As you learned, JMS destinations are normally created as administered objects. JMS also enables you to create a temporary destination (TemporaryQueue and TemporaryTopic), which becomes active only during the session's connection. The JMS provider guaran-tees that the temporary destination is unique across all connections. You create these des-tinations dynamically using the createTemporaryQueue() and createTemporaryTopic() methods of the corresponding session object. The following is an example of creating a TemporaryQueue:

```
TemporaryQueue tempQ = qSession.createTemporaryQueue("myTempQueue");
```

Temporary destinations work in the same fashion as administered destinations.

**Caution**    If you close the connection that the temporary destination belongs to, the
destination is closed and its contents are lost.

When a producer and consumer agree to use a temporary destination, the producer first creates it, and then passes its reference to the consumer. This is accomplished by setting the JMSReplyTo message header field. At the other end, the consumer needs to extract the reference from the message header before using this destination.

# Anatomy of JMS Messages

JMS unifies the content format and structure among various messaging products. It also supports messages containing Java objects. In this regard, it's similar to RMI except that the Java objects are exchanged asynchronously. JMS supports messages containing XML data as well. As shown in Figure 13.6, all JMS messages are composed of the following parts:

- Header: All message types support the same set of header fields, which contain values used to identify and route messages.

- Properties (optional): These are optional header fields added to a message. These properties can be user-defined, JMS standard, or JMS provider-specific.

- Body (optional): This indicates the type of message content used. The message body is usually called the *payload*.

**FIGURE 13.6**

*JMS message structure.*

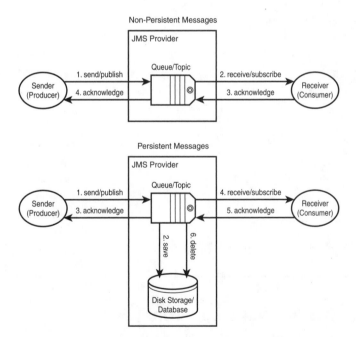

The following sections discuss each part of the message in more detail.

## Message Headers

The message headers are a predefined set of header fields used for routing by the JMS client and provider. Their names follow the pattern JMS<*HEADER*>. The getJMS<*HEADER*>() and setJMS<*HEADER*>() methods of the Message are used as "getter" and "setter" for the field value. Table 13.3 summarizes the header names and how they are set.

**TABLE 13.3**  Summary of JMS Headers

| Header Fields | Set By | Description |
| --- | --- | --- |
| JMSDestination | send() or publish() method | Includes the destination name to which the message is sent. |
| JMSDeliveryMode | send() or publish() method | The value is either persistent or non-persistent. Persistent messages are stored and then forwarded. |
| JMSExpiration | send() or publish() method | Defines the message's time to live. A zero value means the message never expires, which is the default. |
| JMSPriority | send() or publish() method | Specifies the priority level of messages. It has a value of 0–9, 9 is the highest, 4 is the default. |
| JMSMessageID | send() or publish() method | A string that uniquely identifies a message. It's generated by the JMS provider. |
| JMSTimestamp | send() or publish() method | A long value in milliseconds represents the time when the message arrived at the JMS server. |
| JMSCorrelationID | JMS client | An arbitrary string to group messages together; --to an order, for example. |
| JMSReplyTo | JMS client | Represents a JMS destination that the consumer uses to send a reply. |
| JMSType | JMS client | Associates the message to a message type. |
| JMSRedelivered | JMS provider | A flag is set to redeliver the message if the receiver fails to acknowledge. |

## Exploring Message Properties

In addition to the header fields, these optional headers are added to the message by the application developer, the JMS provider, or JMS optional headers. They provide additional information that enhances the flexibility of the JMS API. Properties allow a client, via message selectors (see the "Message Selection" section later today), to have a JMS provider select messages on its behalf using SQL-like criteria. Property values are set prior to sending a message, and cannot be changed by the client receiving it because the client is in read-only mode.

The following sections will shed light on the different types of message properties, and how to use the message selectors to filter only the messages you want to receive.

## User-Defined Properties

Application developers are free to define their message properties. User-defined properties can have any name. Properties are created as name/value pairs. The type of the property is used in the set/get method of the property. JMS provides these types to define application-specific properties: Boolean, Byte, Short, Integer, Long, Float, Double, String, and Object. Here is an example of defining the application property "password" as a String property:

```
TextMessage msg = (TextMessage) qSession.createTextMessage();
msg.setStringProperty("password", password);
sender.send(msg);
```

You can use the method clearProperties() to delete all the message's properties. The method getPropertyNames() returns an Enumeration with the names used in the message.

## JMS-Defined Properties

JMS defines optional headers that start with the prefix "JMSX". They are treated similarly to the user-defined properties mentioned earlier, but are handled by the JMS provider.

## JMS Provider-Specific Properties

JMS allows providers to define their own properties, and each property name must start with the prefix "JMS_<vendor_name>". This is the mechanism a JMS provider uses to make its proprietary message services available to a JMS client.

## Message Selection

Message selection allows clients to set criteria for receiving specific messages. This filtering mechanism enhances performance and adds more flexibility to the applications. This is done by putting the filtering criteria (called the *selector*) in the message header when creating the consumer. This allows the JMS provider to handle the filtering and routing that would otherwise need to be done by the application.

13

The following example defines a `filter` to deliver only messages that belong to the enrollment of `courses` "CS310" and "CS320" to the registration queue "csQueue":

```
String filter = new String("(course = 'CS310') OR (course = 'CS320')");
QueueReceiver receiver = qSession.createReceiver(csQueue, filter);
```

Similarly, for a Pub/Sub model, a subscriber can use the same filter:

```
TopicSubscriber subscriber = tSession.createSubscriber(csTopic, filter);
```

## Message Body

JMS defines six message types; each type depends on the body of the message. Table 13.4 lists the definition of each message type.

**TABLE 13.4**   JMS Message Body Types

| Message Type | Definition |
| --- | --- |
| StreamMessage | Message body contains a stream of Java primitive values. |
| MapMessage | Message body contains a set of name/value pairs in which the name is a `String` and its value is a Java primitive type. |
| TextMessage | Message body contains a `String`. This is the base message type for XML messages. This will likely become the mechanism for representing the content of JMS messages. |
| ObjectMessage | Message body contains a `Serializable` Java object. |
| BytesMessage | Message body contains a stream of uninterpreted bytes. This message type is for literally encoding a body to match an existing message format, such as a Unicode message. |
| Message | Message body contains nothing. Composed of header fields and properties only. This message type is useful when a message body is not required. |

Many JMS providers support the `XMLMessage` type, which extends the `TextMessage` and is not supported directly by JMS. XML is a natural fit into messaging, and adds powerful semantics to message contents.

A message body can be cleared by using the method `clearBody()`. Clearing a message's body does not clear its properties. When a message is received, its body is read-only; any attempt to change the body results in a `MessageNotWriteableException` being thrown.

Each message type must be unpacked to process its body information. Table 13.5 summarizes how to unpack each message type.

**TABLE 13.5**   Unpacking Message Body Types

| Message Type | How to Unpack |
| --- | --- |
| BytesMessage msg | `int length = msg.readBytes(studentInfo);` |
| TextMessage msg | `String name = msg.getText();` |
| MapMessage msg | `String course = msg.getString("Course");` |
| StreamMessage msg | `String name = msg.readString();` |
| ObjectMessage msg | `Student student = (Student) msg.getObject();` |

# Message-Driven Beans

A message-driven bean (MDB) is, by design, an asynchronous message consumer. The container invokes an MDB as the result of the arrival of a JMS message. An MDB has neither a home nor a remote interface, and consists of only the message bean class and a deployment descriptor. The bean class must implement both the `MessageDrivenBean` interface and the `MessageListener` interface. An MDB is container managed, and all configurable administered objects are specified declaratively in the deployment descriptor. A client accesses a message-driven bean through JMS by sending messages to the JMS `Destination` (`Queue` or `Topic`) for which the MDB class is the `MessageListener`. The client has no direct interaction with MDBs (see Figure 13.7).

**Note**

> Other EJB types, such as session and entity beans, are synchronous by design. When they issue an RMI call, they have to wait until they get back a reply. A message-driven bean is designed to handle asynchronous message calls.

Message-driven bean instances are stateless, have no conversational state, and are also anonymous, with no client-visible identity. This makes them an excellent candidate for instance pooling. An MDB is simply a more convenient component to develop a JMS consumer as part of an enterprise application.

The following is an example of an MDB. Note that the `onMessage()` method must be implemented for the `MessageListener` interface. Other methods are implemented for the `MessageDrivenBean` interface.

```
import javax.ejb.*;
import javax.jms.*;
public class RegistrarMDB implements MessageDrivenBean, MessageListener {
```

**13**

```
protected MessageDrivenContext ctx;
public void setMessageDrivenContext(MessageDrivenContext ctx) {
 this.ctx = ctx;
}
public void ejbCreate() {}
public void ejbRemove() {}
public void onMessage(Message message) {
  try {
    TextMessage msg = (TextMessage)message;
    System.err.println("Registrar received a new message: " +
               msg.getText());
  } catch(JMSException e) {
   e.printStackTrace();
  }
 }
}
```

FIGURE **13.7**

*The client view of a message-driven bean.*

**Client View of Message-Driven Beans**

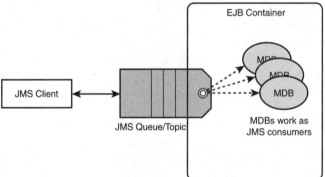

The setMessageDrivenContext() method is called by the EJB container to associate a message-driven bean instance with its context. Also, the onMessage() method is called by the container when a message has arrived for the bean to service. The onMessage method has one argument, which is the incoming message, and it contains the business logic that handles the processing of the message.

Day 14 will discuss message-driven beans in more detail.

# Best Practices

JMS is a versatile API to support the design of reliable, flexible, and high-performance enterprise applications. One of the basic design guidelines is selecting which messaging model the application will use. Another important decision is what type of message is appropriate. Choosing the message size depends on the type of message you decide to use, which in turn has an impact on application performance. Smaller size gives better performance and vice versa. For example, `ByteMessage` takes less memory than `TextMessage` and can support Unicode. `ObjectMessage` carries a serialized Java object, and you need to specify the `transient` keyword for members that need not be exchanged to reduce overhead.

In general, a good practice is closing all resources when you are finished with them. JMS resources such as `Connection`, `Session`, and producer/consumer must be closed after you are finished.

To enhance reliability, use persistent messages, transacted sessions, durable subscribers, and consumer acknowledgment. In addition, set the `TimeToLive` value properly, and receive messages asynchronously. Always remember that reliability works against performance, and depending on your application requirements, you must find the balance between them.

JMS clustering is a critical issue in selecting the right JMS provider. Clustering deals with both load balancing and fail-over. This addresses both performance and reliability, and not all JMS providers support clustering of JMS services.

# Summary

Today you learned about JMS as a unified API to abstract all interfaces and classes to access enterprise messaging requirements. You also learned about JMS architecture, and the two main messaging models supported by JMS: PTP and Pub/Sub. More details were given for the JMS API that supports both messaging models. You explored how to use to use the JMS API to develop JMS clients in both models. You studied the anatomy of a JMS message and explained its constituents. You learned about message types and their usage in enterprise applications. Finally, a brief account of message-driven beans as an asynchronous consumer of messages was given. In Day 14, we'll develop a message-driven bean through a working example.

**13**

# Q&A

**Q How is JNDI used to help make JMS applications more portable?**

**A** JMS depends on two administered objects: `Destination` and `ConnectionFactory`. They are created by the JMS provider administrator, and registered in the JNDI namespace. Later, JMS clients look up the named object in the JNDI and instantiate a resource. This separation between the JMS provider specifics and the JMS API helps make your enterprise application more portable.

**Q  What messaging models are supported by JMS?**

**A**  Point-to-point (PTP) messaging and publish-and-subscribe (Pub/Sub) messaging.

# Quiz

1. Which of the following are JMS administered objects?

   A. `Destination`

   B. `Connection`

   C. `ConnectionFactory`

   D. `Session`

2. Which are JMS messaging models?

   A. Publish-and-subscribe

   B. Point-to-point

   C. Store-and-forward

   D. Peer-to-peer

3. A JMS message is composed of which of the following parts:

   A. Header

   B. Properties

   C. Footer

   D. Body

4. Which following services are NOT provided by JMS?

   A. Clustering: Load balancing and fail-over

   B. Asynchronous message delivery

   C. Error notifications

   D. Security

## Quiz Answers

1. A, C

2. A, B

3. A, B, D

4. A, C, D

# Exercises

1. What is JMS used for?

2. What are message-driven beans, and when do you use them?

3. Compare the PTP and Pub/Sub messaging models.

4. What are the types of JMS messages?

5. Is the JMS session object multithreaded? Why?

13

DAY **14**

# Developing Message-Driven Beans

Today, you'll learn how to develop applications using asynchronous messaging. You'll work on a complete example of developing a message-driven enterprise bean (MDB).

In our sample University Registration System, a student selects items from the course catalog, places them in an enrollment cart, and, when she's ready, places an order for the cart contents. After the order is placed, we must verify the student's billing information, the classroom's capacity, and so on. We would like to enable the student to continue browsing the Web site and not require her to wait for the background processing to complete. This asynchronous processing can be best modeled using a message-driven bean. In the sample application, after the student submits an order, a Java Message Service (JMS) message is sent to a destination, where it will be processed by an `OrderVerifier` message-driven bean. An `OrderVerifier` bean is responsible for verifying the order's facts, such as the billing information and so on.

To learn how to develop and deploy an MDB, the following are the activities we'll engage in today:

- Learn the interactions between the client, the JMS Server, the EJB container, and the message-driven bean by looking under the hood of the bean
- Show you how to implement the message-driven bean class and write its deployment descriptor
- Explore how to compile, package, and deploy the bean in a container
- Learn how to write a client that sends a message to a JMS Destination for which the message-driven bean is the consumer
- Examine the life cycle of a message-driven bean instance

# Looking Under the Hood of an MDB

Figure 14.1 shows the interactions between the client, the JMS service, the EJB container, and the message-driven bean.

**FIGURE 14.1**

*Under the hood of a message-driven bean.*

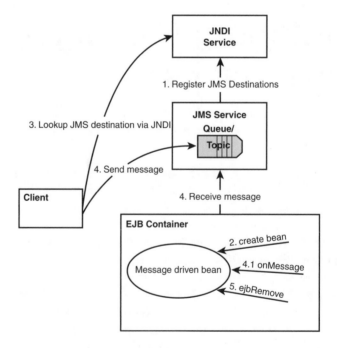

The following steps describe the sequence of interactions in detail:

1. At startup, the JMS service registers all JMS `Destinations` (`Topic` or `Queue`) with the Java Naming and Directory Interface (JNDI) service. The EJB container also registers the message-driven beans as JMS consumers with the JMS service.

2. The EJB container decides to instantiate a message-driven bean based on the caching policy. For example, the EJB container instantiates the `OrderVerifierMDB` bean using the `Class.newInstance("OrderVerifierMDB.class")` and then calls the `setMessageDrivenContext()` and `ejbCreate()` methods on the instance. The bean instance is now ready to accept and process a message. The instance enters the pool of method-ready instances.

3. The client looks up the JMS `Destination` associated with a message-driven bean by using JNDI. For example, the `OrderVerifierTopic` `Topic` associated with the `OrderVerifierMDB` bean can be located using the following code segment:

```
Context initialContext = new InitialContext();
Topic topic = (javax.jms.Topic) initialContext.lookup
        ("jms/OrderVerifierTopic");
```

4. The client sends a message to the JMS `Destination`. For example, the client sends a message to the `Topic` as follows:

```
TextMessage tm = session.createTextMessage();
tm.setText("1234");
publisher.publish(tm);
```

When a client sends a message to a `Destination` for which a message-driven bean is the consumer, the EJB container selects one of its method-ready instances and invokes the `onMessage()` method on the bean instance passing the client's message.

5. The EJB container decides to terminate the session bean instance by calling the `ejbRemove()` method of the bean instance. This happens when the container needs to reduce the number of instances in the method-ready pool.

**Note**

According to EJB 2.0, message-driven beans support only JMS services, and process standard JMS messages such as `TextMessage` and `ByteMessage`. With the advent of Web Services, EJB 2.1 (which was a work in progress at the time this book was written) extends the use of message-driven beans to support Java API for XML Messaging. This will allow message-driven beans to process messages, which conform to Simple Object Access Protocol (SOAP) 1.1. Message-driven beans will also support one-way messages and the blocking of request-response messages.

14

# Designing the Message-Driven Bean

Figure 14.2 shows the design of the `OrderVerifier` component. The `OrderVerifierMDB` message-driven bean implements the `javax.ejb.MessageDrivenBean` and `javax.jms.MessageListener` interfaces. It implements the methods `setMessageDrivenContext()` and `ejbRemove()` as defined in the `javax.ejb.MessageDrivenBean` and the `onMessage()` method, as defined in the `javax.jms.MessageListener` interface. It also implements the `ejbCreate()` method.

**FIGURE 14.2**

`OrderVerifierMDB`
*message-driven bean design.*

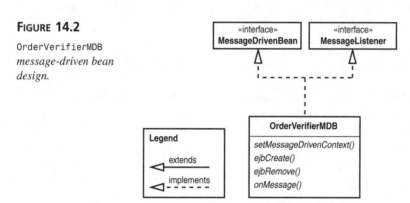

The `OrderVerifier` bean expects the text message to contain the primary key of the order. It locates the order in the database by using its primary key and checks the student billing information and so on. After the order information is verified, it changes the order's status to "`Verified`." For simplicity, we don't write code to verify the student information, but merely set the order status to `Verified`. The `OrderVerifier` component uses the `Order` component that you developed and deployed on Day 11, "Developing Container-Managed Persistence Entity Beans."

**Note**

Clients don't access message-driven beans through interfaces. Unlike session and entity beans, message-driven beans have neither a home nor a component interface. A client accesses a message-driven bean through JMS by sending messages to the JMS `Destination` (`Queue` or `Topic`) for which the MDB class is the `MessageListener`.

# Implementing the Enterprise Bean Class

Table 14.1 shows a summary of message-driven bean methods.

**TABLE 14.1**   Summary of Message-Driven Bean Methods

| Method | Purpose | What You Need to Do |
|---|---|---|
| `setMessageDrivenContext` `(MessageDrivenContext)` | The EJB container calls this method to associate the bean instance with its context maintained by the container. | You must store the reference to the message-driven context in an instance variable if you need to access the run-time context, such as accessing or changing the transaction context. |
| `ejbCreate()` | The EJB container calls this method so that you can initialize your bean instance. | You initialize the bean here. You also allocate any resources that are to be held for the instance's lifetime.<br><br>Each message-driven bean must have only one `ejbCreate()` method with no arguments. |
| `onMessage(Message)` | This method is called by the EJB container when a message has arrived for the bean to service. | You must code the business logic that handles the processing of the message. |
| `ejbRemove()` | The EJB container calls this method before it ends the life cycle of the instance. | You must release any resources that the instance is holding. |

Listing 14.1 shows the `OrderVerifierMDB` bean class. The `OrderVerifierMDB` message-driven bean implements the `javax.ejb.MessageDrivenBean` and `javax.jms.MessageListener` interfaces. It implements the methods `setMessageDrivenContext()`, `ejbRemove()`, and `onMessage()`. In the `onMessage()` method, the bean retrieves the order ID from the text message. It uses the helper method `verifyOrder()` to process the order. The `verifyOrder()` method locates the order by using its primary key from the database, and sets the order's status to `Verified`.

**LISTING 14.1**   The Full Text of day14/OrderVerifierMDB.java

```
package day14;

import javax.jms.*;
import javax.ejb.*;
import javax.naming.*;
import java.rmi.*;
import javax.rmi.*;

import day11.OrderHome;
```

**14**

**LISTING 14.1**    continued

```
import day11.Order;

public class OrderVerifierMDB implements
MessageDrivenBean, MessageListener {
    private MessageDrivenContext ctx;
    public void setMessageDrivenContext(MessageDrivenContext ctx) {
        print("setMessageDrivenContext called.\n");
        this.ctx = ctx;
    }
    public void ejbCreate() {
        print("ejbCreate() called.\n");
    }
    public void ejbRemove() {
        print("ejbRemove() called.\n");
    }
    public void onMessage(Message msg) {
        print("OrderVerifierMDB: onMessage() called.\n");
        if(!(msg instanceof TextMessage)){
            throw new EJBException
                ("OrderVerifierMDB handles only Text Messages.");
        }
        try {
            TextMessage tm = (TextMessage) msg;
            String orderId = tm.getText();
            verifyOrder(orderId);
        } catch(Exception ex) {
            ex.printStackTrace();
            throw new EJBException(ex);
        }
    }
    private void verifyOrder(String orderId) throws FinderException,
        NamingException, RemoteException {
        print("Verifying order Id:" + orderId);
        Context context = new InitialContext();
        OrderHome orderHome = (OrderHome) PortableRemoteObject.narrow
            (context.lookup("day11/Order"),OrderHome.class);
        Order order = orderHome.findByPrimaryKey(orderId);

        /* Now we can verify things such as the class capacity,
           students billing information etc.,
           Here we merely set the order status to "verified"
        */
        print("Changing order status to Verified");
        order.setStatus("Verified");
    }
    void print(String s) {
        System.out.println(s);
    }
}
```

Note that the bean throws `EJBException` on encountering any error.

> **Note**
>
> Message-driven bean methods, unlike the methods of session and entity beans, do not throw application exceptions and can't throw exceptions to the client. The `onMessage()` method should not throw application exceptions or the `java.rmi.RemoteException`.
>
> Message-driven beans can throw only system exceptions from their methods. In such situations, the EJB container performs the following: log the exception; on error, roll back the current transaction, if any; and discard the instance.
>
> However EJB 2.1 removed the restriction that the methods of a message listener interface must not throw application exceptions.

> **Note**
>
> In EJB 2.1, a JMS message-driven bean implements the `javax.jms.MessageListener` interface and a JAXM message-driven bean implements the `javax.xml.messaging.OnewayListener` or `javax.xml.messaging.ReqRespListener` interface. Also, the message-driven bean can implement more than one type of message listener interface.
>
> In addition, in EJB 2.1, a message-driven bean can implement the `javax.ejb.TimedObject` interface for time-based event notifications. The EJB container invokes the bean instance's `ejbTimeout()` method when the timer for the bean has expired.

# Declaring the Deployment Descriptor

Listing 14.2 shows the `ejb-jar.xml` deployment descriptor for the `OrderVerifier` enterprise bean. `ejb-jar.xml` describes the enterprise bean's deployment properties, such as its bean type and structure. The file also provides the EJB container with information about where it can find and then load the bean class. Message-driven beans don't have home or component interfaces, so you don't specify them in the deployment descriptor. The deployment descriptor may specify the JMS `Destination` type (`Queue` or `Topic`) to which the bean should be assigned.

**LISTING 14.2**    The Full Text of day14/ejb-jar.xml

**14**

```
<!DOCTYPE ejb-jar PUBLIC
  "-//Sun Microsystems, Inc.//DTD Enterprise JavaBeans 2.0//EN"
  "http://java.sun.com/dtd/ejb-jar_2_0.dtd">

<ejb-jar>
```

**LISTING 14.2** continued

```
<enterprise-beans>
  <message-driven>
    <ejb-name>OrderVerifierMDB</ejb-name>
    <ejb-class>day14.OrderVerifierMDB</ejb-class>
    <transaction-type>Container</transaction-type>
    <message-driven-destination>
      <destination-type>javax.jms.Topic</destination-type>
      <subscription-durability>NonDurable</subscription-durability>
    </message-driven-destination>
  </message-driven>
</enterprise-beans>
</ejb-jar>
```

The `ejb-jar.xml` declares `OrderVerifierMDB` as the name of the message-driven bean. The `transaction-type` element specifies that this bean uses container-managed transactions. Container-managed transactions are discussed in detail on Day 17. The `destination-type` element within the `message-driven-destination` element specifies that the bean consumes topic messages. The `subscription-durability` element specifies that the message-driven bean's subscription to the `Topic` is `NonDurable`. This means the messages may be missed when the EJB server goes down for any period of time.

Listing 14.3 shows the `weblogic-ejb-jar.xml` deployment descriptor that is specific to WebLogic Server. The `destination-jndi-name` element specifies that `OrderVerifierMDB` subscribes to the `OrderVerifierTopic` Topic.

**LISTING 14.3** The Full Text of `day14/weblogic-ejb-jar.xml`

```
<?xml version="1.0"?>
<!DOCTYPE weblogic-ejb-jar PUBLIC
'-//BEA Systems, Inc.//DTD WebLogic 7.0.0 EJB//EN'
'http://www.bea.com/servers/wls700/dtd/weblogic-ejb-jar.dtd'>
<weblogic-ejb-jar>
  <weblogic-enterprise-bean>
    <ejb-name>OrderVerifierMDB</ejb-name>
    <message-driven-descriptor>
      <pool>
        <max-beans-in-free-pool>20</max-beans-in-free-pool>
        <initial-beans-in-free-pool>5</initial-beans-in-free-pool>
      </pool>
      <destination-jndi-name>OrderVerifierTopic</destination-jndi-name>
    </message-driven-descriptor>
    <jndi-name>day14/OrderVerifier</jndi-name>
  </weblogic-enterprise-bean>
</weblogic-ejb-jar>
```

Listing 14.4 shows the `jboss.xml` deployment descriptor specific to the JBoss server. The `destination-jndi-name` element specifies that `OrderVerifierMDB` subscribes to the `topic/OrderVerifierTopic` Topic.

**LISTING 14.4**    The Full Text of `day14/jboss.xml`

```xml
<?xml version="1.0" encoding="UTF-8"?>
<jboss>
  <enterprise-beans>
    <message-driven>
     <ejb-name>OrderVerifierMDB</ejb-name>
<destination-jndi-name>topic/OrderVerifierTopic</destination-jndi-name>
    </message-driven>
  </enterprise-beans>
</jboss>
```

Later today, you'll learn how to configure a topic in both WebLogic Server and JBoss.

# Writing a Client

Listing 14.5 demonstrates how a client sends a message to the JMS `Destination`.

**LISTING 14.5**    The Full Text of `day14/Client.java`

```java
package day14;

import javax.jms.*;
import javax.naming.*;
import javax.ejb.*;
import java.util.*;

import day11.OrderHome;
import day11.Order;

public class Client {
public static void main(String[] args) {
   print("Starting Client . . .");
   try {
      String orderVerifierJndiName = args[0];
      String connectionFactoryJndiName = args[1];
      print("Looking up the JMS destination(Topic) via JNDI.");
      Context context = new InitialContext();
      Topic topic = (Topic) context.lookup(orderVerifierJndiName);

      print("Locating connection factory.");
      TopicConnectionFactory connectionFactory = (TopicConnectionFactory)
         context.lookup(connectionFactoryJndiName);
```

**14**

LISTING **14.5** continued

```
        print("Creating a connection  and establishing a session.");
        TopicConnection connection =
           connectionFactory.createTopicConnection();
        TopicSession session = connection.createTopicSession
           (false,Session.AUTO_ACKNOWLEDGE);
        TopicPublisher publisher = session.createPublisher(topic);

        print("Creating an order with status:Submitted");
        Context initialContext = new InitialContext();
        Object object = initialContext.lookup("day11/Order");
        OrderHome orderHome = (OrderHome)
           javax.rmi.PortableRemoteObject.narrow(object,OrderHome.class);
        Order order = (Order)orderHome.create
                     ( "1", "Submitted", 100);
        String orderId = order.getOrderId();
        print("Order id " + orderId + " is created");
        print("Creating a text message with order id and publishing it.");
        TextMessage tm = session.createTextMessage();
        tm.setText(orderId);
        publisher.publish(tm);
        print("Sleeping for 2 sec.");
        Thread.sleep(2000);
        print("Now the order status is:" + order.getStatus());
     }
     catch(Exception ex) {
        System.err.println(ex);
        ex.printStackTrace();
     }
  }
  static void print(String s) {
     System.out.println(s);
  }
  }
```

The client accepts two command-line arguments: the Topic JNDI name and the connection factory JNDI name. The client locates the Topic via JNDI. It locates the connection factory in the JNDI name space, creates a TopicConnection, and establishes a TopicSession. It then uses that TopicSession to create a TopicSubscriber so that we can publish messages.

The code creates a sample order and marks its status as Submitted. Before publishing the message, the client creates a text message and populates it with the order ID. The client then publishes the message. As you know, the OrderVerifier bean receives the message and changes the order status to Verified. Finally, the client prints the order status.

# Packaging and Deploying the Enterprise Bean

This section describes the steps to package and deploy the `OrderVerifier` message-driven bean, and also to build the client for both WebLogic Server and JBoss application servers. These steps assume that you packaged and deployed the `Order` entity bean that we discussed on Day 11.

You can run the following commands for WebLogic Server:

```
C:\>cd styejb\examples
```

```
C:\styejb\examples>setEnvWebLogic.bat
```

```
C:\styejb\examples>cd day14
```

```
C:\styejb\examples\day14>buildWebLogic.bat
```

You can run the following commands for JBoss:

```
C:\>cd styejb\examples
```

```
C:\styejb\examples>setEnvJboss.bat
```

```
C:\styejb\examples>cd day14
```

```
C:\styejb\examples\day14>buildJboss.bat
```

# Running the Example

The following steps describe how to start the PointBase database server, WebLogic Server, configure a JMS topic in WebLogic, and run the sample client:

1. Start PointBase server in a new command window as follows:

   ```
   C:\>cd styejb\examples
   ```
   ```
   C:\styejb\examples>setEnvWebLogic.bat
   ```
   ```
   C:\styejb\examples>startPointBase.bat
   ```

2. Start WebLogic Server in a new command window as follows:

   ```
   C:\>cd styejb\examples
   ```
   ```
   C:\styejb\examples>setEnvWebLogic.bat
   ```
   ```
   C:\styejb\examples>startWebLogic.bat
   ```

3. Open the WebLogic Administration Console by opening a Web browser and typing the URL `http://localhost:7001/console`. When prompted, enter the username and the password you have created when you installed the WebLogic Server (refer to Appendix A, "Weblogic Application Server 7.0").

**14**

Set up a JMS server as follows:

1. In the left pane, expand Services > JMS.

2. Click Servers.

3. In the right pane, click Create a New JMSServer.

4. Enter or select these values:

   Name: **styejbJMS**

   Store: **(none)**

   Paging Store: **(none)**

   Temporary Template: **(none)**

5. Click Create. Figure 14.3 shows the corresponding screenshot.

FIGURE **14.3**

*Configuring a JMS server in WebLogic Server.*

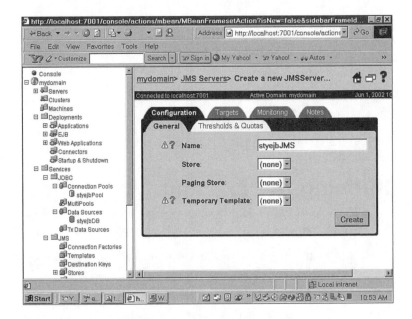

6. Click the Targets tab.

7. Select myserver in the Target combo box.

8. Click Apply. Figure 14.4 shows the corresponding screenshot.

Set up a JMS Destination as follows:

1. In the left pane, expand Services > JMS > Servers > styejbJMS.

2. Click Destinations.

FIGURE **14.4**

*Assigning the JMS server to the target server.*

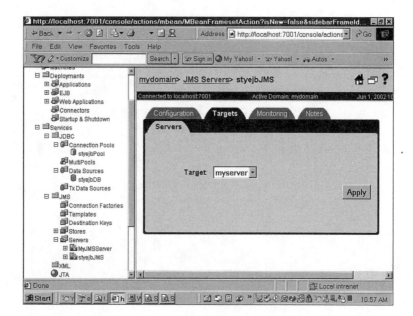

3. In the right pane, click the Configure a New JMSTopic link.

4. Enter or select these values:

   Name: **OrderVerifierTopic**

   JNDIName: **OrderVerifierTopic**

   Enable Store: **default**

   Template: **(none)**

5. Click Create. Figure 14.5 shows the corresponding screenshot.

You can run the client in the same window you used to package the bean and build the client by using the following command:

```
C:\styejb\examples\day14>runClientWebLogic.bat
```

Running the client produces the following output:

```
Starting Client . . .
Looking up the JMS destination(Topic) via JNDI.
Locating connection factory.
Creating a connection  and establishing a session.
Creating an order with status:Submitted
Order id 1029463968627 is created
Creating a text message with order id and publishing it.
Sleeping for 2 sec.
Now the order status is:Verified
```

14

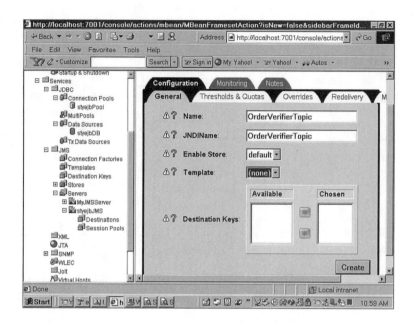

The following steps describe how to start JBoss server, configure a JMS Topic in JBoss, and run the sample client:

1. Start the JBoss server in a new command window as follows:

```
C:\>cd styejb\examples

C:\styejb\examples>setEnvJBoss.bat

C:\styejb\examples>startJBoss.bat
```

2. Edit the file server\default\deploy\jbossmq-destinations-service.xml under the JBoss home directory to create a new JMS Topic as follows:

```
<server>
. . .
<mbean code="org.jboss.mq.server.jmx.Topic"
       name="jboss.mq.destination:service=Topic,name=OrderVerifierTopic">
    <depends
       optional-attribute-name=
          "DestinationManager">jboss.mq:service=DestinationManager</depends>
</mbean>
. . .
</server>
```

Add the text shown in bold to the file. This creates an OrderVerifierTopic Topic and binds it to the JNDI name topic/OrderVerifierTopic.

3. You can run the client in the same window you used to package the bean and build the client by using the following command:

```
C:\styejb\examples\day14>runClientJBoss.bat
```

# Examining the Life Cycle of a Message-Driven Bean

Figure 14.6 shows the life cycle of a message-driven bean instance.

**FIGURE 14.6**

*Message-driven bean life cycle.*

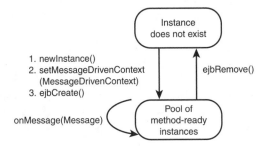

1. newInstance()
2. setMessageDrivenContext (MessageDrivenContext)
3. ejbCreate()

onMessage(Message)

Instance does not exist

ejbRemove()

Pool of method-ready instances

The following sequence describes the life cycle of a message-driven bean instance:

- The bean instance's life cycle starts when the container decides to instantiate a bean instance. The container instantiates the bean using the newInstance() method and then calls the setMessageDrivenContext() and ejbCreate() methods. Now the instance is ready to process a message sent to its Destination by any client.

- When a client sends a message to a Destination, the container selects one of its method-ready instances and calls the instance's onMessage() method.

- The container decides to remove the bean instance. This could be because the container wants to reduce the number of instances in the method-ready pool. The container calls the ejbRemove() method of the bean instance.

 **Caution**

> You cannot rely on the container to call the ejbRemove() method. The container might not call ejbRemove() in the following scenarios: a shutdown or crash of the container, or a system exception thrown from the instance's method. If your instance frees up resources in the ejbRemove() method, those resources are not freed in the preceding scenarios. You should provide some mechanism to periodically clean up the unreleased resources.

14

# Best Practices

As mentioned on Day 2, "Understanding EJB Types and Interfaces," you should consider using a message-driven bean when you want to develop loosely coupled systems and process asynchronous messages.

Consider using message-driven beans, instead of standard JMS consumers, in situations in which you need the power of EJBs, such as security and transaction management. Another benefit is that the EJB container can create multiple instances of a message-driven bean to process large volumes of messages concurrently. On the other hand, a message-driven bean can be associated with a single JMS `Destination` (`Topic` or `Queue`). So, if your application requires a single JMS consumer to process messages from multiple `Topic`s or `Queue`s, you must use a standard JMS consumer or deploy multiple message-driven bean classes.

Consider tuning the message-driven bean's instance pool size. For best performance, the maximum number of beans in the pool should be equal to the maximum number of concurrent messages. If the pool size is less than the number of concurrent messages, messages have to wait for an available bean, which degrades performance.

# Summary

Today you wrote a message-driven enterprise bean that processes messages asynchronously. The enterprise bean consists of bean class and deployment descriptors. When a client sends a message to a `Destination` for which a message-driven bean is the consumer, the EJB container calls the `onMessage()` method on the bean instance passing the client's message. The `onMessage()` method of the enterprise bean class contains business logic to process the message. The enterprise bean doesn't provide home and component interfaces for client access. You also learned how to package and deploy the enterprise bean, and then you wrote and ran a client that accessed the enterprise bean.

# Q&A

**Q  What files do I need to write for a message-driven bean?**

**A**  Unlike other enterprise beans, message-driven beans consist of enterprise bean class and deployment descriptors. They do not provide home or component interfaces.

**Q  Can a message-driven bean contain a state that's specific to a client?**

**A**  A message-driven bean can't contain a state that is specific to a client. However, the instance variables of the message-driven bean instance can contain a state across the handling of client messages. Examples of such a state include socket connections, database connections, and references to `EJBObject`.

# Quiz

1. A message-driven bean implements which of the following interface(s)?

    A. `javax.ejb.EnterpriseBean`

    B. `javax.ejb.MessageDrivenBean` and `javax.ejb.MessageListener`

    C. `javax.ejb.MessageDrivenBean` and `javax.jms.MessageListener`

    D. `javax.ejb.MessageDrivenBean`

2. Which one of the following statements is true for message-driven beans?

    A. MDBs provide only local interfaces for client access.

    B. MDBs provide only remote interfaces for client access.

    C. MDBs can provide either local or remote interfaces for client access.

    D. MDBs do not provide either local or remote interfaces for client access.

3. Which one of the following message-driven bean methods is called by the EJB container when a message has arrived for the bean to service?

    A. `ejbCreate()`

    B. `setMessageDrivenContext()`

    C. `onMessage()`

    D. `ejbRemove()`

## Quiz Answers

1. C
2. D
3. C

# Exercise

To extend your knowledge of the subjects covered today, try the following exercise:

Modify the `OrderVerifier` message-driven bean to consume messages from a `Queue` instead of a `Topic`. You need to configure a `Queue` in the server, and modify the `OrderVerifier` deployment descriptor and the client scripts as part of this exercise.

14

# WEEK 3

# Advanced EJB Applications

15

16

17

18

19

20

21

# DAY 15

# Understanding J2EE Architecture

In Day 1, "Understanding EJB Architecture," you learned that Enterprise JavaBean (EJB) technology is part of the J2EE architecture, and that it's the standard for developing and deploying enterprise applications and components. Enterprise applications can be assembled from standard components and then deployed on varieties of J2EE-compliant application servers. Today, you'll explore the big picture of the J2EE platform. We'll cover the rationale behind the Java 2 Platform, Enterprise Edition (J2EE), and the set of standard APIs that constitute its framework. You'll study the evolution of the multitier architecture as the basis for the J2EE platform. By the end of the day, you'll have learned how your projects can benefit from the J2EE design patterns. You'll also learn how J2EE applications are deployed in the appropriate container.

Today's road map is to explore the J2EE architecture and platform; to that end, you'll

- Learn what J2EE is, and what its objectives are
- Learn the evolution of the J2EE architecture from two-tier to multitier

- Understand the container model and the types of containers used in the J2EE platform
- Explore the J2EE standard common services
- Learn the different J2EE protocols and interactions between tiers
- Understand how J2EE applications are partitioned into modules and deployed into containers
- Understand J2EE design patterns and best practices

# J2EE Overview

Java is one of the most commonly used and mature programming languages for building enterprise applications. Over the years, Java development has evolved from small applets run on a Web browser to large enterprise distributed applications run on multiple servers. Now, Java has three different platforms, or flavors, and each addresses certain programming requirements:

- The Java 2 Platform, Standard Edition (J2SE) is the underlying base platform for the J2EE. Therefore, a brief discussion on the J2SE platform is relevant to our discussion of the J2EE platform. The J2SE platform consists of the Java 2 Software Development Kit (SDK) and the Java 2 Runtime Environment (JRE). J2SE includes tools and application programming interfaces (APIs) for developing client applications with graphical user interfaces (GUIs), database access, directory access, Common Object Request Broker Architecture (CORBA), fine-grained security, input/output functions, and many other functions. It's the most widely used Java platform.
- The Java 2 Platform, Enterprise Edition (J2EE) is a platform for building server-side components and applications. It provides the infrastructure needed for these applications through a set of common services.
- The Java 2 Platform, Micro Edition (J2ME) helps with building Java applications for micro-devices with limited display and memory requirements (the entire API fits into 1KB), such as wireless devices, PDAs, and network devices.

Today, our focus is on the J2EE platform and its common services offerings.

J2EE is a platform and an industry-accepted standard that enables solutions for developing and deploying multitier enterprise applications. It provides a unified platform for building distributed, server-centric systems. J2EE is a set of standard APIs that is offered by a vendor through products and tools to be used by the enterprise. It was developed to meet recent enterprise requirements, such as diversity of both applications and data, in addition to the complexity of business processes. The J2EE standard is defined through a set of related specifications, such as the J2EE specification, the Enterprise JavaBeans specification, the Java Servlet specification, and the JavaServer Pages (JSP) specification.

The J2EE platform offers the following benefits to the enterprise and to product vendors:

- Establishes standards for database connectivity, Web components, business logic components, message-oriented middleware (MOM), communication protocols, and interoperability.

- Provides a standard for avoiding vendor lock-in and building portable applications and components that are flexible, expandable, and reliable. This also helps in developing secure, scalable, and transactional applications.

- Decreases time-to-market because much of the infrastructure and common services are provided by vendors' products that are implemented according to the standard J2EE specification. IT organizations can get out of the middleware business and concentrate on building applications for their business.

- Increases developer productivity because Java programmers can relatively easily learn J2EE technologies based on the Java language. All enterprise software development can be accomplished under the J2EE platform, using Java as the programming language.

- Promotes interoperability within existing heterogeneous systems, such as CORBA and J2EE.

- Enables developers to focus on supporting business process requirements rather than building the in-house application infrastructure. The application server handles the complex tasks of multithreading, synchronization, transactions, resource allocation, and life cycle management.

In general, the J2EE platform helps the enterprise to overcome certain issues such as programming productivity, application reliability, availability, security, scalability, and integration with existing systems.

# The Evolution of J2EE Architecture

The client/server application architecture, which was a two-tier architecture, evolved over time to a multitier architecture. This natural progression occurred as additional tiers were introduced between the end-user clients and back-end systems. Although a multitier architecture brings greater flexibility of design, it also increases the complexity of building, testing, deploying, administering, and maintaining application components.

In the next few sections, we'll discuss the evolution of the multitier architecture.

## Two-Tier Architecture

The two-tier architecture is also known as the client/server architecture. It consists mainly of two tiers: data and client (GUI). The application logic can be located in either the client tier, which results in a fat client, or located in the data tier, which results in a fat server (see Figure 15.1).

FIGURE **15.1**

*Two-tier architecture.*

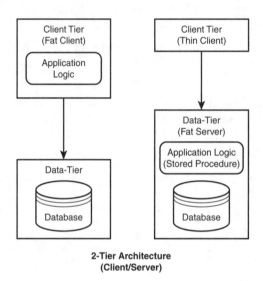

This type of architecture suffers from a lack of scalability because both the client and the server have limited resources, in addition to the negative effect of network traffic to transfer data to the fat client. Another issue is maintainability; you have to roll out the new system version to all system users.

## Three-Tier Architecture

To address the issues of the two-tier architecture, the application logic will be placed in its own tier. Thus applications can be portioned into three tiers. The first tier is referred to as the *presentation layer*, and consists of the application GUI. The middle tier, or the *business layer*, consists of the business logic to retrieve data for the user requests. The back-end tier, or *data layer*, consists of the data needed by the application. Figure 15.2 illustrates the three-tier architecture.

The decoupling of application logic from either presentation or data increases the flexibility of the application design. Multiple views or a GUI can be added without changing the existing application logic. Similarly, multiple applications can be created using the same data model. Changing the components of one tier should not impact the other two tiers. For example, any change to the data or GUI will not affect the application logic.

**FIGURE 15.2**

*Three-tier architecture.*

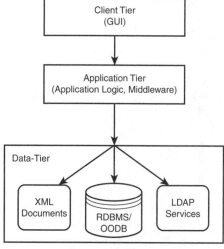

3-Tier Architecture

**Note**

> The three-tier architecture is the basis for J2EE applications, in which EJBs provide a mechanism to build application logic, while JSPs and servlets abstract the presentation layer and allow interaction with the business layer.

One important feature of the three-tier architecture is sharing system resources by all clients, which results in highly efficient, scalable, secure, and reliable applications.

## Multitier J2EE Architecture

Multitier (or *n*-tier) architecture differs from the three-tier architecture in viewing each tier logically rather than physically. The application logic, for example, can be split into more than one layer; the business logic tier and the presentation logic tier. Similarly, the user interface is partitioned into the client tier and the presentation tier. A multitier architecture determines where the software components that make up a computing system are executed in relation to each other and to the hardware, network, and users.

J2EE is a multitier architecture, which partitions the application into client, presentation logic, business logic, and enterprise information tiers. Figure 15.3 depicts the J2EE as a multitier architecture.

The following gives a brief summary of each tier of the J2EE architecture:

- Client tier—This tier interacts with the user and displays information from the system to the user. J2EE supports different types of clients—both inside and outside enterprise firewalls—including Web clients (HTML and Java applets) and Java applications.

**FIGURE 15.3**

*Multitier J2EE architecture.*

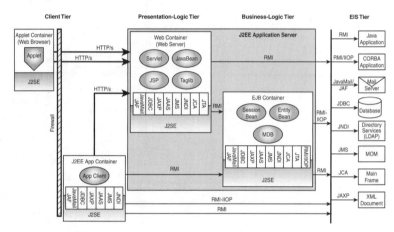

Multitier J2EE Architecture

- Web tier—This tier accepts user requests and generates responses using the presentation logic. In the J2EE platform, servlets and JSPs in a Web container implement this tier, as explained on Day 7, "Designing Web Applications."

- Business logic tier—This tier handles the core business logic of the application. The business components are typically implemented as EJB components with support from an EJB container, which provides the component life cycle and manages persistence, transactions, security, and resource allocation.

- EIS tier—This tier is responsible for the enterprise information systems, including different database systems, transaction processing systems, legacy systems, message-oriented middleware, and enterprise resource planning systems (ERPs). The EIS tier is the point at which J2EE applications integrate with non-J2EE or legacy systems.

**Note**

The J2EE platform is designed not only to support a multitier architecture to partition applications, but also to provide infrastructure common services to reduce the complexity of developing and deploying these applications.

Other than multitier, the J2EE architecture provides the enterprise with common infrastructure services which help in developing and deploying portable, secure and transactional applications. The J2EE architecture partitions enterprise applications into three fundamental parts: components, containers, and connectors. Components are the key focus of application developers, whereas system vendors implement containers and connectors to hide complexity and enhance portability. Enterprise Java applications can run on any J2EE-compliant application server.

**Note**

> Multitier distributed applications follow the Model-View-Controller (MVC) paradigm, discussed earlier on Days 1 and 7. This design pattern provides clean separation between tiers. Using this paradigm, the model (data tier) is separated from the view (client and presentation tiers). Similarly, the controller (the application logic tier) is separated from both the view and the model.

Containers transparently provide common services, including transaction, security, persistence, and resource pooling, to both clients and components. A container allows the configuration of applications and components at deployment, rather than hard-coding them in program code. Connectors extend the J2EE platform by defining a portable client service API to plug into existing enterprise vendor products. Connectors promote flexibility by enabling a variety of implementations of specific services.

# Understanding the J2EE Container Model

Containers are vital to J2EE components. Containers are the run-time environments that provide standard common services to the deployed components. Containers are implemented and offered by various vendors in the form of J2EE-compliant Application Servers. Containers also provide unified access to enterprise information systems, such as access to relational data through the Java Database Connectivity (JDBC) API, or to legacy systems through J2EE Connector Architecture (JCA) API. In addition, containers provide a declarative mechanism for configuring applications and components at assembly or deployment time through the use of deployment descriptors. Features that can be configured at deployment time include security authorization and validation, transaction management, and other tasks. Figure 15.4 depicts the J2EE container model.

Each tier of the J2EE architecture may consist of more than one container. For example, the Web tier may consist of a servlet container (or engine) and a JSP container, which together make a Web container. Similarly, each EJB type runs on its own container, which is commonly known as an EJB container. Some Application Servers are offered with both a Web container and an EJB container.

FIGURE 15.4

*J2EE container model.*

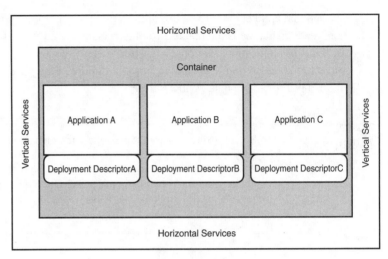

J2EE Container Model

 **Note**

> Some Application Servers, such as WebLogic Server, run all the Web compo-
> nents in the Web container, which is different from the proxy server that's
> used as a gateway to pass requests and responses. All requests are processed
> in the Web container using servlets and JSPs.

A Java Application Server is a platform for developing and deploying multitier distributed J2EE-compiant enterprise applications. It centralizes application services such as
Web server functionality, business components, and access to back-end enterprise systems. It uses technologies such as caching and connection pooling to enhance resource
utilization and application performance. An Application Server also provides control
over performance, transaction, security, scalability, and reliability. Application Servers
provide infrastructure support to an enterprise, which not only reduces the cost of its
applications, but also reduces the time-to-market. Each Application Server has its own
advantages and disadvantages.

**Note**

> No two Application Servers are completely alike. There are many factors in
> selecting the appropriate Application Server that fits your enterprise needs.
> Some of those factors are performance, scalability, and J2EE-compliance.
> Some Application Servers are based on Java, CORBA, or different languages.

The following sections discuss each container used in the J2EE multitier architecture.

**15**

# Applet Container (Web Browser)

Web browsers are standard clients for e-commerce applications. Web-based applications built with standard Web technologies are flexible, maintainable, and portable. In Web-based applications, the user interface is represented by HTML documents, images, form fields, and Java applets. The Web browser contains the logic to render the Web page on the user's computer from the HTML description.

# J2EE Client Application Container

This is a Java client program that cannot run on a Web browser, and must supply its own code for rendering the user interface. Nonbrowser clients usually provide their own presentation and rendering logic. They depend on the Application Server for business logic and access to back-end services. They are more difficult to develop and deploy than Web-based clients. Any client applications written in Java can use an Application Server's common service over RMI (Remote Method Invocation).

RMI allows a client program to execute methods on an Application Server object the same way it does locally. Java applications can use the Java Swing classes to create powerful, portable, and sophisticated user interfaces. Java applications can be used effectively in the enterprise behind firewalls to avoid network issues. They can be integrated with CORBA-based applications by using the RMI/IIOP (Internet Inter-ORB Protocol) protocol.

# Web Container

Web containers provide runtime support for responding to HTTP requests. They process requests by invoking JSP pages or a servlet, and returning results to the client. In addition, Web containers provide APIs to support user session management. Servlet containers and JSP containers, which collectively are called *Web containers*, host Web components. You learned about Web containers on Day 7.

# EJB Container

As you learned on Day 1, EJB containers host EJB components. EJB containers provide automated support for transaction, security, persistence, and life cycle management of deployed components. EJBs are the business logic components for J2EE applications.

# Clustering of J2EE Components and Services

An Application Server cluster is a group of Application Server instances that work together to provide scalable and reliable J2EE applications. A cluster of servers is transparent to its clients and perceived as a single server in delivering its consolidated services. The major two capabilities that a cluster provides are load balancing, and fail-over. Load balancing provide services that result in higher application scalability, while fail-over enhances the reliability and availability of the running applications.

All instances (also called *nodes* or *members*) of a cluster work together by replicating all components and services across them. Not all components and common services can be clustered. Each Application Server product provides unique capabilities for clustering objects. Should one member of a cluster fails, another member takes over the load to preserve the running services. This increases the availability of the application to its users.

Not all J2EE components and services are suitable for clustering. Some types of EJB, such as stateless session beans, read-only entity beans are highly clusterable objects, and can always be clustered. Services such as JMS and JNDI are suitable for clustering. On the other hand, great care must be provided when clustering stateful session beans, which are clustered using in-memory replication to provide failover. In-memory replication of state is a technique used to have multiple instances (called *replicas*) of the same component deployed across different nodes of the cluster. This is more efficient than replication done using persistence through the database. Read-write entity beans are always anchored to one member of the cluster on which they are instantiated. If this member fails, the application responsibility has to create a new instance.

JDBC connection pools can be clustered across multiple servers in an Application Server environment. When a client requests a connection from the pool, the cluster selects the server that will provide the connection, allowing load balancing and protection against server failure. After a client has a connection, the state maintained by the JDBC driver makes it necessary to pin the client to the host Application Server.

Java Message Service (JMS) objects also can be clustered among the different members of a cluster. Both JMS connection factories and JMS destinations (topic or queue) can be deployed on multiple members of a cluster. Such distribution of JMS resources throughout a cluster will enhance both load-balancing and fail-over of JMS services.

**Note**

J2EE doesn't specify any rules for clustering Application Servers, and left this feature to be offered by the J2EE application server provider. Such added value is not part of the standard, but it provides tremendous capability and a key differentiator to the application server when deployed in production environments.

## Load Balancing

You can configure multiple Application Servers to share large volumes of user requests. This is accomplished by using a proxy server (Web server) to perform load balancing by distributing requests across the multiple nodes in the tier behind it.

> **Note**
>
> The most commonly used proxy servers are Apache, Netscape, and Microsoft Web server. The proxy server in this case affects the load balancing of both the Web tier and the EJB tier.

In large enterprise applications, multiple proxy servers (called a *Web server farm*) are used. The load on the proxy servers is distributed by an external load balancer. The most common load balancer is from Cisco.

### Failover and Replication

Application Server provides session replication to ensure that a client's session state remains available. When the node managing the client session fails, the proxy server sends subsequent requests to the replica in the cluster. Session replication is done behind the scenes using the cluster software.

Session replication can be either in-memory or persistent replication. In-memory replication uses fewer resources and is more efficient than persistent replication, which is the most commonly used. Persistence replication writes the session data to a database; therefore, it's far less efficient and has a negative impact on the user's response time.

# Exploring J2EE Protocols

Client applications connect with a J2EE Application Server using standard networking protocols over TCP/IP. Application Server listens for connection requests at a network address that can be specified as part of a Uniform Resource Identifier (URI), which is a standardized string that specifies a resource on a network, including the Internet.

Web-based clients communicate with Application Server using the Hypertext Transfer Protocol (HTTP). Java clients connect using the Java RMI, which allows a Java client to execute objects in Application Server. CORBA-enabled clients access Application Server RMI objects using RMI/IIOP, which allows them to execute Application Server objects using standard CORBA protocols.

The following sections summarize the protocols used by the J2EE platform to transfer data between its multiple tiers.

## Transport Control Protocol over Internet Protocol

TCP/IP, or Transport Control Protocol (TCP) over Internet Protocol (IP), provides reliable delivery of streams of data from one host to another. IP is the basic protocol of the Internet, which enables the unreliable delivery of packets from one host to another. IP makes no guarantees to deliver packets, or that packets will arrive in the order in which they were sent. The TCP adds the notions of connection and reliability, which are responsible for the guaranteed delivery of packets.

## Hypertext Transfer Protocol

HTTP is the Internet protocol used to transfer hypertext objects from remote hosts to requesting clients. It is a generic, stateless, object-oriented protocol that may be used for many similar tasks, such as DNS and distributed object-oriented systems. HTTP messages consist of requests from the client to the HTTP server, and responses from the server to the client. Application Server always responds to an HTTP request by executing a servlet, a JSP, or static HTML, which returns results to the client. An HTTP servlet is a Java class that can access the contents of an HTTP request received over the network and return an HTTP-compliant result to the client. You learned about HTTP, JSP, and servlets on Day 7.

## Secure Sockets Layer

Secure Sockets Layer (SSL) is a security protocol that provides privacy over the Internet. The protocol allows client/server applications to communicate in a way that cannot be eavesdropped on or tampered with. Servers are always authenticated, and clients are optionally authenticated. Data exchanged with the HTTP protocol can be encrypted with the SSL protocol.

 **Note**

Using SSL assures the client that it has connected with an authenticated server and that data transmitted over the network is private. You'll learn more about SSL on Day 19, "Understanding Security," when we study security for J2EE applications.

## Remote Method Invocation

RMI is the standard Java facility for distributed applications. RMI allows one Java program, called a *server*, to publish Java objects that another Java program, called a *client*, can execute. In most applications, Application Server is the RMI server and a Java client application is the client. But the roles can be reversed; RMI allows any Java program to play the role of server. You learned about RMI on Day 2, "Understanding EJB Types and Interfaces."

## JavaIDL

JavaIDL (Java Interface Definition Language) provides a mechanism to Java clients in defining interfaces to access methods on CORBA objects. JavaIDL consists of a collection of CORBA classes and interfaces. An enterprise application developer uses the IDL compiler to generate code for a Java client stub to access a CORBA object, which is defined by the IDL. The Java client is then linked with the stub and uses the CORBA interfaces to access the CORBA object.

## RMI/IIOP

RMI/IIOP is basically a bridge between RMI (the Java native protocol) and IIOP (the CORBA native protocol). IIOP is short for CORBA's Internet Inter-ORB Protocol. RMI/IIOP provides applications developer to write remote interfaces in the Java programming language. The remote interface can then be converted to IDL and implemented in any of the languages that are supported by CORBA mapping and an Object Request Broker (ORB) for that language. This mapping translates objects and primitive data types of one language to CORBA-compliant data types.

Clients and servers can be written in any language using IDL derived from the RMI interfaces. When remote interfaces are defined as Java RMI interfaces, RMI over IIOP provides interoperability with CORBA objects implemented in any language.

RMI is discussed in more details on Day 2, "Understanding the Fundamentals of Enterprise JavaBeans."

# Understanding the J2EE Common Services APIs

The J2EE architecture allows applications to access a wide range of services in a uniform manner. This section describes the technologies that provide access to infrastructure services such as databases, transactions, XML processing, naming and directory services, and enterprise information systems. As such, many J2EE APIs are available for use by developers and management by Application Server. Those of particular interest are summarized in the following sections.

## Java Naming and Directory Interface

The Java Naming and Directory Interface (JNDI) is an API that provides applications with unified methods for performing standard naming and directory services. JNDI standardizes access to directory services, such as associating attributes with objects and searching for objects using their attributes. With JNDI, an application can store and retrieve any named Java object in a standard fashion. You learned about JNDI on Day 4, "Using JNDI for Naming Services and Components."

## Java Database Connectivity

Java Database Connectivity (JDBC) is an API that provides database-independent connectivity between the J2EE platform and a wide range of data sources. JDBC allows J2EE applications to connect to databases and perform all required operations through a standard set of APIs. You learned about JDBC on Day 9, "Using JDBC to Connect to a Database."

## Enterprise JavaBeans

This is the component framework that allows the development and deployment of multi-tier distributed enterprise applications. It provides a standard for building server-side components and specifies rich run-time common services and infrastructure support of deploying components.

## JavaServer Pages

The JSP specification provides template-driven Web application development to deliver dynamic content. You learned about JSP on Day 7.

## Java Servlet

The Servlet API provides an object-oriented abstraction for building Web applications to deliver dynamic content. You learned about the Servlet API on Day 7.

## Java Message Service

The JMS API allows J2EE applications to access enterprise message-oriented middleware systems such as IBM's MQ Series and TIBCO's Rendezvous. JMS messages contain well-defined information that describes specific business actions.

Through the exchange of these messages, applications track the progress of enterprise activities. The JMS API supports both point-to-point and publish-subscribe styles of messaging. You learned about JMS on Day 13, "Understanding JMS and Message-Driven Beans."

## Java Authentication and Authorization Service

The Java Authentication and Authorization Service (JAAS) API provides security-checking mechanisms, such as authentication and authorization, to J2EE applications. You'll learn about JAAS on Day 19.

## JavaMail

The JavaMail API provides a set of abstract classes and interfaces that comprise an electronic mail system. The abstract classes and interfaces support many different implementations of message stores, formats, and transports. Many simple applications will need to interact with the messaging system only through these base classes and interfaces.

The abstract classes in the JavaMail API can be subclassed to provide new protocols and add functionality when necessary. In addition, the JavaMail API includes concrete subclasses that implement widely used Internet mail protocols and conform to specifications RFC822 and RFC2045. They are ready to be used in application development. Developers can subclass JavaMail classes to provide implementations of particular messaging systems, such as IMAP4 (Internet Message Access Protocol version 4), POP3 (Post Office Protocol version 3), and SMTP (Simple Mail Transfer Protocol). You'll learn about JavaMail on Day 21, "Developing a Complete Enterprise Application."

# JavaBeans Activation Framework

The JavaBeans Activation Framework (JAF) API integrates support for MIME (Multipurpose Internet Mail Exchange) data types into the Java platform. JavaBeans components can be specified for operating on MIME data, such as viewing or editing the data. The JAF API also provides a mechanism to map filename extensions to MIME types.

The JAF API is required by the JavaMail API to handle the data included in e-mail messages. Typical applications won't need to use the JAF API directly, although applications making sophisticated use of e-mail might need it.

# Java Transaction API

The Java Transaction API (JTA) specification allows applications to perform distributed transactions independent of specific implementations. JTA specifies standard Java interfaces between a transaction manager and all participants involved in a distributed transaction. Such participants are typically the J2EE application server, the resource managers, and the application components sharing the transaction. You'll learn about JTA in Day 16, "Understanding Transactions."

# Java API for XML Parsing

The Java API for XML Parsing (JAXP) technology provides abstractions for XML parsers and transformation APIs. It supports the processing of XML documents using the Document Object Model (DOM) and Extensible Stylesheet Language Transformation (XSLT) transformations. JAXP enables applications to parse and transform XML documents independent of a particular XML processing implementation.

> **Note**
>
> We won't cover JAXP in this book, but a brief summary of XML can be found in Appendix C, "Understanding XML." More information about JAXP can be found at `http://java.sun.com/products/jaxp`.

> **Note**
>
> Web Services are new technology that allows applications to communicate with each other over the Web. They typically communicate by passing messages. The XML-based SOAP 1.1 protocol over HTTP transport is becoming a popular and standard way exchanging messages between these applications. WSDL (Web Services Description Language) can be used to describe abstractly a Web service and can bind it to a network endpoint. EJB 2.1 is implementing Web services using stateless session beans. Session beans define a Web service interface and implements that interface in the bean class conforming to the JAX-RPC rules. The interface is specified as a service endpoint in the deployment descriptor. The session bean can get the SOAP message and the properties using the `MessageContext` interface available from `SessionContext` interface. From the client's point of view, the session bean is completely hidden behind the Web service endpoint. Java clients, including all enterprise beans, can locate an endpoint using JNDI and accesses the interface by means of the JAX-RPC API.

## J2EE Connector Architecture

The J2EE Connector Architecture (JCA) is a standard API for connecting the J2EE platform to enterprise information systems (EIS), such as enterprise resource planning (ERP), mainframe transaction processing, and database systems. The architecture addresses the issues involved when integrating existing EIS, such as SAP, CICS, legacy applications, and nonrelational databases, with an EJB server and enterprise applications. The JCA defines a set of scalable, secure, and transactional mechanisms for integrating an EIS with a J2EE platform.

The J2EE Connector Architecture is implemented both in Application Server and in an EIS-specific resource adapter (RA). A resource adapter is a system library specific to an EIS and provides an interface to the EIS. A resource adapter is analogous to a JDBC driver. The interface between a resource adapter and the EIS is specific to the underlying EIS, and can be a native interface. The JCA comprises the system-level contracts between Application Server and a given resource adaptor, a common interface for clients to access the adaptor, and interfaces for packaging and deploying resource adaptors to J2EE applications.

**Note**

> We don't cover the JCA API in this book. More information about JCA can be found at http://java.sun.com/products/jca.

**15**

## Summary of the J2EE APIs

Table 15.1 summarizes the J2EE APIs and the container from which they can be used. It also references the day in which the API is covered in this book (also refer to Figure 15.3).

**TABLE 15.1**   Summary of J2EE APIs and Containers

| API | Applet Container | Application Client Container | Web Container | EJB Container | Day |
|---|---|---|---|---|---|
| JNDI | - | Y | Y | Y | 4 |
| JDBC | - | Y | Y | Y | 9 |
| JTA | - | - | Y | Y | 16 |
| JSP | - | - | Y | - | 7 |
| Servlet | - | - | Y | - | 7 |
| EJB | - | Y | Y | Y | Many |
| RMI/IIOP | - | Y | Y | Y | 3 |
| JMS | - | Y | Y | Y | 13 |
| JavaMail | - | Y | Y | Y | 20 |
| JAF | - | Y | Y | Y | 20 |
| JAXP | - | Y | Y | Y | - |
| JAAS | - | Y | Y | Y | 19 |
| JCA | - | - | Y | Y | - |

**Note**

> In EJB 2.1, EJB container provides timer services to enterprise beans for scheduling business tasks based on time events. Both stateless session beans and entity beans can utilize the timer services provided by the container. The EJB container invokes the callback method of the enterprise bean at a specified time or after a specified duration or in specified time intervals for enterprise beans that register with the container. The timer method of an enterprise bean implements the business logic to handle the timeout event. The timer services, however, are not intended for modeling real-time events. The EJB container provides reliable timer services that can survive container crashes, activation/passivation, and load/store cycles of enterprise beans. Further the containers manage timers that are part of transactions. The containers allow enterprise beans to create, locate, and cancel timers.

# Exploring the J2EE Data Formats

Data formats define the types of data that can be exchanged between different components residing in different tiers. The J2EE architecture supports for the following data formats:

- HTML documents—The markup language used to define hypertext documents accessible over the Internet. HTML enables many display elements to be included in a Web page, such as images, sounds, video, form fields, references to other HTML documents, and basic ASCII data. HTML documents are located by URLs.

- Images—The J2EE platform supports both the GIF (Graphics Interchange Format), and JPEG (Joint Photographic Experts Group) images.

- Class files—The format of a compiled Java file into a bytecode format.

- JAR files—A platform-independent file format (compressed files) that permits many files to be aggregated into one file. Other types of JAR files are Web Archives (WARs), Enterprise Archives (EARs), and Resource Archives (RARs). (See the "Packaging J2EE Applications" section later today for more information.)

- XML documents—A well-formed text-based markup language that is used to define data elements based on a schema. Unlike HTML, XML tags describe the data, rather than the format for displaying it. XML is covered in Appendix C.

# Packaging J2EE Applications

The J2EE platform simplifies the deployment of enterprise applications. This is accomplished by packaging applications and components into independent modules. Each module contains all the components along with a deployment descriptor. The deployment descriptor, as its name implies, describes each component's properties, the relationship between components, and the customized common services to be provided by the container at runtime. Typically, all components of one tier are packaged into a separate module.

A J2EE application consists of one or more J2EE modules and one J2EE application deployment descriptor. An application deployment descriptor contains a list of modules and how to configure them. A J2EE application is represented by an EAR file, which must contain at least one JAR file. In addition, an EAR file might contain any number of WAR files and RAR files, or none at all (see Figure 15.5). The standard deployment descriptor for the J2EE application is application.xml, and is located in the META-INF directory of the EAR file.

Each J2EE module consists of one or more J2EE components for the same container type and one component deployment descriptor of that type.

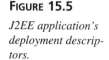

**FIGURE 15.5**

*J2EE application's deployment descriptors.*

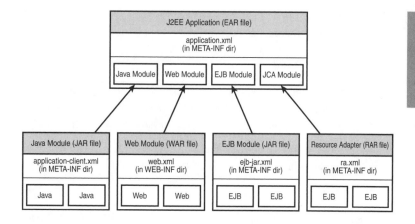

The three types of J2EE modules are

- Application client modules—Contain class files and a deployment descriptor. Application client modules are packaged as JAR files with a `.jar` extension, which will be deployed into the client application container. The standard deployment descriptor for this module is `application-client.xml`, and is located in the `META-INF` directory of the JAR file.

- Web modules—Consist of JSP files, class files for servlets, GIF and HTML files, and a Web deployment descriptor. Web modules are packaged as JAR files with a `.war` extension, which will be deployed into the Web container. The standard deployment descriptor for this module is `web.xml`, and is located in the `WEB-INF` directory of the WAR file.

- EJB modules—Consist of class files for all the deployed EJBs and a deployment descriptor. EJB modules are packaged as JAR files with a `.jar` extension, which will be deployed into the EJB container. The standard deployment descriptor for this module is `ejb-jar.xml`, and is located in the `META-INF` directory of the JAR file.

- Resource adapter modules—Comprise all Java interfaces, classes, native libraries, and the resource adapter deployment descriptor. Resource adapter modules are packaged as RAR files with an `.rar` extension. The standard deployment descriptor for this module is `ra.xml`, and is located in the `META-INF` directory of the JAR file.

# Designing J2EE Applications

In designing J2EE applications, care must be taken to avoid many recurring problems, most of which are related to optimizing remote calls between client and the requesting service. For example, fulfilling a request by making one trip to the database is much more efficient than making several trips. This enhances the network traffic and optimizes repeated resource allocations. These recurring problems and issues in designing applications are gathered and documented in a catalog of design patterns.

Patterns are typically written in a structured format. A design pattern is identified by a name, problem statement, and the solution to that problem. Design patterns are developed to prevent reinventing the wheel; therefore, they are reusable artifacts. They exist at different levels of abstraction, and they communicate designs and best practices. In enterprise applications, you can join design patterns together to solve a larger problem.

By now, you have already been introduced to the MVC design pattern. Today, you'll learn few more patterns that can be applied in designing J2EE applications.

> **Note**
>
> For more details about a large catalog of design patterns, refer to the classic book, *Design Patterns: Elements of Reusable Object-Oriented Software*, by Erich Gamma, Richard Helm, Ralph Johnson, and John Vlissides (ISBN 0-201-63361-2). These four authors are also known as the GOF (Gang of Four).

## Session Façade Design Pattern

The J2EE specification doesn't restrict access to entity beans by any client components. EJB clients, such as Java applications from the client tier, and servlets and JSP from the Web tier, can have direct access to entity beans. Access of entity beans directly over the network takes more remote calls and imposes network overhead. Again, in minimizing remote calls, a session bean can be used as a façade in the EJB tier to mediate access on behalf of the client (see Figure 15.6).

**FIGURE 15.6**

*Session façade pattern*

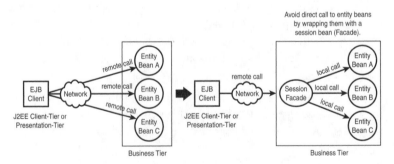

Session Facade Design Pattern

An EJB client accesses the session bean (Façade) instead of entity beans through a coarse-grained method call to accomplish a business process. Wrapping entity beans with a Session Façade reduces network traffic, which is reflected in positive performance.

## Service Locator Design Pattern

The Service Locator pattern addresses the issue of the usage of JNDI to look up different resources and services. These resources can be any of the EJBHome objects, DataSource objects, or JMS ConnectionFactory objects. Each lookup is an expensive remote call in terms of network traffic. To minimize remote calls, a service locator object is created locally to maintain a cache of these service objects (see Figure 15.7).

**FIGURE 15.7**

*Service Locator pattern.*

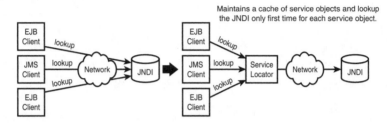

Session Locator Pattern

Any lookup for a JNDI remote object is done only the first time; subsequent lookups access the local cache of service objects.

## Message Façade Design Pattern

Because methods of both session and entity beans are executed synchronously, a client method call has to wait until a value is returned. Some e-commerce applications, such as checking a customer's credit, require waiting for an approval before proceeding. Using synchronous session or entity beans in such situations will not be efficient because the client has to wait for a reply. This situation can be resolved by using a message-driven bean, waiting for a reply, and delivering it to the client through an e-mail (see Figure 15.8).

**FIGURE 15.8**

*Message façade pattern.*

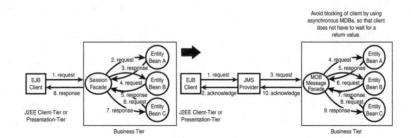

Message Facade Design Pattern

Using message-driven beans implies the use of the JMS product, which is assumed as part of the enterprise infrastructure.

## Value Object Design Pattern

The Value Object design pattern is used to transfer remote, fine-grained data by sending a coarse-grained or bulk view of that data.

**Note** We briefly discussed the concept of a *data bean*, during the discussion of JavaBeans on Day 7. A data bean is a typical implementation of this pattern.

The main advantage of this pattern is to make one trip to the remote EJB tier, and bring a coarse-grained (bulky) object of data to the local machine. Again, this reduces network traffic, and enhances your application performance (see Figure 15.9).

**FIGURE 15.9**

*Value object pattern.*

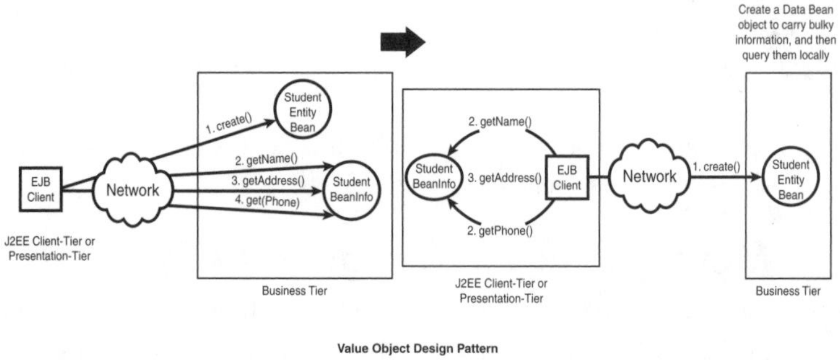

Value Object Design Pattern

# Best Practices

J2EE has many best practices applied to designing applications and components. The main keys in them are the design patterns covered in the previous section. Most best practices focus on minimizing remote calls, which reduce network traffic and enhance the performance of your applications. Both the Service Locator pattern and the Session Façade pattern address remote calls by creating an object local to the service you're trying to access. Caching is another technique used to reduce network traffic in distributed applications.

Not all solutions are synchronous; some elegant solutions use an asynchronous messaging paradigm. Using message-driven beans to delivering solutions in which clients do not have to wait for an immediate response is more efficient.

J2EE best practices is a subject by itself, and requires more study and architectural experience. Each component, application, and tier has its own design considerations, which we try to cover across our journey of 21 days.

15

Clustering of services and components across multiple tiers has great impact on the scalability and availability of your applications. Both load balancing and failover are used in clustering technology to meet heavy load situations.

# Summary

Today, you explored the J2EE platform and the rationale behind its architecture. You learned about different type of containers and the common services that are available for use by the components hosted in that container. J2EE container is a runtime environment and provides several levels of abstractions. You also learned a brief description of the common services available in the J2EE platform. You recognized the J2EE modules necessary to build and deploy J2EE applications. We covered some of the design patterns used in the J2EE platform, such as the Session Façade and the Service Locator.

# Q&A

**Q What are the main tiers of the J2EE architecture?**

**A** The J2EE architecture consists of four tiers: the client tier, presentation tier, business logic tier, and the EIS tier.

**Q Why should I use design patterns?**

**A** Design patterns are reusable artifacts, and proven solutions that can be directly applied to solve certain problems. Design patterns are gained by experience and documented for use by architects and designers of enterprise applications.

# Quiz

1. Which J2EE APIs are used to send an e-mail message to a user?

    A. Java Message Service (JMS)

    B. JavaMail

    C. JavaBean Activation Framework (JAF)

    D. JavaServer Pages (JSP)

2. Which container is most recommended to access a database?

    A. Web container

    B. EJB container

    C. Web browser

    D. Client application container

3. To minimize remote calls, which design patterns are recommended?

    A. Session Façade

    B. MVC

    C. Message Façade

    D. Service Locator

## Quiz Answers

1. B, C
2. B
3. A, D

# Exercises

1. What are the main components included in a WAR file?

2. What is the advantage of using the Session Façade pattern?

3. What is the main difference between a three-tier architecture and a multitier architecture, with respect to the MVC paradigm?

4. What are the common services available to the J2EE platform?

# DAY 16

# Understanding J2EE Transactions

Today, we'll cover both local and global J2EE transactions. On Day 9, "Using JDBC to Connect to a Database," you learned how to use local transactions to handle JDBC calls, and on Day 13, "Understanding JMS and Message-Driven Beans," you learned local transaction to handle Java Message Service (JMS) messages. Today, we will focus on both local and distributed transactions through components and applications across all J2EE tiers. We will discuss the Java Transaction API (JTA), and show how it abstracts transaction management and makes this complex task completely transparent to developers. Concepts such as transaction level of isolation, transaction attributes, and demarcation managements will be highlighted. We will also shed light on both bean-managed transactions and container-managed transactions, which are the subjects of the next two days.

The following summarizes the activities that you'll be learning today:

- Understand transaction fundamentals
- Understand the basic types of transactions: local and distributed

- Learn about the JTA, which manages transactions in J2EE applications
- Learn how to use transactions across all J2EE tiers
- Give a working example of distributed transactions using both JMS and JDBC resources in one global transaction

# Understanding Transaction Fundamentals

A *transaction* is a set of one or more SQL statements that are executed together as a unit of work, so either all the statements are executed or none of the statements are executed. In addition to grouping statements together for execution as a unit, a transaction becomes the fundamental unit of recovery, consistency, and concurrency in reliable J2EE applications.

One of the primary objectives of EJB architecture is to provide transaction services through the EJB container. This relieves the application programmer from dealing with the complex issues of failure recovery, concurrency, and multi-user programming. The transaction simplifies the task of building a sophisticated enterprise application, and it is the foundation for dealing with complex B2B (Business-to-Business) and B2C (Business-to-Consumer) applications.

The following two sections discuss transaction properties, and the transaction models used in transactional applications.

## The ACID Properties

Enterprise transactions share certain characteristics, commonly known as ACID properties, which are important for data integrity and consistency:

- Atomic: All operations of the transaction must be performed successfully or not at all.
- Consistent: The transaction must transition the data from one consistent state to another, preserving the data's semantic and referential integrity. Access should not be allowed to inconsistent data.
- Isolated: Transactions may run concurrently, but any changes made to data by a transaction are invisible to other concurrent transactions until the transaction commits. Isolation requires that several concurrent transactions must be repeatable, (that is, they must produce the same results in the data as same transactions executed serially, and in any order).
- Durable: After the transaction is committed, the resultant data should be permanent. This implies that data for all committed transactions can be recovered after a system crash or media failure.

In summary, an ACID transaction ensures the consistency and integrity of the persistent data. It also assumes a stable set of inputs and working data, and that the data changes are recoverable after system failure.

## Exploring the Transaction Models

Generally, a transaction model describes the main entities that constitute a transaction, and defines when a transaction starts, when it succeeds, and what to do in case of failure. A transaction consists of group of statements, such as database SQL, logical operations, or messages sent to a queue. There are two transaction models: flat and nested.

**16**

### Flat Transactions

In this simple model, a transaction consists of a series of operations. It can be either local or global (distributed). If all the operations succeed, the transaction is committed. If one operation fails, the whole transaction rolls back to the same state before it started. The EJB architecture supports flat transactions, which we will cover today.

### Nested Transactions

This model allows new transactions to be spawned as children, inside another transaction. This is similar to a tree of transactions: The root transaction contains sub-transactions, and so on. Each sub-transaction can be rolled back individually. The whole nested transaction commits if and only if all the sub-transactions succeed.

| Caution | Currently, the EJB specification supports only flat transactions and not nested transactions. As the EJB specification is a work in progress, future versions of the EJB specification might support nested transactions. |
|---|---|

# Types of Transactions

Transactions can be either local (also called *standard*) or global (also called *distributed*), depending on the resources and the data sources involved. Most enterprise applications use some sort of transactions. J2EE applications and components are designed with transactions in mind. In the following sections, we will cover both types of transaction types with respect to JDBC and JMS applications.

## Local Transactions

A local transaction deals with a single resource manager. Each resource manager provides access to a single external resource through a collection of configurations and processes (see Figure 16.1). A resource manager enforces the ACID properties for a specific external resource, such as an RDBMS or a JMS provider. J2EE applications access the resource manager through a resource adapter. For example, a transaction-aware JDBC API is a common resource adapter. A JMS API is another resource adapter that provides access to a messaging system (JMS provider). The JCA (J2EE Connector Architecture) is a common adapter that provides access to legacy systems (ERP or CRM systems) through a JCA adapter.

**FIGURE 16.1**

*Local transactions.*

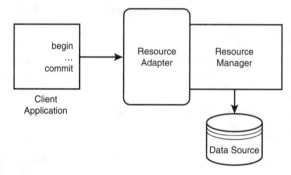

Local transaction uses only one resource manager

*Transaction demarcation* denotes the events—such as the begin, commit, and rollback events—that occur at each transaction boundary. J2EE applications and components provide two methods of transaction demarcation, either programmatically or declaratively. In the programmatic description, the bean's developer explicitly demarcates the transaction boundary in the bean's code. This type of transaction demarcation is called a *bean-managed transaction*. The declarative approach is when the demarcation is specified in the beanís deployment descriptor. The EJB container will manage all transaction demarcation, and will propagate the transaction context across different beans, and even across EJB containers. This type of transaction demarcation is called a *container-managed transaction*.

We will cover local transactions with respect to JDBC and JMS. JCA transactions are beyond the scope of this book.

## JDBC Local Transactions

As you learned on Day 9, JDBC controls local transactions through the `Connection` object. Both transaction settings and transaction demarcations are performed on the `Connection` object. By default, all database operations through the JDBC driver are transactional. To change this behavior, you learned to use `setAutoCommit(false)` on the `Connection` object to manage your transactions. You also learned to set other transaction demarcations using the `commit()` or `rollback()` method on the `Connection` object.

## Transaction Levels of Isolation

To control concurrency among different transactions in accessing shared data, the DBMS provides the concept of *locking*. Locking protects data integrity and consistency. On the other hand, it is a costly operation and has a negative impact on overall performance. Transaction levels-of-isolation is the concept by which components can be set to control the multiple interactions with the shared resource. The transaction level of isolation is set by the application server to control the application behavior. The levels of isolation depend on the application, the nature of the data, and the frequency of updates.

**16**

 **Note**

> Note that in auto-commit mode, in which each Statement is considered a transaction, locks are held for only one Statement. After a lock is set, it will remain until the transaction is committed or rolled back.

Here are some of the issues related to transaction isolation:

- A *dirty read* occurs when the first transaction reads uncommitted changes made by the second transaction. If the second transaction is rolled back, the data read by the first transaction becomes invalid because the rollback undoes the changes.

- A *phantom read* occurs when new records added to the database are detectable by transactions that started prior to the insert.

- A *repeatable read* is when the data read is guaranteed to look the same if read again during the same transaction. This occurs when each transaction is Serializable.

How locks are set is determined by the *transaction isolation level*, which can range from not supporting transactions at all to supporting transactions that enforce very strict access rules.

Table 16.1 summarizes the transaction isolation levels, from the least restrictive to the most restrictive. It lists also how the transaction isolation level affects system performance.

**TABLE 16.1**    Transaction Isolation Levels

| Transaction Level | Dirty Read | Phantom Read | Nonrepeatable | Restriction | Performance |
|---|---|---|---|---|---|
| TRANSACTION_NONE | N/A | N/A | N/A | Lowest | Fastest |
| TRANSACTION_UNCOMMITTED | Yes | Yes | Yes | Low | Faster |

**TABLE 16.1**    continued

| Transaction Level | Dirty Read | Phantom Read | Nonrepeatable | Restriction | Performance |
|---|---|---|---|---|---|
| TRANSACTION_READ_COMMITED | No | Yes | Yes | High | Fast |
| TRANSACTION_REPEATABLE_READ | No | Yes | No | Higher | Medium |
| TRANSACTION_SERIALIZABLE | No | No | No | Highest | Slow |

From Table 16.1, you can see that as the isolation levels become more restrictive, the performance of the transaction decreases. A TRANSACTION_SERIALIZABLE isolation level, for example, involves more locks in the database; therefore, it has a greater impact on the transaction's performance.

You can control the transaction isolation level using the method setTransactionIsolation() of the Connection object. You also can examine the transaction level for a connection using the getTransactionIsolation() method. Here is an example:

```
// Begin a new transaction by disable transaction
// auto-mode on the Connection object
conn.setAutoCommit(false);
// Set transaction isolation level on the Connection object
conn.setTransactionIsolation(Connection.TRANSACTION_READ_COMMITTED);
// Create a Statement object using the Connection object
Statement stmt = conn.createStatement();
try {
  stmt.executeUpdate("UPDATE Student set fname='Laura' where id =5");
  conn.commit();
} catch (SQLException ex) {
  conn.rollback();
  stmt.close();
}
```

**Note**    Transaction isolation level cannot be set during a transaction.

In EJB, for container-managed transactions, isolation levels are set in the bean's deployment descriptor. However, in a bean-managed transaction, the bean's developer sets the transaction isolation level in the bean's code. These approaches will be covered in next two days (Days 17 and 18).

**Caution**

Different EJB containers allow different levels of granularity for setting isolation levels; some containers defer this responsibility to the database. In some containers, you might be able to set different isolation levels for different methods, whereas other products might require the same isolation level for all methods in a bean or, possibly, all beans in the container.

**Note**

If a JDBC Connection participates in a distributed transaction, the JTA transaction manager will ignore both the auto-commit mode and isolation level settings during the distributed transaction. Distributed transactions will be covered in the next section.

**16**

## JMS Local Transactions

As you learned on Day 13, JMS controls local transaction demarcation through the Session object (QueueSession in PTP mode; TopicSession in Pub/Sub mode). By default, a new session created from its corresponding connection is *not* transactional. To change this behavior, create a transacted session by setting the transacted parameter to true of the method createQueueSession(true) or createTopicSession(true). A transaction will be committed only when you use the method commit() or rollback() on the session object. In JMS, transactions are chained, which means that a new transaction automatically starts as soon as the current transaction is committed or rolled back.

In JMS, local transactions are handled by a JMS producer or consumer, or, in some cases, a JMS router (a combined producer and consumer). The following is an example of a local transaction used by a JMS's queue sender:

```
// Create a transacted session for a QueueSender
QueueSession qSession =
    qCon.createQueueSession (true, Session.AUTO_ACKNOWLEDGE);
QueueSender qSender = qSession.createSender (myQueue);
qSender.send(msg);
qSession.commit();
```

In the preceding example, the message msg will not be delivered until the commit() is completed. Here is another example of a QueueReceiver in a transacted session:

```
// Create a transacted session for a QueueReceiver
QueueSession qSession =
        qCon.createQueueSession (true, Session.AUTO_ACKNOWLEDGE);
QueueReceiver qReceiver = qSession.createReceiver (myQueue);
TextMessage msg = (TextMessage) qRec.receive();
qSession.commit();
```

A *message router* (sometimes called a *message broker*) is a common application used to deliver messages between multiple producers and multiple consumers. Here is an example of a transacted session in a message-router scenario:

```
// Create a transacted session for a message router
QueueSession qSession =
        qCon.createQueueSession (true, Session.AUTO_ACKNOWLEDGE);
QueueReceiver qReceiver = qSession.createReceiver (myQueue);
TextMessage msg = (TextMessage) qReceiver.receive();
QueueSender qSender = qSession.createSender(myQueue);
qSender.send(msg);
qSession.commit();
```

Similarly, a transacted session can be created using a `TopicSession` in the Pub/Sub model.

## Distributed Transactions

A distributed transaction executes operations on different resources to accomplish its workflow requirement. Database and middleware vendors have developed the X/Open Distributed Transaction Protocol (DTP) model to define the rules and guidelines for distributed transactions.

### Two-Phase Commit Protocol

To perform a distributed transaction, the transaction manager coordinates the transaction execution across multiple resource managers. Because all participant resource managers are not aware of each other, an algorithm has been established, as a standard protocol, to control the interactions of all participants. The two-phase commit (2PC) protocol enforces the ACID properties and is implemented into two phases:

- Phase 1: This is the preparation phase. The transaction manager, or coordinator, asks each resource manager to prepare to commit (also called *vote to commit*). This involves assigning locks to shared resources without actually writing data to permanent storage. Each resource manager replies with its readiness to execute.

- Phase 2: If all the resource managers reply with successful preparation, the transaction manager requests all to commit their changes; otherwise, it tells them all to roll back and indicates transaction failure to the application. The transaction will succeed if and only if all resource managers commit successfully.

Some variants of the 2PC implementation allow for full transaction success, even if one resource manager fails. The transaction manager saves the failed part to be recovered later.

**Note**     If there is only one participant in the transaction, the transaction manager avoids the 2PC, and uses the local transaction's single-phase commit protocol.

## Distributed Transaction Model

**16**

A distributed transaction often spans multiple resource managers. Each resource manager may be hosted on a heterogeneous processing node, manages its own threads of control, and has a different resource adapter. According to DTP, a distributed transaction model is more complex than a local one; more participants are involved in a distributed transaction model. The following list describes the participants in a distributed transaction:

- Transaction Originator: The client initiates the transaction. It can be a Java application in the client tier, a servlet in the Web tier, or a session bean in the EJB tier. It also can be a JMS producer/consumer in the Web tier or the EJB tier.

- Transaction Manager: Manages transactions on behalf of the originator. It enforces the transaction ACID properties by coordinating access across all participating resource managers. When resource managers fail during transactions, transaction managers help resource managers decide whether to commit or roll back pending transactions. JTA implements the transaction manager in J2EE architecture.

- Recoverable Resource: Provides persistent storage for transaction data to ensure durability of the transaction. In most cases, this is often a database or a flat file resource.

- Resource Manager: One of the aforementioned transaction-aware types. This can manage a DBMS, a JMS provider, or a JCA resource.

Figure 16.2 summarizes the protocols and interactions among all participants of a distributed transaction.

The transaction manager interacts with all participant resource managers through the XA protocol (defined by X/Open to implement the 2PC algorithm). Each of the resource adapters complies with the XA protocol by providing XA-compliant interfaces. Both JDBC API and JMS API provide XA-compliant interfaces that are designed to be used by the container vendor and not by the application developer. Application clients interface with the transaction manager through the TX protocol (which includes all the transaction demarcation events).

In the case of local transactions, applications interact directly with the resource manager. But in distributed transactions, applications are required to interface with the transaction manager, which coordinates all transaction demarcations among multiple resource managers. This decoupling of transaction management simplifies the task of writing complex enterprise applications.

**FIGURE 16.2**

*Distributed transaction model.*

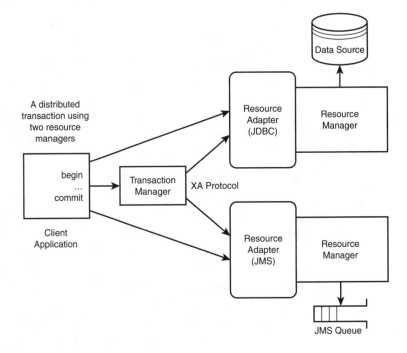

## Java Transaction API

J2EE implements the DTP model using JTA, in which the transaction manager is represented by `javax.transaction.UserTransaction`. JTA enforces the transaction ACID properties between multiple resource managers. The JTA transaction manager is implemented by the EJB container vendor (application server vendor), and registered in the JNDI namespace. A client creates a distributed transaction context by looking up the JNDI namespace for the named resource `UserTransaction`, which acts as a factory of distributed transactions. The `UserTransaction` interface abstracts all the classes and interfaces of managing a J2EE distributed transactions. The application and component developer needs only to use the `begin()`, `commit()`, and `rollback()` methods of the `UserTransaction` context.

The `begin()` method *explicitly* starts a distributed transaction and associates the transaction with a calling thread. The transaction manager transparently (that is, behind the scenes) manages transactional access to any XA-compliant resource managers that the application uses. This clean isolation of responsibilities makes it easier to develop portable and complex enterprise applications.

**Note**

To start a distributed transaction, developers issue an explicit `begin()` method. This is somewhat different in a local transaction, where a transaction is implicitly started in the method `setAutoMode(false)` of a JDBC `Connection`, or `createQueueSession(true)` of a JMS `Connection`.

16

The following code demonstrates how the named resource `UserTransaction` is looked up in the default JNDI service, and a context is established for the transaction manager. Applications and components of the Web tier use this context to control the behavior of the distributed transaction. The body of the distributed transaction can be any code designed to access one or more resource manager.

```
Context ctx = new InitialContext();
UserTransaction utx =
        (UserTransaction) ctx.lookup("java:comp/UserTransaction");
utx.begin();
// use multiple resources, such as databases (JDBC),
// messaging (JMS), and integrations (JCA)
utx.commit();
```

**Note**

The transaction manager interacts with the XA-compliant resource adapter transparently. Implicitly, it uses a transaction ID to identify each transaction thread of execution. Applications do not need to know about this transaction ID.

The previous code snippet demonstrates how to establish a `UserTransaction` context from a Web tier component (a JSP or a servlet). A `UserTransaction` context is established differently in the EJB tier, as explained later.

Three different types of resource manager are defined and supported by the J2EE architecture: JDBC-compliant databases, JCA adapters, and JMS providers. All three types of resource managers may be used within the scope of a single distributed transaction.

**Note**

We discuss only resource managers and resource adapters for JDBC and JMS. The JCA adapter and resource manager are beyond the scope of this book.

The main benefit of JTA is to combine multiple components and enterprise applications into a single distributed transaction with minor programming effort. Transactions are propagated automatically between multiple components and J2EE applications. As mentioned before, in a container-managed transaction, all demarcations are handled declaratively using the deployment descriptor. Bean-managed transactions use explicit demarcation in the bean's code.

**Note**    JTA can be used by an EJB to access a single resource. In this case, the JTA driver is intelligent enough to switch to local transaction mode, and uses the one-phase commit protocol.

There are many scenarios in which JTA can be used to access multiple resources in a single distributed transaction context. Here are the most commonly used scenarios in enterprise applications. Figure 16.3 illustrates these scenarios.

**FIGURE 16.3**

*Scenarios of distributed transactions.*

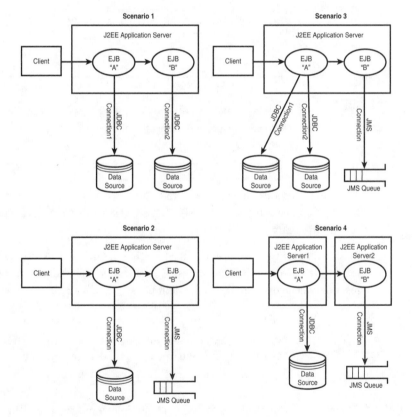

- Scenario 1: A distributed transaction spans two EJBs: A and B. Each has its JDBC `Connection` to a `DataSource`. Each database instance has its own connection pool, which is defined separately in the JNDI service. The JTA transaction context propagates from EJB A to EJB B. This scenario is useful in updates of two databases simultaneously, as one unit of work.

- Scenario 2: A distributed transaction spans two EJBs: A and B. The first has its JDBC `Connection` to a `DataSource`, whereas the second has its connection to a JMS provider. The JTA transaction context propagates from EJB A to EJB B. This scenario is useful in updating a database, while ensuring the delivery of a JMS message.

- Scenario 3: Similar to Scenario 2, except that EJB A has access to two data sources; each has its connection pool. JTA transaction context propagates from EJB A to EJB B.

- Scenario 4: The JTA transaction manager propagates the transaction context across the EJB container (application server) boundary to another J2EE-compliant container. These containers can be of the same vendor or of different vendors.

You see from these scenarios that the distributed transaction context is propagated from one component to another. You need to keep in mind that JTA is working behind the scenes through the EJB container to control transaction behavior.

 **Note**

> While a JMS resource manager is participating in a distributed transaction, the JTA driver will ignore a JMS transacted `Session` setting. This setting will be resumed after the distributed transaction is completed. Similarly, a local transaction setting of the JDBC resource manager will be ignored by the JTA driver during the course of the distributed transaction, and will resume its setting after the transaction is completed.

## JTA Exception Handling

Few JTA exceptions are required to be handled while processing a distributed transaction. Table 16.2 summarizes JTA exceptions as part of the `javax.transaction` package.

**TABLE 16.2**   JTA Exceptions

| Exception | Description |
| --- | --- |
| RollbackException | Thrown to indicate that the transaction has been rolled back rather than committed. |

**TABLE 16.2**    continued

| Exception | Description |
| --- | --- |
| HeuristicMixedException | Thrown to indicate that a heuristic decision was made and that some relevant updates have been committed, whereas others have been rolled back. |
| HeuristicRollbackException | Thrown to indicate that a heuristic decision was made and that some relevant updates have been rolled back. |
| SystemException | Thrown if the transaction manager encounters an unexpected error condition. |

**Note**    JTA transactions are automatically rolled back if a SystemException is thrown from a bean method. Transactions are not automatically rolled back, however, if an application exception is thrown.

## Java Transaction Services

The Java Transaction Service (JTS) API is a Java binding of the CORBA Object Transaction Service (OTS) specification. JTS provides transaction interoperability using the standard IIOP protocol for transaction propagation between servers. The JTS API is intended for vendors who implement transaction-processing infrastructure for enterprise middleware. For example, an EJB Server vendor may use a JTS implementation as the underlying transaction manager.

EJB containers are not required to support the JTS interfaces; they are only required to support the JTA and the Java Connector APIs. The JTS interfaces are low-level APIs between a J2EE server and enterprise information system (EIS) resource managers, and they are not intended for the use by application developers.

# Exploring Transactions Across the J2EE Tiers

Distributed transactions in J2EE applications are supported by the EJB container (application server). Both the Web tier, and the EJB tier can provide distributed transaction capability, which means that they can access the UserTransaction interface. Applets and J2EE client applications are not required to provide distributed transaction support (and doing so is not recommended). We strongly recommend using distributed transactions through the EJB tier. As explained on Day 9, placing all your JDBC calls in EJBs ensures a high degree of server application portability. This relieves application developers from having to manage transaction control with explicit JDBC calls or JMS messages.

In the Web tier, a client component (such as a JSP or servlet) can obtain a `UserTransaction` using JNDI `Context`, as explained in the previous section. Transaction demarcation should start and complete in the servlet's `service()` method.

**Caution**

Few architects encourage the use of distributed transactions in the Web tier through the use of a servlet or a JSP, which are not transactional by design. On the other hand, EJBs are transactional components that can be managed by the EJB container or by the bean code itself.

16

## Learning Bean-Managed Transactions

Only session beans and message-driven beans can manage transactions programmatically. All transaction demarcations are managed by the bean's code. Session beans and MDBs can establish a `UserTransaction` context from `EJBContext`. The bean then uses the context in other transactional demarcation.

**Note**

EJBs establish transaction context from `EJBContext`, and not through looking up the JNDI service, as in the case of a JSP or servlet. The container passes the bean's transaction context secretly to the bean's context.

```
public class UserManagerBean implements SessionBean {
    SessionContext ctx = null;
    public void setSessionContext(SessionContext ctx) {
      this.ctx = ctx;}
    // Implement other methods such as ejbCreate, ejbRemove,
    ...
    public void connectUserManager(){
      // Create a UserTransaction context from the EJB context
      UserTransaction utx = ctx.getUserTranssaction();
      utx.begin();
      // Access multiple resources as one unit-of-work
      utx.commit();
      ...
    }
// other methods of the class
}
```

Only session beans and message-driven beans can use bean-managed transaction demarcation. Entity beans must always use a container-managed transaction demarcation.

To control the bean access performance, the transaction isolation level can be set programmatically using the setTransactionIsolation() method on the Connection object. Full coverage of bean-managed transactions is in Day 17.

# Container-Managed Transactions

In a container-managed transaction, the EJB container manages the transaction demarcation for each method of the bean. Transaction behavior is described in the bean's deployment descriptor. *Transaction attributes* determine how the EJB container handles transactions with each bean's method invocation. Each method can be associated with only a single transaction. A transaction begins just before the method starts, and commits just before it exits. Not all methods of the bean are associated with transactions, only those specified in the bean's deployment descriptor by transaction attributes. The following section introduces the transaction attributes that are vital in configuring the bean's methods participating in a container-managed transaction.

## Transaction Attributes

For a bean participating in a container-managed transaction, transaction attributes are set in the bean's deployment descriptor. It is possible to set a transaction attribute for the whole bean or for only individual methods. A transaction attribute must be specified for the methods in the remote interface of a session bean, and for the methods in the home and remote interfaces of an entity bean. Transactional behavior of the bean can be controlled declaratively by changing the transaction attributes in the deployment descriptor. Table 16.3 summarizes the transaction attributes of a container-managed transaction.

**TABLE 16.3**  Container-Managed Transaction Attributes

| Attribute | Description |
| --- | --- |
| NotSupported | The bean does not support transactions. Transactions will not be propagated through the bean. If the client is associated with a transaction context, the container will suspend the transaction before invoking the bean's method. After the method completes, the container resumes the suspended transaction association. |
| Supports | If the client is associated with a transaction context, it will be propagated through the bean's method. If the client is not associated with a transaction context, it will be suspended. |
| Required | The bean will always be part of a JTA transaction. If the client is associated with a JTA transaction, the context will be propagated to the bean's method. If the client is not associated with a transaction, the container begins a new transaction, and commits when the method returns. |

**TABLE 16.3**    continued

| Attribute | Description |
|---|---|
| RequiresNew | The EJB container always begins a new transaction before invoking the bean's method, and commits upon the method's return. If the calling client is associated with a transaction context, the container suspends the transaction with the current thread before starting the new transaction. When the method and the transaction complete, the container resumes the suspended transaction. |
| Mandatory | The calling client must be associated with a transaction; otherwise, invoking the bean's method will fail, throwing a `TransactionRequiredException`. |
| Never | The calling client must not be associated with a transaction; otherwise, invoking the bean's method will fail, throwing a `RemoteException`. |

The following is an example of a deployment descriptor of a stateful session bean with a container-managed transaction demarcation:

```
<?xml version="1.0"?>
<!DOCTYPE ejb-jar PUBLIC
'-//Sun Microsystems, Inc.//DTD Enterprise JavaBeans 2.0//EN'
'http://java.sun.com/dtd/ejb-jar_2_0.dtd'>
<ejb-jar>
  <enterprise-beans>
    <session>
      <ejb-name>EnrollmentCart</ejb-name>
      <home>EnrollmentCartHome</home>
      <remote>EnrollmentCart</remote>
      <ejb-class>EnrollmentCartBean</ejb-class>
      <session-type>Stateful</session-type>
      <transaction-type>Container</transaction-type>
    </session>
  </enterprise-beans>
  <assembly-descriptor>
    <container-transaction>
      <method>
        <ejb-name>EnrollmentCart</ejb-name>
        <method-intf>Remote</method-intf>
        <method-name>getCourses</method-name>
        <method-params/>
      </method>
      <trans-attribute>Required</trans-attribute>
    </container-transaction>
  </assembly-descriptor>
</ejb-jar>
```

Notice that only the `getCourses()` method is specified with the transaction attribute `Required`.

It's always recommended to use container-managed transactions in a J2EE application if possible. Container-managed transactions are easy to implement. They keep your applications more portable and flexible in deployment. Container-managed transactions will be covered in more detail in Day 18.

16

> **Note**
>
> It is also recommended that an EJB component always access a data source under the scope of a transaction because this provides some guarantee of the integrity and consistency of the data.

# Example of Distributed Transactions

Today's example is to implement a distributed transaction that accesses two resource managers: a JDBC resource manager and a JMS provider. The example runs in both the WebLogic and JBoss server environments. The PointBase database is used for the WebLogic Server, and the HyperSonic database for JBoss server, whereas each server provides JMS service separately.

The example consists of a stateless session bean, UserManager, which uses JTA's distributed transaction to perform the following tasks as one unit of work:

- Updates the database with student information
- Sends a JMS message to the registration office

The registration office is modeled as a message-driven bean: RegistrarMDB.

Figure 16.4 depicts the components used in the example. Each component is described later in a separate listing.

**FIGURE 16.4**

*Example of the UserManager EJB.*

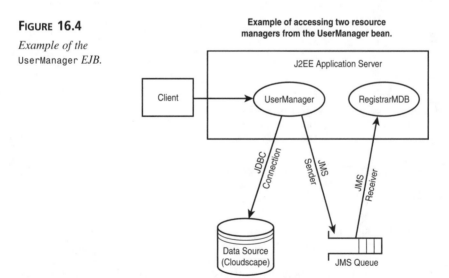

Listing 16.1 is for the remote interface UserManager, which lists all the business methods used in our example.

**LISTING 16.1**   The Remote Interface `UserManager.java`

```
package day16;
import javax.ejb.EJBObject;
import java.rmi.RemoteException;
public interface UserManager extends EJBObject {
  public void connectUserManager()
        throws RemoteException;
  public void addCourse(String studentID, String courseID)
        throws RemoteException;
  public void notifyRegistrar(String studentID, String courseID)
        throws RemoteException;
  public void disconnectUserManager()
        throws RemoteException;
}
```

The home interface `UserManagerHome` in Listing 16.2 lists all the lifecycle methods used to manage the bean.

**LISTING 16.2**   The Home Interface `UserManagerHome.java`

```
package day16;
import java.rmi.RemoteException;
import javax.ejb.*;
public interface UserManagerHome extends EJBHome {
    UserManager create() throws RemoteException, CreateException;
}
```

Listing 16.3 is the bean class `UserManagerBean`, which implements all the business methods listed in the remote interface and the callback methods to manage the bean's lifecycle by the container.

**LISTING 16.3**   The `SessionBean` Class `UserManagerBean.java`

```
package day16;

import javax.ejb.*;
import javax.transaction.*;
import javax.sql.*;
import java.sql.*;
import javax.jms.*;
import javax.naming.*;

public class UserManagerBean implements SessionBean {
    private SessionContext ctx = null;
    private UserTransaction ut = null;
```

**LISTING 16.3**   continued

```java
private java.sql.Connection conn = null;
private QueueSession qSession= null;
private QueueConnection qConn = null;
private Queue que = null;

// Prepares the UserManager for use by starting a
// new distributed transaction.
public void connectUserManager(){
    try {
        // Establish a UserTransaction context from EJBContext
        ut = ctx.getUserTransaction();
        // Begin the distributed transaction
        System.out.println("Begin JTA distributed transaction. . .");
        ut.begin();
        // Setup database connection
        InitialContext jndiCtx = new InitialContext();
        // Create a handle to the DataSource
        System.out.println("  Connecting to JDBC data store...");
        DataSource ds =
            (DataSource)jndiCtx.lookup("java:comp/env/jdbc/styejbDB");
// Obtain a connection from the pool
        conn = ds.getConnection();

    } catch(Exception e) {
        try {
            ut = ctx.getUserTransaction();
            ut.rollback();
        } catch(Exception e2) {
            System.err.println(e2);
        }
    }
}

// Add a new course into the student account.
// This can be called several times within the same transaction.
public void addCourse(int studentID, String courseID){

    try {
        Statement stmt = conn.createStatement();
        try {
            System.out.println("  Trying to drop table StudentCourse...");
            stmt.execute("drop table StudentCourse");
            System.out.println("  Table StudentCourse dropped successfully...");
        } catch (SQLException e) {
            System.out.println("  Table StudentCourse did not exist.");
        }
        stmt.execute("create table StudentCourse " +
            " (id int, courseID varchar(6), is_registered varchar(1))");
```

LISTING **16.3** continued

```
            System.out.println("  Created new StudentCourse table.");
            stmt.execute("insert into StudentCourse values(" +
                        studentID + ",'" + courseID +  "','F')");
            System.out.println("  A new record is inserted " +
                        "into table StudentCourse. . .");
        } catch(Exception e) {
            try {
                ut = ctx.getUserTransaction();
                ut.rollback();
            } catch(Exception e2) {
                System.err.println(e2);
            }
        }
    }
    // Notify registration office by sending a copy of the enrolled course.
    // This can be called several times within the same transaction.
    public void notifyRegistrar(int studentID, String courseID){
        System.out.println("  Notify registration...");
        try {
            // Setup queue connection
            System.out.println("  Connecting to JMS destination...");
            InitialContext jndiCtx = new InitialContext();
            QueueConnectionFactory qcf = (QueueConnectionFactory)
                        jndiCtx.lookup ("ConnectionFactory");
            qConn = qcf.createQueueConnection();
            Queue que = (Queue)jndiCtx.lookup("java:comp/env/jms/RegistrarQ");
            qSession = qConn.createQueueSession(true,
                            QueueSession.AUTO_ACKNOWLEDGE);
            qConn.start();
            Thread.sleep(1000);
            QueueSender sender = qSession.createSender(que);
            TextMessage message = qSession.createTextMessage();
            message.setText("Student id=" + studentID +
                            " is enrolled in course=" + courseID);
            sender.send(message);
            System.out.println("  Message sent: " + message.getText());
        } catch(Exception e) {
            try {
                ut = ctx.getUserTransaction();
                ut.rollback();
            } catch(Exception e2) {
                System.err.println(e2);
            }
            System.err.println(e);
        }
    }
}
    // Close and commit the transaction
```

**LISTING 16.3**    continued

```
public void disconnectUserManager(){
   try {
      // Get the UserTransaction instance
      ut = ctx.getUserTransaction();
      System.out.println("Committing the transaction. . .");
      // Commit the distributed transaction
      qConn.stop();
      conn.close();
      ut.commit();
   } catch(Exception e) {
      try {
         ut = ctx.getUserTransaction();
         ut.rollback();
      } catch(Exception e2){
         System.err.println(e2);
      }
      System.err.println(e);
   }
}
// The following methods to implement the SessionBean
public void setSessionContext(SessionContext ctx) { this.ctx = ctx;}
public void ejbCreate() {};
public void ejbActivate() {};
public void ejbPassivate() {};
public void ejbRemove() {};
}
```

Listing 16.4 is the client to test the developed beans.

**LISTING 16.4**    The Client Code to Access UserManager Client.java

```
package day16;

import javax.naming.*;
import javax.rmi.PortableRemoteObject;

public class Client {
   public static void main(String argv[]) {
   // A simple client deligates the UserManager session bean
   // to perform a JTA transaction. The JTA transaction will
   // be started in one method, then the context will be
   // propagated to other methods of the bean. Multiple resources:
   // a JDBC and a JMS resource manager are invloved in the
   // same distributed transaction.
      System.out.print("Demonstration the use of JTA \n");
   try {
      InitialContext ctx = new InitialContext();
```

**LISTING 16.4** continued

```
            Object obj = ctx.lookup("day16/UserManagerHome");
            UserManagerHome userHome = (UserManagerHome)
                PortableRemoteObject.narrow(obj, UserManagerHome.class);
            UserManager user = userHome.create();
            // Delegate a UserManager to start a JTA transaction
            System.out.println("\nStart global transaction...");
            user.connectUserManager();
            // Connect to a JDBC DataSource and add the enrolled course
            System.out.println("Adding courses to database...");
            user.addCourse(1, "CS310");
            // Connect to a JMS destination and send a message
            System.out.println("Notifying registrar queue...");
            user.notifyRegistrar(1, "CS310");
            // Commit the JTA transaction and release resources
            Thread.sleep(1000);
            System.out.println("Committing transaction...");
            user.disconnectUserManager();
        } catch(Exception e) {
            System.err.println(e.toString());
        }
    }
}
```

Listing 16.5 is the JMS receiver, a simple message-driven bean to receive the message and log it on the screen. This can be part of another distributed transaction, but we left this as an exercise for you. See the "Exercises" section at the end of the day.

**LISTING 16.5** The JMS Receiver `RegistrarMDB.java`

```
package day16;

import javax.ejb.MessageDrivenBean;
import javax.ejb.MessageDrivenContext;
import javax.ejb.EJBException;

import javax.jms.JMSException;
import javax.jms.Message;
import javax.jms.MessageListener;
import javax.jms.Queue;
import javax.jms.QueueConnection;
import javax.jms.QueueConnectionFactory;
import javax.jms.QueueSender;
import javax.jms.QueueSession;
import javax.jms.TextMessage;
import javax.naming.InitialContext;
import javax.naming.NamingException;
```

16

**LISTING 16.5**    continued

```
public class RegistrarMDB implements MessageDrivenBean, MessageListener{
  private MessageDrivenContext mctx =null;
  public void setMessageDrivenContext(MessageDrivenContext ctx) {mctx = ctx;}
  public void ejbCreate() {
        System.out.println("Instance of RegistrarMDB is created...");
  }
  public void ejbRemove() {}

  public void onMessage(Message message) {
    System.out.println("RegistrarMDB.onMessage: started..");
    try {
      TextMessage msg = (TextMessage)message;
      System.out.println("RegistrarMDB: Registrar received message: " +
                         msg.getText());
    } catch(JMSException e) {
      e.printStackTrace();
    }
  }
}
```

The deployment descriptor in Listing 16.6 combines the deployment information about
both the UserManager and the RegistrarMDB.

**LISTING 16.6**    Standard Deployment Descriptor ejb-jar.xml

```
<?xml version="1.0"?>

<!DOCTYPE ejb-jar PUBLIC
'-//Sun Microsystems, Inc.//DTD Enterprise JavaBeans 2.0//EN'
'http://java.sun.com/dtd/ejb-jar_2_0.dtd'>

<ejb-jar>
  <enterprise-beans>
    <session>
      <ejb-name>UserManager</ejb-name>
      <home>day16.UserManagerHome</home>
      <remote>day16.UserManager</remote>
      <ejb-class>day16.UserManagerBean</ejb-class>
      <session-type>Stateful</session-type>
      <transaction-type>Bean</transaction-type>
      <resource-env-ref>
          <resource-env-ref-name>jdbc/styejbDB</resource-env-ref-name>
      <resource-env-ref-type>javax.sql.DataSource</resource-env-ref-type>
      </resource-env-ref>
      <resource-env-ref>
          <resource-env-ref-name>jms/RegistrarQ</resource-env-ref-name>
```

**LISTING 16.6** continued

```
        <resource-env-ref-type>javax.jms.Queue</resource-env-ref-type>
          </resource-env-ref>
      </session>
      <message-driven>
        <ejb-name>RegistrarMDB</ejb-name>
        <ejb-class>day16.RegistrarMDB</ejb-class>
        <transaction-type>Container</transaction-type>
        <message-driven-destination>
          <destination-type>javax.jms.Queue</destination-type>
        </message-driven-destination>
        <resource-ref>
          <res-ref-name>jms/QCF</res-ref-name>
          <res-type>javax.jms.QueueConnectionFactory</res-type>
           <res-auth>Container</res-auth>
        </resource-ref>
      </message-driven>
    </enterprise-beans>
  </ejb-jar>
```

The deployment descriptor for WebLogic Server and JBoss are listed in Listings 16.7 and 16.8.

**LISTING 16.7** WebLogic Deployment Descriptor `weblogic-ejb-jar.xml`

```
<?xml version="1.0"?>
<!DOCTYPE weblogic-ejb-jar PUBLIC
'-//BEA Systems, Inc.//DTD WebLogic 6.0.0 EJB//EN'
'http://www.bea.com/servers/wls600/dtd/weblogic-ejb-jar.dtd'>

<weblogic-ejb-jar>
  <weblogic-enterprise-bean>
    <ejb-name>UserManager</ejb-name>
    <reference-descriptor>
      <resource-env-description>
        <res-env-ref-name>jdbc/styejbDB</res-env-ref-name>
        <jndi-name>jdbc.styejbDB</jndi-name>
      </resource-env-description>
      <resource-env-description>
        <res-env-ref-name>jms/RegistrarQ</res-env-ref-name>
        <jndi-name>RegistrarQ</jndi-name>
      </resource-env-description>
    </reference-descriptor>
    <jndi-name>day16/UserManagerHome</jndi-name>
  </weblogic-enterprise-bean>
  <weblogic-enterprise-bean>
    <ejb-name>RegistrarMDB</ejb-name>
```

**LISTING 16.7**  continued

```
      <message-driven-descriptor>
        <pool>
         <max-beans-in-free-pool>5</max-beans-in-free-pool>
         <initial-beans-in-free-pool>1</initial-beans-in-free-pool>
        </pool>
        <destination-jndi-name>RegistrarQ</destination-jndi-name>
      </message-driven-descriptor>
     <reference-descriptor>
       <resource-description>
         <res-ref-name>jms/QCF</res-ref-name>
    <jndi-name>ConnectionFactory</jndi-name>
       </resource-description>
     </reference-descriptor>
     <jndi-name>RegistrarQ</jndi-name>
     </weblogic-enterprise-bean>
  </weblogic-ejb-jar>
```

**LISTING 16.8**  JBoss Deployment Descriptor `jboss.xml`

```
    <?xml version="1.0" encoding="UTF-8"?>

  <jboss>
    <enterprise-beans>
      <session>
        <ejb-name>UserManager</ejb-name>
        <jndi-name>day16/UserManagerHome</jndi-name>
         <resource-env-ref>
           <resource-env-ref-name>jdbc/styejbDB</resource-env-ref-name>
            <jndi-name>java:/styejbDB</jndi-name>
         </resource-env-ref>
         <resource-env-ref>
           <resource-env-ref-name>jms/RegistrarQ</resource-env-ref-name>
            <jndi-name>queue/RegistrarQ</jndi-name>
         </resource-env-ref>
      </session>
      <message-driven>
       <ejb-name>RegistrarMDB</ejb-name>
        <destination-jndi-name>queue/RegisterQ</destination-jndi-name>
        <resource-ref>
          <res-ref-name>jms/QCF</res-ref-name>
          <jndi-name>ConnectionFactory</jndi-name>
        </resource-ref>
      </message-driven>
     </enterprise-beans>
    </jboss>
```

Part of making your application portable is to use a `<resource-env-ref>` element in your standard deployment descriptor (`ejb-jar.xml`) to define a logical name used by the application. Then you need to map this logical name to a `<reference-descriptor>` in your server-specific deployment descriptor. An example is the usage of the logical name `"jdbc/styejbDB"` for the JDBC `DataSource`, which is shown above in bold in Listing 16.6, 16.7, and 16.8.

# Build and Run the Example

To build the example, a build script is provided for WebLogic Server and the JBoss server.

1. Configure both the connection pool `styejbPool` and the JDBC DataSource `styejbDB` as described in Day 9.

2. Configure both the `ConnectionFactory` and the Destination `Queue` as described in Day 14.

3. Build the example for the appropriate application server. From the directory `Day16`, run the build script. This creates a subdirectory named `build` that contains all the compiled code:

```
c:\>cd c:\styejb
c:\styejb>setEnvWebLogic.bat
c:\styejb>cd day16
c:\styejb\day16>buildWebLogic.bat
```

4. To run the example, use the appropriate script for each server. Set up the environment for the client in a new command window, and then use the run script in the `Day16` directory:

```
c:\styejb>setEnvWebLogic.bat
c:\styejb>cd day16
c:\styejb\day16> runClientWebLogic.bat
```

In order to run the example on the JBoss application server, use the appropriate scripts in the same directory.

The following is the expected output of the example on the server side:

```
Begin JTA distributed transaction. . .
   Connecting to JDBC data store...
   Trying to drop table StudentCourse...
      table StudentCourse dropped successfully...
   Created new StudentCourse table.
   A new record is inserted into table StudentCourse. . .
   Notify registration...
   Connecting to JMS destination...
   Message sent: Student id=1 is enrolled in course=CS310
Committing the transaction. . .
```

16

On the client side, this is the expected output:

```
Start global transaction...
Adding courses to database.
Notifying registrar queue..
Committing transaction...
```

# Best Practices

We always recommend using JTA's `UserTransaction` context in accessing enterprise data. This will ensure both data consistency and data integrity when multiple components are accessing the same data. If the resource adapter doesn't support JTA, local transactions are recommended for accessing enterprise data.

Container-managed transactions are more optimized because they are handled by the container. They are also easier to manage and deploy because transaction attributes are set in the deployment descriptor. The default transaction attribute should be `Required`. Using this attribute ensures that the methods of an enterprise bean are invoked under a JTA distributed transaction.

# Summary

Today you learned what transactions are, and why they are important in J2EE applications. Both local (standard) and distributed (global) transaction types were discussed with the emphasis on distributed transactions. The JTA API was outlined, and you were shown how it is used in managing distributed transactions among multiple resource managers. We highlighted how transactions work across all J2EE tiers. Both bean-managed transaction and container-managed transaction were explained. An example of distributed transaction was given, where two resource manager are used: a JDBC resource manager and a JMS resource manager. The example used bean-managed transaction demarcation.

# Q&A

**Q How is a local transaction different from a distributed transaction?**

**A** A local transaction manages only a single resource manager, such as a database or a JMS provider. This is managed by setting methods of the JDBC `Connection` object or the JMS `Session` object. On the other hand, a distributed transaction is a global in a sense, and is used to access multiple resource managers. JTA is used to coordinate and manage both local and distributed transaction through the `UserTransaction` interface.

**Q** **What are the main resource managers used in a J2EE distributed transaction?**

**A** Three types of resource-managers can participate in a J2EE distributed transaction: JDBC, JMS, and JCA resource managers.

# Quiz

1. Which of the following bean types can use bean-managed transaction demarcation?

    A. Stateless session beans

    B. Stateful session beans

    C. Entity beans

    D. Message-driven beans

2. Transaction isolation levels in EJBs are

    A. Set by the bean developer for a bean-managed transaction

    B. Set by the deployer for a container-managed transaction

    C. Specified to the bean's method level

    D. Specified on the session to the database

3. Which transaction attribute is mostly recommended in an XA-compliant resource manager?

    A. `RequiredNew`

    B. `Required`

    C. `Mandatory`

    D. `Supported`

## Quiz Answers

1. A, B, D

2. A, D

3. B

# Exercise

Modify today's example to include a distributed transaction in the JMS consumer. This requires modifying the message-driven bean `RegistrarMDB` by adding a JDBC connection to the database `styejbDB`. Updating the data element `is_registered` to be `'T'` of same record received in the table `StudentCourse` is also required.

# WEEK 3

# DAY 17

# Building Container-Managed Transaction Beans

On Day 16, "Understanding Transactions," you learned about both the programmatic and the declarative approaches to transaction management. Today, we'll focus on developing EJBs that use the declarative approach of transaction demarcation. In this approach, the EJB container manages that transaction boundary on behalf of the EJB, behind the scenes, according to the setting found in the bean's deployment descriptor. On Day 18, "Building Bean-Managed Transaction Beans," you'll learn how to develop an EJB with bean-managed transaction demarcation, which is a topic for advanced developers. One of the powerful features of the Java 2 Enterprise Edition (J2EE) architecture is to let the EJB container manage all the common services, such as transaction, security, and persistence. Doing so reduces your development efforts, yet adds robustness and flexibility to your applications.

The following summarizes what you will be learning today to build applications with container-managed transactions:

- Learn why you would use container-managed transactions
- Explore which EJB types can use container-managed transactions, and their restrictions
- Learn to define the home and component interfaces, and implement an EJB class with a container-managed transaction
- Learn to write the deployment descriptor for an EJB with a container-managed transaction
- Learn to compile, package, and deploy an EJB in a container
- Learn to write a client that accesses an EJB with a container-managed transaction

# Understanding Container-Managed Transactions

In an EJB with container-managed transactions (CMT), the EJB container sets the boundaries of the transactions. This simplifies application development because the EJB developer does not include code that begins, commits, and rolls back the transaction. Implicitly, the container begins a transaction immediately before an EJB method starts, and commits the transaction just before the method exits. Each method can be associated with a single transaction. Nested or multiple transactions are not allowed within a method. Container-managed transactions do not require all methods to be associated with transactions. When deploying a bean, you specify which of the bean's methods are associated with transactions by setting the transaction attributes in the EJB's deployment descriptor.

 **Note**

In an EJB with container-managed transactions, each business method can be associated with *only* a single transaction.

In an EJB with container-managed transaction, you must set the value of the `<transaction-type>` of the standard deployment descriptor `ejb-jar.xml` to the value `Container`. Here is an example:

```
<ejb-jar>
  <enterprise-beans>
    <session>
      ...
```

```
    <transaction-type>Container</transaction-type>
    </session>
  </enterprise-beans>
</ejb-jar>
```

Bean-managed transaction demarcation, on the other hand, is the programmatic approach in which the EJB code manages the transaction boundary (you'll learn this approach on Day 18). In developing enterprise applications, the container-managed transaction demarcation is the preferred approach of the J2EE platform for managing the transaction boundary. This allows applications to be more flexible and portable, and easier to develop, deploy, and maintain.

All EJB types can use container-managed transactions, but that is not true for bean-managed transactions. Entity beans *must* use container-managed transactions. Session and message-driven beans may use either container-managed transactions or bean-managed transactions. Figure 17.1 summarizes the taxonomy of the various transaction options available to each EJB type.

**17**

**FIGURE 17.1**

*Taxonomy of transaction options with EJB types.*

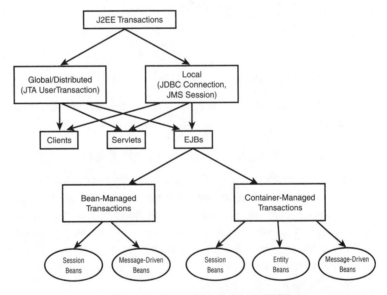

Taxonomy of Transactions Options and EJB Types

In Figure 17.1, you can see that an EJB with bean-managed transactions may choose to implement either Java Database Connectivity (JDBC) transactions or Java Transaction API (JTA) transactions. JDBC transactions involve the use of the `java.sql.Connection` interface (refer to Day 9, "Using JDBC to Connect to a Database"), whereas JTA

transactions involve the use of the `javax.transaction.UserTransaction` interface
(refer to Day 16). Again, the J2EE architecture strongly encourages the use of JTA transaction options.

## Using JDBC in CMT

The following is an example of a business method in an EJB with CMT demarcation.
The business method updates two databases using JDBC connections. The container provides transaction demarcation per the assembler.

```
public class MySessionEJB implements SessionBean {
    EJBContext ctx;
    public void methodA(...) {
        Connection conn;
        Statement stmt;
        conn = ...;
        stmt = conn.createStatement();
        // Perform some updates on conn. The Container
        // automatically enlists conn with the container-
        // managed transaction.
        stmt.executeQuery(...);
        // release connections
        conn.close();
    }
    ...
}
```

The preceding code uses no explicit transaction demarcation, such as `commit()` or
`rollback()`.

## Using Isolation Levels with CMT

As you learned on Day 16, the isolation level describes the degree to which access to a
resource manager can be controlled among concurrently executing transactions. Isolation
level is resource manager–specific, and the J2EE architecture does not define an API for
managing the isolation level. In EJB with bean-managed transactions, you set the transaction isolation level in the application code, or in programmatic fashion. Most resource
managers require that all access to the resource manager within a transaction be done
with the same isolation level.

For container-managed transactions, you set the transaction isolation level in the vendor-
specific deployment descriptor, or in declarative fashion. For example, in the WebLogic
Server environment, the `<transaction-isolation>` element of the `weblogic-ejb-
jar.xml` deployment descriptor is used to set these values, which correspond to the con-
stant values of the isolation level of the `Connection` interface (refer to the "Transaction

Isolation Level" section on Day 16). The following code shows how you can set the value of the `<transaction-isolation>` tag to `Serializable`:

```
<weblogic-ejb-jar>
  <transaction-isolation>
   <isolation-level>Serializable</isolation-level>
     <method>
        <ejb-name>...</ejb-name>
        <method-intf>...</method-intf>
        <method-name>...</method-name>
        <method-params>...</method-params>
     </method>
  </transaction-isolation>
</weblogic-ejb-jar>
```

WebLogic passes this value to the underlying database. The behavior of the transaction depends on both on the EJB's isolation level setting and the concurrency control of the underlying database.

**17**

> Many database vendors provide limited support for detecting serialization issues. Therefore, even if you set the isolation level to `TRANSACTION_SERIALIZABLE`, you might experience serialization problems due to the limitations of the database. Consult your DBMS documentation for more details about isolation level support.

The container uses the transaction isolation level attribute as follows:

- Session beans, message-driven beans, and entity beans with bean-managed persistence (BMP): For each database connection used by the bean, the container sets the transaction isolation level at the start of each transaction.
- Entity beans with container-managed persistence (CMP): The classes generated by the application server manage transaction isolation. The application server responsibility is to control the isolation level according to the setting in its configuration files.

# Reviewing Transaction Attributes with CMT

Transaction attributes were briefly covered on Day 16. Here you'll learn more about using transaction attributes to control the scope of a container-managed transaction. When `methodA` of `EJB1` invokes `methodB` of `EJB2` (see Figure 17.2), the scope of the transaction depends on the transaction attribute setting of `methodB` in the deployment descriptor of `EJB2`.

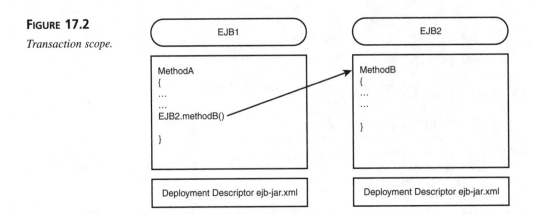

FIGURE 17.2

*Transaction scope.*

Table 17.1 summarizes the effects of the transaction attribute of methodB on the scope of the originated transaction. In this table, both T1 and T2 are transactions that are controlled by the container. The T1 transaction is associated with EJB1, which calls methodB in EJB2. The container starts the T2 transaction just before methodB executes. Depending on the transaction attribute setting of methodB, the container will propagate the context of transaction T1's scope, or start a new T2 transaction. Notice that in some cases, methodB does not execute within a transaction controlled by the container, as specified by N/A in the table. EJB components inherit the transaction of the caller even if the caller is a distributed client. The EJB container propagates the transaction context across EJB components and J2EE-compliant application servers.

**TABLE 17.1**   Transaction Attributes and Scope

| Transaction Attribute | EJB1.method | EJB2.methodB |
|---|---|---|
| Required | None | New transaction: T2 |
|  | T1 | T1 |
| RequiresNew | N/A | New transaction: T2 |
|  | T1 | New transaction: T2 |
| Mandatory | N/A | TransactionRequiredException |
|  | T1 | T1 |
| NotSupported | N/A | N/A |
|  | T1 | N/A |
| Supports | N/A | N/A |
|  | T1 | T1 |
| Never | N/A | N/A |
|  | T1 | TransactionRequiredException |

As you can see in Table 17.1, based on the transaction attribute settings, the EJB container takes an appropriate action. For example, if the setting is `Required`, the EJB container invokes the method within the existing transaction context (T1). But if the client `methodA` calls without a transaction context, the EJB container begins a new transaction (T2) before executing `methodB`. In another example, if the transaction attribute is `Mandatory`, the EJB container invokes `methodB` within the existing transaction context (T1). But if the client calls without a transaction context, the EJB container throws the `TransactionRequiredException` exception of the `UserTransaction` interface.

## Setting Transaction Attributes

Transaction attributes control the method behavior of an EJB, and are stored in the standard deployment descriptor `ejb-jar.xml`. They can be changed during several phases of J2EE application development, application assembly, and deployment. As an EJB developer, it is your responsibility to specify these attributes when creating the bean. Only an application developer who is assembling components into larger applications should modify the attributes. The J2EE deployer is not expected to modify these attributes.

You can specify the transaction attributes for the entire EJB methods or just for individual methods. If you've specified one attribute for a method and another for the entire EJB as a default, the attribute for the method takes precedence. When specifying attributes for individual methods, the requirements for session and entity beans vary. Session beans need the attributes defined for business methods, but do not allow them for the create methods. Entity beans require transaction attributes for the business, create, remove, and finder methods.

The assembler uses the `<container-transaction>` element to define the transaction attributes for the methods of session and entity beans' home and component interfaces, and for the `onMessage()` methods of message-driven beans. Each `<container-transaction>` element consists of a list of one or more `<method>` elements and the `<trans-attribute>` element. The `<container-transaction>` element specifies that all the listed methods must be assigned the specified transaction attribute value. It is required that all the methods specified in a single `<container-transaction>` element be methods of the same EJB. The `<method>` element uses the `<ejb-name>`, `<method-name>`, and `<method-params>` elements to denote one or more methods of an EJB's home and component interfaces. In the following sections, you'll learn three different styles of how to compose the `<method>` element to specify a transaction attribute.

**17**

**Tip**

> Specifying container-managed transactions with the `Required` transaction attribute is the easiest way to handle transaction management in the application, and works in most cases.

## Setting Transaction Attributes for the Entire EJB

This style is used to specify a default value of the transaction attribute for all the methods of the EJB. The <method-name> tag is assigned the value * (asterisk) to indicate that all methods have the transaction attribute Required:

```
<ejb-jar>
   ...
   <assembly-descriptor>
     ...
     <container-transaction>
      <method>
        <ejb-name> myEJB </ejb-name>
        <method-name> * </method-name>
        <trans-attribute>Required</trans-attribute>
      </method>
      ...
   </assembly-descriptor>
   ...
</ejb-jar>
```

## Setting a Transaction Attribute for a Specific Method

This style is used for referring to a specific method of a home or component interface of the specified EJB:

```
<ejb-jar>
   ...
   <assembly-descriptor>
     ...
     <container-transaction>
      <method>
        <ejb-name> myEJB </ejb-name>
        <method-name> methodA </method-name>
        <trans-attribute>Supports</trans-attribute>
      </method>
      ...
   </assembly-descriptor>
   ...
</ejb-jar>
```

## Setting a Transaction Attribute for an Overloaded Method

If there are multiple overloaded methods (that is, the same method name with different parameter types), this style uses the <method-params> tag to differentiate which method to set:

```
<ejb-jar>
   ...
   <assembly-descriptor>
     ...
```

```
   <container-transaction>
    <method>
      <ejb-name> myEJB </ejb-name>
      <method-name> methodA </method-name>
      <method-params>
         <method-param> java.lang.Object </method-param>
         ...
         <method-param> java.lang.String </method-param>
      </method-params>
      <trans-attribute>RequiredNew</trans-attribute>
    </method>
    ...
  </assembly-descriptor>
  ...
</ejb-jar>
```

17

**Caution**   In specifying the data type in the `<method-param>` tag, use the fully qualified class name; for example, `java.lang.String`.

The optional `<method-intf>` element can be used to differentiate between methods with the same name and signature that are multiply defined across the component and/or home interfaces:

```
<ejb-jar>
   ...
   <assembly-descriptor>
     ...
     <container-transaction>
       <method>
         <ejb-name>MyEJB</ejb-name>
         <method-intf>Remote</method-intf>
         <method-name>methodA</method-name>
         <method-params>
            <method-param>java.lang.String</method-param>
         </method-params>
       </method>
       <trans-attribute>Required</trans-attribute>
     </container-transaction>
     ...
   </assembly-descriptor>
   ...
</ejb-jar>
```

# Performing Nontransactional Execution

Some EJBs might need to access resource managers that do not support an external transaction manager. The container cannot manage the transactions for such EJBs with

CMT. Therefore, the EJB developer should assign the NotSupported transaction attribute to all the EJB's methods.

## Rolling Back a Container-Managed Transaction

You might wonder how a container-managed transaction is rolled back. There are two ways to roll back a CMT:

- When a System exception is thrown, the container automatically rolls back the transaction, which means that it will try to call the associated method again.

- Application exceptions do not automatically cause a rollback. The EJB must invoke the setRollbackOnly() method of the EJBContext interface to notify the container to roll back the transaction.

The following example demonstrates both system- and application-level exception handling in rolling back a CMT:

```
public class RegistrarEJB implements SessionBean{
  SessionContext ctx;
  ...
  public void registerForCourse(String courseID)
    throws InsufficientRoomException {
  try {
      rs = updateCourse(courseID);
      if (rs < 0) {
      // Application-level exception
        ctx.setRollbackOnly();
            throw new InsufficientRoomException();
      }
  } catch (SQLException ex) {
      // This is a system-level exception
      throw new EJBException
      ("Transaction rollback due to SQLException: "+ ex.getMessage());
  }
 }
 ...
}
```

The registerForCourse() method of the RegistrarEJB example illustrates the setRollbackOnly() method. If the updateCourse() method returns with insufficient room, the application exception InsufficientRoomException will be thrown. If the updates fail for any reason, these methods throw a SQLException and the registerForCourse() method throws an EJBException. Because the EJBException is a system exception, it causes the container to automatically rollback the transaction.

There are special considerations for entity beans, session beans, and message-driven beans in the event of a roll back of a CMT:

- For a stateful session bean, the SessionSynchronization interface can be implemented to explicitly reset a bean's instance variables.

- For an entity bean, when a rollback occurs, the EJB container will invoke ejbLoad(), which has the effect of reloading the bean's instance variables from the database.

# Transaction Semantics for CMT

The J2EE architecture describes semantics that govern transaction-processing behavior based on the EJB type (entity bean, stateless session bean, or stateful session bean) and the transaction type (container-managed or bean-managed). These semantics describe the transaction context at the time a method is invoked, and define whether the EJB can access methods in the javax.transaction.UserTransaction interface. EJB applications must be designed with these semantics in mind. For container-managed transactions, transaction semantics vary for each bean type. The following sections discuss these transaction semantics with respect to each EJB type.

**17**

## Implementing Session Beans with CMT

Stateless session beans can be pooled together and reused by different users. The duration of a container-managed transaction is tightly coupled with the  duration of a single method call.

Because stateful session beans are not shared between multiple users, they are not transactional by design. Member variables (or the bean's state) cannot be rolled back when a transaction aborts. On the other hand, session beans can propagate transaction context to other resources they interface with, such as a database or a Java Message Service (JMS) queue. Only beans that manage their own transactions have access to the UserTransaction via the EJBContext. EJBs that do not manage their transaction can access only the setRollbackOnly() and getRollbackOnly() methods of the EJBContext. In a stateful session bean, the life cycle of a container-managed transaction is *not* tightly coupled with the life cycle of the EJB.

**Note**

According to the EJB architecture, all methods on a stateful session bean must support one of the following transaction attributes: RequiresNew, Mandatory, or Required.

## Synchronizing the State of a Session Bean

The EJB architecture allows stateful session beans to optionally synchronize their state. This is accomplished by implementing the SessionSynchronization interface (in the package javax.transaction). The EJB container notifies the EJB with the beginning and end of a transaction demarcation through the callback methods of the SessionSynchronization interface. Any information that might have been cached in its state by the EJB can be committed when the transaction completes. In addition, in the case of a rollback, a stateful session bean might want to refresh any required instance variables of its state from the database because the container will not perform this automatically.

Use of the SessionSynchronization interface by an stateful session bean implies the implementation of the callback methods afterBegin(), beforeCompletion(), and afterCompletion(). Figure 17.3 summarizes the life cycle of a stateful session bean implementing the SessionSynchronization interface. Refer to Day 6 for more details about stateful session beans.

**FIGURE 17.3**

*Stateful session bean life cycle with* SessionSynchron- ization.

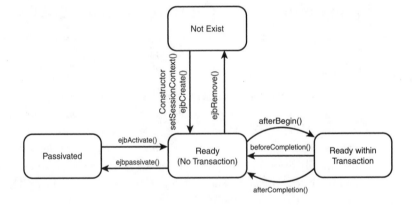

**Stateful session Bean Life cycle with SessionSynchronization**

The afterBegin() method is called by the container after a new transaction is started but before the business method is invoked, so it's a good place to synchronize the instance variables of the session bean with the state of the database. The session bean also has a chance to roll back in the beforeCompletion() method. In the afterCompletion() method, the session bean can check whether a rollback occurred

and respond accordingly. The following example demonstrates the use of the
`SessionSynchronization` interface with the stateful session bean `MyStatefulEJB`:

```
public class MyStatefulEJB implements SessionBean, SessionSynchronization {
    private SessionContext ctx;
    private boolean isFailed = false;
...
    public void afterBegin() {}

    public void beforeCompletion() {
        if ( isFailed ) {
            ctx.setRollbackOnly();
        }
    }
    public void afterCompletion(boolean success) {
        if (!success)
        //rollback occurred
    }
...
}
```

17

In the preceding example, the `afterCompletion()` method indicates that the transaction
has completed. It has a single `boolean` parameter, `success`, whose value is `true` if the
transaction was committed and `false` if it was rolled back. If a rollback occurs, the session bean can refresh its instance variables from the database in the `afterCompletion()`
method.

## Methods Not Allowed in CMT

As a general rule, you shouldn't invoke any method that might interfere with the transaction boundaries set by the container. Table 17.2 summarizes the methods that JB developers should avoid calling while developing an EJB with CMT.

**TABLE 17.2**    Summary of Prohibited Methods with CMT

| Interface | Methods |
| --- | --- |
| Java.sql.Connection | commit(), setAutoCommit(), rollback() |
| javax.ejb.EJBContext | getUserTransaction() |
| All methods | javax.transaction.UserTransaction |

Bean-managed transactions do not have these restrictions. You may, however, use these
methods to set boundaries in bean-managed transactions. For more information about
bean-managed transaction, see Day 18.

## Message-Driven Beans with CMT

The EJB architecture allows message-driven beans (MDBs) with CMT to use either the Required or the NotSupported transaction attribute:

- Required: The EJB container automatically starts a transaction, and a message receipt from a JMS queue or topic is included in the transaction. The onMessage() method is called automatically by the container within this transaction context. When onMessage() returns, the EJB container automatically commits the transaction. If the transaction fails, the message stays in the queue until it is delivered to the message-driven bean. The container handles message acknowledgement automatically on behalf of the MDB.

- NotSupported: The EJB container does not start a transaction before calling onMessage(). MDBs rely on message acknowledgement mechanisms used by the JMS provider. Refer to Day 13, "Understanding JMS and Message-Driven Beans," for more information about JMS.

## Entity Beans

Entity beans are always container-managed. The ejbLoad() callback method loads the current state of an entity row from the database. The ejbStore() method updates the current state onto the database. Because an entity bean is a proxy representation of a table row in a database, the ejbLoad() method is the first method that a container calls in a transaction, and ejbStore() is the last method called before the end of a transaction. The business methods are called inbetween. An entity bean cannot be a bean-managed transaction because a bean cannot call either ejbLoad() or ejbStore() method to synchronize its state.

**Note**    Both ejbLoad() and ejbStore() are callback methods and can be called only by the container from within a transaction.

## Summary of Transaction Options for EJBs

Table 17.3 lists the types of transactions that are allowed for the different types of EJBs. An entity bean must use container-managed transactions. With container-managed transactions, you specify the transaction attributes in the deployment descriptor, and you roll back a transaction with the setRollbackOnly() method of the EJBContext interface.

**TABLE 17.3**    Transaction Options for EJB Types

| Bean Type | Container-Managed Transaction | Bean-Managed Transaction | |
|---|---|---|---|
| | | JTA | JDBC |
| Entity | Yes | No | No |
| Session | Yes | Yes | Yes |
| Message-driven | Yes | Yes | Yes |

## Setting WebLogic-Specific Transactions

Because our examples use WebLogic, we must discuss a few parameters in respect to WebLogic transactions. The following sections describe how to set these parameters in the vendor-specific deployment descriptor `weblogic-ejb-jar.xml`.

### Setting Transaction Timeouts

An EJB developer can specify the timeout period for transactions in enterprise applications. If the duration of a transaction exceeds the specified timeout setting, the transaction manager rolls back the transaction automatically. In a bean-managed transaction, this is done programmatically in the code. The transaction timeout is set before the transaction begins. See Day 18 for more information about bean-managed transactions.

In container-managed transactions, the EJB developer sets the transaction timeout in the vendor-specific deployment descriptor. For WebLogic, the `<trans-timeout-seconds>` tag of the `weblogic-ejb-jar.xml` deployment descriptor is used:

```
<weblogic-ejb-jar>
   <transaction-descriptor>
      <trans-timeout-seconds>5<trans-timeout-seconds>
   </transaction-descriptor>
</weblogic-ejb-jar>
```

Only EJBs with container-managed transactions are affected by the `<trans-timeout-seconds>` attribute. For EJB with BMT, you invoke the `setTransactionTimeout()` method of the `UserTransaction` interface (in JTA transactions).

## Example for Developing EJB with CMT

For EJB applications with container-managed transactions, a basic transaction works in the following way:

1. In the EJB's standard deployment descriptor, the EJB developer or assembler specifies the transaction type by setting the `<transaction-type>` tag with the value `Container` (for CMT).

2. In the standard deployment descriptor, the EJB developer or assembler specifies the transaction attribute by setting the value of the `<trans-attribute>` tag to one of the following values: `NotSupported`, `Required`, `Supports`, `RequiresNew`, `Mandatory`, or `Never`. This tag enables you to set a default value for all methods of the entire EJB, or a value for each specific method of the EJB. Refer to the "Setting Transaction Attributes" section earlier today for more information.

> **Note**
>
> On invoking a method in the EJB, the EJB container checks the `<trans-attribute>` setting in the deployment descriptor for that method. If no setting is specified for the method, the EJB uses the default `<trans-attribute>` setting for that EJB.

3. Depending on the `<trans-attribute>` setting, the EJB container takes the appropriate action (refer to Table 17.1).

4. During the execution of the business method, if it is determined (by the application logic) that a rollback is required, the business method calls the `setRollbackOnly()` method of the `EJBContext`. This will notify the EJB container that the transaction is to be rolled back at the end of the business method.

> **Note**
>
> Calling the `setRollbackOnly()` method of the `EJBContext` is allowed only for EJB with CMT.

5. At the end of the business method (and before it returns), the EJB container completes the transaction either by committing the transaction or rolling it back (if the `setRollbackOnly()` method was called in step 4).

6. You can also control transaction timeouts by setting its attribute in the vendor-specific deployment descriptor.

## Defining the Bean's Remote Interface

For this example, the `EnrollmentCart` EJB is implemented as a stateful session bean with container-managed transaction, the remote interface `EnrollmentCart` defines all business methods, and is stored on disk in the file `EnrollmentCart.java`, as shown in Listing 17.1.

**LISTING 17.1**   The Full Text of day17/EnrollmentCart.java

```
package day17;
import java.util.*;
import javax.ejb.*;
import java.rmi.RemoteException;
/**
  EnrollmentCart is the remote interface for enrollment cart
  stateful session bean.
 */
public interface EnrollmentCart extends EJBObject
{
    public void addEnrollment(EnrollmentInfo enroll) throws RemoteException;
    public void deleteEnrollment(int itemId) throws RemoteException;
    public Collection getEnrollments() throws RemoteException;
    public void emptyCart() throws RemoteException;
    public void register() throws InsufficientRoomException, RemoteException;
}
```

17

The remote interface uses the EnrollmentInfo class as a helper class to transfer data between the EJB tier and the client tier. The InsufficientRoomException is an application exception to detect any failure to register for a course due to insufficient room in the enrolled class.

## Defining the Bean's Home Interface

The home interface is stored in the file EnrollmentCartHome.java, and defines the life cycle method of the EJB, as shown in Listing 17.2.

**LISTING 17.2**   The Full Text of day17/EnrollmentCartHome.java

```
package day17;
import java.rmi.RemoteException;
import javax.ejb.*;
/**
  EnrollmentCartHome is the remote home interface for
  the enrollment cart stateful session bean.
 */
public interface EnrollmentCartHome extends EJBHome
{
    EnrollmentCart create() throws CreateException, RemoteException;
}
```

## Implementing the Bean's Class

The bean class implements all the methods in both the remote and home interfaces of EnrollmentCart EJB, as shown in Listing 17.3.

**LISTING 17.3**  The Full Text of day17/EnrollmentCartEJB.java

```java
package day17;

import java.util.*;
import javax.ejb.*;
import javax.naming.*;
import java.sql.*;
import java.rmi.RemoteException;

/**
    EnrollmentCartEJB is stateful session bean, representing  the
    private conversation of a specific client. It keeps track of the
    user's current selection of courses.
 */

public class EnrollmentCartEJB implements SessionBean, SessionSynchronization
{
    private SessionContext ejbCtx;
    private HashSet cart;
    private boolean isFailed = false;

    public EnrollmentCartEJB(){}
    // SessionSynchronization methods
    public void afterBegin() {}
    public  void beforeCompletion() {
         if (isFailed)
             ejbCtx.setRollbackOnly();
    }
    public  void afterCompletion(boolean committed) {
        if (committed == false)
          throw new EJBException("Transaction afterCompletion failed");
        System.out.println("afterCompletion: Transaction succeeds...");
     }
    // Business methods
    public void addEnrollment(EnrollmentInfo enroll) throws RemoteException {
        cart.add(enroll);
    }
    public void register() throws InsufficientRoomException, RemoteException {
        java.sql.Statement stmt = null;
        java.sql.Statement stmt2 = null;
        java.sql.Connection conn = null;
        System.out.println("register: started..");
        try{
            InitialContext initCtx  = new InitialContext();
          javax.sql.DataSource ds = (javax.sql.DataSource)
          initCtx.lookup ("java:comp/env/jdbc/styejbDB");
          conn = ds.getConnection();
          stmt = conn.createStatement();
          stmt2 = conn.createStatement();
        } catch (Exception e){
          e.printStackTrace();
```

LISTING 17.3    continued

```
      }
      try{
       Iterator it = cart.iterator();
       while (it.hasNext()){
         EnrollmentInfo enroll=(EnrollmentInfo)it.next();
         ResultSet rs = stmt.executeQuery
            ("SELECT * FROM COURSES WHERE COURSEID='" +
                   enroll.getCourseId()+"'");
         while (rs.next()){
              int mlimit = rs.getInt("MAX_LIMIT");
              int curr   = rs.getInt("CURR");
              if (mlimit < curr + 1){
                isFailed = true;
                ejbCtx.setRollbackOnly();
                throw new InsufficientRoomException();
              }else{
                curr++;
                stmt2.executeUpdate("UPDATE COURSES SET CURR =" + curr
                  + " WHERE COURSEID='" + enroll.getCourseId()+"'");
                System.out.println("register: Database updated for: "+
                      enroll.getCourseId());
              }
          }
        }
       }
       System.out.println("register: success..");
      }catch (SQLException ex){
       // This is a system level exception
       throw new EJBException
       ("Transaction rollback due to SQLException: "+ ex.getMessage());
      }
    }
    public Collection getEnrollments() throws RemoteException {
       return cart;
    }

    public void emptyCart() throws RemoteException {
       cart.clear();
    }
    public void deleteEnrollment(int itemId) throws RemoteException {
        for(Iterator i = getEnrollments().iterator(); i.hasNext(); ) {
           EnrollmentInfo tmpEnrol = (EnrollmentInfo) i.next();
           if (tmpEnrol.getItemId() == itemId) {
              getEnrollments().remove(tmpEnrol);
              break;
           }
        }
     }
     // EJB methods
     public void setSessionContext(SessionContext ctx){
        this.ejbCtx = ctx;
```

17

Listing 17.3   continued

```
  }
  public void ejbCreate() throws CreateException{
     cart = new HashSet();
  }
  public void ejbRemove() {}
  public void ejbActivate(){}
  public void ejbPassivate(){}
}
```

In the preceding code, the business method register() of the EnrollmentCart is executed within a transaction that is maintained by the container. The EJB implements the
SessionSynchronization interface to synchronize its state with the database. An application exception will be raised if any course is out of room while registering all the
selected courses in the enrollment cart.

## Developing Helper Classes

Listing 17.4 is the code of the helper class EnrollmentInfo, which is used as a data container to transfer data between the EJB tier and the client tier. The EnrollmentInfo class
implements the java.io.Serializable interface in order to use it for transferring data
across tiers.

**Listing 17.4**   The Full Text of day17/EnrollmentInfo.java

```
package day17;
public class EnrollmentInfo implements java.io.Serializable {
  public int itemId = 0;
  public int studentId = 0;
  public String courseId = null;
  public EnrollmentInfo (int itemId, int studentId, String courseId) {
    this.itemId = itemId;
    this.studentId = studentId;
    this.courseId = courseId;
  }
  public int getItemId(){
        return itemId;
  }
  public int getStudentId(){
        return studentId;
  }
  public String getCourseId(){
        return courseId;
  }
 }
}
```

Listing 17.5 is the code for the `InsufficientRoomException` used as an application exception.

**LISTING 17.5**  The Full Text of day17/InsufficientRoomException.java

```
package day17;
public class InsufficientRoomException extends Exception {
   public InsufficientRoomException() {
      super();
   }
   public InsufficientRoomException(Exception e) {
      super(e.toString());
   }
   public InsufficientRoomException(String s) {
      super(s);
   }
}
```

## Packaging the Beans into a JAR File

The deployment descriptor for the EnrollmentCart EJB is listed in Listing 17.6. The EJB developer sets the `<session>` tag, with the `<transaction-type>` to be set to `Container` for the EJB to manage its own state. There is no mechanism for an application assembler to affect enterprise beans with bean-managed transaction demarcation. The application assembler must define transaction attributes for an enterprise bean with container-managed transaction demarcation. We use only the default `Required` transaction attribute for all methods of the EJB. Listing 17.6 displays the `ejb-jar.xml` file.

**LISTING 17.6**  The Full Text of day17/ejb-jar.xml

```
<?xml version="1.0"?>

<!DOCTYPE ejb-jar PUBLIC
'-//Sun Microsystems, Inc.//DTD Enterprise JavaBeans 2.0//EN'
'http://java.sun.com/dtd/ejb-jar_2_0.dtd'>

<ejb-jar>
  <enterprise-beans>
    <session>
       <ejb-name>EnrollmentCart</ejb-name>
       <home>day17.EnrollmentCartHome</home>
       <remote>day17.EnrollmentCart</remote>
       <ejb-class>day17.EnrollmentCartEJB</ejb-class>
       <session-type>Stateful</session-type>
       <transaction-type>Container</transaction-type>

        <resource-env-ref>
```

17

**LISTING 17.6**      continued

```
            <resource-env-ref-name>jdbc/styejbDB</resource-env-ref-name>
            <resource-env-ref-type>javax.sql.DataSource</resource-env-ref-type>
          </resource-env-ref>
      </session>
  </enterprise-beans>
    <assembly-descriptor>
      <container-transaction>
        <description>no description</description>
        <method>
          <ejb-name>EnrollmentCart</ejb-name>
          <method-name>*</method-name>
        </method>
        <trans-attribute>Required</trans-attribute>
      </container-transaction>
    </assembly-descriptor>
</ejb-jar>
```

For WebLogic Server, Listing 17.7 shows the vendor-specific `weblogic-ejb-jar.xml` that is used to set the transaction timeout and isolation level.

**LISTING 17.7**      The Full Text of `day17/weblogic-ejb-jar.xml`

```
<?xml version="1.0"?>

<!DOCTYPE weblogic-ejb-jar PUBLIC
'-//BEA Systems, Inc.//DTD WebLogic 6.0.0 EJB//EN'
'http://www.bea.com/servers/wls600/dtd/weblogic-ejb-jar.dtd'>

<weblogic-ejb-jar>
  <weblogic-enterprise-bean>
    <ejb-name>EnrollmentCart</ejb-name>
      <stateful-session-descriptor>
        <stateful-session-cache>
          <max-beans-in-cache>5</max-beans-in-cache>
        </stateful-session-cache>
      </stateful-session-descriptor>
      <transaction-descriptor>
       <trans-timeout-seconds>60</trans-timeout-seconds>
      </transaction-descriptor>
      <reference-descriptor>
        <resource-env-description>
          <res-env-ref-name>jdbc/styejbDB</res-env-ref-name>
          <jndi-name>jdbc.styejbDB</jndi-name>
        </resource-env-description>
      </reference-descriptor>
    <jndi-name>day17/EnrollmentCartHome</jndi-name>
  </weblogic-enterprise-bean>
    <transaction-isolation>
```

LISTING 17.7     continued

```
        <isolation-level>TRANSACTION_SERIALIZABLE</isolation-level>
          <method>
              <ejb-name>EnrollmentCart</ejb-name>
              <method-name>*</method-name>
          </method>
      </transaction-isolation>
  </weblogic-ejb-jar>
```

## Developing and Testing the Client

Listing 17.8 is the client program to test the EnrollmentCart EJB (as saved in the Client.java file). The client adds the selected courses as enrollments, and then tries to register all the courses. If one of the courses cannot be registered due to insufficient room in the class, an exception will be raised by the EJB and printed by the client in the catch clause.

17

LISTING 17.8     The Full Text of day17/Client.java

```
package day17;
import java.util.*;
import java.rmi.*;
import java.io.*;
import javax.naming.*;
import javax.ejb.*;

/*
  This client demonstrates usage of stateful session bean with
  CMT and SessionSynchronization
 */
public class Client
{

  public static void main(String[] argv){
     System.out.print("Day 17: Demonstration the use of CMT\n");
     try{
     Context initialContext = new InitialContext();
     Object object = initialContext.lookup("day17/EnrollmentCartHome");
     EnrollmentCartHome enrollmentCartHome = (EnrollmentCartHome)
      javax.rmi.PortableRemoteObject.narrow(object, EnrollmentCartHome.class);
     EnrollmentCart enrollmentCart = (EnrollmentCart)
                           enrollmentCartHome.create();
     // Add enrollment courses
     enrollmentCart.addEnrollment(new EnrollmentInfo(1, 15, "CS201"));
     enrollmentCart.addEnrollment(new EnrollmentInfo(2, 15, "CS205"));
     enrollmentCart.addEnrollment(new EnrollmentInfo(3, 15, "CS231"));
     // register the courses
     enrollmentCart.register();
```

**LISTING 17.8** continued

```
    print("Following courses are registered successfully:");
    Collection coll = enrollmentCart.getEnrollments();
    for (Iterator i = coll.iterator(); i.hasNext();){
        EnrollmentInfo enroll = (EnrollmentInfo) i.next();
        print("Course id: " + enroll.getCourseId());
        }
    enrollmentCart.remove();
    }
    catch ( Exception e){
        print("Enrolled courses failed to register.\n");
    e.printStackTrace();
    }
 }
 static void print(String s){
    System.out.println(s);
 }
}
```

# Build and Run the Example

To build the example, a build script is provided for WebLogic Server and the JBoss
server.

1. Configure both the JDBC DataSource and connection pool as described on Day 9.

2. Build the example for the appropriate application server. From the directory Day17,
   run the build script. This creates a subdirectory named build that contains all the
   compiled code:

   c:\>**cd c:\styejb**

   c:\styejb>**setEnvWebLogic.bat**

   c:\styejb>**cd day17**

   c:\styejb\day17>**buildWebLogic.bat**

3. To run the example, use the appropriate script for each server. Set up the environment for the client in a new command window, and then use the run script in the
   Day17 directory:

   c:\styejb>**setEnvWebLogic.bat**

   c:\styejb>**cd day17**

   c:\styejb\day17> **runClientWebLogic.bat**

# Best Practices

The J2EE architecture encourages the use of container-managed transaction demarcation. It's the preferred approach over bean-managed transaction. Use container-managed transaction demarcation unless you have a specific need for bean-managed transactions. CMT should be used wherever possible to minimize the overhead of writing code to a transaction management service API. Not only will this result in less work for you as a programmer, but it will also reduce the possibility of errors in the final code. For example, it will keep you from accidentally not committing a transaction or committing too early. It also enables you to change the behavior without programmatic changes. Never demarcate transactions from an EJB with container-managed transactions. Bean-managed transactions will be covered on Day 18.

Do not invoke any resource-manager-specific transaction demarcation, such as `commit()` and `rollback()` of the `Connection` interface, and avoid using the `UserTransaction` interface.

The way to implement rollbacks is by calling the `setRollBackOnly()` method of the `EJBContext` and then throwing an application exception. This enables you to handle exceptions at the client code.

To optimize transaction use on your system, always follow an inside-out approach to transaction demarcation. Transactions should begin and end at the inside (the database) of the system where possible, and move outside (toward the client application) only as necessary.

Many RDBMS provide high-performance locking systems for Online Transaction Processing (OLTP) transactions. If your underlying database is capable of demarcating transactions automatically, use them when possible.

A scenario in which you must use bean-managed transactions is when you define multiple transactions from within a single method. An EJB container limits transactions demarcation on a per-method basis. However, even in this scenario, you can still use container-managed transaction demarcation by breaking the method into multiple methods instead of using multiple transactions in a single method, and also using container-managed transactions by setting the transaction attribute for each individual method.

Generally, client applications are not guaranteed to stay active over long periods of time. When a client starts a transaction and then exits before committing, it wastes valuable transaction and connection resources in the EJB container. Moreover, even if the client does not exit during a transaction, the duration of the transaction might be unacceptable if it relies on user activity to commit or roll back data. Make your methods in an EJB

17

with CMT as short as possible and split large methods into smaller ones with distinct functions. The primary purpose is that shorter transactions reduce contention in your application because database locks are held for shorter time periods. Set transaction time-out to a reasonable value for the application server you're using.

## Summary

Today we have covered the important aspects of the J2EE architecture: understanding and developing an EJB with container-managed transactions (CMT). We explored all EJB types that can use CMT with either JDBC or JTA. We explained how to configure the transaction isolation level required by the application, and set its value in the vendor-specific deployment descriptor of the EJB. We also have focused on how to configure an EJB to work as a CMT, and set the fine-grained transaction attribute for each method of the EJB. Some restrictions applied in using resource-manager specific transaction demarcation are discussed. The topic of using the SessionSynchronization interface by a stateful session bean is covered.

## Q&A

**Q  Which type of EJBs can use container-managed transactions? And with which transaction option?**

A  All types of EJBs (session, message-driven, and entity beans) can use container-managed transactions, with either the JDBC or JTA transaction option.

**Q  What are the acceptable values of the transaction attribute?**

A  There are six values that can be specified for the transaction attribute: Required, RequiresNew, NotSupported, Mandatory, Never, and Supports.

**Q  How do you configure the EJB to be a CMT?**

A  You must set the <transaction-type> element in the standard deployment descriptor ejb-jar.xml to the Container value. You must also specify the <transaction-attribute> for either the entire EJB or for specific methods of the EJB.

## Quiz

1. Which of the following methods can be used only in CMT?

    A. begin() and commit()

    B. commit() and rollback()

    C. getStatus() and getRollback()

    D. `getRollbackOnly()` and `setRollbackOnly()`

2. When using JTA for your transactions, which transaction attributes would you require?

    A. `Supports`

    B. `Never`

    C. `RequiresNew`

    D. `Mandatory`

3. If a `System` exception is thrown from within an EJB with CMT, which of the following is handled automatically by the container?

    A. Stateful session beans

    B. Stateless session beans

    C. Message-driven bean

    D. Bean-managed persistence bean

## Quiz Answers

1. D
2. C
3. A, B, C

# Questions

1. Why is CMT used in enterprise applications?
2. How can you set the transaction isolation level for CMT?
3. Which methods and interfaces cannot be used within an EBJ with CMT?
4. Which EJB type can use the `SessionSynchronization` interface? Why?

# Exercises

Change the client code of today's example (`Client.java`) to start a JTA transaction to call the `EnrollmentCart` EJB. Then change the `<transaction-attribute>` in the `ejb-jar.xml` to `Never`. Rebuild and run the example using the same scripts. Comment on the exceptions that you're getting when running the code.

Where applicable, exercise solutions are offered on the book's Web site at `www.ejb21days.com`.

# DAY **18**

# Building Bean-Managed Transaction Beans

On Day 17, "Building Container-Managed Transaction Beans," we covered EJBs with container-managed transactions (CMTs). Today we'll closely examine the other type of transaction demarcation, the bean-managed transaction (BMT), which is the programmatic approach of performing transaction demarcation on the Java 2 Enterprise Edition (J2EE) platform. This will be illustrated through an example of how to develop, deploy, and run an EJB with bean-managed transaction demarcation. We'll explore the types of beans that can perform bean-managed transactions and the transaction semantics of each method that we use. We'll discuss the situations in which you can use this type of transaction and any restrictions you might encounter when using it. You'll also learn how to deploy such a bean into application servers and how to set its deployment descriptors.

Toward the end of learning to implement bean-managed transactions in your enterprise applications, the following is a summary of today's activities:

- Learn when and why to use bean-managed transactions
- Review the type of transactions used in a bean-managed transaction

- Learn which types of EJBs support bean-managed transactions
- Work through a step-by-step example of developing an EJB with the bean-managed transaction demarcation
- Deploy the example on our two application server environments

# Why Bean-Managed Transactions?

EJB with bean-managed transactions is the programmatic approach in which the EJB code invokes methods that mark the boundaries of the transaction. On Day 17, you learned about container-managed transactions. CMT is the declarative approach in transaction demarcation in which the container manages the transaction behind the scenes on behalf of the EJB, and according to the configuration of the EJB's deployment descriptor. You also learned that container-managed transaction is the approach that J2EE encourages you to use.

You might ask yourself why you should study bean-managed transactions. The answer is simple: Sometimes a container-managed transaction is not sufficient or adequate to perform certain transactional tasks you are trying to accomplish. For example, a method of your EJB must be associated with either a single transaction or no transaction at all. In this situation, due to the limitations of container-managed transactions to set these conditions in the EJB's deployment descriptor, you might consider using bean-managed transactions.

Enterprise applications use BMT to perform fine-grained control of transaction boundaries in business methods. For situations in which distributed transactions are managing multiple resources, bean-managed transaction may also be used. The following pseudo-code illustrates the workflow of a business method controlling transaction boundaries across multiple resource managers. Based on certain conditions, the code decides whether to begin a new transaction or end different transactions within the same method.

```
businessMethod(...)
...
  begin transaction
    ...
    update database tableA
    send message to a queueA
    ...
  if (conditionA)
      send message to dead-letter queue
      commit transaction
  else
      rollback transaction
      begin transaction
```

```
            update database tableA
            send another message to queueB
            commit transaction
    end if
....
end method
```

Traditionally, transactional applications are responsible for managing their transactions. These applications demand a very skilled developer to perform tasks such as creating transaction objects, explicitly starting a transaction, keeping track of the transaction context, and committing the transaction when all updates have completed. The EJB architecture provides the BMT for advanced developers to carry on the same traditions.

# Using Local or Global Transactions in BMT

When coding a bean-managed transaction, you need to decide whether to use Java Database Connectivity (JDBC) for local transaction or the Java Transaction API (JTA) for distributed and global transactions. On Day 9, "Using JDBC to Connect to a Database," you learned how to use JDBC transactions, and on Day 16, "Understanding J2EE Transactions," you learned how to use JTA transactions. You also learned that JTA is the approach recommended by the J2EE platform and should be used whenever possible. In the next sections, we'll review both transaction management mechanisms, and discuss the rationale behind using either mechanism for BMT.

18

## Using JDBC Transactions in BMT

A JDBC transaction is controlled by the resource manager of the underlying DBMS. With JDBC, you invoke the `setAutoCommit(false)` method of the `javax.sql.Connection` interface before you start demarcating a transaction with the `commit()` and `rollback()` methods. The beginning of the transaction is implicit; a new transaction starts by the first SQL call following the most recent `getConnection()`, `commit()`, or `rollback()` method.

The isolation level describes the degree to which a transaction's access to a resource manager is isolated from the access to the resource manager by other concurrently executing transactions. The API for managing an isolation level is resource manager–specific. That means the EJB architecture does not define an API for managing the isolation level. For session beans and message-driven beans with bean-managed transaction demarcation, the EJB developer can specify the desirable isolation level programmatically in the enterprise bean's methods by using the resource manager–specific API. For example, you can use the `setTransactionIsolation(int iLevel)` method of the `Connection` interface to set the appropriate isolation level for database access.

The following code illustrates a session bean that uses the `Connection` interface's methods to demarcate bean-managed transactions:

```
public class MySessionBeanA implements SessionBean {
...
  public void businessMethodA(...){
    // Using JDBC to perform local transaction on connection
    conn.setAutoCommit(false);
    // Set transaction isolation level on the Connection object
    conn.setTransactionIsolation(Connection.TRANSACTION_READ_COMMITTED);
    // JDBC transaction begins implicitly here...
    Statement stmt = conn.createStatement();
    try {
      ...
      conn.commit();
    } catch (SQLException ex) {
      conn.rollback();
      stmt.close();
    }
  }
...
}
```

The method starts by invoking `setAutoCommit()` on the `Connection` object. This invocation tells the DBMS not to automatically commit every SQL statement. Next, the same method calls routines that update the database tables. If the updates succeed, the transaction is committed. But if an exception is thrown, the transaction is rolled back.

You might want to use JDBC transactions when wrapping legacy code inside a session bean.

## Using JTA Transactions in BMT

JTA implements global transactions for J2EE components and applications in which all resource managers are registered with the global transaction manager that handles the transactions. For a global transaction, the enterprise bean never makes calls directly on a database connection or a JMS session. In JTA, transactions are demarcated by `begin()`, `commit()`, and `rollback()` methods of the `UserTransaction` interface.

 **Caution**

While an EJB instance is in a transaction, the instance must not attempt to use the resource manager–specific transaction demarcation API. That means it must not invoke the `commit()` or `rollback()` method on the `java.sql.Connection` interface or on the `javax.jms.Session` interface.

The available methods of the `UserTransaction` interface support demarcation of a transaction, setting transaction timeout, and rolling back a transaction. A client program with BMT can use explicit transaction demarcation to perform, throughout EJB, atomic updates across multiple databases connected to multiple EJB containers, (see Day 16). Table 18.1 lists a summary of the methods of the `UserTransaction` interface used by BMT components to demarcate transaction boundaries.

**TABLE 18.1**    Summary of `UserTransaction` Methods

| Method | Description |
|--------|-------------|
| `void begin()` | Creates a new transaction and associates it with the current thread. |
| `void commit()` | Completes the transaction associated with the current thread. |
| `int getStatus()` | Obtains the status of the transaction associated with the current thread. See Table 18.2 for the status constants and their meanings. |
| `void rollback()` | Rolls back the transaction associated with the current thread. |
| `void setRollbackOnly()` | Modifies the transaction associated with the current thread such that the only possible outcome of the transaction is to roll back the transaction. |
| `void setTransactionTimeout(int seconds)` | Modifies the timeout value associated with transactions started by subsequent invocations of the begin method. |

You should avoid calling the `getRollbackOnly()` and `setRollbackOnly()` methods of the `EJBContext` interface for BMT. An EJB with BMT has no need to use these methods because it can obtain the status of a transaction by using the `getStatus()` method, and also can roll back a transaction using the `rollback()` method of the `UserTransaction` interface if required.

 **Caution**   As you learned on Day 17, the methods `getRollbackOnly()` and `setRollbackOnly()` of the `EJBContext` interface are for the use of EJB with CMT only.

When an application needs to know about the status of its transaction, it can query the transaction manager by invoking the `getStatus()` method on the `UserTransaction` object. A summary of the JTA transaction statuses is listed in Table 18.2, where each status constant is represented as `static int`.

**TABLE 18.2**   Summary of JTA Transaction Status

| Status Constant | Meaning |
| --- | --- |
| STATUS_ACTIVE | Transaction is in the active state. |
| STATUS_COMMITTED | Transaction has been committed. |
| STATUS_COMMITTING | Transaction is in the process of committing. |
| STATUS_MARKED_ROLLBACK | Transaction has been marked for rollback. This could be a result of using the `setRollbackOnly()` method. |
| STATUS_NO_TRANSACTION | No transaction is currently associated with the target instance. |
| STATUS_PREPARED | Transaction has been prepared. |
| STATUS_PREPARING | Transaction is in the process of preparing. |
| STATUS_ROLLEDBACK | Transaction manager determined that the transaction state is a rollback. |
| STATUS_ROLLING_BACK | Transaction is in the process of rolling back. |
| STATUS_UNKNOWN | Current status of transaction cannot be determined. |

The following example demonstrates the use of a JTA transaction in an EJB with bean-managed transaction demarcation:

```
SessionContext ctx;
...
// Using JTA for distributed transaction.
public void businessMethodB(){
   try {
      // Establish a UserTransaction context from EJBContext
      UserTransaction ut = ctx.getUserTransaction();
      // Begin the distributed transaction
      ut.begin();
      ...
      ut.commit();
   } catch(Exception e) {
      ut.rollback();
   }
...
```

In the preceding example, the transaction context ut is obtained from the EJBContext (in this case, the SessionContext) because the EJB container maintains such context for transaction propagation across components and applications.

## Setting Transaction Timeouts with BMT

The transaction timeout is a useful mechanism of specifying an expected period for a transaction to execute. This gives application code more control over managing transactions. EJB developers specify the timeout period for transactions in EJB with BMT by calling the setTransactionTimeout() method of the UserTransaction interface. If the duration of a transaction exceeds the specified timeout setting, the transaction manager rolls back the transaction automatically. Here is an example of setting the transaction timeout to 30 seconds:

```
// obtain user transaction context
   ut = ejbContext.getUserTransaction();
// set transaction timeout before beginning a transaction
   ut.setTransactionTimeout(30);
// start a transaction
   ut.begin();
   ...
```

18

 **Note**   You must set the timeout before you begin the transaction. Setting a timeout does not affect a transaction that has already started.

# Which Types of EJBs Can Use BMT?

An EJB with BMT must be either a session bean or a message-driven bean. Entity beans use only container-managed transaction demarcation. Because the EJB architecture does not support nested transactions, your EJB instance that starts a transaction must complete that transaction before it starts a new transaction. Your transaction is completed when it is either committed or rolled back. The EJB container manages client invocations to an EJB with BMT. When writing code for a client, you invoke a business method via the EJB's home or component interface; the EJB container suspends any transaction that might be associated with the client request. If a transaction is associated with the instance, the container associates the method execution with this transaction. As you learned from Day 16, the EJB container propagates transactions implicitly. That means you don't have to explicitly pass the transaction context as a parameter because the EJB container handles this task for you transparently.

 **Note**   You should keep in mind that clients such as JavaServer Pages (JSPs) and servlets are not designed to be transactional components. Use EJBs to perform transactional work, and then you can invoke such EJBs from either a servlet or a JSP.

In the following sections, you'll learn about the transaction semantics for methods specific to each type of bean using BMT. You'll also learn the restrictions that are imposed when an EJB of a certain type uses bean-managed transactions.

## Understanding Transaction Semantics in BMTs

As you learned on Day 17, transaction semantics govern the behavior of transaction processing, which are based on the EJB type and the transaction type. These semantics describe the transaction context at the time a method is invoked, and define whether the EJB can access methods in the UserTransaction interface. EJB applications must be designed with these semantics in mind. For BMT, the transaction semantics differ between stateful session, stateless session, and message-driven beans. For entity beans, transactions are never bean-managed. Entity beans may choose to manage their own persistence mechanism (CMP or BMP), but must leave transaction demarcation to the EJB container.

## Session Beans with BMT

Both stateful and stateless session beans can use bean-managed transaction demarcation. In a session bean with BMT, it is a common practice to use either JDBC or JTA transactions. As mentioned earlier, JTA transactions are recommended wherever possible.

You learned in the previous section that you must obtain the transaction context from the EJBContext, which in turn is obtained by the setSessionContext() method of the EJB.

The EJB code starts a transaction using the begin() method of the UserTransaction object. All operations in an EJB execute within the scope of a transaction. The commit() method causes the EJB container to call the transaction manager to complete the transaction. In case of failure, exceptions can be caught and the transaction can be rolled back using the rollback() method of the UserTransaction object.

## Stateless Session Bean with BMT

In a stateless session bean with BMT, a business method must commit or roll back a transaction before returning. The EJB container detects the case in which a transaction was started but not completed, rolls back the transaction, and then throws the `java.rmi.RemoteException` to the client if the client is a remote client, or throws the `javax.ejb.EJBException` if the client is a local client.

In developing a stateless session bean with BMT, the EJB's deployment descriptor must be specified through a bean-managed demarcation, as follows:

```
<ejb-jar>
   <enterprise-beans>
      <session>
         ...
         <session-type>Stateless</session-type>
         <transaction-type>Bean</transaction-type>
         ...
      </session>
   </enterprise-beans>
</ejb-jar>
```

**TABLE 18.3**   Transaction Semantics for Stateless Session Beans

| Method | Can the Method Access `UserTransaction`? |
| --- | --- |
| `create()` | No |
| `setSessionContext()` | Yes |
| `ejbCreate()` | Yes |
| `ejbRemove()` | Yes |
| Business method | Yes |

Only the constructor `create()` of the stateless session bean is not allowed to access methods on the `UserTransaction` interface.

## Stateful Session Bean with BMT

In a stateful session bean with a JTA transaction, the association between the bean instance and the transaction is retained across multiple client calls. Even if each business method called by the client opens and closes the database connection, the association is retained until the instance completes the transaction. There is no restriction that a business method must commit or roll back a transaction before returning, as in the case of a stateless session bean.

In a stateful session bean with a JDBC transaction, the JDBC connection retains the association between the bean instance and the transaction across multiple calls. If the connection is closed, the association is not retained. A stateful session bean instance may, but is not required to, commit a started transaction before a business method returns. If a transaction has not been completed by the end of a business method, the container retains the association between the transaction and the instance across multiple client calls until the instance eventually completes the transaction.

 **Caution**

> Stateful session beans that implement the `SessionSynchronization` interface cannot use bean-managed transaction demarcation. The reason for such a restriction is that they are in full control of committing the transaction, and thus would create a conflict between the container and the EJB.

In developing a stateful session bean with BMT, the EJB's deployment descriptor must be specified with a bean-managed demarcation, as follows:

```
<ejb-jar>
   <enterprise-beans>
      <session>
         ...
         <session-type>Stateful</session-type>
         <transaction-type>Bean</transaction-type>
         ...
      </session>
   </enterprise-beans>
</ejb-jar>
```

In the case of a stateful session bean, it is possible that the business method that started a transaction can complete without committing or rolling back the transaction. In such a case, the container must retain the association between the transaction and the instance across multiple client calls until the instance commits or rolls back the transaction. When the client invokes the next business method, the EJB container must invoke the business method in this transaction context.

The following example illustrates a stateful session bean that retains the transaction context across two data sources, using three client calls, invoked in the order methodA, methodB, and methodC:

```
public class MySessionEJB implements SessionBean {
   EJBContext ctx;
   DataSource ds1;
   DataSource ds2;
```

```
Connection con1;
Connection con2;
methodA(...) {
   Statement stmt;
   InitialContext initCtx = new InitialContext();
   // obtain distributed transaction context
   ut = ctx.getUserTransaction();
   // start transaction explicitly
   ut.begin();
   // do some work using con1 here
   ds1 = (javax.sql.DataSource)
              initCtx.lookup("java:comp/env/jdbc/myDB1");
   con1 = ds1.getConnection();
   stmt = con1.createStatement();
   stmt.executeUpdate(...);
   // The container retains the transaction associated with the
   // instance to the next client call [which is methodB(...)]
}
methodB(...) {
   Statement stmt;
   InitialContext initCtx = new InitialContext();
   // make some work using con2 here...
   ds2 = (javax.sql.DataSource)
         initCtx.lookup("java:comp/env/jdbc/myDB2");
   con2 = ds2.getConnection();
   stmt = con2.createStatement();
   stmt.executeUpdate(...);
   // The container retains the transaction associated with the
   // instance to the next client call [which is methodC(...)].
}
methodC(...) {
   Statement stmt;
   // obtain again the same transaction contex
   ut = ctx.getUserTransaction();
   // make some more work using con1 and con2
   stmt = con1.createStatement();
   stmt.executeUpdate(...);
   stmt = con2.createStatement();
   stmt.executeUpdate(...);
   // commit the transaction
   ut.commit();
   // release connections
   con1.close();
   con2.close();
}
...
}
```

In this example, the transaction begin() in methodA and the container maintain the transaction context after the EJB returns from the method. The EJB calls commit() to commit the transaction in `methodC`, where it restores the "same" transaction context from the `EJBContext`.

Transactions are expensive and use critical resources; therefore, it is recommended that an EJB open and close a database connection in each business method rather than hold the `Connection` open until the end of the transaction. The following is an example of a stateful session bean that starts a transaction in `methodA` and commits in `methodC`:

```
public class MySessionEJB implements SessionBean {
    EJBContext ctx;
    InitialContext initCtx;
    methodA(...) {
        Statement stmt;
        // obtain distributed transaction context
        ut = ctx.getUserTransaction();
        // start a transaction
        ut.begin();
    }
     methodB(...) {
        DataSource ds;
        Connection con;
        Statement stmt;
        // open connection
        ds = (javax.sql.DataSource)
                initCtx.lookup("java:comp/env/jdbc/myDB");
        con = ds.getConnection();
        // make some updates on con
        stmt = con.createStatement();
        stmt.executeUpdate(...);
        // close the connection
        stmt.close();
        con.close();
    }
    methodC(...) {
        // obtain same distributed transaction context
        ut = ctx.getUserTransaction();
        // commit the transaction
        ut.commit();
    }
...
}
```

In the preceding example, if the sequence of execution were `methodA`, `methodB`, `methodB`, and `methodC`, and all the database updates were done by the multiple invocations of `methodB`, these methods would be performed in the scope of the same transaction with optimum resource usage.

Table 18.4 summarizes the transaction semantics of stateful session beans with bean-managed transactions.

**TABLE 18.4**    Transaction Semantics for Stateful Session Beans

| Method | Can Access UserTransaction Methods? |
| --- | --- |
| create(...) | No |
| setSessionContext() | Yes |
| ejbCreate() | Yes |
| ejbRemove() | Yes |
| ejbActivate() | Yes |
| ejbPassivate() | Yes |
| Business method | Yes |
| afterBegin() | N/A |
| beforeCompletion() | N/A |
| afterCompletion() | N/A |

Because a stateful session bean with bean-managed transaction cannot implement the SessionSynchronization interface, the methods afterBegin(), beforeBegin(), and afterCompletion() of the SessionSynchronization are not applicable.

## Message-Driven Beans with BMT

As you learned on Day 14, "Developing Message-Driven Beans," there is no direct communication between a client and a message-driven bean, except through a JMS message. Therefore, no client transaction context is available when a message-driven bean is invoked because a distributed transaction context does not flow with a JMS message. When a message-driven bean with BMT uses the UserTransaction interface to specify transactions, the message receipt that causes the onMessage() method of the bean to be invoked is not part of the transaction. A container-managed transaction with the Required transaction attribute must be used if receipt of a message is to be part of a transaction. A message-driven bean instance must commit a transaction before the onMessage() method returns. The EJB container detects the case in which a transaction was started, but not completed, in the onMessage() method, and rolls back the transaction.

**Caution**

The EJB developer must not send a JMS message followed by synchronous receipt of a reply to that message within a single transaction. Because a JMS message is not delivered to its final destination until the transaction commits, the receipt of the reply within the same transaction will never take place.

18

The container makes the UserTransaction interface available to the EJB's business method or the onMessage() method via the EJBContext interface and under the environment entry "java:comp/UserTransaction". When an instance uses the UserTransaction interface to demarcate a transaction, the container must enlist all the resource managers used by the instance between the begin() and commit() or rollback() methods with the transaction. When the instance attempts to commit the transaction, the container is responsible for global coordination of committing the transaction.

 **Caution**  |  In MDB with BMT, the acknowledge() method should not be used within a transaction.

In developing a message-driven bean with BMT, the EJB's deployment descriptor must be specified with a bean-managed demarcation, as follows:

```
<ejb-jar>
  <enterprise-beans>
    ...
    <message-driven>
      ...
      <transaction-type>Bean</transaction-type>
      ...
    </message-driven>
    ...
  </enterprise-beans>
</ejb-jar>
```

Table 18.5 describes the transaction semantics for message-driven beans in bean-managed transactions.

**TABLE 18.5**   Transaction Semantics for Message-Driven Beans

| Method | Can Access UserTransaction Methods? |
| --- | --- |
| create() | No |
| setMessageDrivenContext() | Yes |
| ejbCreate() | Yes |
| ejbRemove() | Yes |
| onMessage() | Yes |
| Business method | Yes |

# Handling Exceptions in BMT

EJB must catch and handle specific exceptions thrown during transactions. EJBs can throw either application or system-level exceptions, or both, whenever they encounter errors while handling transactions. Application-level exceptions arise from errors in the business logic. The calling application must handle them. System-level exceptions, such as runtime errors, transcend the application itself and can be handled by the application, the enterprise bean, or the EJB container. An EJB must declare application-level exceptions and system-level exceptions in the throws clauses of its remote interface. You must test for checked exceptions in your client application's try-catch block before calling the bean's methods.

When an instance attempts to start a transaction using the begin() method of the UserTransaction interface while the instance has not committed the previous transaction, the container must throw the javax.transaction.NotSupportedException in the begin() method.

The container must throw the java.lang.IllegalStateException if an instance of a bean with BMT attempts to invoke the setRollbackOnly() or getRollbackOnly() method of the EJBContext interface.

## System-Level Exceptions

An EJB throws a system-level exception to indicate an unexpected system-level failure. For example, it throws an exception if it can't open a database connection. System-level exceptions are usually a java.ejb.EJBException if the method is local and a java.rmi.RemoteException is the method is remote.

**Note**   java.ejb.EJBException is a runtime exception and it isn't required to be listed in the throws clause of the bean's business methods.

System-level exceptions usually require the transaction to be rolled back. Often the container managing the EJB does the rollback. Sometimes the client must roll back the transaction, especially if the transactions are bean-managed.

## Application-Level Exceptions

The bean's business methods use application exceptions to report abnormal application conditions, such as unacceptable input values or amounts beyond acceptable limits. These are business logic errors, not system problems. Application-level exceptions are exceptions other than java.ejb.EJBException. For example, a bean method that debits an account balance might throw an application exception to report that the account balance isn't sufficient to permit a particular debit operation. When an application-level exception occurs, the enterprise bean instance doesn't automatically roll back the client's transaction. The client then has the knowledge and the opportunity to evaluate the error message, take the necessary steps to correct the situation, and recover the transaction.

# Developing an EJB with BMT

Today we'll develop an EJB with BMT through an example adapted from our university registration system. We'll also demonstrate the use of servlets as controllers in the Web tier, and use a JavaBean object to transfer data between the EJB tier and the Web tier.

The following are the main steps required in developing an EJB component with BMT:

1. In the EJB's deployment descriptor, the bean developer sets the transaction type in the <transaction-type> tag to the value Bean to specify a bean-managed demarcation.

2. The client application uses JNDI to obtain an object reference to the UserTransaction object to establish a transaction context.

3. The client application begins a transaction using the begin() method of the UserTransaction object, and issues a request to the EJB through the EJB container. All operations on the EJB execute within the scope of a transaction. If a call to any of these operations raises an exception (either explicitly or as a result of a communication failure), the exception can be caught and the transaction can be rolled back using the rollback() method of the UserTransaction object. If no exceptions occur, the client application commits the current transaction using the commit() method. This method ends the transaction and starts the processing of the operation. The transaction is committed only if all the participants in the transaction agree to commit.

4. The commit() method causes the EJB container to call the transaction manager to complete the transaction.

5. The transaction manager is responsible for coordinating with the resource managers to update any databases.

## Developing the Bean's Remote Interface

For our example, you implement the Student EJB as a stateful session bean, where you define all business methods in the Student remote interface. Listing 18.1 shows the remote interface Student.java.

**LISTING 18.1**   The Remote Interface `Student.java`

```
package day18;
import javax.ejb.EJBObject;
import java.rmi.RemoteException;
import java.sql.SQLException;

public interface Student extends EJBObject
{
  public void setupDB() throws RemoteException;
  public StudentInfo getStudent (String id)
      throws RemoteException, SQLException;
  public void addStudent (StudentInfo Student)
      throws RemoteException, SQLException;
  public void updateStudent (StudentInfo Student)
      throws RemoteException, SQLException;
  public void deleteStudent (String id)
      throws RemoteException, SQLException;
}
```

The remote interface uses the `StudentInfo` JavaBean class as a helper class to transfer data between the EJB tier and the Web tier.

## Developing the Bean's Home Interface

The home interface `StudentHome` defines the life cycle methods of the EJB (see Listing 18.2). The home interface is stored in the `StudentHome.java` file.

**LISTING 18.2**   The Home Interface `StudentHome.java`

```
package day18;
import javax.ejb.EJBHome;
import javax.ejb.CreateException;
import java.rmi.RemoteException;
public interface StudentHome extends EJBHome
{
  public Student create () throws RemoteException, CreateException;
}
```

## Developing the Bean's Class

The bean class implements all the methods in both the remote and home interfaces. Listing 18.3 displays the code to implement all business methods and life cycle methods.

**LISTING 18.3**  The Bean Class `StudentBean.java`

```java
package day18;
import java.io.*;
import javax.ejb.*;
import java.sql.*;
import javax.sql.*;
import javax.naming.*;
import java.rmi.RemoteException;
import javax.transaction.*;

public class StudentBean implements SessionBean{
  SessionContext ctx;
  DataSource ds = null;
  String id     = null;
  String fname = null;
  String lname = null;
  String address   = null;

  public void setupDB()
      throws RemoteException
  {
    System.out.println("Settingup Database...");
     try {
       InitialContext ctx = new InitialContext();
       ds = (DataSource)ctx.lookup("java:comp/env/jdbc/styejbDB");
     }catch (Exception ex) {
        ex.printStackTrace();
     }
   }

  public StudentInfo getStudent(String id)
      throws RemoteException, SQLException
  {
    try {
       String sql = "SELECT * " +
         "FROM STUDENTS " +
          "WHERE STUDENT_ID ='";
      Connection conn = ds.getConnection();
      System.out.println("Conntected to DB...");
      Statement stmt = conn.createStatement();
      ResultSet rs = stmt.executeQuery(sql+id+"'");
      System.out.println("Getting Result...");
      while(rs.next()){
        id = rs.getString(1);
        fname = rs.getString(2);
        lname = rs.getString(3);
        address = rs.getString(4);
       }
      conn.close();
       System.out.println("Returning Student Info...");
```

**LISTING 18.3**    continued

```
      return (new StudentInfo (id, fname, lname, address)));

   }catch (java.sql.SQLException e) {
      throw new RemoteException("SQL failed: " + e.getMessage());
   }catch (Exception ex) {
      ex.printStackTrace();
   }
   return null;
}

public void addStudent(StudentInfo st)
    throws RemoteException, SQLException
{
   UserTransaction ut = ctx.getUserTransaction ();
    try {
    System.out.println("addStudent: Starting new transaction...");
 ut.begin ();

 String sql = "INSERT INTO STUDENTS VALUES(" + st.id +
              ",'" + st.fname  +
              "', '" + st.lname +
              "', '" + st.address + "')";
    Connection conn = ds.getConnection();
    Statement stmt = conn.createStatement();
 stmt.executeUpdate(sql);
 ut.commit ();
 stmt.close();
    conn.close();
 System.out.println("addStudent: transaction committed...");
    }catch (java.sql.SQLException e) {
       try{
        System.out.println("addStudent: transaction rolled back...");
         ut.rollback();
       } catch (SystemException ex) {
        throw new RemoteException("Rollback failed: " + ex.getMessage());
        }

    }catch (Exception e) {
      try{
         ut.rollback();
      } catch (SystemException ex) {
        throw new RemoteException("Rollback failed: " + ex.getMessage());
      }
   }
}

public void updateStudent(StudentInfo st)
    throws RemoteException, SQLException
{
```

**LISTING 18.3**  continued

```
UserTransaction ut = ctx.getUserTransaction ();
  try {
    System.out.println("updateStudent: Starting new transaction...");
ut.begin ();

String sql = "UPDATE STUDENTS SET FNAME  ='" + st.fname  +
             "', LNAME ='" + st.lname  +
             "', ADDRESS ='" + st.address     +
      "' WHERE STUDENT_ID=";
    Connection conn = ds.getConnection();
    Statement stmt = conn.createStatement();
stmt.executeUpdate(sql+st.id);
ut.commit ();
stmt.close();
  conn.close();
System.out.println("updateStudent: transaction committed...");
  }catch (java.sql.SQLException e) {
      try{
        System.out.println("updateStudent: transaction rolled back...");
          ut.rollback();
        } catch (SystemException ex) {
          throw new RemoteException("Rollback failed: " + ex.getMessage());
      }

    }catch (Exception e) {
        try{
          ut.rollback();
        } catch (SystemException ex) {
          throw new RemoteException("Rollback failed: " + ex.getMessage());
        }
      }
  }

  public void deleteStudent(String id)
  throws RemoteException, SQLException
  {
    UserTransaction ut = ctx.getUserTransaction ();
  try {
      System.out.println("deleteStudent: Starting new transaction...");
    ut.begin ();
    String sql = "DELETE FROM STUDENTS WHERE STUDENT_ID=";
    Connection conn = ds.getConnection();
     Statement stmt = conn.createStatement();
    stmt.executeUpdate(sql+id);
    ut.commit ();
    stmt.close();
     conn.close();
    System.out.println("deleteStudent: transaction committed...");
  }catch (java.sql.SQLException e) {
          try{
```

**LISTING 18.3** continued

```
            System.out.println("deleteStudent: transaction rolled back...");
              ut.rollback();
            } catch (SystemException ex) {
              throw new RemoteException("Rollback failed: " + ex.getMessage());
        }
      }catch (Exception e) {
          try{
            ut.rollback();
          } catch (SystemException ex) {
            throw new RemoteException("Rollback failed: " + ex.getMessage());
          }
        }
      }
  public void ejbCreate () throws RemoteException, CreateException {}
  public void ejbRemove() {}
  public void setSessionContext (SessionContext ctx) {this.ctx = ctx;}
  public void ejbActivate () {}
  public void ejbPassivate () {}
}
```

In the preceding code, the EJB obtains the transaction context from the EJBContext maintained by the container, and uses it across all methods of the bean.

## Developing Helper Classes

The helper class StudentInfo implemented as a JavaBean, which is used as a data container (data bean) to transfer data between the EJB tier and the Web tier, as shown in Listing 18.4.

**LISTING 18.4** Helper Class StudentInfo.java

```
package day18;

public class StudentInfo implements java.io.Serializable {
  public String fname = null;
  public String lname = null;
  public String id = null;
  public String address = null;
  public StudentInfo (String ID, String fname, String lname, String address){
    this.fname = fname;
    this.lname = lname;
    this.id = ID;
    this.address = address;
  }
}
```

18

# Packaging the Beans into a JAR File

The deployment descriptor for the `Student` EJB is listed in the following code (see Listing 18.5). The EJB developer sets the `<session>` tag with the `<transaction-type>` to `Bean` so that the EJB will manage its own state. There is no mechanism for an application assembler to affect enterprise beans with bean-managed transaction demarcation. The application assembler must not define transaction attributes for an enterprise bean with bean-managed transaction demarcation.

**LISTING 18.5**   Standard Deployment Descriptor `ejb-jar.xml`

```
<?xml version="1.0"?>
<!DOCTYPE ejb-jar PUBLIC
'-//Sun Microsystems, Inc.//DTD Enterprise JavaBeans 2.0//EN'
'http://java.sun.com/dtd/ejb-jar_2_0.dtd'>
<ejb-jar>
   <enterprise-beans>
      <session>
         <ejb-name>Student</ejb-name>
         <home>day18.StudentHome</home>
         <remote>day18.Student</remote>
         <ejb-class>day18.StudentBean</ejb-class>
         <session-type>Stateful</session-type>
         <transaction-type>Bean</transaction-type>
         <resource-env-ref>
           <resource-env-ref-name>jdbc/styejbDB</resource-env-ref-name>
           <resource-env-ref-type>javax.sql.DataSource</resource-env-ref-type>
         </resource-env-ref>
      </session>
   </enterprise-beans>
</ejb-jar>
```

Listing 18.6 displays the vendor-specific `weblogic-ejb-jar.xml`, which is required when you deploy this component in WebLogic Server.

**LISTING 18.6**   Standard Deployment Descriptor `weblogic-ejb-jar.xml`

```
<?xml version="1.0"?>
<!DOCTYPE weblogic-ejb-jar PUBLIC
'-//BEA Systems, Inc.//DTD WebLogic 6.0.0 EJB//EN'
'http://www.bea.com/servers/wls600/dtd/weblogic-ejb-jar.dtd'>

<weblogic-ejb-jar>
  <weblogic-enterprise-bean>
    <ejb-name>Student</ejb-name>
      <reference-descriptor>
```

**LISTING 18.6** continued

```
                    <resource-env-description>
                        <res-env-ref-name>jdbc/styejbDB</res-env-ref-name>
                        <jndi-name>jdbc.styejbDB</jndi-name>
                    </resource-env-description>
                </reference-descriptor>
            <jndi-name>day18/MyStudentHome</jndi-name>
        </weblogic-enterprise-bean>
</weblogic-ejb-jar>
```

## Developing the Testing Client

To test the Student EJB, you need to develop the client application. The client code delegates the Student session bean to update data in the database. The Student EJB performs these tasks through a bean-managed transaction demarcation. Listing 18.7 provides the code you need to use for the client.

**LISTING 18.7** Client for Testing Code Client.java

```java
package day18;
import javax.naming.Context;
import java.rmi.*;
import javax.naming.InitialContext;
import java.util.Hashtable;

public class Client {
  public final static String id = "100";
  public static StudentInfo info = null;
  public static void main (String[] argv) {
   System.out.print("\nDay 18: Demonstration the use of BMT\n");
   try{
    // get handle to the Student object
    System.out.println ("Connecting to a Student EJB..");
    Context ctx = new InitialContext();
    Object obj = ctx.lookup("day18/MyStudentHome");
    StudentHome studentHome = (StudentHome)
        javax.rmi.PortableRemoteObject.narrow(obj, StudentHome.class);
    Student student = (Student) studentHome.create ();
    student.setupDB();
    try{
      System.out.println ("Try deleting student with id="+id);
      student.deleteStudent(id);
    }catch (Exception e){
          System.out.println("Record does not exist...");
    }
```

18

---

**LISTING 18.7**   continued

```
System.out.println ("Try adding a new student");
info = new StudentInfo(id, "Snow", "White", "161 MAIN ST, ELK GROVE, CA");
student.addStudent(info);
System.out.println ("Requesting the student info...");
info = student.getStudent(id);
System.out.println ("Student Info = " +
                         info.id + ", " +
                         info.fname + ", " +
                         info.lname + ", " +
                         info.address);
// Modify student info
info.id = id;
info.fname = "John";
info.lname = "Doe";
info.address="111 CASPER DR, SACRAMENTO, CA";
// Update student in the database
System.out.println ("Updating the student info...");
student.updateStudent (info);
info = student.getStudent (id);
System.out.println ("Student Info = " +
                         info.id + ", " +
                         info.fname + ", " +
                         info.lname + ", " +
                         info.address);
}catch ( Exception e){
       System.out.println("Student transaction failed...");
     e.printStackTrace();
 }
 }
}
```

---

## Deploying and Running the Student EJB

Before deploying the Student EJB, you must first build the example. Build scripts are provided for both WebLogic Server and the JBoss server. The following are the steps required to build and deploy the Student EJB with BMT in any of the servers.

1. Configure both the JDBC DataSource and connection pool as described on Day 9.

2. Build the example for the appropriate application server. From the directory day18, run the build script. This creates a subdirectory named build that contains all the compiled code. The following is an example for WebLogic:

   ```
   c:\>cd c:\styejb
   ```

   ```
   c:\styejb>setEnvWebLogic.bat
   ```

   ```
   c:\styejb>cd day18
   ```

   ```
   c:\styejb\day18>buildWebLogic.bat
   ```

3. To run the example, use the appropriate script for each server. Set up the environment for the client in a new command window, and then use the run script in the `day18` directory:

```
c:\styejb>setEnvWebLogic.bat
c:\styejb>cd day18
c:\styejb\day18> runClientWebLogic.bat
```

Similarly, to set the environment, build and deploy the code, and then run the client in the JBoss server, you must use the scripts `setEnvJboss.bat`, `buildJBoss.bat`, and `runClientJboss.bat`, respectively.

# Best Practices

Bean-managed transaction demarcation is only used by more advanced users who want more control over the application workflow. The J2EE architecture recommends managing transactions through container-managed demarcation. Declarative transaction management provides one of the major benefits of the J2EE platform, by freeing the EJB developer from the burden of managing transactions.

Use JTA, where possible, in managing transaction boundaries in enterprise applications. This guarantees data consistency and integrity, and ensures that work performed by multiple components through multiple resource managers is grouped as an atomic unit.

Only session beans and message-driven beans can use both bean-managed transaction and container-managed transaction demarcation. Entity beans must use only container-managed demarcation.

An EJB should not invoke resource manager-specific transition demarcation API methods, such as `commit()` and `rollback()` of the `Connection` interface, within a transaction. It uses only the methods of the `UserTransaction` interface to manage transaction boundaries.

Stateless session beans should always either commit or roll back a transaction before the business method returns. Stateful session beans do not have this requirement. EJBs with BMT should not invoke the `getRollbackOnly()` and `setRollbackOnly()` methods of the `EJBContext` interface. These methods should be used only in container-managed transactions. For bean-managed transactions, you should invoke the `getStatus()` and `rollback()` methods of the `UserTransaction` interface.

Servlets and JSP are used in nontransactional tasks, such as data presentation and user interaction. Because transactions tend to be associated with business logic, database access and other transactional work should be handled by a transactional EJB.

18

# Summary

Today you learned how to use, develop, and deploy EJBs with bean-managed transaction demarcation. This type of transaction management is the programmatic approach to controlling transaction boundaries in the application code. Transaction demarcations are embedded into the EJB code, whether you try to commit, roll back, or abort a transaction. BMT is used mainly by advanced users who want to have more control over their transactions. You can use either local or global transactions when developing an EJB with BMT.

According to the EJB architecture, only session and message-driven beans can use bean-managed transactions. Entity beans can use only container-managed transactions. A working example was given to illustrate the use of a session bean (Student EJB) with BMT. You also studied the restrictions imposed by the J2EE architecture on the use of BMT, and the transaction semantics of each EJB method.

# Q&A

**Q** **Which types of EJBs can use bean-managed transactions?**

**A** Stateful and stateless session beans, as well as message-driven beans, are the types of EJBs that can use BMT. Entity beans can only use container-managed transaction demarcation.

**Q** **What type of beans can use the SessionSynchronization interface? Why?**

**A** Stateful session beans with CMT can only use the SessionSynchronization interface. EJBs with BMT cannot use the SessionSynchronization interface because they control commitment of the transaction.

# Quiz

1. A developer uses a bean-managed transaction in a stateful session bean when

   A. Accessing legacy systems

   B. Implementing the SessionSynchronization interface

   C. Implementing JTA to control user transactions

   D. Controlling transactions using the setRollBack() method

2. In which one of the following is it appropriate to implement SessionSynchronization?

   A. Stateful session beans

   B. Session beans with container-managed transactions

    C. Container-managed persistent entity beans

    D. Session beans with bean-managed transactions

3. Transaction isolation levels in EJBs are

    A. Set by the EJB developer for bean-managed transactions

    B. Set by the deployer for container-managed transactions

    C. Specified to the method level

    D. Specified to the class level only

## Quiz Answers

1. A, C

2. A

3. A

# Exercises

Modify the earlier example to use a stateless session bean with BMT instead of the stateful session bean Student EJB. Perform any code change necessary to avoid the restrictions imposed by J2EE architecture with respect to a stateless session bean with BMT, as you learned from today's discussions.

18

# DAY **19**

# Understanding Security

Security is an important and sensitive aspect of protecting the enterprise from malicious attacks and threats, such as disclosure of vital information and destruction of assets, which have a negative effect on system availability and integrity. In previous days, we briefly introduced some security aspects. We explored how to use the Java Naming and Directory Interface (JNDI) services to authenticate a user in Day 4, "Using JNDI for Naming Services and Components." Today, we'll go into more detail.

First, we'll explore security concepts that are used in developing applications. Later, we'll focus on Java 2 Enterprise Edition (J2EE) security mechanisms and how they are used in the development and deployment of secure enterprise applications. We'll also explore how J2EE supports container-managed security through a declarative approach and component-managed approach through a programmatic approach. We'll also investigate the Java Authentication and Authorization Service (JAAS) API as a standard API for accessing pluggable security mechanisms. Like other J2EE common services, JAAS allows the development of component-based applications, which are adaptable to the existing security mechanism in place.

In learning the concepts of security in enterprise applications, the following are the main highlights of today's activities:

- Learn the concepts and mechanisms of security in the context of developing J2EE applications
- Learn how security is implemented across all J2EE tiers
- Study the JAAS architecture and concepts
- Learn about the roles and responsibilities for developing and deploying J2EE application
- Learn some of the best practices in applying J2EE security

# Reviewing Security Fundamentals

To build secure enterprise applications, security mechanisms must be established to ensure that enterprise assets and resources are protected from accidental and malicious attacks. Enterprise security addresses data resources, applications, and components, but it also deals with the secure communication between them. Security ensures that information is neither modified nor disclosed except in accordance with the security policy established by the enterprise. Most security measures involve proof material (such as passwords) and *data encryption*, which is the translation of data into a form that cannot be interpreted by an intruder.

We'll start by highlighting the important concepts, entities, and mechanisms used in enterprise security.

## Security Concepts

A special jargon of terms and concepts is used in managing and developing enterprise security. The following sections explore the concepts used in application security and their definitions.

### Resources, Users, and Groups

A *resource* is a critical entity that can be accessed by enterprise applications. Resources can be shared, and their accesses are controlled using sets of permissions. In the context of J2EE applications, the following resources require permissions:

- EJB and Web containers (application server)
- EJBs, servlets, JavaServer Pages (JSPs), HTML pages
- Java Database Connectivity (JDBC) connection pools

- Java Message Service (JMS) destinations
- JNDI contexts

A *user* is an entity that accesses resources. A user can be an application end user (such as a consumer or customer), or it can be a client application (such as a browser or another program). An *administrator* is a special type of user, who has certain capabilities to manage enterprise resources. When a user wants to access a resource, it presents a username and a *credential* (either a password or a digital certificate) to the application server. If the application server can prove the identity of the user Laura, it creates a security context (or a thread) and associates Laura with that context. In the event of any further access to resources, the server performs a security check to see whether Laura has the correct permissions to proceed.

A *group* is a collection of users. It is more efficient to manage a group than to manage a large numbers of users individually. Group members usually have something in common, such as similar permissions to access system resources. The system can be configured to assign users to groups. A person can be defined as both an individual user and a group member. Individual access permissions override any group member access permissions. Groups are defined at the operating system level, and not at the application level.

## Permissions, Access Control Lists, and Realms

*Permissions* represent the privileges given to users to access certain resources. For example, permissions can be a combination of reading, writing, and executing files and directories. Other examples of permissions can be the ability to send and receive messages, load servlets, or connect to a hostname and port of a data source. The system administrator assigns permissions to both users and groups. This administration task is quite complex and prone to errors.

To reduce the complexity of administering security in an enterprise, an administrator protects shared resources by creating lists of users and groups that have the required permissions to access those resources. Such lists are called *access control lists* (*ACLs*). ACLs were first introduced to manage security of the Unix platform. ACLs are configured in the access control properties of the security policy.

A security *realm* is a logical domain of users, groups, permissions, and ACLs defined to protect resources. A user must belong to a realm in order to access resources defined in that realm. Some application servers use local disk storage or a database for storing security realms, but other security realms can use Windows NT, Unix, and Lightweight Directory Access Protocol (LDAP) for storage.

19

## Principals and Roles

A *principal* is a logical entity that is associated with an identity (user, group, program, or organization) as a result of authentication. An identity can be mapped to a different principal based on the security context defined for the application. Thus, a role can have multiple principals when accessing enterprise resources.

A *role* is a logical grouping of users who have similar permissions, at the application level, to access resources. Roles are similar to groups, but roles are defined at the application layer. Roles are mapped to real-world groups and users (defined at the operating system layer) when the bean is deployed. J2EE security authorization is role-driven, and each principal is mapped to a unique role for the purposes of access control.

Figure 19.1 depicts the security concepts discussed so far. A client first must be identified and authenticated by the system before it is allowed access to the authorized resources.

**FIGURE 19.1**

*Security concepts.*

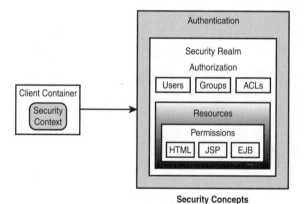

## Learning Security Mechanisms

Security mechanisms provide answers to the following concerns in regard to protecting enterprise resources:

- Identity: Who is supposed to grant access to resources?
- Authority: After the user is identified, what access control is allowed?
- Integrity: How confidential is the data? Are passwords and credit-card numbers protected from being stolen?
- Validity: How can we validate the true identity?
- Audit: How can we discover a security breach?

Building a highly secure system is always costly, but is even harder to define, develop, and deploy. The next few sections answer the preceding list of questions and concerns.

## Authentication

*Authentication* is the mechanism of verifying the identity of the security entity before completing a connection to the resource. The principal is the party whose identity is verified. Associated with a principal is a set of *credentials*, or proof materials such as passwords or digital certificates. More sophisticated credentials include smart cards and biometrics (fingerprint and retinal/iris scans). When the proof is two-way, it is referred to as *mutual authentication*. Authentication is the first layer of a security environment, as depicted in Figure 19.1.

After the user is authenticated, an initial security context is established and maintained by the container, and is associated with that user. Among the possible policies and mechanisms for controlling access to a security context is the Secure Sockets Layer (SSL) protocol (or HTTP over SSL [HTTPS]), which is used to encrypt passwords. This provides an additional level of security to password authentication.

The authentication process can be initiated for Web clients in the Web tier, and also can be started at the EJB container for J2EE client applications. In both cases, the corresponding container for allowing access control to resources will assess security checks. Figure 19.2 depicts the authentication for the two different clients accessing the application server.

**FIGURE 19.2**

*J2EE client authentication.*

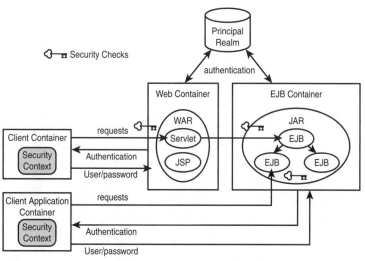

J2EE Authentication

19

Authentication validates the identity of the user, usually via JNDI or JAAS. We explored JNDI authentication in Day 4, and we'll explore authentication across J2EE tiers later today.

## Authorization

*Authorization* is the mechanism that ensures only authenticated principals with the right permissions can access application components. It is a fine-grain security that allows authenticated users and groups (through access control lists) to access the assigned resources.

Roles that are allowed to access a given component are specified in the EJB's deployment descriptor. The deployer maps the roles to actual users using the J2EE server's deployment descriptors. After a user is authenticated, the container maintains a security context of that user. Whenever an attempt is made to access a protected component, the container applies security checks on the roles specified in the deployment descriptor to either grant or deny access to the user.

## Encryption

*Encryption* is the mechanism used to translate data into a form that cannot be interpreted by an intruder. This ensures that data transmitted over the network is intelligible to only the intended recipient. Encryption is useful for securing critical data during communication between applications.

Most J2EE application servers address secure communications through SSL encryption for data integrity and confidentiality across the network. Clients can establish SSL sessions using the Hypertext Transfer Protocol (HTTP) or Remote Method Invocation (RMI) over Internet Inter-ORB Protocol (IIOP). SSL is also used to provide an additional level of security to password authentication in e-commerce applications. Optionally, SSL can be used in mutual authentication between two parties or applications.

## Digital Signing

*Digital signing* is the mechanism of protecting the true identity of the authenticated entity. This is achieved through the use of digital certificates. A *digital certificate* is a statement that is digitally signed from one entity, which could be a person or a company, indicating that the public key of some other entity has some particular value. This is similar to the notary public concept used by banks and lawyers. Certificate interfaces enable developers to build tools for parsing certificates, enforcing their own site-specific certificate policies, and managing local databases of certificates.

The Java 2 Standard Edition (J2SE) Security API introduces certificate interfaces and classes for parsing and managing certificates, and provides an X.509 implementation of the certificate interfaces. The purposes of some of the certificate-related classes are described in Table 19.1.

**TABLE 19.1**   Certificate-Related Classes

| Class | Purpose |
| --- | --- |
| Certificate | A parent class for certificates that have different formats but important common uses. Subclasses are used for X.509 and Pretty Good Privacy (PGP), share general certificate functionality, such as encoding and verifying, and some types of information, such as a public key. |
| CertificateFactory | A class used to generate certificate and certificate revocation list (CRL) objects from their encoding. |
| X509Certificate | A subclass of Certificate for X.509 certificates. It provides a standard way to access all the attributes of an X.509 certificate. |
| Policy | A class that specifies the permissions available for code from various sources. |

## Auditing and Filtering

*Auditing* is the mechanism that allows you to establish watchdog activities and maintain logs of sensitive actions taken for later analysis. Events such as failed login attempts, authentication requests, rejected digital certificates, and invalid ACLs are logged. Auditing is a fundamental mechanism in accountability, which assists in detect intrusion attempts and any security breaches. It helps in detecting errors associated with the application's code or their configurations.

*Filtering* is the mechanism of allowing you to configure your firewall in accepting or rejecting the client request based upon the origin (hostname or IP address) or the protocol used during the client connections. The J2EE platform does not standardize the auditing mechanism, and itís up to the container providerís implementation.

## Administration

Administration is the most complex and costly aspect of application security. As a security administrator, you'll be involved in managing user security realms, repositories, and security policies. Other functions include delegation of administrative privileges, allowing users self-registration, and testing and deployment of new systems. J2EE does not support a standard for administration, and it's up to the J2EE container provider to provide the tools used.

**19**

# Exploring J2EE Security Across All Tiers

The J2EE architecture supports secure deployment of applications and components. It provides you with both programmatic and declarative security approaches. Software problems are magnitudes of times more costly to find and repair after deployment. J2EE emphasizes the cost-effective declarative approach, in which application code is driven and managed according to the security policies. This enhances the portability and flexibility of deploying enterprise applications. Similar to transactions and persistence, J2EE expresses and manages security requirements (roles and access control) outside the application code in XML-based deployment descriptors.

The programmatic security approach explicitly allows you to add security rules and checks to the application code. This is particularly useful in situations in which special security rules across EJB or JSP components' call chains cannot be implemented using the declarative approach. For example, an application might make authorization decisions based on certain factors, such as user information stored in a database.

The J2EE architecture provides an end-to-end global security that spans multiple tiers. It supports the propagation of the security context for components along a call chain, across components that are hosted in different tiers. This eliminates the need for the user information to be passed as parameters in the business method calls, thereby providing reliability and ease of programming. It also supports the concept of a single sign-on (SSO) to access applications. The security context can be propagated across multiple J2EE servers that use different security realms in the production environment. It also propagates the security context to Common Object Request Broker Architecture (CORBA)-based applications over the IIOP protocol through the EJB to CORBA mapping. Figure 19.3 illustrates security context propagation across multiple J2EE components, tiers, and servers.

The following sections will help you examine how the authentication and authorization security mechanisms work across the J2EE tiers. You'll explore each type of applications in each tier, and the recommended security mechanisms.

## Client Tier Security

Security on the client tier is applied to either a standalone Java application or to a J2EE client application that runs on its own container. The other type of client is a Web-based client that runs within the browser container, which will be discussed in the section on Web tier security.

**FIGURE 19.3**

*J2EE security context propagation.*

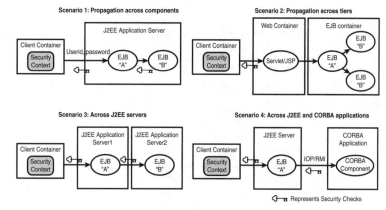

Scenarios of Propagation of J2EE Security Context
Across Components, Tiers, and Applications

## J2EE Client Application

A J2EE client application is a J2EE component that's deployed in the J2EE client container. When a J2EE client application is launched, a login window provided by the EJB container pops up and asks the user to input his user ID and password. After the user is authenticated, the application is started and its components become functional. The authenticated user security context is established at the EJB tier and propagated across other tiers or servers as needed. The J2EE architecture encourages the use of a J2EE client application rather than a standalone Java application. This method of authentication is best used in highly customized Intranet applications. A J2EE client application can use JAAS authentication, which will be discussed later today.

## Standalone Java Application

J2EE does not specify how to authenticate users with standalone Java applications. However, some J2EE container providers use the JNDI authentication mechanism, as discussed in Day 4, to authenticate standalone users.

# Web Tier Security

J2EE supports both authentication and authorization for Web tier components. The Web tier is probably the first entry point for most browser-based applications, and is where user authentication takes place. In the next few sections, we'll explore the methods of authentication at the Web tier, and we'll highlight the use of the declarative and programmatic approaches in authorization.

**19**

## HTTP BASIC Authentication

This is the simplest type of authentication. The keyword BASIC is used in the <auth-method> element. When a user attempts to access any secure resource, the Web container uses the browserís login screen to solicit the user ID and password from the user in order to perform authentication. This is also considered to be a part of the client tier authentication mechanism for a Web-based client application.

```
<web-app>
. . .
<login-config>
   <auth-method>BASIC</auth-method>
   <realm-name>default</realm-name>
</login-config>
. . .
</web-app>
```

## Form-Based Authentication

Form-based authentication is another declarative authentication approach available to the Web tier for configuring a login method. In the web.xml deployment descriptor of the WAR file, the value of the <auth-method> subelement is set to FORM. Here's an example of the <login-config> element of the web.xml file:

```
<web-app>
. . .
  <login-config>
    <auth-method>FORM</auth-method>
      <form-login-config>
        <form-login-page>login.jsp</form-login-page>
        <form-error-page>error.jsp</form-error-page>
      </form-login-config>
  </login-config>
. . .
</web-app>
```

In the preceding example, the user will be automatically presented with the login.jsp page for authentication, if not already authenticated.

Form-based authentication is used if an application requires a special login screen. The web.xml deployment descriptor must specify the login form page using the <form-login-page> element, and the error page using <form-error-page> element, as specified in the FORM authentication shown earlier. When a user attempts to access a secure resource, the Web container presents the login form as specified in the deployment descriptor. The following is an example of a JSP page incorporating form-based security authentication:

```
<form method="POST" name="Login" action="j_security_check">
```

```
      <input type="text" name="j_username">
      <input type="password" name="j_password">
      <input type="submit" value="Login" name="Submit">
</form>
```

**Note**

In the preceding form-based authentication example, the form named Login must contain fields named precisely j_username and j_password to represent the username and password, respectively.

**Caution**

Neither HTTP BASIC authentication nor form-based authentication is secure—the content of the user dialog is sent as plain text, and the target server is not authenticated.

## HTTPS Authentication

The HTTP over SSL protocol can be used for authentication purposes. SSL is a powerful mechanism, which requires the user's public key to encrypt passwords. This is commonly used for Web-based e-commerce applications as well as single sign-on requirements. This is accomplished by simply running an instance of the HTTPS server for authentication purposes.

## Hybrid Authentication

In both BASIC and form-based authentication, passwords are not encrypted. This deficiency can be overcome by running HTTP BASIC and form-based authentication mechanisms over SSL. In general, the use of the CONFIDENTIAL flag in the <transport-guarantee> element of the web.xml ensures the use of SSL for data transmission.

```
<web-app>
. . .
<security-constraint>
. . .
   <user-data-constraint>
     <transport-guarantee>CONFIDENTIAL</transport-guarantee>
   </user-data-constraint>
</security-constraint>
. . .
</web-app>
```

19

**Note**

> This technique is different from HTTPS authentication, which is based on running a separate instance of the HTTPS server. The hybrid technique is based on the deployment descriptor setting, which will be enforced by the Web container.

Most Web container providers support the concept of a single sign-on, so that one login session can propagate across multiple applications. A flag of NONE means that the application does not require any transport guarantee, whereas a flag of INTEGRAL means that transmitted data cannot be changed in transit.

## Web Component Declarative Authorization

In a Web application, authorization is performed by defining roles, and then specifying how these roles are allowed accessing to the protected resources (such as JSPs and servlets). The role is defined using the <role-name> element of the web.xml deployment descriptor:

```
<web-app>
   . . .
   <security-role>
     <role-name>Registrar</role-name>
   </security-role>
   . . .
</web-app>
```

Resources are protected by using one or more <web-resource-collection> elements. Each <web-resource-collection> element contains an optional series of <url-pattern> elements followed by an optional series of <http-method> elements. The <url-pattern> element value specifies a URL pattern, which must match for the request to access the protected resource. The <http-method> element value specifies a type of HTTP request to allow (GET or POST). The following is an example of declarative authorization to the welcomeServlet resource:

```
<web-app>
   . . .
<security-constraint>
    <web-resource-collection>
      <web-resource-name>Welcome Servlet</web-resource-name>
      <url-pattern>/welcomeServlet</url-pattern>
      <http-method>GET</http-method>
    </web-resource-collection>
    <auth-constraint>
      <role-name>Registrar</role-name>
    </auth-constraint>
   . . .
```

```
</security-constraint>
. . .
</web-app> .
```

Developers may declare one or more `<security-role-ref>` elements to protect their Web components in the application's deployment descriptors. These elements are used to reference an existing `<role-name>` value set by the application assembler.

A more flexible approach of deploying secure Web applications, the `<role-name>` element value can be linked (by the deployer) to an already defined `<security-role>` element through the `<role-link>` element. The following is an example of a `web.xml` deployment descriptor to illustrate these concepts:

```
<web-app>
. . .
 <servlet>
   <servlet-name>HelloServlet</servlet-name>
 </servlet>
   ...
 <security-role-ref>
   <role-name>Registrar</role-name>
   <role-link>AdminRole</role-link>
 </security-role-ref>
...
</web-app>
```

## Web Component Programmatic Authorization

This section discusses the programmatic approach to use for cases in which the declarative approach is not sufficient. The `getRemoteUser()`, `getUserPrincipal()`, and `isUserInRole()` methods are available in the `HttpServletRequest` interface to provide servlets and JSPs with access to security context information.

The `getRemoteUser()` method obtains the name of the authenticated user, whereas the `getUserPrincipal()` method returns the principal object associated with the authenticated user. The `isUserInRole(String roleName)` queries the underlying security realm to determine whether the authenticated caller belongs to a given security role. This may be useful for dynamically verifying that a `Registrar` role, for example, should be able to update or delete data.

In the `HelloServlet` code that follows, we use the `HttpServletRequest` to access `CallerPrincipal`. Also, to perform sensitive operations, we check on the user role as specified in the `web.xml`.

```
// Obtain the principal from the HTTPServletRequest object
CallerPrincipal callerPrincipal = request.getCallerPrincipal();
// obtain the caller principal's name
out.println("User name :" + callerPrincipal.getName());
```

19

```
// Check if the caller belongs to <role-name>
if (request.isUserInRole("Registrar")) {
    // do things only allowed to the Registrar
}
```

 **Note** | The preceding example uses both the declarative and programmatic approaches of security authorization.

## EJB Tier Security

The EJB container supports both declarative and programmatic authorization approaches. When an EJB business method invokes another EJB using the other bean's home or component interface, the EJB container propagates the security context, including the principal and roles, from the invoking EJB to the invoked EJB. In the following sections, you will learn how to declare security rules in the EJB deployment descriptor ejb-jar.xml file. First, you'll learn how to define a security role, and reference it from your code. You also will learn how to link roles and how to secure EJB methods.

### Defining Security Roles

The application assembler can optionally define one or more security roles in the ejb-jar.xml deployment descriptor. This definition uses the <role-name> element of the deployment descriptor. In the following snippet, the role name Registrar is defined as part of the <assembly-descriptor> tag:

```
<ejb-jar>
. . .
  <assembly-descriptor>
    <security-role>
      <description>
        This role is only allowed to Registrar
      </description>
      <role-name>Registrar</role-name>
    </security-role>
  <assembly-descriptor>
. . .
</ejb-jar>
```

 **Note** | The description tag is optional in all elements of deployment descriptors.

The deployer then maps the physical groups and user accounts defined in the operational environment to the security roles defined by the application assembler. This is performed using the vendor-specific deployment descriptor. For example, WebLogic Server uses the `weblogic-ejb-jar.xml` deployment descriptor to map the role named `Registrar` to the principal `Laura`:

```
<weblogic-ejb-jar>
. . .
  <security-role-assignment>
    <role-name>Registrar</role-name>
    <principal-name>Laura</principal-name>
  </security-role-assignment>
</weblogic-ejb-jar>
```

As your learned earlier today, multiple principals can be assigned to the same role (in case one is on vacation!), as illustrated by following examples:

```
<weblogic-ejb-jar>
. . .
  <security-role-assignment>
    <role-name>Registrar</role-name>
    <principal-name>Laura</principal-name>
    <principal-name>Lillian</principal-name>
    <principal-name>Rudy</principal-name>
  </security-role-assignment>
</weblogic-ejb-jar>
```

## Declaring Security Role References

The EJB developer is responsible for setting the `<security-role-ref>` elements of the deployment descriptor and the security role names used in the EJB code. Here's an example:

```
<ejb-jar>
 <enterprise-beans>
  ...
  <session>
   <ejb-name>UserManagerEJB</ejb-name>
   ...
   <security-role-ref>
    <description>
       This security role should be assigned to the
       Registrar of the registration office.
    </description>
    <role-name>Registrar</role-name>
   </security-role-ref>
  </session>
  ...
 </enterprise-beans>
 ...
</ejb-jar>
```

19

**Note**
The declared name must be the security role name that is used as a parameter to the isCallerInRole(String *roleName*) method.

## Linking Security Role References to Security Roles

Declaring the security role references in the preceding code allows the assembler or the
deployer to link the names of the security roles used in the code to the security roles
defined for an assembled application through the defined <security-role> elements.

The application assembler links each security role reference to a security role using the
<role-link> element. The value of the <role-link> element must be the name of one
of the security roles defined in a <security-role> element. The following deployment
descriptor example shows how to link the security role reference named Registrar to
the security role named registration-office:

```
<ejb-jar>
...
 <enterprise-beans>
   ...
  <session>
   <ejb-name>UserManagerEJB</ejb-name>
   ...
   <security-role-ref>
     <description>
       This role should be assigned to the
       Registrar of the registration office.
       The role has been linked to the
       Registration-office role.
     </description>
     <role-name>Registrar</role-name>
     <role-link>registration-office</role-link>
   </security-role-ref>
   ...
  </session>
  ...
 </enterprise-beans>
...
</ejb-jar>
```

## Securing EJB Methods

The EJB container authorizes access to EJB components based on the user's security
context, in conjunction with the permissions configured in the ejb-jar.xml deployment
descriptor. The assembler is responsible for setting the method permissions, which is

achieved by using both the `<role-name>` and `<method-permission>` elements of the `<assembly-descriptor>` tag.

The following `ejb-jar.xml` fragment grants permissions to an authenticated user in the role of `Registrar` for all the methods (indicated by the `*`) of the home and remote interfaces of the `UserManagerEJB` bean:

```
<ejb-jar>
...
  <assembly-descriptor>
    . . .
    <method-permission>
      <role-name>Registrar</role-name>
      <method>
        <ejb-name>UserManagerEJB</ejb-name>
        <method-name>*</method-name>
      </method>
    </method-permission>
  </assembly-descriptor>
. . .
</ejb-jar>
```

You can selectively specify certain methods when granting access. The following example grants permissions to only the `enrollStudent()` method of the same `UserManagerEJB`:

```
<method-permission>
    <role-name>student</role-name>
    <method>
      <ejb-name>UserManagerEJB</ejb-name>
      <method-name>enrollStudent</method-name>
    </method>
</method-permission>
```

A more fine-grained level, when you need to grant access to a certain overloaded method (which has the same name but different parameters), is to specify the parameter types of the method in a group of the `<method-param>` elements:

```
<method-permission>
    <role-name>student</role-name>
    <method>
        <ejb-name>UserManagerEJB</ejb-name>
        <method-name>enrollStudent</method-name>
        <method-params>
            <method-param> java.lang.String </method-param>
            <method-param> java.lang.Integer </method-param>
        </method-params>
    </method>
</method-permission>
```

19

You must specify the full class name for each parameter of the method.

## Using `<run-as>` to Delegate Security

The application assembler can use the `<run-as>` element to define a run-as identity for an EJB in the deployment descriptor. This applies to all the methods of the EJB or to the `onMessage()` method of a message-driven bean, and all internal methods of the invoked beans.

Because the application assembler does not, in general, know the security environment of the operational environment, the run-as identity is designated by a logical `<role-name>`, which is delegated to one of the security roles defined by the application assembler in the deployment descriptor. The deployer then assigns a security principal defined in the operational environment to be used as the principal for the run-as identity.

The `<run-as>` element in the following example is used to provide access to *only* the `Registrar` role. This type of exclusionary access is useful in situations in which you want to protect internal EJBs from external user access.

```
<ejb-jar>
...
<enterprise-beans>
   ...
   <session>
     <ejb-name>UserManagerEJB</ejb-name>
     ...
     <security-identity>
       <run-as>
         <role-name>Registrar</role-name>
       </run-as>
     </security-identity>
     ...
   </session>
   ...
</enterprise-beans>
...
```

## EJB Component Programmatic Authorization

Similar to Web components, EJB components can perform programmatic authorization. The `EJBContext` provides EJB components access into the security and transaction contexts. `EJBContext` provides two methods to allow programmatic authorization: `getCallerPrincipal()` and `isCallerInRole()`.

getCallerPrincipal() allows the EJB component to obtain the principal object associated with the caller. getCallerPrincipal() is commonly used from within a session bean to access another entity bean using the principal as the primary key. This approach allows sensitive data for retrieval purposes to be obtained from the EJBContext. The method isCallerInRole(String roleName) is used in the same fashion as in the "Web Component Programmatic Authorization" section earlier today. The following example illustrates the use of the getCallerPrincipal() method:

```
// Obtain the default initial JNDI context.
Context ctx = new InitialContext();
// Look up the remote home interface of the StudentEJB
Object ojb = ctx.lookup("java:comp/env/ejb/StudentEJB");
// Convert obj to the proper type.
StudentHome student = (StudentEJBHome)
        javax.rmi.PortableRemoteObject.narrow(obj, StudentEJBHome.class);
// obtain the caller principal, and name
CallerPrincipal callerPrincipal = ejbContext.getCallerPrincipal();
String callerKey = callerPrincipal.getName();
// use the name as primary key to StudentEJB finder
StudentEJB myStudent = student.findByPrimaryKey(callerKey);
// update the studentís phone number
myStudent.changePhoneNumber(...);
```

The preceding code fragment obtains the principal name of the current caller by using the ejbContext to locate the student, and updates the student's phone number.

> **Note**
> Although J2EE emphasizes the use of declarative authorization, we explained programmatic authorization for completeness.

**19**

## EIS Tier Security

J2EE supports both declarative and programmatic approach in the EIS tier. In the declarative approach, the application component requests a connection to an EIS resource using JNDI authentication (the JNDI access mechanism was covered in Day 4). With this approach, the container manages the authentication of the EIS resource. The container determines the username and password for establishing a connection to an EIS instance from the configuration files or from the command line.

With the programmatic approach, the component manages the authentication to the EIS resource. We explored the programmatic approach to accessing a JDBC resource in Day 4, in the section "Using JNDI in User Authentication." The programmatic approach to accessing a JMS resource is explained in Day 13, "Understanding JMS and Message-Driven Beans," in the section "Step 2: Create a QueueConnection."

# JAAS Security

The Java Authentication and Authorization Service, as its name implies, consists of two main components: authentication and authorization components. The authentication is performed in a pluggable fashion because JAAS implements the standard Pluggable Authentication Module (PAM) framework, which is common on Unix platforms. This allows application code to be independent from the underlying security realm in the physical environment. Therefore, any new authentication mechanism can be plugged in as a module (similar to a driver) into the JAAS framework. Sample authentication mechanisms exist today for JNDI, Unix, and Windows NT.

After the user executing the code has been authenticated, the JAAS authorization component uses the access control model to protect access to sensitive resources. JAAS authorization is a user-based authorization with fine-grain permissions. Figure 19.4 illustrates JAAS architecture components.

FIGURE **19.4**

*JAAS architecture.*

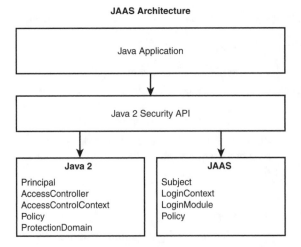

JAAS provides a means to enforce access controls based on where code came from and who signed it. JAAS is applied to all the Java 2 platform including applets, servlets, and EJBs.

## JAAS Concepts

The JAAS API is provided by the `javax.security` package. The key JAAS class is `Subject`, which represents a grouping of related information for a single entity such as a person, organization, or a program. It encompasses the entity's principals, public credentials, and private credentials. The `LoginContext` interface is used to authenticate a `Subject`. Table 19.2 summarizes the interfaces and classes used in the `java.security` package.

**TABLE 19.2**  Main JAAS Interfaces and Classes

| Interface | Description |
| --- | --- |
| `Subject` | Represents the principal source of the request and can be any entity. A `Subject` object is created at the completion of a successful user authentication or login. |
| `LoginContext` | Represents the security context and is used to initiate login, logout, and acquire the authenticated `Subject` for the purpose of authorization checking. |
| `Configuration` | Provides the `getConfiguration()` method for the purpose of obtaining a list of `LoginModules` provided in a particular implementation. |
| `LoginModule` | Implements different authentication mechanisms, such as the JNDI `LoginModule` or the Unix `LoginModule`. |
| `Callback` | Collects input, such as a password, from the user and passes it to the client. |
| `CallbackHandler` | A method that the `LoginModule` calls to communicate with a `Subject` to obtain authentication information. |

The `LoginContext` represents the initial security context established in the application code, and encapsulates the underlying security realm. The main methods of the `LoginContext` interface are `login()`, `logout()`, and `getSubject()`. The main exception of the security package is `LoginException`.

The `LoginModule` class abstracts the authentication mechanism, and is similar to the driver or adapter that the JAAS API uses to access a particular authentication mechanism or realm. The EJB developer does not usually interface directly with the `LoginModule` unless it's required to develop a customized module for a new mechanism. The container provider is usually responsible for providing a `LoginModule` for each supported security realm.

After the `Subject` is authenticated, the access controls can be placed on that `Subject` by invoking the `doAs()` method of the `Subject` class. The `doAs()` method associates the specified `Subject` with the current security context. If the `Subject` has the necessary access controls, the action is completed; however, if the `Subject` does not have the necessary access controls, a security exception is raised.

During authentication, the `Subject` is populated with associated identities, or principals. A `Subject` may have many principals. For example, a student may have the name principal `Laura Ghaly`, the Social Security number principal `11-222-3333`, and the user ID principal `lghaly`, all of which help distinguish this `Subject` from other `Subjects`. The

19

Subject class provides a method getPrincipals() to query all of them.

FIGURE **19.5**

*JAAS pluggable
authentication.*

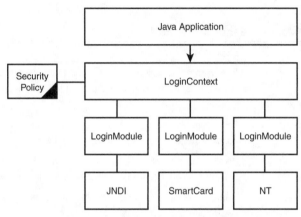

JAAS Pluggable Authentication

The following example utilizes the doAs() method. We assume that a LoginContext has
authenticated a Subject with the principal named Laura Ghaly.

```
// JAAS Authentication and Authorization
import java.security.*;
public class JAASClient extends Object {
   public static void main(){
// Establish an initial security context
   LoginContext logCtx = new LoginContext("Laura Ghaly");
// Authenticate the subject by try to login
   try{
      logCtx.login();
      System.out.println("Login succeeded");
   }  catch (LoginException le) {
      System.out.println("Login failed");
   }
   // Retrieve the authenticated subject from the context
   Subject laura = logCtx.getSubject();
   Subject.doAs(laura, new SimpleAction());
     // Perform the SimpleAction as the authenticated subject: laura
   // Try to logout after finish
   try{
      logCtx.logout();
      System.out.println("Logout succeeded");
   }  catch (LoginException le) {
      System.out.println("Logout failed");
   }
}
```

In the preceding example, the security context will be propagated from the current code to the instantiated Java class `SimpleAction` on behalf of the principal `Laura Ghaly`.

# Security Responsibilities

The goal of security in the J2EE architecture is to reduce the effort required by the EJB developer to secure the application by allowing greater coverage from more qualified EJB roles. The EJB container provides the implementation of the security infrastructure, whereas the deployer and the system administrator define the security policies. This eliminates any hard-coded security in the EJB code, and allows portability across multiple EJB servers that use different security mechanisms.

The application assembler (which could be the same party as the EJB developer) defines the security roles for an application composed of one or more EJBs, JSPs, and/or servlets. The assembler defines (declaratively in the deployment descriptor) method permissions for each security role. Method permissions are the permissions to invoke a specified group of methods of the EJB's home and component interfaces. The assembler also sets delegated security using the run-as identity.

The deployer is responsible for mapping the principals and groups of principals defined in the target operational environment to the security roles defined by the application assembler for the EJBs in the deployment descriptor. The deployer is also responsible for mapping principals for the run-as identities specified by the application assembler. The deployer is also responsible for configuring other aspects of the security management of the enterprise beans, such as the principal mapping for inter-EJB calls, and the principal mapping for resource manager access, such as JMS and JDBC access. At runtime, a client will be allowed to invoke a business method only if the deployer has assigned the principal associated with the client call to at least one security role.

The container provider is responsible for enforcing the security policies at runtime, providing the tools for managing security at runtime, and providing the tools used by the deployer to manage security during deployment.

# Best Practices

In this section, we'll summarize the best practices mentioned throughout the day:

- Use the declarative approach when it is sufficient; otherwise, use the programmatic approach for business rules.

- Component developers should neither implement security mechanisms nor hard-code security policies in the EJB's business methods. Rather, developers should rely on the security mechanisms provided by the container, and should let the application assembler and deployer define the appropriate security policies for the application.

- Use encryption (SSL and digital certificates) to secure sensitive data such as passwords and credit-card numbers.
- Use auditing, filtering, and monitoring of your enterprise applications to prevent any security breaches.
- Use the JAAS API in authentication and authorization whenever possible.

# Summary

Today, you learned the concepts and mechanisms of J2EE security, and how to apply both programmatic and declarative approaches. J2EE emphasizes a role-based, declarative security mechanism that can be propagated from one component to another, or across multiple tiers and multiple J2EE application servers. This container-managed and cost-effective approach increases the flexibility and portability of deploying secure enterprise applications. You also explored the JAAS security API as the forthcoming standard for authentication and authorization.

# Q&A

**Q** **What is the main difference between the declarative and programmatic security approaches?**

**A** The declarative security approach is a container-managed approach in which security rules are configured outside application code, in the deployment descriptor. This helps make the application more portable and flexible. J2EE emphasizes the declarative approach because it reduces the cost of deploying enterprise applications. On the other hand, the programmatic approach is a component-managed approach in which EJBs, JSPs, and servlets maintain the security rules in the component's code. This is useful in applying business rules when the declarative approach is not adequate.

**Q** **What is the main purpose of the JAAS API?**

**A** The JAAS API extends the security architecture of standard Java with additional support to authenticate and enforce access controls upon users. JAAS enables developers to authenticate users and enforce access controls on those users in their applications. It simplifies application development by serving as a building block for developers. By abstracting the complex underlying authentication and authorization mechanisms, JAAS minimizes the risk of creating dangerous but subtle security vulnerabilities in application code. JAAS is considered the upcoming standard in securing Java applications.

# Quiz

1. When a user is authenticated using JAAS security, which of the following statements are true?

   A. An initial context is established

   B. A `Subject` object is created and mapped to a principal

   C. A principal is mapped to the user

   D. A `LoginModule` is created

2. In the programmatic approach, which of the following methods are used to check user authorization?

   A. `isCallerInRole()` of the `HttpServletRequest` in the Web container

   B. `isCallerInRole()` of the `EJBContext` in the EJB container

   C. `login()`

   D. `LoginContext()`

## Answers

1. A, B
2. A, B

**19**

# Exercises

1. What is the difference between groups and roles?
2. What is the key class, and what are its methods in the JAAS API?
3. Why does J2EE emphasize the security declarative approach?
4. What are the main responsibilities of the application assembler in enterprise security?
5. Briefly describe the concept of single sign-on in the context of J2EE security.
6. Explain the concept of security context propagation.

# Day 20

# Implementing JavaMail in EJB Applications

JavaMail is one of the common services of the J2EE architecture that is responsible for reading, composing, and sending e-mail messages from enterprise applications. JavaMail enables you to implement a Mail User Agent (MUA), similar to the familiar Microsoft Outlook, Pine, and Eudora. Today you'll explore the benefits and features that the JavaMail API offers, and how you can use them in a simple EJB: the Emailer EJB. First, you'll be exposed to the main concepts (classes and interfaces) of the JavaMail API. JavaMail basically provides a set of classes that model a mail system. The API provides a platform- and protocol-independent framework to build Java-technology-based mail and messaging applications. At the end of the day, you'll apply this to some of the scenarios we use in our university registration system. JavaMail is implemented as a Java platform optional package and is also available as part of the J2EE.

Today you'll explore the JavaMail API and use it to develop a sample full J2EE application that includes components in the EJB tier, Web tier, and client tier.

Throughout today's activities, you'll learn

- What JavaMail is, and the different protocols it can handle
- What the JavaMail API is, and the concepts it implements
- How to compose, send, and read e-mail messages with different scenarios (forward; reply; nontext messages; multilingual messages; messages with attachments) that are similar to a real e-mail system
- How to develop and deploy a full portable J2EE enterprise application based on the MVC pattern to demonstrate the use of the JavaMail API
- How to deploy the J2EE application on both the WebLogic Server and the JBoss server environments, and configure each server's environment to run the portable application

# Understanding JavaMail

JavaMail is a unified service for abstracting an electronic mail (e-mail) system. It has pre-built implementations of some of the most popular protocols for mail transfer and provides an easy way to use them. The JavaMail API is designed to provide protocol-independent access for sending and receiving messages. However, it does not include any facilities for adding, removing, or changing user accounts. There are no standards to accomplish these tasks, and every e-mail system handles them differently.

You probably already know the most common e-mail agents (clients), such as Eudora, Outlook, Netscape, and other modern e-mail clients, which let you send both text and HTML e-mails. E-mail messages were originally limited to plain text and they did not support bold, italics, or hyperlinks. Modern e-mail agents recognize HTML, so you can now send either plain text messages or rich-content documents languages that aren't Latin based, such as Japanese and Chinese.

The JavaMail API provides a set of abstract classes and interfaces that comprise an electronic mail system. The abstract classes and interfaces support many different implementations of message stores, formats, and transports. Many simple applications will need to interact with the messaging system only through these base classes and interfaces.

 **Note**

> JavaMail helps create an e-mail agent (or mail client), and does not provide any mail server functionality. So, you must have access to a mail server before you try using JavaMail.

The abstract classes in the JavaMail API are expandable, and they can be subclassed to provide new protocols and add new functionality when necessary. In addition, JavaMail API includes concrete subclasses that implement the most widely used Internet mail protocols, such as Internet Message Access Protocol (IMAP), Post Office Protocol (POP), and Simple Mail Transfer Protocol (SMTP). They are ready to be used in application development. Developers can subclass JavaMail classes to provide the implementations of particular messaging systems, other than these protocols.

## JavaMail Architecture

JavaMail is designed to standardized access to a variety of e-mail services. The JavaMail architecture provides a protocol-independent access for sending and receiving messages. This abstract mechanism is similar to other J2EE APIs, such as JDBC, JNDI, and JMS. Similarly, the JavaMail API is divided into two main parts: an application-independent part, and a service-dependent part. Your applications are written in a standard way to use the application-independent part of the JavaMail API, which transparently calls the underlying protocol or e-mail service. A JavaMail-compliant service must implement part of the JavaMail API. Here is a brief description of the two parts that comprise the JavaMail architecture:

- An application-programming interface (API): This API is used by the application components to send and receive mail messages, independent of the underlying provider or protocol used.

- A service provider interface (SPI): This part of the API speaks the protocol-specific languages, such as SMTP, POP, IMAP, and Network News Transfer Protocol (NNTP). It is used to plug in a provider of an e-mail service to the J2EE platform.

Figure 20.1 illustrates the JavaMail architecture and the interaction of the two main APIs.

As you learned from Day 15, "Understanding J2EE Architecture," JavaMail can be used from within components of either the Web tier or the EJB tier. It can't be used from J2EE client applications or applets.

**20**

## Comparing JavaMail and JMS

JavaMail and JMS have something in common: both Both are used for delivering asynchronous messaging in J2EE applications. However, there are many differences between the two APIs, including the purpose and the implementations.

Java JMS is used as a unified API to access a MOM (Message-Oriented Middleware) provider, whereas JavaMail is used to access an e-mail system provider. JMS is designed to produce and consume messages by applications, and not by users, as is the case in JavaMail.

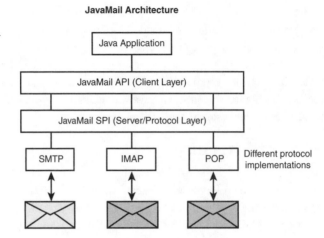

FIGURE 20.1

*The JavaMail architecture.*

Both JMS and JavaMail are used to design loosely coupled applications, which is different from those tightly coupled applications built using RMI/IIOP. In asynchronous communication, users or components send messages, and they do not have to wait for an immediate response. You've covered JMS in detail on Day 13, "Understanding JMS and Message-Driven Beans."

## JavaBeans Activation Framework

The JavaBeans Activation Framework (JAF) API integrates support for MIME (Multipurpose Internet Mail Extensions) data types into the Java platform. This means that you are not limited to using only plain text e-mail messages. You can use many different content types, such as HTML, images, sound, and video. JavaBeans components can be specified for particular MIME data operations, such as viewing or editing the data. The JAF API also provides a mechanism to map filename extensions to MIME types, which is useful in sending messages with attachments.

The JAF API is used by the JavaMail API to handle the data included in e-mail messages. Typical applications will not need to use the JAF API directly, although applications making sophisticated use of e-mail might need it. Later today, you'll learn how to use JAF in conjunction with JavaMail to process HTML e-mail messages and messages with attachments.

## Reviewing Basic Protocols

The JavaMail API is designed to use the most common protocols for exchanging e-mail messages. Each of the following subsections briefly discusses one of these protocols. A good understanding of the basics of these protocols will help you grasp how to use the

JavaMail API. Although the API is designed to be protocol-independent, you can't overcome the limitations of the underlying protocols. Certain protocols support more capabilities than others.

## Simple Mail Transfer Protocol

SMTP is the mechanism for delivery of e-mail. This protocol is used for sending outgoing messages from your applications. Your JavaMail-compliant client will communicate with the SMTP server of your company or a particular ISP to deliver e-mail messages to the specified destinations. JavaMail uses the term *transport* for the service of sending an e-mail message. The SMTP server relays the message to the SMTP server at the destination, and the recipients retrieve the messages through the use of POP, IMAP, or other protocols, as described in the next two sections.

## Post Office Protocol

Also known as POP3, this protocol is used to store and retrieve mail to and from an SMTP server. Similar in concept to the U.S Post Office, it defines support for a single mailbox for each user. JavaMail applications connect to a mailbox to retrieve, read, and delete e-mail messages using POP. Other functionality, such as counting unread messages, can also be accomplished from the application. With POP3, the server provides a folder that stores messages as they arrive. When a client connects to a POP3 server, it specifies the folder from which it retrieves the messages and transfers them to a message store on the client.

## Internet Message Access Protocol

IMAP (currently in version 4 and called IMAP4) is a more advanced protocol than POP for storing and retrieving e-mail messages. It can access messages from more than one computer, which has become extremely important as reliance on e-mail messaging and use of multiple computers have increased. Additionally, JavaMail applications can take advantage of the fact that users can have multiple folders on the server and multiple users can share those folders. With IMAP, message folders are stored on the mail server, including folders that contain incoming messages and folders that contain archived messages.

20

## Multipurpose Internet Mail Extensions

MIME is not a mail transfer protocol, per se. Instead, it defines the content of the messages to be handled, such as the format and the attachments. As a user of the JavaMail API, you usually don't need to worry about these formats. However, these formats do exist and are used by your programs. To handle non-plain text mail content, the JavaBeans Activation Framework is required, as we discussed earlier today.

## NNTP and Others

The JavaMail architecture provides support for new mechanisms and protocols to be added to the existing family of protocols. This is due to the separation of the JavaMail API into application-specific and provider-specific APIs. Some of the newly added protocols are the S/MIME (Secure Multipurpose Internet Mail Extensions) protocol, NNTP (which is used for newsgroups), and more.

# Learning the JavaMail API

The JavaMail API consists of some interfaces and classes used to send, read, and delete e-mail messages. The `javax.mail` and `javax.mail.internet` packages contain all the JavaMail core classes. The `javax.mail.activation` package represents the JavaBean Activation Framework.

## Exploring the Core Classes

The JavaMail core classes, which belong to the `javax.mail` package, are `Session`, `Message`, `Address`, `Authenticator`, `Transport`, `Store`, and `Folder`. Table 20.1 gives a brief description of each core class.

**TABLE 20.1**    Summary of JavaMail Core Classes

| Class | Description |
| --- | --- |
| Session | The key class of the API. A multithreaded object represents the connection factory. |
| Message | An abstract class that models an e-mail message. Subclasses provide the actual implementations. |
| Address | An abstract class that models the addresses (*from* and *to* addresses) in a message. Subclasses provide the specific implementations. |
| Authenticator | An abstract class used to protect mail resources on the mail server. |
| Transport | An abstract class that models a message transport mechanism for sending an e-mail message. |
| Store | An abstract class that models a message store and its access protocol, for storing and retrieving messages. A Store is divided into Folders. |
| Folder | An abstract class that represents a folder of mail messages. It can contain subfolders. |

In the following sections, you'll learn these core classes in more detail. After that, you'll learn how to use those classes to perform e-mail system agent functionality, such as sending, reading, and deleting messages.

### Session

The `Session` class is the primary class of the JavaMail API. It defines a basic mail session. The `Session` object acts as the connection factory for the JavaMail API, which handles both configuration setting and authentication. It is through the `Session` object that everything else works. To create a `Session` object, you look up the administered object stored in the JNDI service, as mentioned on Day 4, "Using JNDI for Naming Services and Components."

```
InitialContext ctx = new InitialContext();
Session session = (Session) ctx.lookup("ursMailSession");
```

In the preceding snippet, `ursMailSession` is the JNDI name object used as the administered object for the `Session` object. `ursMailSession` can be created and configured with the required parameters as name/value pairs, including information such as the mail server hostname, the user account sending the mail, and the protocols supported by the `Session` object. Using this declarative approach as the default method when creating a `Session` object helps makes your application portable by not hardcoding any parameters inside your applications. Later today, we'll explain how to configure this administered `Session` object, in the WebLogic Server and JBoss server environments.

> **Note**
>
> As you learned on Day 4, the J2EE specification recommends that all resource manager connection factory references be organized in the subcontexts of the application component's environment, using a different subcontext for each resource manager type. According to Table 4.2, connection factories of JavaMail should be declared in the `java:comp/env/mail` subcontext.

**20**

The other method of creating the `Session` object is based on the programmatic approach in which you can use a `java.util.Properties` object to override some of the default information, such as the mail server name, username, password, and other information that can be shared across your entire application. As you learned, J2EE promotes portability, and always recommends the declarative approach over the programmatic approach to avoid hardcoding parameters.

Because the constructors for the `Session` class are private, you can get a single default `Session` that can be shared with other components using the `getDefaultInstance()` method:

```
Properties props = new Properties();
// Override props with your customized data
props.put("mail.transport.protocol", "smtp");
props.put("mail.host", "acme");
Session session = Session.getDefaultInstance(props, null);
```

Similarly, to create a unique `Session` object (not shared), you use the `getInstance()` method:

```
Session session = Session.getInstance(props, null);
```

In both cases, the `null` argument is an `Authenticator` object. More information about the `Authenticator` object will be given shortly.

In most cases, it's sufficient (also efficient) to use a shared `Session`, even if you're working with mail sessions for multiple user mailboxes. You can add the username and password combination at a later step in the communication process and keep everything separate.

### Message

The `Message` object is the container for all parts of the e-mail message. After you've created a `Session` object, you can start composing messages to send. This is accomplished by using a concrete subclass of `Message`. Because `Message` is an abstract class, you must work with a subclass; in most cases, you'll use a `MimeMessage` (in `javax.mail. internet`). A `MimeMessage` is an e-mail message that understands MIME types and headers. Message headers are restricted to ASCII characters only, although non-ASCII characters can be encoded in certain header fields. `MimeMessage` acts as a container to hold all the parts of the message.

To create a `Message`, you pass the `Session` object as an argument to the `MimeMessage` constructor:

```
MimeMessage msg = new MimeMessage(session);
```

After you've created a new `MimeMessage`, you can start filling its parts. The `Message` class implements the `Part` interface (with `MimeMessage` implementing `MimePart`). To set the content, you use the `setContent()` method with arguments for the content and the MIME type. Here's an example of setting the message body with a plain text message:

```
msg.setContent("Hello World", "text/plain");
```

The special method `setText()` is used to set the text content (with MIME type of text/plain):

```
msg.setText("Hello World");
```

The `setContent()` method is used to set other kinds of MIME types, such as HTML e-mail messages.

The method `setSubject()` is used to set the subject of the message:

```
message.setSubject("Just Say Hello");
```

Other methods used to set various message properties will be discussed in the next sections.

## Address

`Address` is an abstract class that represents an e-mail address, such as john.doe@acme.com. This represents any sender address (*from*) or recipient address (*to*). To create an `Address` object, you pass the e-mail address as a parameter to the `InternetAddress` subclass constructor:

```
Address address = new InternetAddress("john.doe@acme.com");
```

If you want the name to appear next to the e-mail address, you can pass that name along to the constructor:

```
Address address = new InternetAddress("john.doe@acme.com", "John Doe");
```

This method is used to create a valid e-mail address, whether you need to create address objects for the message's *from* field or the *to* field.

 **Note**
You can send a message that appears to be from anyone, unless the mail server prevents you from doing so for security reasons.

**20**

You use the `setFrom()` method to set the sender address, and the `setReplyTo()` method to set the address to which the reply should be directed (where from and to are of type Address):

```
msg.setFrom(from);

msg.setReplyTo(to);
```

Not all message types allow the `setReplyTo()` method to be specified separately from the sender of the message.

You can send a message from multiple senders simply by creating the following:

```
Address address[0] = address1;
Address address[1] = address1;
...
msg.addFrom(address);
```

To set the message recipients, you use the `addRecipient()` method. This method requires a `Message.RecipientType` in addition to the address.

```
message.addRecipient(type, address)
```

The three predefined address *type*s are objects with one of these values:

- `Message.RecipientType.TO` for a primary recipient
- `Message.RecipientType.CC` for a carbon copy recipient
- `Message.RecipientType.BCC` for a blind carbon copy recipient

For example, to send a message to our friend John Doe and carbon copy support@acme.com, the following would be appropriate:

```
Address toAddress = new InternetAddress("john.doe@acme.com");
Address ccAddress = new InternetAddress("support@acme.com");
message.addRecipient(Message.RecipientType.TO, toAddress);
message.addRecipient(Message.RecipientType.CC, ccAddress);
```

The JavaMail API provides no mechanism to check for the validity of an e-mail address. This is left to the e-mail server provider.

### Authenticator

The JavaMail API can use an `Authenticator` object to access the e-mail server by using a username and password. Because it's an abstract class, you create a subclass `PasswordAuthentication`, passing a username and password to its constructor. You must register the `Authenticator` with the session when you create it, by replacing the null in the example shown in the "Session" section earlier today. Here's an example with the user `jDoe` and his `pswrd`:

```
Properties props = new Properties();
// Override props with any customized data
PasswordAuthentication auth = new PasswordAuthentication("jDoe", "pswrd")
Session session = Session.getDefaultInstance(props, auth);
```

## Transport

The last task in sending an e-mail message is to use the `Transport` class. This class normally uses the SMTP protocol to send a message. An easy way to send a message is to use the `default` version of the class by calling the static `send()` method:

```
Transport.send(msg);
```

Here the static `send()` method makes a separate connection to the e-mail server for each method call. To enhance your application performance, we recommended keeping your connection to the mail server alive when sending multiple messages. To do so, you need to create a specific instance of the `Transport` object and not the default object. You pass the protocol along with the hostname, username, and password, send the messages, and then close the connection, as shown here:

```
MimeMessage msg1, msg2;
// ... Create and populate messages ...
Transport trans = session.getTransport("smtp");
trans.connect("mail.acme.com", "jDore", "pswrd");
trans.sendMessage(msg1, msg1.getAllRecipients());
trans.sendMessage(msg2, msg2.getAllRecipients());
trans.close();
```

To monitor your mail server while sending messages, you turn on your debug flag by using the `setDebug()` method of the `Transport` class:

```
session.setDebug(true);
```

The default parameter value is `false`, which turns off debugging.

## Store and Folder

When you store and retrieve messages from your e-mail server, you must connect to a `Store`. A `Store` holds messages in different `Folders` on your server. After you create a `Session` object, you connect to a `Store`, and identify the e-mail server host, user ID, and password. Both the `Transport` and `Store` classes extend the `Service` class, which defines the `connect()` and `close()` methods. You need to tell the `Store` what protocol to use:

```
Store store = session.getStore("pop3");
store.connect(host, userid, password);
```

After you connect to a `Store`, you can get a `Folder`, open it, and start reading messages. The following is an example of how to read messages from the (reserved name) `INBOX` folder:

```
Folder folder = store.getFolder("INBOX");
folder.open(Folder.READ_ONLY);
Message message[] = folder.getMessages();
```

**20**

**Note**

The only folder available in POP3 is INBOX. If you're using IMAP, you can have other folders available.

The folder name is case sensitive. You open a folder in a read only or read/write mode. The latter mode enables you to delete messages. To create a new folder under the current folder, use the create() method. The delete() and the exists() methods delete and check whether a folder exists, respectively.

To read the contents of a message, use the getContent() method (without the message's header). The writeTo() method writes the message, including the message header, to a stream.

```
System.out.println(((MimeMessage)message).getContent());
```

After you've finished reading your e-mail, close the connection to the folder and store:

```
folder.close(true);
store.close();
```

In the preceding snippet, the true parameter value of the close() method indicates the removal of all deleted messages. *Expunge* is another term used to describe the deletion of messages.

## The JavaBean Activation Framework

The JAF API is used by the JavaMail API to manage MIME data. The DataSource interface provides the JAF with an abstraction of some arbitrary collection of data. The FileDataSource class implements a simple DataSource object that encapsulates a file. This helps you include attachments of different file types in your messages. The following section demonstrates the use of these interfaces and classes to send messages with attachments.

# Using the JavaMail API

The previous section summarizes all the main classes of the JavaMail API, and in this section, you'll learn how to connect all the pieces together to perform the regular operations of e-mail services. You'll explore how to send, reply, and forward messages, in addition to finding out how to read or retrieve and delete them.

## Sending Messages with JavaMail

Sending an e-mail message can vary between sending a plain text message and a rich-content message. The next sections shed light on how to send messages in languages that aren't Latin based. Forwarding and replying to messages are also implemented by sending messages. You'll learn how to send messages with attachments.

## Sending a Text Message

This is the most common method of sending e-mail messages. Here are the steps to send a message with JavaMail from within you application components in the Web tier or the EJB tier:

1. Import the JNDI (naming), JavaBean activation, and JavaMail packages. You'll also need to import `java.util.Properties`:

   ```
   import java.util.*;
   import javax.activation.*;
   import javax.mail.*;
   import javax.mail.internet.*;
   import javax.naming.*;
   ```

2. Look up the mail session in the JNDI service by using the default context:

   ```
   InitialContext ic = new InitialContext();
   Session session = (Session) ic.lookup("ursMailSession");
   ```

3. Use the properties to override the default `Session` by creating a `Properties` object and adding the properties you want to override. Then call `getInstance()` to get a new `Session` object with the new properties.

4. Construct a `MimeMessage` with the recipient's address, subject, and body parts of the message. Create an `Address` for each recipient of the message:

   ```
   String body = "Welcome to the new world of JavaMail";
   Message msg = new MimeMessage(session);
   Address to = new InternetAddress("john.doe@acme.com");
   msg.setFrom();
   meg.addRecipient(Message.RecipientType.TO, to);
   msg.setSubject("Hello");
   msg.setSentDate(new Date());
   msg.setText(body);
   ```

   In the `setFrom()` method, the value of the attribute is obtained implicitly from the `mail.user` property, which is set during the configuration of the mail `Session`. If this property is absent, the system property `user.name` is used.

5. Send the message.

   ```
   Transport.send(msg);
   ```

**20**

If the JNDI lookup fails, the `NamingException` will be thrown; if JavaMail transport fails, the `MessagingException` will be thrown. You must put your code in a `try` block and catch these exceptions.

## Replying to Messages

To reply to a message, you must create a new message from the original by using the `reply()` method. You also need to set the new `Message` with the proper recipient and subject, and add the `"Re: "` if it isn't already there. The `reply()` method copies the `from` or `reply-to` header to the new recipient. It doesn't add any content to the original message, so you need to set the body of the new message. The method also takes a Boolean parameter indicating whether to reply to only the sender (`false`) or reply to all the recipients (`true`). The following is an example of replying only to the sender:

```
MimeMessage reply = (MimeMessage) msg.reply(false);
reply.setFrom(new InternetAddress("john.doe@acme.com"));
reply.setText("Have Fun!");
Transport.send(reply);
```

To set the `reply-to` address when sending a message, use the `setReplyTo()` method.

## Forwarding Messages

To forward a message to a new recipient, you must construct a new message and then populate its parts. An e-mail message can be made up of multiple parts. Each part is a `MimeBodyPart`, and the different body parts are combined into a container called a *MimeMultipart*. To forward a message, you create one part for the text of your message and a second part with the message to forward, and then combine the two into a multipart message. Then you add the multipart message to a properly addressed message and send it. Here's an example of forwarding a message:

```
Address to = new InternetAddress("john.doe@acme.com");
Message forward = new MimeMessage(session);
forward.setSubject("Fwd: " + msg.getSubject());
forward.setFrom(new InternetAddress(msg.getFrom()));
forward.addRecipient(Message.RecipientType.TO, new InternetAddress(to));
// Construct the message part of the text
BodyPart mbp1 = new MimeBodyPart();
mbp.setText("fyi");
// Create a multi-part to combine the parts
Multipart mp = new MimeMultipart();
mp.addBodyPart(mbp1);
// Construct the message part of the forwarded content
BodyPart mbp2 = new MimeBodyPart();
mbp2.setDataHandler(msg.getDataHandler());
mp.addBodyPart(mbp2);
// Associate the multipart with the message
forward.setContent(mp);
// Send the message
Transport.send(forward);
```

## Sending a Message with Attachments

Resources can be attached to and detached from messages using the JavaMail API. Attachments are resources that are associated with a mail message, and are usually kept outside of that message; for example, a text file, a Word document, or an image. A message with attachments is represented as a MIME multipart message in which the first part is the main body of the message and the other parts are the attachments. Sending a message with an attachment is similar to forwarding a message; here's an example:

```
Message msg = new MimeMessage(session);
String filename="c:\myfiles\notes.doc";
Multipart mp = new MimeMultipart();
// Construct the message text part
mp.addBodyPart("Attached find my document.");
// Construct the attachment part
MimeBodyPart mbp = new MimeBodyPart();
DataSource source = new FileDataSource(filename);
mbp.setDataHandler(new DataHandler(source));
mbp.setFileName(filename);
mp.addBodyPart(mbp);
msg.setContent(mp);
Transport.send(msg);
```

The FileDataSource is part of the Java Activation Framework, and its constructor accepts a String that indicates the full filename on the disk.

## Sending Messages as HTML and Images

New e-mail systems support HTML and image content. To send an HTML file, you use the more generic setContent() method, and set the MIME type to text/html, as follows:

```
String html = "<HTML><H1> Welcome to the new world of JavaMail</H1></HTML>";
Message msg = new MimeMessage(session);
msg.setContent(html, "text/html");
```

On the other hand, if you want your HTML content message to be complete with embedded images included as part of the message, you must treat those images as attachments and reference each one with a special content ID (CID) URL, where the CID is a reference to the Content-ID header of the image attachment:

```
Message msg = new MimeMessage(session);
BodyPart mbp = new MimeBodyPart();
String html = "<H1>Welcome to the world of JavaMail</H1>" +
              "<img src=\"cid:img1\">";
mbp.setContent(html, "text/html");
// Create a related multi-part to combine the parts
MimeMultipart mp = new MimeMultipart("related");
mp.addBodyPart(mbp);
```

20

```
// Create part for the image
mbp = new MimeBodyPart();
// Fetch the image and associate to part
DataSource img = new FileDataSource("images/logo.gif");
mbp.setDataHandler(new DataHandler(img));
mbp.setHeader("Content-ID","img1");
// Add part to multi-part
mp.addBodyPart(mbp);
// Associate multi-part with message
msg.setContent(mp);
```

## Sending Message Content Based on Locale

Situations sometimes arise in which you need to send a message in a language other than a Latin-based script (char set). This is common in internationalization (i18n) efforts of enterprise applications. To accomplish this, you must set the message to the right locale for the language. The following example is set to send an e-mail message based on the Japanese locale (ISO-2022-JP):

```
Message msg = new MimeMessage(session);
msg.setSubject(subject, "ISO-2022-JP");
msg.setText(body, "iso-2022-jp");
```

**Note**

Some Web servers are familiar only with the ISO-8859-1 (Western European) char set, and they can't decode messages written in other char sets. You might need to check the Web server documentation before sending messages using different char sets.

# Reading Messages with JavaMail

Reading mail messages involves fetching the messages from the message store. The JavaMail API enables you to connect to a message store, which could be an IMAP server or POP3 server. The JavaMail API provides several options for reading messages, such as reading a specified message number or range of message numbers, or prefetching specific parts of messages into the folder's cache. Here's an example of reading incoming messages on a POP3 server:

```
Store store = session.getStore("POP3");
store.connect(host, userid, password);
Folder mbox = store.getFolder("INBOX");
mbox.open(Folder.READ_ONLY);
Message msg[] = mbox.getMessages();
//...process each message according to requirements...
mbox.close(false);
store.close();
```

Each message in the preceding snippet is processed according to your business requirements.

> **Note**　Reading messages from an IMAP server is similar to reading messages from a POP3 server. With IMAP, however, the JavaMail API provides methods to create and manipulate folders and transfer messages between them. If you use an IMAP server, you can implement a full-featured, Web-based mail client with much less code than if you use a POP3 server.

## Deleting Messages and Flags

To delete a message, you must connect to the message store and open the message folder using READ_WRITE mode. You must flag the message with the Flags.Flag.DELETED flag (too many flags!). When you've processed all the messages, close the folder, and pass in a true value to expunge the deleted messages. The following code snippet demonstrates how to delete a message:

```
mbox.open(Folder.READ_WRITE);
Message msg = mbox.getMessage(1);
msg.setFlag(Flags.Flag.DELETED, true);
mbox.close(true);
```

The setFlag() method does not delete the message, it only marks the message for deletion. The close() method with the true parameter value is where messages are deleted or expunged.

# Developing JavaMail Applications

Today you'll develop the Emailer EJB, which is responsible in our university registration system for sending e-mails to students when they submit courses at enrollment time, and for notifying them again when they are approved for registration.

Our example today uses the Model-View-Controller (MVC) architecture pattern to design a JavaMail application. The servlet component in the Web tier represents the controller, which acts as a client to the EJB tier. The Emailer EJB in the EJB tier represents the model, which handles business logic (primarily sending an e-mail message). The view is represented by an HTML form (which could be a JSP) that interacts with the servlet. Figure 20.2 illustrates the use of the MVC pattern in designing our JavaMail application.

**20**

**FIGURE 20.2**

*Using the MVC pattern in the JavaMail application.*

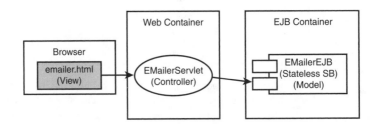

MVC pattern and the EmailerEJB Example

The example also partitions the application into a Web tier module (packaged into a WAR file) as well as an EJB module (packaged into a JAR file). You'll learn how to create and deploy an EAR file, which combines both the JAR file and the WAR file into an enterprise application.

Figure 20.3 summarizes the sequence diagram of the sample application in sending an e-mail message. The student interacts with the `EmailerServlet` using the `emailer.html` HTML form. The `EmailerServlet`, on behalf of the client, relays the request to the `Emailer` EJB, which sends the e-mail to the recipient through the e-mail server.

**FIGURE 20.3**

*The sequence diagram for sending an e-mail message.*

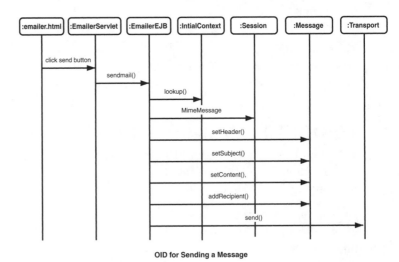

OID for Sending a Message

Here's a summary of the steps required to develop your JavaMail application of today's example:

1. Develop the EJB tier components. You need to develop only one component: the `Emailer` session bean.

2. Package the EJB tier into an EJB module (JAR file).

3. Develop the Web tier components. You need to develop the `EmailerServlet`.

4. Package the Web tier components into a Web module (WAR file).

5. Package the modules into an application (EAR file).

6. Develop an HTML form (this could be a JSP) as a GUI to make requests to the Web tier.

7. Create and configure the JavaMail `Session` on both the WebLogic Server and JBoss server environments.

8. Deploy and run the application on each server.

The following sections give you more details about performing each of the steps mentioned in this list. As usual, the full application code listing, and scripts for compiling and deploying into the WebLogic Server and JBoss server environments can be downloaded from our Web site.

## Developing the EJB Tier Components

The EJB tier contains only the `Emailer` EJB, and we selected a stateless session bean to model its activities. The main business method is the `sendMail()` method, which sends e-mail messages to students. To optimize the `Emailer` EJB, you can cache the mail `Session` object so that you don't have to look it up every time you send a message.

As you learned on previous days, we need to develop the remote interface, home interface, and the bean class. The following listings provide the code for these components.

Listing 20.1 is for the remote interface `Emailer`, which lists all the business methods used in our example.

**LISTING 20.1**   The Remote Interface `Emailer.java`

```
package day20;
import java.rmi.RemoteException;
import javax.ejb.EJBObject;
// Provides a method to send mail messages
public interface Mailer extends EJBObject {
    public void sendMail(String to, String body)
        throws RemoteException, URSMailerException;
}
```

20

Listing 20.2 shows the home interface `EmailerHome`, which lists all the life cycle methods used to manage the bean.

**LISTING 20.2**   The Home Interface `EmailerHome.java`

```
package day20;
import java.rmi.RemoteException;
import javax.ejb.CreateException;
import javax.ejb.EJBHome;
// The Home interface for MailerEJB
public interface MailerHome extends EJBHome {
    public Mailer create() throws RemoteException, CreateException;
}
```

Listing 20.3 is the bean class `EmailerEJB`, which implements all the business methods listed in the remote interface and the callback methods to manage the bean's life cycle by the container.

**LISTING 20.3**   The Bean Class `EmailerEJB.java`

```
package day20;
import java.util.Date;
import java.util.Locale;
import java.util.Properties;
import javax.naming.InitialContext;
import javax.activation.DataHandler;
import javax.mail.Message;
import javax.mail.MessagingException;
import javax.mail.Transport;
import javax.mail.Session;
import javax.mail.Multipart;
import javax.mail.internet.MimeMultipart;
import javax.mail.internet.MimeBodyPart;
import javax.mail.internet.MimeMessage;
import javax.mail.internet.InternetAddress;
import java.rmi.RemoteException;
import javax.ejb.EJBException;
import javax.ejb.FinderException;
import javax.ejb.SessionBean;
import javax.ejb.SessionContext;

// Session Bean implementation of MailerEJB.
// Used to send a mail message confirmation such as an email
// to a student after a registration into courses is completed.

public class MailerEJB implements SessionBean {
    private Session mailSession = null;
    public void sendMail(String to, String body)throws URSMailerException {
      try {
```

**LISTING 20.3**    continued

```
            MimeMessage msg = new MimeMessage(mailSession);
            msg.setFrom();
            InternetAddress dest = new InternetAddress(to);
            msg.setSubject("Testing STYEJB JavaMail");
            msg.setRecipient(Message.RecipientType.TO, dest);
            msg.setSentDate(new Date());
            msg.setHeader("X-Mailer", "JavaMailer");
            msg.setContent(body, "text/plain");
            Transport.send(msg);
        } catch (Exception e) {
            e.printStackTrace();
            throw new URSMailerException("Failure while sending email");
        }
    }

    public void ejbCreate() {
        try {
            InitialContext ctx = new InitialContext();
            mailSession = (Session) ctx.lookup("java:comp/env/mail/Mail");
        } catch (javax.naming.NamingException e) {
            e.printStackTrace();
        }
    }
    public void ejbPostCreate() {}
    public void ejbActivate() {}
    public void ejbPassivate() {}
    public void ejbRemove() {}
    public void setSessionContext(javax.ejb.SessionContext ec) {}
}
```

Notice that we've created the Session object in the ejbCreate() method, and cached it into the session instance variable. This will enhance the application's performance, and can handle a larger number of students.

## Packaging the Emailer EJB into an EJB Module

For large applications, all the components of the EJB tiers are packaged into one JAR file, along with its deployment descriptors. For our example today, you need to package only one component.

To build the example for the appropriate application server, you need to be in the Day20 directory, and then run the build script provided for this server. This will create a build subdirectory that contains all the compiled code. The script will then package the EJBs with the deployment descriptor (see Listing 20.4) into an EJB module (JAR file).

**20**

**LISTING 20.4**    The Deployment Descriptor `ejb-jar.xml`

```xml
<?xml version="1.0"?>

<!DOCTYPE ejb-jar PUBLIC
'-//Sun Microsystems, Inc.//DTD Enterprise JavaBeans 2.0//EN'
'http://java.sun.com/dtd/ejb-jar_2_0.dtd'>

<ejb-jar>
  <enterprise-beans>
    <session>
      <ejb-name>MailerEJB</ejb-name>
      <home>day20.MailerHome</home>
      <remote>day20.Mailer</remote>
      <ejb-class>day20.MailerEJB</ejb-class>
      <session-type>Stateless</session-type>
      <transaction-type>Container</transaction-type>
      <resource-env-ref>
          <resource-env-ref-name>mail/Mail</resource-env-ref-name>
          <resource-env-ref-type>javax.mail.Session</resource-env-ref-type>
      </resource-env-ref>
    </session>
  </enterprise-beans>
</ejb-jar>
```

You must provide a server-specific deployment descriptor for each application server; they are included in your download (`jboss.xml` for the JBoss server and `weblogic-ejb-jar.xml` for the WebLogic Server). For the sake of making your application portable, you must specify the `<resource-env-ref>` element in your `ejb-jar.xml` deployment descriptor, as you learned on Day 4.

## Developing the Web Tier Components

This example includes a servlet component in the Web tier to act as a client to the `Emailer` EJB in the EJB tier. Students first interact with the servlet (through the HTML form discussed in the next section), and requests are relayed back to the EJB tier to execute the required business logic. Listing 20.5 is the `EmailerServlet`.

**LISTING 20.5**    The Servlet `EmailerServlet.java`

```java
package web;
import java.io.IOException;
import java.io.PrintWriter;
import java.util.Hashtable;
import javax.naming.InitialContext;
import javax.rmi.PortableRemoteObject;
```

**LISTING 20.5** continued

```
import javax.servlet.ServletException;
import javax.servlet.http.HttpServlet;
import javax.servlet.http.HttpServletRequest;
import javax.servlet.http.HttpServletResponse;
import day20.*;

// This Servlet will call the MailerEJB with the email address.
public class MailerServlet extends HttpServlet
{
    private MailerHome mailerHome = null;
    // Looks up the MailerHome interface and saves it for use in doGet().
    public void init() throws ServletException{
        try{
            InitialContext jndiCtx = new InitialContext();
            Object ref = jndiCtx.lookup("day20/Mailer");
            mailerHome = (MailerHome)
                PortableRemoteObject.narrow(ref, MailerHome.class);
        }
        catch(Exception e){
            throw new ServletException("Failed to lookup Mailer", e);
        }
    }

    public void doPost(HttpServletRequest request, HttpServletResponse response)
        throws ServletException, IOException{
        String title = "Servlet client to Mailer EJB";
        String toAddress = request.getParameter("toAddress");
        String mailMsg = request.getParameter("message");
        response.setContentType("text/html");
        PrintWriter out = response.getWriter();
        out.println("<HTML><HEAD><TITLE>");
        out.println(title);
        out.println("</TITLE></HEAD><BODY>");
        out.println("<H1>" + title + "</H1>");
        out.println("<H2>Calling EJB...</H2>");
        try{
            Mailer bean = mailerHome.create();
            bean.sendMail(toAddress, mailMsg);
            out.println("Mail Message is sent....");
        }
        catch(Exception e){
            out.println(e.toString());
        }
        finally{
            out.println("</BODY></HTML>");
            out.close();
        }
    }
}
```

20

## Packaging the `EmailerServlet` into a WAR File Module

All components in the Web tier (such as JSP, servlets, and TagLibs), along with a `web.xml` deployment descriptor, should be packaged into a Web module (WAR file). You must also provide a server-specific Web deployment descriptor. The `jboss-web.xml` file is included for the JBoss server, and `weblogic.xml` is provided for WebLogic Server.

The script provided for each server will create a `web` subdirectory that contains all the compiled code. It will then package the `EmailerServlet` component and the deployment descriptor `web.xml` into a Web module (WAR file).

Listing 20.6 provides the `web.xml` deployment descriptor.

**LISTING 20.6**    The Web Deployment Descriptor `web.xml`

```xml
<?xml version="1.0" encoding="ISO-8859-1"?>

<!DOCTYPE web-app
    PUBLIC "-//Sun Microsystems, Inc.//DTD Web Application 2.3//EN"
    "http://java.sun.com/dtd/web-app_2_3.dtd">

<web-app>
    <servlet>
        <servlet-name>MailerServlet</servlet-name>
        <servlet-class>MailerServlet</servlet-class>
    </servlet>
    <servlet-mapping>
        <servlet-name>MailerServlet</servlet-name>
        <url-pattern>/MailerServlet</url-pattern>
    </servlet-mapping>
    <welcome-file-list>
      <welcome-file>index.html</welcome-file>
    </welcome-file-list>
</web-app>
```

# Building the EAR File

The modules created in the previous sections—one for the Web tier and one for the EJB tier—can be combined into an application file (EAR file). For the sake of convenience, both scripts are also combined into one script to package the application into an EAR file. Listing 20.7 shows the `application.xml` deployment descriptor that will combine both WAR and JAR files into an enterprise application.

**LISTING 20.7**   The EAR Deployment Descriptor `application.xml`

```xml
<?xml version="1.0" encoding="UTF-8"?>
<!DOCTYPE application PUBLIC
    '-//Sun Microsystems, Inc.//DTD J2EE Application 1.3//EN'
      'http://java.sun.com/dtd/application_1_3.dtd'>

<application>
    <display-name>STYEJB JavaMail Application</display-name>
    <module>
    <web>
        <web-uri>mailer.war</web-uri>
        <context-root>day20</context-root>
    </web>
    </module>
    <module>
        <ejb>mailer.jar</ejb>
    </module>
</application>
```

Listing 20.8 provides the build script for the WebLogic Server application server. The script for JBoss is included in the downloaded files.

**LISTING 20.8**   The Build Script for WebLogic Server `buildWebLogic.bat`

```
@echo Compiling EJB tier files...
rem "Cleaning previous build (if any)"
rmdir /s/q build build1

rem "Creating a staging area for the build"
mkdir build build\META-INF

rem "Copying deployment files to META-INF directory"
copy %STYEJB_HOME%\day20\ejb-jar.xml build\META-INF
copy %STYEJB_HOME%\day20\weblogic-ejb-jar.xml build\META-INF

rem "Compiling  EJB classes and interfaces"
javac -g -d build URSMailerException.java \
        Mailer.java MailerHome.java MailerEJB.java

rem "Creating the EJB's deployment Jar file"
cd build
jar cv0f tmp_mailer.jar META-INF day20
cd ..

rem "Compiling the container classes"
java weblogic.ejbc -keepgenerated -g \
        -deprecation build\tmp_mailer.jar build\mailer.jar

@echo Compiling Web tier files...
```

**20**

**LISTING 20.8**    continued

```
rem "Cleaning previous build (if any)"
rmdir /s/q web
mkdir web web\WEB-INF web\WEB-INF\classes

copy GUI\MailerServlet.java web\.
copy GUI\*.html web\.
javac -g -d web\WEB-INF\classes -classpath %CLASSPATH%;build \
      URSMailerException.java Mailer.java MailerHome.java MailerEJB.java
javac -g -d web\WEB-INF\classes \
      -classpath %CLASSPATH%;web\WEB-INF\classes;build web\*.java

rem Copying Web Deployment Descriptor...
copy web.xml web\WEB-INF
copy weblogic.xml web\WEB-INF

jar cf mailer.war -C  web .
mkdir build1 build1\META-INF
move mailer.war build1

@echo Creating Enterprise Archive (EAR) file ...
copy application.xml build1\META-INF
copy build\mailer.jar build1\
jar cf mailer.ear -C build1 .

@echo Moving Enterprise archive file in to build directory...
move mailer.ear build1
rem "Deploying the war file"
copy build1\mailer.ear  %APPLICATIONS%
```

# Implementing the Client

The Web client for the `EmailerServlet` is an HTML form (see Listing 20.9) for testing our JavaMail application. The HTML form (see Figure 20.4) makes a request with the recipient's e-mail address and the body of the message to be sent.

**LISTING 20.9**    The HTML Form `index.html`

```
<html>
  <head>
    <title>JavaMailer EJB Form</title>
  </head>
  <body>
    <h1>Send Message Using JavaMail Form</h1>
    <form method="POST" action="MailerServlet">
      <table cellspacing="2" cellpadding="2" border="0">
        <tr><td>To:</td>
```

**LISTING 20.9**   continued

```
                <td><input type="text" name="toAddress" size="40"></td>
          </tr>
          <tr><td>Message:</td>
             <td>
               <textarea name="message" cols="50" rows="10"></textarea>
             </td>
          </tr>
          <tr><td><input type="submit" name="Send" value="Send"></td>
             <td><input type="Reset"></td>
          </tr>
        </table>
      </form>
    </body>
 </html>
```

## Configuring the Mail Session in WebLogic

Before running the JavaMail application, you must create and configure a JavaMail
Session into a JNDI service in the WebLogic Server Administration Console
(`http://localhost:7001/console`). This allows server-side components and applications to access JavaMail services with JNDI. In our example, you create a mail `Session`
by specifying the default mail user, mail host, transport, and store protocols in the
Administration Console so that components that use JavaMail do not have to set these
properties (see Figure 20.4).

**FIGURE 20.4**

*WebLogic Server
Administration
Console.*

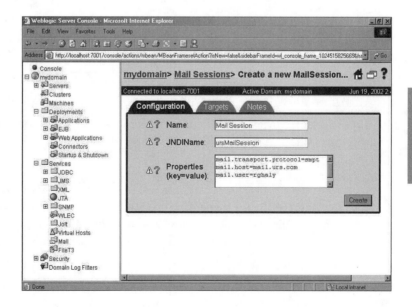

20

Applications that are heavy e-mail users benefit because WebLogic Server creates a single `Session` object and makes it available via JNDI to any component that needs it.

1. In the Administration Console, click on the Mail node in the left pane.

2. Click Create a New Mail Session.

3. In the Name field, enter a name for the new session. Enter **MailSession**.

4. In the JNDIName field, enter a JNDI lookup name. Use `ursMailSession`. Your code uses this string to look up the `javax.mail.Session` object.

5. In the Properties field, enter properties to configure the `Session`. Use Table 20.2 to set the required fields. In our example, you set the protocol, mail server host, and username as shown in Figure 20.4.

**TABLE 20.2**   Summary of Mail Session Property Fields

| Property | Description |
| --- | --- |
| `mail.store.protocol` | The protocol to use to retrieve e-mail. The default is IMAP. |
| `mail.transport.protocol` | The protocol to use to send e-mail. SMTP is the default. |
| `mail.host` | The name of the mail host machine. |
| `mail.user` | The name of the default user for retrieving e-mail. |
| `mail.protocol.host` | The mail host for a specific protocol. For example, you can set `mail.SMTP.host` and `mail.IMAP.host` to different machine names. |
| `mail.protocol.user` | The protocol-specific default user name for logging in to a mailer server. For example, `mail.smtp.user=styejb`. |
| `mail.from` | The default return address. |
| `mail.debug` | Set to `True` to enable JavaMail debug output. |

 **Note**

You can override any properties set in the mail `Session` in your code by creating a `Properties` object that contains the properties you want to override. Then, after you look up the mail `Session` object in JNDI, call the `Session.getInstance()` method with your `Properties` to get a customized `Session`.

To configure the JBoss environment, you must customize the entries in the `mail-service.xml` file in the `<JBOSS_HOME>/server/default/deploy` directory. The `README.TXT` file provides more information about how to configure these parameters.

# Running the JavaMail Application

To run the JavaMail application, you must deploy the emailer.ear file into the appropriate application server. The following steps show you how to deploy the EAR file into WebLogic Server:

c:\styejb>**setEnvWebLogic.bat**

c:\styejb>**cd day20**

c:\styejb\day20> **runWebLogic.bat**

Similarly, you can deploy the application into the JBoss server using the runJboss.bat script.

After you deploy the application on WebLogic Server, you can run the client from your Web browser by putting the following URL in the address field: http://localhost:7001/day20/index.html. On the JBoss server, you need to use the URL http://localhost:8080/day20/index.html.

As shown in Figure 20.5, fill the e-mail address with your e-mail address, and a message of your choice, and then click on the Send button. Check your e-mail for the delivered message.

**FIGURE 20.5**

*HTML form to send e-mail messages.*

20

# Best Practices

Reading messages from an IMAP server is similar to reading messages from a POP3 server. With IMAP, however, the JavaMail API provides methods to create and manipulate folders and transfer messages between them. If you use an IMAP server, you can implement a full-featured, Web-based mail client with much less code than if you use a POP3 server. With POP3, you must provide code to manage a message store through your application server, possibly using a database or file system to represent folders.

One of J2EE's objectives is portability, and it always recommends a declarative approach over a programmatic approach to avoid hardcoding parameters. Avoid the programmatic approach as much as possible. Create and configure the Session object in a JNDI service as an administered object, so that you can tune it or change its parameters without changing any code.

It's always more efficient to use a shared Session object among all your components, even if you're working with mail sessions for multiple user mailboxes.

# Summary

Today you explored the JavaMail API classes and their use. You started by learning the protocol used in e-mail systems, and the difference between sending an e-mail message and a JMS message. You also learned how to send, read, and delete e-mail messages, using the JavaMail and JAF APIs. Through a working example, you explored how to develop a simple JavaMail application. You also found out how to develop a complete enterprise application by portioning the application into a Web module (WAR file) and a EJB module (JAR file), and then combining them into an EAR file. You learned how to test your application from your browser through the use of an HTML form.

# Q&A

**Q What are the main differences among SMTP, POP, and IMAP?**

**A** SMTP is a protocol used to send outgoing messages, whereas POP and IMAP are used to retrieve and read incoming messages.

**Q What are the steps involved in sending an e-mail message through the JavaMail API?**

**A** The main steps involved in sending an e-mail message are as follows:

1. Create a Session object, usually by looking it up in JNDI services.

2. Create a MimeMessage from the session, as a container to your contents.

3. Set the to, subject, and content using the `addRecipient()`, `setSubject()`, and `setContent()` methods respectively.

4. Send the message using `Transport.send()`.

# Quiz

1. When sending mail, which of the following is the proper sequence of working with classes?

   A. `Session, Authenticator, Message, Transport`

   B. `Authenticator, Message, Session, Transport`

   C. `Authenticator, Session, Message, Transport`

   D. `Session, Transport, Message, Authenticator`

2. When forwarding a message, you need to

   A. Create a new message from the original message, and copy over its content.

   B. Create a multipart message, and construct two parts—one for the text message and one for the original message—and combine them together.

   C. Create a blank message and copy the original content over.

   D. Use the original message object and set its new recipients.

3. When retrieving an e-mail message, which of the following is the proper order of working with classes?

   A. `Store, Folder, Message`

   B. `Session, Store, Folder, Message, Transport`

   C. `Session, Folder, Message, Transport`

   D. `Session, Store, Folder, Message`

4. Which of the following are part of the JavaBeans Activation Framework (JAF)?

   A. `Transport`

   B. `DataSource`

   C. `FileDataSource`

   D. `Session`

20

# Answers

1. A

2. A

3.  D
4.  B, C

## Exercises

In today's example, modify the index.html file to add the following fields to the form: From, CC, BCC, and Subject. Also add Read, Forward, Reply, and Delete buttons. Modify the EmailerServelet and Emailer EJB accordingly. The read function will retrieve the next unread message, which can then be forwarded to a recipient, replied to the sender, or deleted using the appropriate button.

# DAY **21**

# Developing a Complete Enterprise Application

Today, you'll develop a complete enterprise application. You'll apply different concepts you learned in the previous days to build an application that consists of Web components (JSPs and servlets), EJB components (session, entity, and message-driven enterprise beans), and the EIS tier (database tables).

The sample university registration system is an end-to-end application that handles the online course registration and enrollment process in a transactional e-commerce environment.

Today you'll see how to perform analysis, design, implementation, and deployment of the sample application. You'll undertake each of the following:

- Understand the application requirements
- Perform use case analysis
- Decide on a system architecture that meets the application requirements
- Identify the components in the multitier architecture and the interactions among these components
- Implement the components, and package and deploy the application

# Understanding the Application

The university registration system is a typical e-commerce application. The application has a Web site that enables students to browse the course catalog and register for courses online. Figure 21.1 shows an overview of the system.

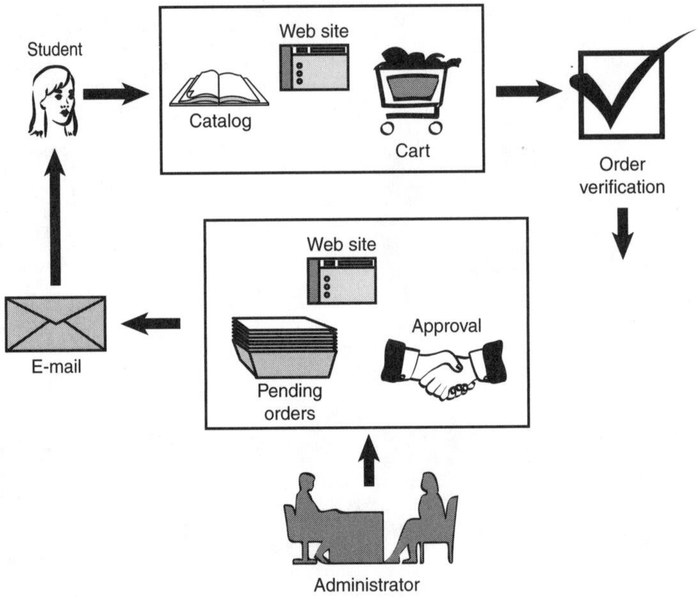

FIGURE 21.1

*University registration
system.*

The application provides the following functionality:

- Student registration—This functionality enables new students to create and maintain their account information. The account information includes the student's first name, last name, address, e-mail, login name, and password.

- Student authentication—This module handles the student login process, such as verifying the login name and password. This ensures that only registered students browse the course catalog and purchase courses for enrollment.

- Course catalog browsing—The Web site displays the current course offerings in the university and their details. The course details include the course title and fee.

- Enrollment cart—The enrollment cart module enables students to place their course selection in a shopping cart while browsing the course catalog, and later to view the cart contents before placing an order.

- Order processing—The order module enables students to place their orders, and performs the necessary verification before approving them.

- Administrator interface—This functionality allows the administrator to view and approve orders for enrollment.
- Notification—This functionality causes the system to send e-mail to students when they have enrolled for a course.

# Analyzing the Application

Use case analysis is the standard technique for analyzing the requirements of an application. A use case diagram shows the interaction between the system and actors. An *actor* is a role that human and/or nonhuman users of the system play when interacting with use cases. Figure 21.2 shows a high-level use case diagram of the university registration system.

**FIGURE 21.2**

*Use case diagram.*

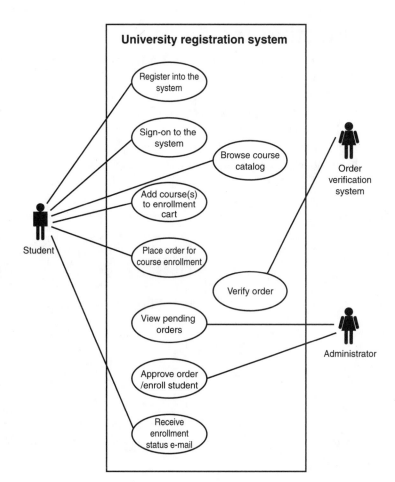

21

The use case diagram in this case consists of actors, such as student, administrator, and order verification system. The following describes the use cases:

- New students register with the system.
- Existing students log on to the system and can browse the course catalog.
- A student can select courses and add them to the enrollment cart.
- A student places an order for the enrollment cart contents.
- The system verifies the order in the background.
- An administrator can view the verified orders that need approval for enrollment.
- An administrator approves the order and enrolls the student in the courses.
- The system notifies the student of enrollment via e-mail.

# Architecting the System

*Architecting* consists of deciding what tiers are needed for the application, what services are required at each tier, and how the application logic will be spread across different tiers. As you learned on Day 15, "Understanding J2EE Architecture," the J2EE architecture is designed for multitier applications. In a multitier architecture, the business logic can be split into more than one layer. In the sample application, logic is partitioned into the business logic tier and the presentation logic tier. The user interface is partitioned into the client tier and the presentation tier. The application-persistent data is stored in the EIS tier. Figure 21.3 shows the architecture of the system.

**FIGURE 21.3**

*Architecture diagram.*

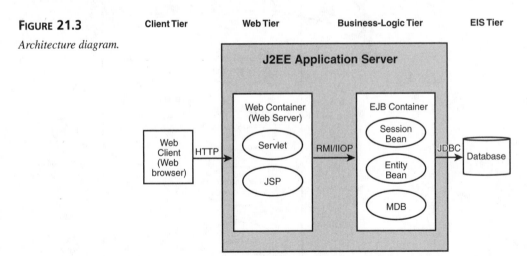

The sample architecture consists of the following tiers:

- Client tier—Students and administrators use the client tier to interact with the system. The client tier is provided by a Web browser, such as Internet Explorer or Netscape Navigator. The client tier communicates with the Web tier by using the HTTP protocol.

- Web tier—This tier accepts user requests and generates responses using the presentation logic. The sample application uses both servlets and JSPs in a Web container. The Web tier communicates with the business logic tier using RMI/IIOP protocol.

- Business logic tier—This tier handles the core business logic of the application. The business components are implemented as EJB components with support from an EJB container.

- EIS tier—The EIS tier consists of the database in which the sample application's permanent data is stored. The business-logic tier communicates with the EIS tier using JDBC.

**Note**

J2EE offers flexibility in partitioning the application logic across tiers. For example, you have a choice between Web-centric and EJB-centric design. In the Web-centric design, the Web tier components are responsible for most of the application's functionality. The Web tier components communicate directly with the EIS tier using container services such as the JDBC API. In the EJB-centric design, the enterprise beans encapsulate the core application logic. Web tier components communicate with EJB tier components instead of accessing the EIS tier directly.

The decision between the Web-centric and EJB-centric approaches depends on factors such as application functionality and scalability requirements. The Web-centric approach offers a quick start for small applications, but can rapidly become complex and difficult to maintain for large applications. The EJB-centric approach offers advantages such as automatic handling of transactions, distributed processing, security, and so on, and can stay manageable as applications grow more complex. The sample application uses the EJB-centric approach.

# Designing the Application

Next, you must decide what components are needed in each tier and how they interact with each other to achieve the required functionality.

21

Figure 21.4 shows the high-level design of the application. Please note that this diagram does not show all the components and their interactions. The diagram shows JSPs, servlets, enterprise beans, and database tables. The following sections discuss the various components in detail.

**FIGURE 21.4**

*Application design.*

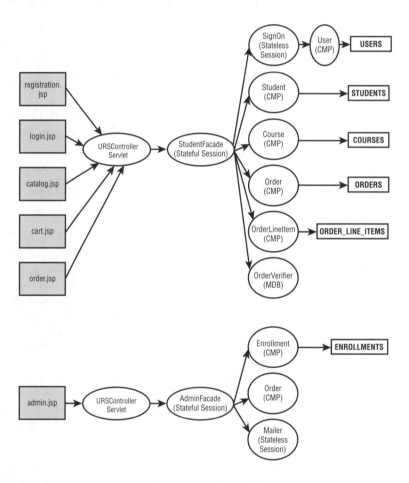

## Designing the Business Logic Tier Components

The following discusses the key enterprise beans in the business logic tier:

- The concept of the student is central to the university registration application. Multiple clients must share behavior, such as creating a student account, verifying an existing account, and updating account information. Updates to the state of a student object must be written to the persistent store. The student object must live even when the client's session with the server is over. Therefore, the `Student` component is modeled as a container-managed persistence entity bean.

- `SignOn` is the authentication component that verifies the user login name and password. This component uses the `User` component to retrieve and store the user's login name and password. Such a component doesn't need to maintain client-specific state information across method invocations, so the same bean instance can be reused to service other client requests. This can be modeled as a stateless session bean.

- The `Course` component models the courses offered by the university. Because courses are persistent objects, `Course` is modeled as a container-managed persistence entity bean.

- `EnrollmentCart` models the shopping cart concept in a typical e-commerce Web site. While browsing the course catalog, a student can add courses to and remove courses from the `EnrollmentCart`. A cart must be allocated by the system for each student concurrently connected to the Web site. All the selected courses of a student will be added to the temporary cart. This cart is not a persistent object because the student can choose to abandon the cart. Therefore, in the application, `EnrollmentCart` is modeled as a stateful session bean. Alternatively, if you want the enrollment cart to survive a client machine or server crash, you must model it as an entity bean.

- A student places an order when he/she is ready to purchase the enrollment cart contents. The `Order` component must live even when the student's session with the application is over. Therefore, the `Order` component is modeled as a container-managed persistence entity bean.

- A student's order consists of one or more line items. Each line item represents a single course item that the student has ordered. This is modeled as the `OrderLineItem` component. Similar to `Order`, `OrderLineItem` must persist even when the student's session with the application is over. Therefore, `OrderLineItem` is modeled as a container-managed persistence entity bean. Also, the `Order` entity bean has a one-to-many bidirectional relationship with `OrderLineItem`. This relationship is modeled as a container-managed relationship.

- The `OrderVerifier` component is responsible for verifying the order's facts, such as the student's billing information, the classroom's capacity, and so on. We would like to enable the student to continue browsing the Web site and not require her to wait for the background processing to complete. This asynchronous processing can be best modeled using a message-driven bean. In the sample application, after the student submits an order, a Java Message Service (JMS) message is sent to a destination, where it will be processed by an `OrderVerifier` message-driven bean.

21

- A student can enroll in multiple courses and each course can have many students enrolled in it. The Enrollment CMP component models the join relationship between the students and the courses. The Student entity bean has a one-to-many relationship with Enrollment and the Course has a one-to-many relationship with Enrollment.

- The Mailer component is the stateless session bean responsible for sending e-mail messages. The AdminFacade component uses Mailer to send an e-mail confirmation to the student when the administrator approves the order for enrollment.

- The StudentFacade component provides a unified interface to student functionality. Instead of communicating directly with enterprise beans such as Student and Order, clients go through the simpler interface of StudentFacade. StudentFacade is modeled as a stateful session bean.

- The AdminFacade component provides a unified interface to the administrator functionality. Web components use a single AdminFacade component to access the administrator functionality. This component is modeled as a stateful session bean.

> **Note**  The sample application uses the following approach for the business logic tier design.

- Provides a simple interface to complex functionality by using session bean façades.

  The session bean façades front the entity beans. For example, the StudentFacade session bean provides a simple interface to student functionality and fronts entity beans such as Order.

- For portability and ease of development, container-managed entity beans are used instead of bean-managed persistence entity beans. Also, all entity beans provide local interfaces for efficient access due to co-location.

- Uses distributed islands of local components. For example, as shown in Figure 21.5, one such island is composed of components such as StudentFacade, SignOn, Course, and Order. All the components within this island communicate with each other by using local interfaces. This offers the benefit of higher performance. An island communicates with a remote island by using remote interfaces, which offers the benefit of scalability.

**FIGURE 21.5**

*Distributed islands of local components.*

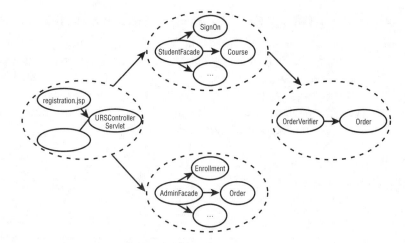

## Designing the Web Tier Components

The following section discusses the Web tier components in the sample application:

- The primary role of `URSControllerServlet` servlet is to act as a controller. This component is responsible for receiving parameters from the client and then invoking the calls to the EJB tier, which handles the business logic. Finally, the servlet receives the result and uses it to provide a response to the user. This servlet usually forwards the response to a JSP to perform a presentation task.

- The application contains the JSP pages, such as the registration page, login page, course catalog page, enrollment cart page, and order confirmation page. These components contain the presentation logic for student-related functionality. In addition, the admin page contains the presentation logic for administrator-related functionality.

**Note**

The sample application uses the MVC (Model-View-Controller) design pattern discussed on Day 7, "Designing Web Applications." The model layer contains the enterprise bean components that handle the core business logic. The view layer contains the JSP pages, whose job is to format and present responses to the client. The controller layer provides the `URSControllerServlet` servlet, which is responsible for receiving the client request, managing screen flow, and selecting an appropriate response.

**21**

## Designing the EIS Tier Database Schema

Figure 21.6 shows the database tables and the relationships between them. Each table is shown as a solid rectangle with two compartments. The top compartment holds the table name and the bottom compartment holds a list of column names. The primary key column(s) uniquely identifies a row in the table. We use the abbreviation PK for the primary key. The foreign key column of a table identifies a row in a different table. We use the abbreviation FK for the foreign key.

**FIGURE 21.6**

*Database schema of the sample application.*

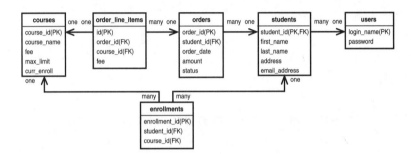

For example, the `enrollments` table consists of the columns `enrollment_id` (primary key), `student_id` (foreign key to `student_id` in the `students` table), and `course_id` (foreign key to `course_id` in the `courses` table).

## Designing the Scenarios

This section examines the interactions between components for key use case scenarios.

### Student Logs On to the System

Figure 21.7 shows the sequence diagram for the use case Student Logs On to the System. The student enters a login name and password, and clicks the submit button in the login page. The browser sends an HTTP `GET` request to the Web server. The `URSControllerServlet` servlet receives the client request and invokes the `validateUser()` method of the `StudentFacade` enterprise bean. The façade delegates the method call of the `SignOn` authentication component, which uses the `User` entity bean to look up and validate the login name and password. Finally, the controller servlet forwards the request to the catalog page, which displays the course catalog.

### Student Places Order

As shown in Figure 21.8, when the student clicks the Place Order button in the enrollment cart page, the `URSControllerServlet` receives the request and invokes the `placeOrder()` method of `StudentFacade`. The façade first creates a new order using the

Order entity bean. The façade then creates multiple line items using the OrderLineItem entity bean and associates the line items with the order. Finally, the façade sends a JMS message to the Destination using the MessageSender component for order verification purposes.

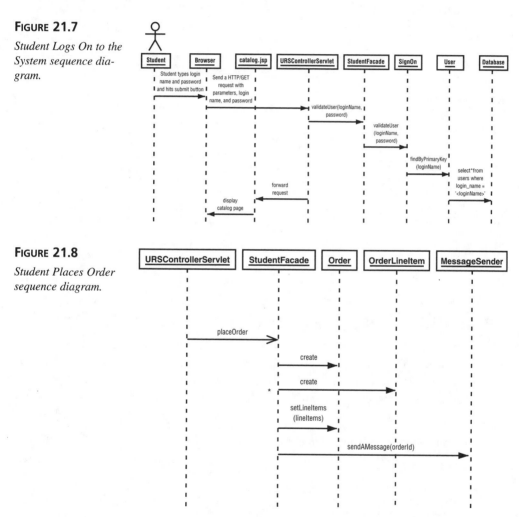

**FIGURE 21.7**

*Student Logs On to the System sequence diagram.*

**FIGURE 21.8**

*Student Places Order sequence diagram.*

## Administrator Approves Order and Enrolls Student in Courses

Figure 21.9 shows the sequence diagram corresponding to the use case Administrator Approves Order and Enrolls Student in Courses. When the administrator approves an order placed by the student, he or she clicks the Approve Order button on the

21

administrator page. The URSControllerServlet receives the corresponding request and invokes the method approvedOrder of AdminFacade. The façade retrieves the order by using its primary key, order_id, and changes the order status to Approved. The façade then enrolls the student in all the courses that are part of the order by using the enrollment component. Finally, the façade sends an e-mail to the student confirming the approval.

**FIGURE 21.9**

*Administrator Approves Order and Enrolls Student sequence diagram.*

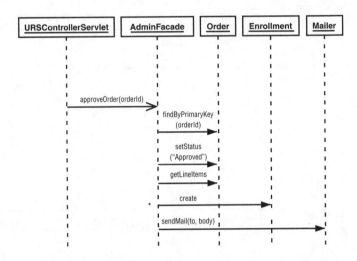

# Packaging and Deploying the Application

This section describes the steps to package and deploy the application for both WebLogic Server and JBoss application servers. These steps assume that you configured OrderVerifierTopic as discussed on Day 14, "Developing Message-Driven Beans," and ursMailSession as discussed on Day 20, "Implementing JavaMail in EJB Applications."

You can run the following commands for WebLogic:

```
C:\>cd styejb\examples
```

```
C:\styejb\examples>setEnvWebLogic.bat
```

```
C:\styejb\examples>cd day21
```

```
C:\styejb\examples\day21>buildWebLogic.bat
```

You can run the following commands for JBoss:

```
C:\>cd styejb\examples
```

```
C:\styejb\examples>setEnvJboss.bat
```

```
C:\styejb\examples>cd day21

C:\styejb\examples\day21>buildJBoss.bat
```

# Running the Sample Application

The following steps describe how to start the PointBase database server and WebLogic Server, and run the sample application:

1. Start PointBase server in a new command window as follows:
```
C:\>cd styejb\examples
C:\styejb\examples>setEnvWebLogic.bat
C:\styejb\examples>startPointBase.bat
```

2. Start WebLogic Server in a new command window as follows:
```
C:\>cd styejb\examples
C:\styejb\examples>setEnvWebLogic.bat
C:\styejb\examples>startWebLogic.bat
```

3. Open the university registration system URL, **http://localhost:7001/urs**, using a Web browser. This will display the main page as shown in Figure 21.10.

**FIGURE 21.10**

*Sample application main page.*

21

4. Register a new student by clicking the New students register here link. Enter **tom** for the login name and **tom** for the password. Enter a first name, last name, address, and email for the student. Figure 21.11 shows the corresponding screenshot. Click the Register button.

**FIGURE 21.11**

*Sample application registration page.*

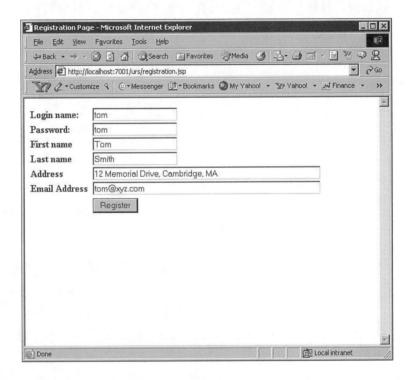

5. Figure 21.12 shows the course catalog page. Add a couple of courses to the enrollment cart by clicking the Add to cart link that corresponds to each course. Click the View your enrollment cart link to view the enrollment cart.

6. Figure 21.13 shows the enrollment cart page. Click the Place Order link to purchase the cart contents.

7. Now we'll explore the administrator functionality. Open the URL **http://localhost:7001/urs**. Click the Administrator click here link. Figure 21.14 shows the administrator page displaying the verified order(s). Click the Approve link to approve the order and enroll the student in the courses.

FIGURE **21.12**

*Sample application
course catalog page.*

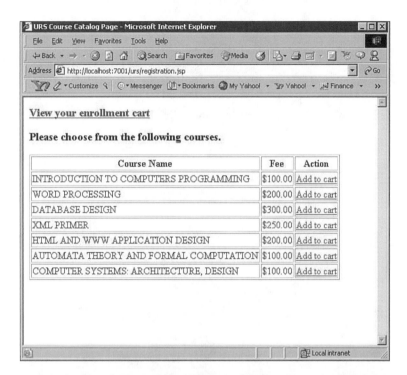

FIGURE **21.13**

*Sample application
enrollment cart page.*

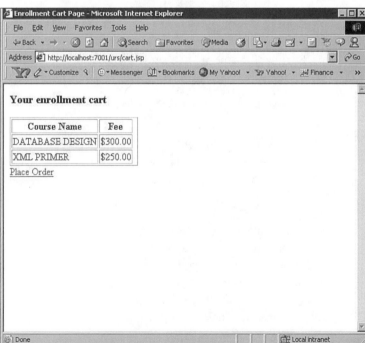

21

**FIGURE 21.14**

*Sample application administrator page.*

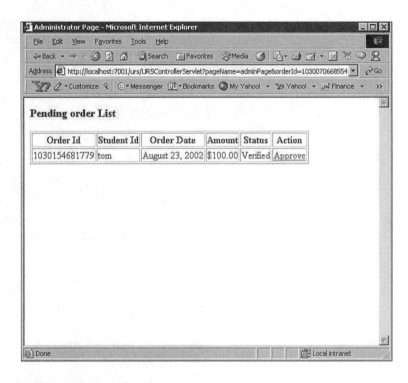

The following steps describe how to start the JBoss server and run the sample application:

1. Start the JBoss server in a new command window as follows:

```
C:\>cd styejb\examples
C:\styejb\examples>setEnvJBoss.bat
C:\styejb\examples>startJBoss.bat
```

2. Open the university registration system URL, **http://localhost:8080/urs**, using a Web browser. This will display the main page as shown in Figure 21.10. The remaining steps are similar to those listed for WebLogic Server's steps 4 through 7.

# Best Practices

Local architecture is implemented with local enterprise beans. Distributed architecture is implemented with remote enterprise beans. Local architecture offers the benefit of higher performance for the same hardware, but it's harder to scale and cluster. On the other hand, distributed architecture is easier to scale and cluster, but results in reduced performance for the same hardware. One possible solution is to create distributed islands of local components as in the sample application.

# Summary

Today, you worked on a complete sample application. We explored the requirements of the sample university application and analyzed them using a use case approach. We decided to use the multitier architecture that J2EE offers. We also decided to use an EJB-centric design in which the enterprise beans encapsulate the core application logic. We identified those components and their interactions. Finally, we packaged, deployed, and ran the sample application.

# Q&A

**Q In which tier should I implement the referential integrity constraints?**

**A** It's generally best to implement referential integrity constraints logic in the EIS tier rather than the EJB tier. Implementing the constraints in the EIS tier means that they can be used by non-J2EE applications and offer greater performance and reliability. Implementing such constraints in the EJB tier duplicates logic and makes maintenance difficult. On the other hand, EIS tier constraints such as database procedural triggers are not portable across database vendors.

# Quiz

1. Which of the following approaches is best for building large-scale enterprise applications?

    A. Web-centric approach

    B. EJB-centric approach

    C. EIS-centric approach

2. Which of the following approach is true?

    A. Local architecture offers best performance for the same hardware.

    B. Distributed architecture offers best performance for the same hardware.

    C. Local architecture is easier to scale and cluster.

## Quiz Answers

1. B
2. A

21

# Exercises

To extend your knowledge of the subjects covered today, try the following exercise:

Add functionality so that a student can view his or her course enrollments. Add a View Course Enrollments link to the catalog page, and develop an `enrollment.jsp` that displays the student enrollments. In addition, add a `Collection getStudentEnrollments()` method to the `Student` component. This method invokes the method `Collection findStudentEnrollment(String studentId)` of the `Enrollment` component. Package, deploy, and run the application.

# Appendixes

A

B

C

D

E

# APPENDIX A

# WebLogic Application Server 7.0

For the WebLogic Server examples in this book, you'll need to download, install, and configure BEA WebLogic Server version 7.0. This appendix is provided to help you do so.

## Downloading and Installing WebLogic 7.0

You can download WebLogic Server from the BEA site at www.bea.com. BEA provides you with a fully functional trial version of this server for 30 days (from the installation date), which provides ample time for running the examples within this book at the suggested pace of 21 days. BEA also provides thorough online documentation for WebLogic Server and its services at www.weblogic.com. BEA also provides a suite of examples included when you download the server. We advise you to learn the examples in this book before you run other examples.

At www.bea.com, click on the Download link to download BEA WebLogic Server 7.0. If you aren't a registered user, you must register first, and then log in to the site. You proceed by choosing the platform that you'll be installing the WebLogic Server under from the Choose A Platform drop-down list. In this appendix, we'll cover an installation for the Microsoft Windows 2000 platform. For other platforms, please follow the installation instructions provided by BEA (for which a link will be provided on the download page). With that mentioned, please proceed by picking Microsoft Windows NT/2000 from the Choose A Platform list.

Click on the NET INSTALLER link, and when requested, save the file net_platform701_win32.exe to your hard drive. You may select the directory of your choice. However, we recommend using the c:\temp\ directory of your computer as a temporary holding ground. When the download is complete, work through the following list to complete the installation process:

1. Double-click on the downloaded file net_platform701_win32.exe; the Installer will prompt you to select the BEA home directory, and the components you want to install. Select c:\bea as the BEA home directory, which we call BEA_HOME directory. Check only on the "WebLogic Server" components to be installed. (If you've previously installed any BEA product, you already have a BEA home directory; in that case, you should use the same home directory for this server's installation. Otherwise, create a new BEA home directory.)

2. Later, the installer will ask you where you would like to keep the installation temporary files. Use the same directory as before (c:\temp\). When you are presented with the option of whether to perform a typical installation or a custom installation, elect to perform the typical installation and resume by clicking the Next button. When downloading the archives is completed, the Installer will prompt you to enter the server installation directory. You choose c:\bea\weblogic701, which we call the WEBLOGIC_HOME directory.

3. Next, the file installation will begin. When it completes, you'll be presented with the Run Configuration Wizard, to start configuring your server.

# Configuring WebLogic 7.0

When the installation is complete, you must configure the WebLogic Server environment. From the Start menu, select Programs, BEA WebLogic Platform 7.0, and choose the Configuration Wizard application. You'll be presented with the screen in Figure A.1.

Select the WLS Domain template and give it the name mydomain. Choose the Single Server (Standalone Server) server type and click Next. Notice that for the purpose of the examples in this book, you're using a single server configuration. However, for real-world enterprise applications in a production environment, you would probably install the clustered version, where load-balancing and failover capability can be utilized for high performance and fully redundant services (see Figure A.2).

**FIGURE A.1**

*Domain selection dialog.*

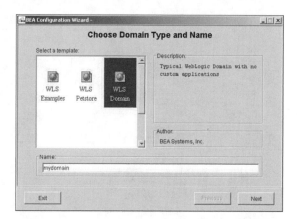

**FIGURE A.2**

*Server type dialog.*

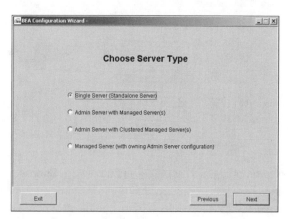

The screen in Figure A.3 will prompt you for the location of your domain. Input the following path **<bea-home>\weblogic701\config**. So, if your BEA home directory were c:\bea, the domain location would be c:\bea\weblogic701\config.

Next, you'll be presented with the server configuration parameters. You shouldn't change the default parameters provided because they are the most common and safest configuration for the listen ports. The listen address is not provided with a default value, and if you leave it blank, you'll be able to access your server through the URL http://localhost:7001/. Your configuration should look like the one shown in Figure A.4.

FIGURE A.3

*Domain location dialog.*

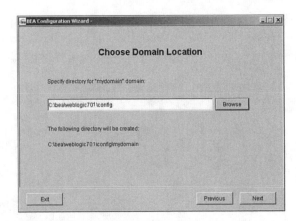

FIGURE A.4

*Server type selection dialog.*

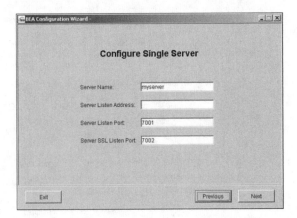

Now you'll be prompted for a username and password. Choose a username and password that you'll remember—you won't be able to run or administer the server without them. We recommend using the username **system**, and the password **administrator** for this installation or WebLogic. After you've entered that information, proceed by clicking Next. When prompted to choose whether you would like to run the server as a Windows service, you may choose No for the purposes of running the examples in this book. Proceed by clicking Next.

Now you'll be prompted to choose whether to install this server on the Windows Start menu. You may choose No for the purposes of this book. Proceed by clicking Next. Finally, you're presented with the Configuration Summary page shown in Figure A.5, which contains the information that you have previously entered.

Click the Create button to proceed. Configuration is now complete for the domain and server you'll use to run examples in this book. Now you can choose End Configuration Wizard, and click the Next button to finish.

**FIGURE A.5**

*Configuration
Summary screen.*

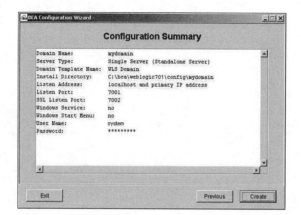

A

Congratulations! After you've entered your server's configuration parameters in the
setEnvWeblogic.bat file located in the examples' root directory (as per the instructions
contained in README.txt located in the same directory), you can start running the examples provided with this book.

Note

> If you choose a different installation directory than the one we suggested
> earlier (c:\bea), you must set the environment variable WEBLOGIC_HOME (in
> the setEnvWebLogic.bat script) to the new location. Other parameters, such
> as STYEJB_HOME (location of your examples root directory), WLS_USER (for the
> username) and WLS_PW (for the password)  also must be set.

# APPENDIX **B**

# JBoss Application Server 3.0

JBoss is an open-source, J2EE-compliant application server, which is currently distributed for free. For the JBoss server examples in this book, you'll need to download, install, and configure JBoss version 3.0. This appendix is provided to help you do so.

## Downloading and Installing JBoss 3.0

You can download JBoss from `http://sourceforge.net/projects/jboss`. JBoss provides you with a fully functional, free version of this server. JBoss also provides thorough online documentation for the JBoss server and its services for nominal fees. If you encounter difficulties in running any of the examples, or you would like to learn more specifics about the JBoss server, we recommend that you consult this suite of documentation.

At the Web site `http://sourceforge.net/projects/jboss`, click on the Files menu link to download JBoss 3.0.1. Select the version that is integrated with Tomcat Web server: `jboss-3.0.1_tomcat-4.0.4.zip`. You proceed by selecting the mirror site that is geographically nearest to you. In this appendix, we'll cover the installation of JBoss for the Microsoft Windows 2000 platform. For other platforms, please follow the installation instructions provided by JBoss.

After you've downloaded `jboss-3.0.1_tomcat-4.0.4.zip`, you can unzip it into the directory of your choice. However, we recommend that you use the `c:\` directory of your computer as the installation or home directory for JBoss. We also recommend to rename the directory to a shorter name, such as "`c\jboss3.0.1`" directory to be the `<JBOSS_HOME>`, which you'll use to set up your sample scripts.

By uncompressing the downloaded file, the installation step is completed. Let's now configure the JBoss server.

> The installation step will install not only the JBoss application server, but also the Tomcat Web server under the `catalina` subdirectory.

# Configuring JBoss 3.0

After the installation is completed, you must edit a few configuration parameters before you start running the JBoss server. The main configuration parameter you need to edit is where JBoss can find the Java 1.3 installation directory. Here are the steps required to add the Java installation directory to the JBoss server environment:

> We assume that you already have Java 1.3 installed on your machine. If you have not already done so, download and install the Java SDK 1.3 from `http://java.sun.com/j2se/1.3/download.html`, and select Windows (all languages).

1. Open the file `<JBOSS_HOME>\bin\run.bat` using a text editor such as Notepad.
2. Set your Java home directory by inserting the following line at the beginning of the file (where `c:\java131` is the directory of Java home on your drive):
   ```
   set JAVA_HOME=c:\java131
   ```
3. Save the file with the new setting.

By identifying where Java is located on your machine, you've completed the configuration steps.

# Running and Testing JBoss 3.0

To run and test JBoss, go to the directory <JBOSS_HOME>, and type **run**. For example, if your <JBOSS_HOME> is c:\jboss30, you should open a command window and type the following commands:

`C:\cd \jboss30\bin>`

`C:\jboss30\bin>`**run**

The command window will display all the actions on the screen.

To test the JBoss server, open your browser and enter the URL http://localhost:8080/jmx-console, which will connect to the JBoss server, and should display something similar to Figure B.1.

**FIGURE B.1**

*Testing JBoss.*

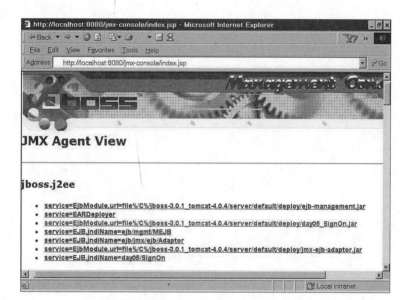

Congratulations! After you have entered your server's configuration parameters in the setEnvJBoss.bat file located in the examples root directory (as per the instructions contained in the README.txt located in the same directory), you can start running the examples provided with this book. For your convenience, we also provide the startJBossServer.bat script from the same examples directory to run the JBoss server.

# APPENDIX C

# Understanding XML

Extensible Markup Language (XML) is a markup language for describing and defining structured data independent from application logic. XML is a subset of the more versatile Standard Generalized Markup Language (SGML), which has been the standard, vendor-independent way to maintain repositories of structured documents for more than a decade. Due to its complexity, SGML is not well suited to serving documents over the Internet. XML was developed to include all the important features of SGML, but to leave behind all the drawbacks. Thus, XML retains the power and flexibility of SGML without any of SGML's complexity.

XML is a project of the World Wide Web Consortium (W3C), and the development of the specification is being driven by the XML Working Group. XML is not a single, predefined markup language; rather, it's a meta language in the sense that it enables you to design your own markup. A markup language is a mechanism to identify structures in a document, such as HTML and RTF.

XML, like HTML, is descended from SGML, and both consist of tags. Unlike HTML, however, XML itself doesn't predefine any tags, rather it provides a way to create user-defined tags and the structural relationships between them.

The semantics of an XML document either will be defined by the applications that process them or by stylesheets. The elements of HTML are used for presentation and display purposes, whereas elements of XML are used to describe structured data and contents. This appendix covers the fundamentals of XML to help you understand the deployment descriptors of EJBs and applications, which were discussed earlier in the book. For more details, we recommend that you refer to the book, *Sams Teach Yourself XML in 24 Hours* (ISBN: 0672322137).

# Exploring an XML Document

The XML specification defines a standard way to add markup to documents. XML users can create their own tags, which relate to their content. Here is an example of an address book, which shows a complete XML document with user-defined tags:

```xml
<?xml version="1.0"?>

<classlist>
  <student gender="m">
    <name>
      <firstname>John</firstname>
      <middleinitial>M</middleinitial>
      <lastname>Doe</lastname>
    </name>
    <address>
      <street>10 Main St.</street>
      <city>Sacramento</city>
      <state>CA</state>
      <zip>95814</zip>
    </address>
    <phone areacode="916">123-4567</phone>
    <email>john.doe@acme.com</email>
  </student>
</classlist>
```

The preceding XML document contains data about a class list, marked up with tags that describe their contents. The `<classlist>` tag is the root tag, and the `<name>`, `<address>`, `<phone>`, and `<email>` tags are used to describe different properties of the `<student>`'s tag. For example, the `<name>` tag consists of the `<firstname>`, `<middleinitial>`, and `<lastname>` tags, which contain the person's first name, middle initial, and last name, respectively.

## Parts of an XML Document

An XML document consists of a prolog and a body. The prolog is used for declarations, and it consists of two internal blocks: the XML version and Document Type Declaration

(DTD). The *XML version* is an optional block, which defines the version of the XML specification used in the document. The XML version is the first line of the document. Here's an example of a version declaration:

```
<?xml version = "1.0" ?>
```

The second block declares the data type declaration used. The DTD block is also optional; it defines a set of rules to which the XML document conforms. DTD will be covered in more detail later in this appendix.

The body of an XML document contains the root element tag that encompasses all other markup used for other contents in the document. The earlier listing is an example of the body section, with the `<classlist>` as the root tag. Figure C.1 depicts all the parts of a XML document.

**FIGURE C.1**

*The parts of an XML document.*

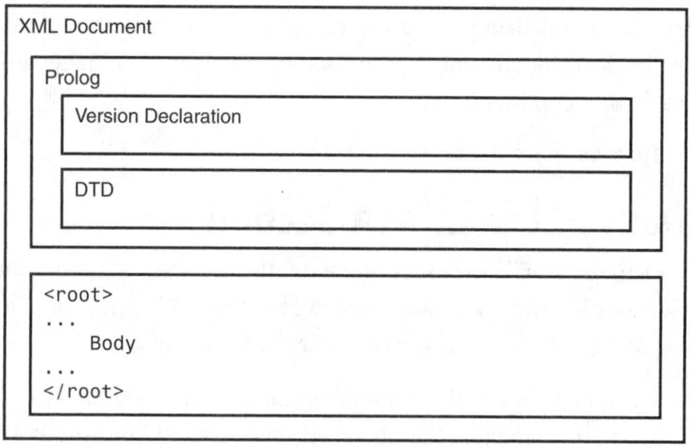

Parts of XML Document

# Summary of XML Document Markups

XML documents are composed of markup and content. Six kinds of markup can occur in an XML document: elements, attributes, comments, marked sections, entity references, and document type declarations. The following sections introduce each of these markup concepts. All the markups are case-sensitive; that means, for example, the tag `<FirstName>` is different from `<firstname>`.

## Building Elements

Elements are the building blocks of an XML document. The content of an element is surrounded by a start tag and an end tag. Some elements may be empty; in which case, they have no content. If an element is not empty, it begins with the start tag, `<element>`, and ends with the end tag, `</element>`. An empty element, however, is represented with a one-tag format, such as `<element/>`. The `<name>`. . .`</name>` tags, in the earlier listing, are an example of an element that contains subelements.

## Adding Attributes

Attributes are name-value pairs that occur inside the start tags of the element. Attributes are additional information to the element. For example, in the start tag `<student gender="m">`, the attribute `gender` with the value `"m"` is added to the `student` element. In XML, all attribute values must be quoted.

## Adding Comments to Your Documents

Comments begin with `"<!--"` and end with `"-->"`. Comments can contain any data except the literal string `"--"`. You can place comments anywhere in your document. When an XML document is processed by a parser, comments are ignored. Here's an example of a comment:

```
<!-- This is just a comment -->
```

## What's in the CDATA Section

In a document, a CDATA section instructs the parser to ignore markup characters within the section; in effect, markup characters within a CDATA section look like comments to the parser. CDATA stands for (unparsed) *character data*.

Consider a mathematical equation, or source code, as content in an XML document. It might contain characters that the XML parser would ordinarily recognize as markup (> and &, for example). To prevent this, a CDATA section can be used. Consider the following example:

```
<![CDATA[
    if (a>5) (b = 3);
]]>
```

All character data between the start of the section, `<![CDATA[`, and the end of the section, `]]>`, is passed directly to the application without parsing.

## Understanding Document Type Declaration

As mentioned earlier, the DTD defines the rules of the XML document. A DTD has a different syntax from that of an XML document.

A DTD can be either an internal or an external file. It can be declared internally within the XML document type declaration block. An externally declared DTD can be stored in a file (here we're using a file named student.dtd), as in the following example:

```
<!DOCTYPE classlist [
<!ELEMENT student (name, address?, phone?, email?)>
<!ELEMENT name (firstname, middleinitial?, lastname)>
<!ELEMENT address (street, city, state, zipcode)>
<!ELEMENT phone (#PCDATA)>
<!ELEMENT email (#PCDATA)>
<!ELEMENT street (#PCDATA)>
<!ELEMENT city (#PCDATA)>
<!ELEMENT state (#PCDATA)>
<!ELEMENT zipcode (#PCDATA)>
<!ATTLIST student gender CDATA #REQUIRED>
<!ATTLIST phone areacode CDATA #REQUIRED>
]>
```

Elements are declared using the <!ELEMENT > tag. Special characters play an important role in DTD syntax. For example, parentheses ( ) are used to group names, and the ? character indicates that the middleinitial name is optional, and can appear once or not at all. PCDATA stands for *parsed character data*. Here's how to use this file in the declaration block of an XML document:

```
<!DOCTYPE classlist SYSTEM "student.dtd">
<classlist>
```

## Including Entity References

In XML, entities are used to represent special characters, which are used to refer to repeated or varying text and to include the content of external files.

Every entity must have a unique name. You can define your own entity in the document declaration section. Here's an example of an entity definition:

```
<!DOCTYPE state[
<!ENTITY ca "California">
]>
```

To use an entity, you simply reference it by name. Entity references begin with an ampersand and end with a semicolon. The following is an example of using the defined entity ca:

```
<state> &ca; </state>
```

The preceding line is equivalent to writing

```
<state> California </state>
```

XML also uses predefined entities, such as &gt; (for the greater than character, >), &lt; (for the less than character, <), and &amp; (for the ampersand, &).

## XML Schema

A DTD is not a typed language because every element is specified as text, and its syntax is not XML-based. An XML schema, on the other hand, is a strongly typed language in which each element can be specified with a type, such as string or integer. It also enables users to define their own types as structures of other types.

An XML schema follows the same syntax as the XML standard. This gives XML more power to handle more data semantics, but without the burden of having to learn a new language's syntax. The trend in the industry today is to use XML schemas instead of DTDs.

# Characteristics of XML Documents

An XML document must be well formed and valid. For a document to be well formed, it must contain a root element, which is unique and surrounds the whole document, and all other elements must be within the root element with no overlapping. There should be no unclosed tags. Every start tag must have an end tag. The address book example earlier is a well-formed document.

A valid document, on the other hand, must be not only well formed, but also have a DTD to which the well-formed document conforms. This means that the XML document must use only the elements that have been declared in the DTD.

Some advantages of XML technology are that it is platform and system independent; enables you to define your own tags; allows multiple displays for the same XML document; supports the Unicode standard; and is easy to understand even for people who don't have any prior knowledge of it. The main disadvantages of XML are the time and expense required in converting the existing information to XML, and that only newer software will be able to read and understand XML.

## Processing XML Documents with XML Parsers

A *parser* is a piece of software that processes the XML document and checks whether it is valid or at least well formed. Several parsers are available today, including Microsoft's MSXML and IBM's XML4J (same as Apache's Xerces).

## Supporting the Unicode Standard

XML supports documents written and authored in languages that aren't Latin-based. Like Java, XML supports the Unicode standard ISO 10646. Unicode is a standard to support most languages on the globe, which some of them have very large character sets. This means you can include structured contents in an XML document using either a single-byte character set (such as English, French, or Hebrew) or a double-byte character set (such as Japanese, Chinese, or Korean). The following declaration is used for documents with the Latin-1 character set (Western European languages):

```
<?xml version = "1.0" encoding="ISO-8859-1"?>
```

For the full XML 1.0 specification, see http://www.w3.org/XML/.

C

# APPENDIX D

# Introduction to UML Notation

UML stands for *Unified Modeling Language*. UML is a widely used notation for describing the analysis, design, and architecture of software systems. It's the modeling language used in visualizing, specifying, building, and documenting software components and applications.

In this appendix, we present the fundamentals of class diagrams, sequence diagrams, and state transition diagrams, which are needed to understand the UML notation used in the book. For more details, we recommend that you to refer to *Sams Teach Yourself UML in 24 Hours* (ISBN: 0672322382).

## Class Diagrams

A class diagram describes the static structure of the system, and provides the domain view of the real-world entities. It consists of classes, their structure, and their relationships to other classes. The following sections describe the notation of a class and the type of relationships that can exist between classes.

# Class Notation

A class represents both the properties (attributes) and the behavior (operations) of a domain entity. In UML, a class is modeled as a solid rectangle with three compartments. The top compartment holds the class name and other general properties of the class. The middle compartment holds a list of attributes. The bottom compartment holds a list of operations.

For example, Figure D.1 shows the `EnrollmentCartEJB` class. It consists of the attributes `ctx` (of type `SessionContext`) and `cart` (of type `HashSet`). The class also contains the operations `addCourses` and `getCourses`. The parameters and return type can be shown for operations. For example, the method `addCourses` accepts the input parameter `courseIds` and returns `void`.

FIGURE D.1

*Class example.*

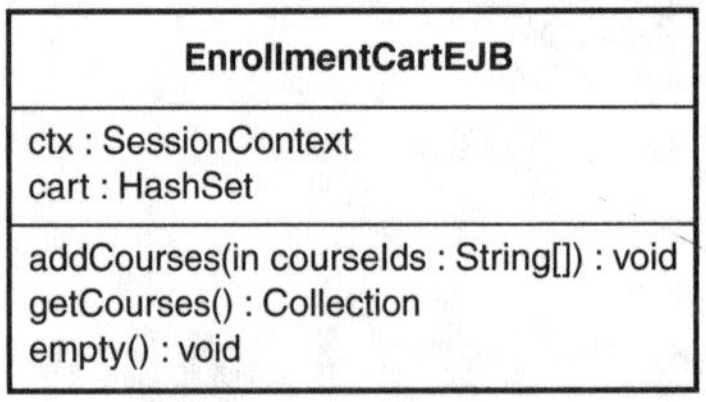

```
+---------------------------------------------+
|              EnrollmentCartEJB              |
+---------------------------------------------+
| ctx : SessionContext                        |
| cart : HashSet                              |
+---------------------------------------------+
| addCourses(in courseIds : String[]) : void  |
| getCourses() : Collection                   |
| empty() : void                              |
+---------------------------------------------+
```

The attribute and operation compartments can be suppressed to reduce detail in an overview.

# Stereotype Notation

A stereotype is an extension of the vocabulary of the UML that enables you to create a new kind of building block. It represents the subclassification of a model element.

A stereotype is shown in angle brackets (<<*name*>>). For example, an interface is displayed by using class notation with the stereotype <<interface>>. Figure D.2 shows `SessionBean` is an interface.

FIGURE D.2

*Stereotype example.*

```
+------------------+
|   «interface»    |
|   SessionBean    |
+------------------+
```

# Generalization/Inheritance Relationship Notation

A generalization relationship between classes shows that the subclass shares the structure or behavior defined in superclasses. A generalization relationship is drawn as a solid line with an arrowhead pointing to the superclass. For example, Figure D.3 shows that `EnrollmentCart` inherits from `EJBObject`.

**FIGURE D.3**

*Generalization relationship example.*

## Association Relationship Notation

An association represents a semantic connection between two classes. Associations are bidirectional. Figure D.4 shows the association between the Person and Company classes.

The association name describes the nature of the relationship. You can also show the direction in which to read the name. Figure D.4 shows the name of the association is works for and also shows the direction in which to read the association.

Association roles describe the "faces" that classes present to each other within an association. Figure D.4 shows the role of the Person is employee and the role of the Company is employer for this association.

Multiplicity indicates how many instances of one class may be associated with a single instance of another class. Multiplicity values are specified in the format *lower-bound..upper-bound*. An unlimited multiplicity value is denoted by an *. Figure D.4 shows that a Person is employed by one Company; a Company employs one or more Persons.

**FIGURE D.4**

*Association relationship example.*

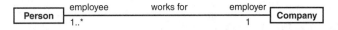

## Aggregation/Composition Relationship Notation

An aggregation relationship is used to show a whole or partial relationship within which one class represents a larger thing that consists of smaller things.

An aggregation relationship is shown as a solid line with a diamond at one end. The diamond end designates the whole thing.

Composition is a special form of aggregation within which the parts are inseparable from the whole. The lifetime of the part is coincident with the lifetime of the whole. A composition relationship is shown as a solid line with a filled diamond at one end.

For example, Figure D.5 shows that OrderEJB is composed of many LineItemEJBs, and that the name of the composition relationship is Order-LineItem.

**FIGURE D.5**

*Composition relation-
ship example.*

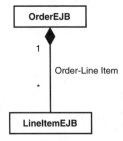

**Realization Relationship Notation**

A *realization* is a relationship between an interface and the class that provides the interface's services. A realized interface is represented by a dashed line with an arrowhead
pointing to the interface.

Figure D.6 shows that the class `EnrollmentCartEJB` implements the interface
`SessionBean`.

**FIGURE D.6**

*Realization relation-
ship example.*

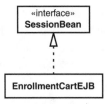

# State Diagrams

A state diagram describes the life history of objects of a given class.

A state diagram is used to show the following:

- The state space of a given class
- The events that cause a transition from one state to another
- The actions that result from a state change

A state diagram is a directed graph of states connected by transitions.

## State Notation

A *state* is a condition in which an object can reside during its lifetime while it satisfies
some condition, performs an activity, or waits for an event. A state icon is a rounded rectangle with a name and a compartment.

For example, Figure D.7 shows the state diagram of a stateful session bean instance. It consists of three states: Instance does not exist, Ready, and Passive.

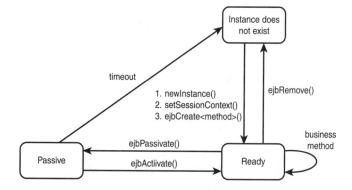

## Transition Notation

A *transition* is a relationship between two states. It indicates that an object in the first state will perform certain actions, and will then enter the second state when a given event occurs. The icon for a state transition is a line with an arrowhead pointing toward the next state. For example, Figure D.7 shows that the object in the Ready state enters the Passive state when the ejbPassivate() event occurs.

# Sequence Diagrams

A sequence diagram describes the dynamic aspects of the software system. A sequence diagram, (also known as an *object interaction diagram* or *OID*) consists of objects (not classes) and their interactions, which are arranged in time sequence. In particular, it shows the objects participating in the interaction and the sequence of the method calls between them.

As shown in Figure D.8, users (also called actors) interact with the system through sending a message (method call) to Object1, which in turn interacts with other objects in a chain reaction. The vertical dotted lines mark the lifelines that are stemmed from each object. Horizontal arrows represent the messages (method calls) including parameters, if any. A sequence diagram always represents a use case or a scenario of the system.

**FIGURE D.8**

*Sequence diagram example.*

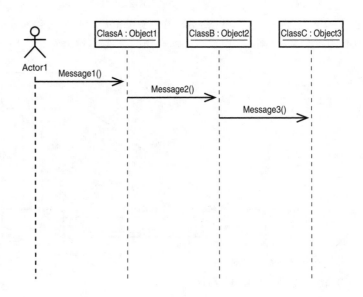

# APPENDIX E

# Glossary of Terms

**abort**   An operation to terminate a transaction in such a way that the values assigned to all protected resources are unchanged from the beginning of the transaction.

**Access Control List (ACL)**   The methods by which interactions with resources are limited to collections of users or programs for the purpose of enforcing integrity, confidentiality, or availability constraints.

**ACID properties**   The acronym for the four properties guaranteed by transactions: atomicity, consistency, isolation, and durability.

**activation**   The process of transferring an enterprise bean from secondary storage to memory. See *passivation*.

**adapter**   A software component that provides an interface from the enterprise application to an enterprise information system (EIS), such as database or legacy system.

**applet**   A Java program that can be downloaded over the network and executed by a browser. In contrast to Java applications, which are loaded from a disk and running on an operating system shell, Java applets are programs that are loaded from a Web site to run on a Web browser.

**applet container**    A container that includes support for the applet programming model, such as a Web browser.

**application assembler**    An EJB role that composes components and modules into larger deployable application units.

**application client**    A client-tier component that executes in its own Java Virtual Machine. Application clients have access to some J2EE platform APIs (JNDI, JDBC, RMI/IIOP, JMS).

**application client container**    A container that supports application clients and provides a federated view of the J2EE platform APIs.

**application client module**    A software unit that consists of one or more classes and an application client deployment descriptor.

**application component**    A server-side component, such as an EJB, JSP, or servlet, that is deployed, managed, and executed on an application server. It can also be a client-side component such as a Java applet.

**Application Programming Interface (API)**    A set of classes and interfaces that specify a particular functionality; for example, the JDBC API.

**application server**    A server that shares and processes application logic and connections to back-end resources. It provides infrastructure with common services to access resources such as databases, ERP applications, and traditional mainframe applications. It also provides a mechanism to deploy J2EE applications.

**asynchronous**    An event that occurs at a time that is unrelated to the time at which another event occurs. The relationship between the times at which they occur is unpredictable.

**atomicity**    A property of a transaction in which all changes made to a database are made permanent; otherwise, all changes are rolled back.

**authentication**    The process used by a server to verify the identity of an entity, such as a user, a process, or a computer.

**authorization**    The process of determining which services may be accessed by a particular entity, such as a user, a process, or a computer, and giving that entity permission to access those services.

**base class**    A class from which other classes or beans are derived. A base class may itself be derived from another base class.

**bean-managed persistence (BMP)**   A relationship in which the transfer of data between an entity bean instance's variables and the underlying resource manager is managed by the entity bean.

**bean-managed transaction (BMT)**   A transaction in which an Enterprise JavaBean (EJB) controls the transaction boundaries. In a bean-managed transaction, controls can be specified using JTA.

**Binary Large Object (BLOB)**   An advanced SQL data type, which is part of SQL-3.

**browser**   An Internet-based tool that enables users to browse Web sites.

**business logic**   The code that implements the functionality of an application. In the EJB architecture, this logic is implemented by the methods of an EJB.

**business method**   A method of an EJB that implements the business logic of an application. Usually defined in the component interface and implemented by the bean class of an EJB.

**bytecode**   The compiled format for Java programs that can be run (interpreted) on any computer with a Java virtual machine (JVM).

**callback method**   The method in a component called by the container to notify the component of important events in its life cycle.

**caller principal**   A principal that is associated with an application component instance during a method invocation. For example, an EJB instance can call the `getCallerPrincipal()` method to get the principal associated with the current security context.

**certificate**   A digital statement that associates a particular public key with a name or other attributes. The statement is digitally signed by a certificate authority (CA).

**certificate authority (CA)**   A well-known and trusted entity that issues public key certificates. A certificate authority attests to a user's real-world identity, somewhat like a notary public.

**Character Large Object (CLOB)**   An advanced SQL data type that is part of SQL-3.

**cipher**   In cryptography, a coding system used to create encrypted messages.

**cipher text**   In cryptography, text that is encrypted.

**class**   A category of objects used in object-oriented programming. A class defines instances and class variables and methods, and specifies the interfaces and class implementations and the immediate super class of the class.

E

**class hierarchy**    The relationships between classes that share a single inheritance. All Java classes inherit from the Object class.

**class method**    A method that is invoked without reference to a particular object. Class methods affect the class as a whole, not a particular instance of the class. Also called a *static method*.

**class variable**    A data item associated with a particular class as a whole—not with particular instances of the class. Also called a *static field*.

**CLASSPATH**    An environmental variable that tells the Java virtual machine where to find the class libraries, including user-defined class libraries.

**client**    A process that remotely accesses resources of a server, which has larger computing power and memory capacity.

**client certificate authentication**    An authentication mechanism in which a client uses an X.509 certificate to establish its identity.

**client/server**    The model of interaction in distributed data processing in which a program at one location sends a request to a program at another location and awaits a response. The requesting program is called the *client*, and the responding program is called the *server*.

**client-side program**    A Java program, usually embedded in an HTML page and viewed with a Web browser.

**cluster**    A group of servers that work together to provide an application platform with more powerful and reliable services than a single server. A cluster appears to its clients as a single server but it is, in fact, a group of servers acting as one. Cluster includes both load-balancing and fail-over capabilities.

**commit**    The operation that ends a transaction and updates the database so that other processes can access any changes made.

**Common Object Request Broker Architecture (CORBA)**    A standard from the Object Management Group (OMG) for communicating between distributed objects. CORBA uses IDLs (interface definition languages) and ORBs (object request brokers), and communicates with IIOP (Internet Inter Operability Protocol).

**compiler**    A program to translate source code into code to be executed by a computer. The Java compiler translates source code written in Java into bytecode to run on the JVM.

**component contract**    The contract between a component and its container. The contract includes life cycle management of the component, a context interface that the instance uses to obtain various information and services from its container, and a list of services that every container must provide for its components.

**components-off-the-shelf (COTS)** Components that are provided by EJB providers to be integrated or assembled together into enterprise applications.

**concurrency** A concept that refers to multiple users or programs simultaneously sharing the same database. Transactions and locks are used to give each of these a consistent view of the database.

**connection** A session with a database opened by a JDBC application program, so-called because it represents a connection between the program and a (usually remote) database. At any one time, only one transaction can be associated with a connection.

**connector** A standard extension mechanism for containers to provide connectivity to enterprise information systems (EIS). A connector is specific to an EIS and consists of a resource adapter and application development tools for EIS connectivity.

**consistency** A successful transaction transforms a database from a previous valid state to a new valid state.

**constructor** A special class method that has the same name as the class and is used to construct and possibly initialize objects of its class type.

**container** An entity that provides life cycle management, security, deployment, and runtime services to components. Each type of container (EJB, Web, JSP, servlet, applet, and application client) also provides component-specific services.

**container-managed relationship (CMR)** A declarative relationship between an entity bean and another entity bean to map the join relationship of data records in a database.

**container-managed persistence (CMP)** Data transfer between an entity bean's variables and a resource manager managed by the entity bean's container.

**container-managed transaction (CMT)** A transaction whose boundaries are defined by an EJB container. An entity bean must use container-managed transactions.

**conversational state** The set of all values of members of a session bean that can be stored by serializing the bean instance.

**cookie** A piece of data that the server creates to store user information on the user's disk.

**credentials** The information describing the security attributes of a principal, such as a password. Credentials can be acquired only through authentication or delegation.

E

**cursor**   A cursor is used to reference the current position in a result set of a SQL operation using JDBC connection.

**Customer Information Control System (CICS)**   An IBM-licensed program that enables transactions entered at remote terminals to be processed concurrently by user-written application programs.

**data abstraction**   A data type with a private representation and a public set of operations. The Java language uses the concept of classes to implement data abstraction.

**data bean**   A type of JavaBean component used to transfer data between the EJB tier and the Web tier. It's also a common design pattern called Value Object.

**Data Definition Language (DDL)**   A subset of SQL commands dealing with database objects. The most common DDL commands are CREATE TABLE and DROP TABLE.

**Data Manipulation Language (DML)**   A subset of SQL commands dealing with database objects. The most common DML commands are SELECT, DELETE, and UPDATE.

**database**   A collection of interrelated or independent data items stored together without redundancy to serve one or more applications.

**database management system (DBMS)**   A program or set of programs that enables users to structure and manipulate the data in the tables of a database. A DMBS ensures privacy, recovery, and integrity of data in a multiuser environment.

**database system**   A shorter term for a database management system (DBMS).

**data type**   A programming classification indicating the type of data in a variable. Some commonly used data types are various forms of integers, character, and Boolean.

**deadlock**   A condition that can occur when two or more users are waiting for each other to give up locks. Advanced DBMSs can detect deadlocks and abort one of the user transactions when this happens.

**declaration**   A statement that establishes an identifier and associates attributes with it, without necessarily reserving its storage (for data) or providing the implementation (for methods).

**decryption**   The process of taking cipher text (encrypted data) and a cryptographic key and producing plain text (the original unencrypted data).

**default**   The value of a variable assumed by a program if a value is not supplied by the user.

**delegation**   The act by which a specific principal authorizes another principal to use its identity or privileges. Such authorization can be granted with restrictions.

**Denial of Service (DoS) attack**   A security attack in which an organization's Web site is deprived of the services it offers, caused by an overwhelming false user requests. For example, an enterprise Web site could be forced to cease operation, thus causing the enterprise a great deal of time and money.

**deployer**   An EJB role that installs modules and J2EE applications into an operational environment.

**deployment**   The process of placing an application into a distributed environment and making the application available for use. Deployment can include such tasks as installation, configuration, and administration of various parts of the application.

**deployment descriptor**   An XML file provided with each J2EE module that describes all the runtime properties of components and how they should be deployed into a specific container. The deployment descriptor is processed by the application server's deployment tool before starting to deploy each component with its supplied parameters.

**deprecation**   Refers to an entity that is no longer recommended by the current specification, and it may no longer exist in a future release.

**digital signature**   A string of bits that is computed from the signed data and private key of an entity. A digital signature can be used to verify that the data came from the entity and was not modified in transit.

**dirty read**   A dirty read occurs when a transaction reads data from a database that has been modified by another transaction, and that data has not yet been committed.

**distributed application**   An application made up of distinct components running in separate runtime environments, usually on different platforms connected via a network. Typical distributed applications are two tier, three tier, and multitier.

**distributed computing**   An application design and implementation strategy that separates an application into units that are executed on different computers and communicate through a network. For example, an application can be separated into three distributed units: a user interface unit, a processing unit, and a storage unit.

**distributed object**   An object that can be located anywhere on a network. Distributed objects are packaged as independent units of code that can be accessed by remote clients via method invocations.

**distributed transaction**   Transactions that are demarcated and coordinated by an external transaction manager via the two-phase commit protocol across multiple resource managers. Also known as a *global transaction*.

E

**distributed transaction processing (DTP)**   A form of processing in which multiple application programs update multiple resources (such as databases) in a coordinated manner. Programs and resources can reside on one or more computers across a network.

**document type definition (DTD)**   A file that defines how the markup tags in SGML and XML documents should be interpreted by the application presenting the document.

**domain**   A collection of servers, services, interfaces, machines, and associated resource managers defined by a single configuration file.

**double-byte character set (DBCS)**   A set of characters in which each character is represented by two bytes, commonly called Unicode. Languages such as Japanese and Chinese, which contain more symbols than can be represented by 256 code points, require double-byte character sets. Compare with *single-byte character set*.

**durability**   Changes that a transaction makes to a database will survive future system or media failures.

**EIS resource**   An entity that provides EIS-specific functionality to its clients. Examples are a record or set of records in a database system, a business object in an ERP system, and a transaction program in a transaction processing system.

**EJB container**   A container that implements the EJB component contract of the J2EE architecture. This contract specifies a runtime environment for enterprise beans that includes security, concurrency, life cycle management, transaction, deployment, and other services. An EJB container is provided by an EJB or J2EE server.

**EJB container provider**   A vendor that supplies an EJB container.

**EJB context**   An object that allows an enterprise bean to invoke services provided by the container and to obtain the information about the caller of a client-invoked method.

**EJB home object**   An object that provides the life cycle operations (create, remove, find) for an enterprise bean.

**EJB module**   A software unit that consists of one or more enterprise beans and an EJB deployment descriptor.

**EJB object**   An object whose class implements the enterprise bean's remote interface. A client never references an enterprise bean instance directly; a client always references an EJB object. The class of an EJB object is generated by the container's deployment tools.

**EJB Query Language (EJB-QL)**   A subset of SQL that is used to write declarative queries of a CMP's methods in the bean's deployment descriptor.

**EJB server**   Software that provides services to an EJB container. The J2EE architecture does not specify the contract between EJB server and container. An EJB server may host one or more EJB containers.

**EJB server provider**   A vendor that supplies the EJB server.

**encapsulation**   The hiding of a software object's internal representation. The object provides an interface that queries and manipulates the data without exposing its underlying structure.

**encryption**   The process of scrambling data to prevent unauthorized disclosure, while still preserving access to the original data by authorized users.

**encryption key pair**   An encryption key pair consists of the public key used to encrypt information and a private key used to decipher the information.

**Enterprise Application Archive (EAR) file**   A JAR archive that contains a J2EE application.

**Enterprise Application Integration (EAI)**   A concept in which all services, applications, and products in an enterprise can be integrated to work together.

**enterprise applications**   Applications written using the Enterprise JavaBeans architecture are scalable, transactional, and secure.

**enterprise bean provider**   An application programmer who produces EJB classes, component and home interfaces, and deployment descriptor files, and packages them in an EJB .jar file.

**enterprise information system (EIS)**   The applications that comprise an enterprise's existing system for handling enterprise-wide information. These applications provide an information infrastructure for an enterprise. An EIS offers a well-defined set of services to its clients. Examples of EIS include enterprise resource planning (ERP) systems, mainframe transaction processing systems, and legacy database systems.

**Enterprise JavaBeans (EJB)**   A component architecture for the development and deployment of object-oriented, distributed, enterprise applications. Applications written using the Enterprise JavaBeans architecture are scalable, transactional, and secure.

**enterprise resource planning (ERP)**   A business management system that integrates all facets of the business, including planning, manufacturing, sales, and marketing.

**entity bean**   A type of EJB that represents persistent data maintained in a database. An entity bean can manage its own persistence or it can delegate this function to its container. An entity bean is transactional, and is identified by a primary key. The main two categories of an entity bean are BMP and CMP.

E

**environment variable**  A string of specific value that controls a certain attribute of an application. An environment variable is made available to the application as it starts.

**exception**  An event during program execution that prevents the program from continuing normally; generally, an error. The Java programming language supports exceptions with the try, catch, and throw keywords.

**exception handler**  A block of code that reacts to a specific type of exception. If the exception is for an error that the program can recover from, the program can resume executing after the exception handler has executed.

**Extensible Markup Language**  See *XML.*

**failover**  The ability to transparently handle failure of a service invocation by handing the request off to another service provider.

**firewall**  A firewall monitors traffic between an internal network and the Internet and regulates the type of network traffic that can pass through it.

**foreign key**  A foreign key is an attribute of a table that is used to refer to rows of another table. The attribute value is the primary key value of the other table.

**form-based authentication**  An authentication mechanism in which a Web container provides an application-specific form for logging in.

**garbage collection (GC)**  The automatic detection and freeing of memory that is no longer in use. The Java runtime system performs garbage collection so that programmers never explicitly free objects.

**global transaction**  See *distributed transaction.*

**graphical user interface (GUI)**  Refers to the techniques involved in using graphics, along with a keyboard and a mouse, to provide an easy-to-use interface to some program.

**group**  A set of users that share some characteristics. An ACL can assign permissions to a group, which are applied by default to each user of that group.

**home handle**  An object that can be used to obtain a reference of the EJB's home interface. A home handle can be serialized and stored to stable storage and deserialized to obtain the reference.

**home interface**  One of two interfaces (the home interface and the component interface) for an enterprise bean. The home interface defines zero or more methods for creating and removing an enterprise bean.

**host**  A computer that is attached to a network and provides services other than acting as a communication switch.

**HTTPS**   HTTP layered over the SSL protocol.

**Hypertext Markup Language (HTML)**   The basic language that is used to build hypertext documents on the World Wide Web. It is used in basic, plain ASCII-text documents, but when those documents are processed by a Web browser, the document can display formatted text, color, a variety of fonts, graphics images, special effects, hypertext jumps to other Internet locations, and information forms.

**Hypertext Transfer Protocol (HTTP)**   The Internet protocol, based on TCP/IP, used to fetch hypertext objects from remote hosts.

**infrastructure**   A set of hardware, software, components, and services that support enterprise computing and applications needs.

**inheritance**   A mechanism by which a class can use the attributes and methods defined in its base (super) classes.

**instance method**   Any method that is invoked with respect to an instance of a class. Also called simply a *method*. See also *class method*.

**instance variable**   A data item that is associated with a particular object. Each instance of a class has its own copy of the instance variables defined in the class. See also *class variable*.

**integrated development environment (IDE)**   A programming environment integrated into an application. Examples include JBuilder, Visual Age, and Visual Cafe.

**integration**   The ability of applications to share information or to process independently by requesting services and satisfying service requests. In a well-integrated system, all the parts have a purpose, and the parts combine effectively to achieve the purpose of the overall system.

**interface**   A set of methods defined (declared with its signatures) to be accessed by any class in the class hierarchy.

**Interface Definition Language (IDL)**   APIs written in Java that provide standards-based interoperability and connectivity with CORBA.

**internationalization**   The preparation of software for proper behavior in multiple locales and foreign languages.

**Internet**   A network of networks, consisting of literally millions of hosts around the world. This network uses the TCP family of protocols to communicate.

**Internet Interoperability Protocol (IIOP)**   The protocol used by CORBA clients to communicate with ORBs over the Internet.

**Internet Protocol (IP)**    One of the protocols in the TCP family. IP specifies the format of messages (called *packets*) and the addressing scheme.

**interpreter**    A module that alternately decodes and executes every statement in some body of code. The Java interpreter decodes and executes bytecode for the Java virtual machine. See also *compiler*.

**intranet**    A private network, inside a company or organization, that uses the same kinds of software that you would find on the public Internet.

**invocation**    The process of performing a method call on a distributed object, with or without knowledge of the object's location on the network.

**IP multicast**    A network protocol used in sending out data to distributed servers sharing one subnet. An unreliable packet delivery service supported by all operating systems and most routers, and used in clustering services.

**isolation**    Changes that a transaction makes to a database are not visible to other operations until the transaction completes its work.

**isolation level**    See *transaction isolation level*.

**J2EE application**    Any deployable unit of J2EE functionality. This can be a single module or a group of modules packaged into an .ear file with a J2EE application deployment descriptor. J2EE applications are typically engineered to be distributed across multiple computing tiers.

**J2EE architecture**    Enterprise architecture, based on Java 2, that is used to develop, deploy, and manage enterprise applications. It provides a component-based framework, and infrastructure services through a set of unified APIs.

**J2EE connector architecture (JCA)**    An architecture for integration of J2EE products with enterprise information systems (EISs).

**J2EE product provider**    A vendor that supplies a J2EE product.

**J2EE server**    The runtime portion of a J2EE product. A J2EE server provides Web container and/or EJB container.

**J2EE tool provider**    An organization or software vendor that provides tools used for the development, packaging, and deployment of J2EE applications.

**JAR Java Archive (JAR) file**    A platform-independent file format that permits many files to be aggregated into one file.

**Java**    An object-oriented programming language developed by Sun Microsystems, Inc. A write-once, run-anywhere programming language.

**Java 2 Platform, Enterprise Edition (J2EE platform)**   An environment for developing and deploying enterprise applications. The J2EE platform consists of a set of services, application programming interfaces (APIs), and protocols that provide the functionality for developing multi-tiered, Web-based applications.

**Java 2 Platform, Micro Edition (J2ME)**   J2ME is the Java platform technology developed for consumer wireless devices.

**Java 2 Platform, Standard Edition (J2SE platform)**   The core Java technology platform.

**Java API for XML Processing (JAXP)**   A Java package that is used to parse XML documents in Java applications.

**Java Authentication and Authorization Service (JAAS)**   A Java package that enables services to authenticate and enforce the use of access controls upon users.

**Java Database Connectivity (JDBC)**   An industry standard for database-independent connectivity between the Java platform and a wide range of databases.

**Java Development Kit (JDK)**   A software development environment for writing applets and applications in the Java programming language.

**Java Management Extensions (JMX)**   Java standard API for application management.

**Java Message Service (JMS)**   The Java standard API used to access message-oriented middleware (MOM) by enterprise applications. Includes messaging products such as IBM's MQ Series.

**Java Naming and Directory Interface (JNDI)**   The Java standard API for accessing directory services, such as LDAP, COS Naming, and others.

**Java Remote Method Invocation (RMI)**   A distributed object model for Java program to Java program, in which the methods of remote objects written in the Java programming language can be invoked from other Java virtual machines, possibly on different hosts.

**Java Runtime Environment (JRE)**   A runtime version of the Java Development Kit (JDK) for end users and developers who want to redistribute only the runtime environment. It consists of the JVM, the Java core classes, and supporting files.

**Java Security Manager**   Works with the Java API to define security boundaries and enabling programmers to establish a custom security policy for their Java applications.

**Java Transaction API (JTA)**   A high-level application transaction interface and a Java mapping to XA. Allows an application to control user transaction boundaries through the use of the two-phase commit protocol.

**Java Transaction Service (JTS)** Specifies the implementation of a transaction manager that supports JTA and implements the Java mapping of the OMG Object Transaction Service (OTS) 1.1 specification at the level below the API.

**Java Virtual Machine (JVM)** A software execution engine that safely and compatibly executes the bytecodes in Java class files on a microprocessor (whether in a computer or in another electronic device).

**Java Web Server** A secure, platform-independent HTTP server to speed and simplify the deployment and management of Internet and intranet Web sites.

**JavaBean Activation Framework (JAF)** A Java package to support for MIME (Multipurpose Internet Mail Exchange) data types. It's required by the JavaMail API.

**JavaBeans** JavaBeans is a portable, platform-independent component model written in Java.

**Javadoc** A tool that generates API documentation in HTML format from comments in Java source code.

**JavaMail** An API for sending and receiving email, used by Java applications.

**JavaServer Pages (JSP)** An extensible Web technology that uses template data, custom elements, scripting languages, and server-side Java objects to return dynamic content to a client. Typically, the template data is HTML or XML elements; in many cases, the client is a Web browser.

**JDBC driver** A Java program that implements the JDBC interface. It is loaded by the JDBC driver manager.

**JDBC-ODBC bridge** General database connectivity through the ODBC client library, created as a joint project between Intersolve and JavaSoft. Allows Java connectivity to any relational database.

**JMS queue** A simple data structure to send/receive asynchronous messages from one client to another. See *point-to-point*.

**JMS topic** A simple data structure to publish/subscribe asynchronous delivery of messages from one client to another. See *point-to-point*.

**JSP** See *JavaServer Pages*.

**JSP action** A JSP element that can act on implicit objects and other server-side objects or can define new scripting variables.

**JSP application** A Web application, written using the JSP technology, that can contain JSP pages, servlets, HTML files, images, applets, and JavaBeans components.

**JSP container** A container that provides the same services as a servlet container and an engine that interprets and processes JSP pages into a servlet.

**JSP declaration** A JSP scripting element that declares methods, variables, or both, in a JSP file.

**JSP directive** A JSP element that gives an instruction to the JSP container and is interpreted at translation time.

**JSP element** A portion of a JSP page that is recognized by a JSP translator. An element can be a directive, an action, or a scripting element.

**JSP expression** A scripting element that contains a valid scripting language expression that is evaluated, converted to a string, and placed into the implicit out object.

**JSP file** A file named with a .jsp extension that contains standard HTML tags, core JSP tags, custom JSP tags, and scripting language statements in order to display dynamic pages in a Web browser.

**JSP page** A text-based document using fixed template data and JSP elements that describes how to process a request to create a response.

**JSP scripting element** A JSP declaration, scriptlet, or expression, whose tag syntax is defined by the JSP specification, and whose content is written according to the scripting language used in the JSP page.

**JSP scriptlet** A JSP scripting element containing any code fragment that is valid in the scripting language used in the JSP page.

**JSP tag** A piece of text between a left angle bracket and a right angle bracket that is used in a JSP file as part of a JSP element.

**JSP tag library** A collection of tags identifying custom actions described via a tag library descriptor (TLD) and Java classes. It can be imported into any JSP file and used with various scripting languages.

**just-in-time (JIT) compiler** A compiler that converts all the bytecode into native machine code just as a Java program is run. This results in run-time speed improvements over code that is interpreted by a Java virtual machine.

**legacy application** An application, often internally developed, on which an organization has invested considerable time and money. Legacy applications may exist with many other similar legacy applications in a centralized environment. While most legacy applications run on mainframes; minicomputers and some large Unix systems can be considered legacy systems using internally developed legacy applications.

E

**Lightweight Directory Access Protocol (LDAP)**   A set of protocols for accessing information directories. These directories can be physically distributed across multiple systems for access by many applications within an enterprise. LDAP is based on the standards contained within the X.500 standard, but is significantly simpler.

**load balancing**   A mechanism to distribute processing and communications activity evenly across a computers sharing the same load. It is part of clustering technology offered by application server vendors.

**local interface**   One of two interfaces for an EJB. The local interface defines the business methods callable by a local client. See *remote interface*.

**local transaction**   A transaction that accesses a single database or file and is controlled by a single, local resource manager as a transaction participant.

**lock**   Locks allow a database transaction to mark data (for example, rows or tables) it is using to exclude a concurrent user from performing certain operations on the same data.

**man-in-the-middle attack**   An attack in which an enemy inserts a machine into a network, and then captures, possibly modifies, and retransmits all messages between two parties.

**message**   A formula for sending data and values across applications. It consists of a header, containing message ID data, and a body containing user-defined information.

**message-driven bean (MDB)**   A type of EJB that handle asynchronous messages received from JMS destination. The message-driven bean selects an instance from a pool to process the message.

**message-oriented middleware (MOM)**   A product used to deliver asynchronous messages from one application to another.

**metadata**   Data about data. It describes, for example, the types of data in the database schema.

**method**   A procedure associated with a class or interface, defining one of the legal operations on instances of the class or interface.

**method call**   A communication from one object to another that requests the receiving object to execute a method. It consists of a method name that indicates the requested method and the arguments to be used in executing the method.

**method permission**   An authorization rule that determines who is permitted to execute one or more EJB methods. It can be specified in the EJB's deployment descriptor.

**Model-View-Controller (MVC)**   An architecture pattern that provides separation of application parts into more independent layers, which can be separately developed, and managed.

**module**   A software unit that consists of one or more J2EE components of the same container type and one deployment descriptor of that type.

**multithreading**   The ability of an operating system to execute different parts of an application, called *threads*, at the same time, allowing the application to perform multiple tasks simultaneously.

**multitier**   An application architecture that includes clients (one tier), middleware (one or more tiers), and brokers, application servers, and other kinds of resources suppliers (one or more tiers).

**mutual authentication**   An authentication mechanism employed by two parties for the purpose of proving each other's identity to one another.

**name binding**   The association of a name with an object reference. Name bindings are stored in a naming context.

**naming context**   A set of associations between distinct, atomic, human-readable identifiers and objects.

**nonrepeatable read**   Data returned by a SQL query that would be different if the query were repeated within the same transaction. Nonrepeatable reads can occur when other users are updating the same data you're reading.

**object**   The building blocks of object-oriented programs. An object is a programming unit consists of data (instance variables) and functionality (instance methods). See also *class*.

**object request broker (ORB)**   A CORBA term designating the means by which objects transparently make requests and receive responses from objects, whether they are local or remote.

**Object Transaction Service (OTS)**   A definition of the interfaces that permit CORBA objects to participate in transactions.

**object-oriented programming (OOP)**   A programming approach based on the concepts of data abstraction, inheritance, and polymorphism.

**online transaction processing (OLTP)**   A method of assuring the integrity of each database transaction, usually through a process called two-phase commit.

**Open Database Connectivity (ODBC)**    A Microsoft-developed C database API that allows access to database management systems using SQL.

**open system**    A system that implements specified common standards across different computer vendors. Implementing open system standards for communication allows computers from different vendors to communicate with each other.

**operation**    A method or service that can be requested of an object.

**overloading**    An object-oriented programming technique that allows redefinition of methods when the methods are used with class types.

**overriding**    Providing a different implementation of a method in a subclass of the class that originally defined the method.

**package**    A program element that contains related classes and interfaces.

**parametric authorization**    The ability to perform authorization decisions on protected resources taking the context and target of the business request into account.

**parent class**    Same as *base class* or *super class*.

**passivation**    The process of transferring an enterprise bean from memory to secondary storage. See *activation*.

**permission**    Defines access to a system resource. In order to allow access to a resource, the corresponding permission must be explicitly granted to the principal attempting access. This is ability to carry out certain operations on certain objects, as defined in an access control list.

**persistence**    The protocol for transferring the state of an entity bean between its instance variables and an underlying data elements in a database.

**phantom read**    A condition occurs when your program fetches a record that has been inserted by another user's transaction, and the other transaction subsequently aborts, erasing the record you fetched.

**platform**    The combination of system hardware and software that supports an application.

**plug-in**    A software module that adds functionality to a larger application.

**point-to-point (PTP)**    A JMS messaging paradigm or model that send and receive asynchronous messages, which are exchanged through a queue. See *JMS queue*.

**portability**    To transfer a program from one hardware or software environment to another by rewriting sections of the code that are machine dependent, and then recompiling the program on the new environment.

**primary key**   An attribute or set of attributes that are unique among rows of a table. A table's primary key is used to refer to rows of the table.

**principal**   The identity assigned to an entity as a result of authentication.

**private key**   An encryption/decryption key known only to the party or parties that exchange secure messages.

**privilege**   A security attribute that does not have the property of uniqueness and that may be shared by many principals.

**process**   A collection of code, data, and other system resources, including at least one thread of execution, that performs a data processing task.

**protocol**   A set of rules that govern the format and timing of messages sent and received over a communication link. For example, TCP/IP, RMI, and IIOP are protocols.

**proxy**   To transfer data processing tasks to another program or device.

**proxy server**   A proxy server sends requests to another server for processing, which is invisible to the end user.

**pub/sub**   A JMS messaging paradigm or model that publish and subscribe asynchronous messages, which are exchanged through a topic. See *JMS topic*.

**public key**   A value provided by a certificate authority that, combined with a private key, can be used to encrypt and decrypt messages.

**public key algorithm**   An algorithm for encrypting or decrypting data with a public or private key. A private key is typically used to encrypt a message digest; in such an application, the public key algorithm is called a message digest encryption algorithm. A public key is typically used to encrypt a content-encryption key, or session key; in such an application, the public key algorithm called a key-encryption algorithm. An example of a public key algorithm is RSA.

**query**   A SQL SELECT statement.

**realm**   A domain for a set of security attributes. The realm organizes security information and defines its range of operations. A realm has its own idea of principals and permissions.

**record**   A row of a table or a row of the result set returned by a query. Also called *tuple*.

**recovery**   In transaction systems, after a failure, the ability to restore the system to the most recently committed, and therefore consistent, state.

E

**re-entrant EJB**   An enterprise bean that can handle multiple simultaneous, interleaved, or nested invocations that will not interfere with each other.

**reference**   A data element whose value is an address.

**referential integrity**   Correctness of foreign keys among table of a database. A DBMS maintains referential integrity by ensuring that there exists a row in the referenced table for every reference to the table.

**relation**   A table, the basic data structure of the relational model.

**relational database management system (RDBMS)**   DBMS for a relational database model.

**reliability**   The extent to which a system produces the correct output on repeated trials while meeting the performance requirement.

**remote interface**   One of two interfaces for an EJB. The remote interface defines the business methods callable by a remote client. See *local interface*.

**remote method invocation (RMI)**   A technology that allows an object running in one Java virtual machine to invoke methods on an object running in a different Java virtual machine.

**remote procedure call (RPC)**   Executing what looks like a normal procedure call (or method invocation) by sending network packets to some remote host.

**remove method**   Method defined in the home interface and invoked by a client to destroy an enterprise bean.

**resource adapter (RA)**   A system-level software driver that is used by an EJB container or an application client to connect to an EIS. A resource adapter is typically specific to an EIS. It is available as a library and is used within the address space of the server or client using it.

**Resource Adapter Archive (RAR)**   A compressed .rar file used to load classes and other files required to run a resource adapter on a resource manager. An interface and associated software that provides access to a collection of information and processes; for example, a database management system.

**resource manager**   Provides access to a set of shared resources. A resource manager participates in transactions that are controlled and coordinated by a transaction manager. A resource manager is typically in different address space or on a different machine from the clients that access it.

**resource manager connection**   An object that represents a session with a resource manager.

**resource manager connection factory**   An object used for creating a resource manager connection.

**RMI/IIOP**   A version of RMI implemented to use the CORBA IIOP protocol. RMI over IIOP provides interoperability with CORBA objects.

**role (development)**   The function performed by a party in the development and deployment phases of an application developed using J2EE technology.

**role (security)**   An abstract logical grouping of users that is defined by the application assembler. When an application is deployed, the roles are mapped to security identities, such as principals or groups, in the operational environment.

**role mapping**   The process of associating the groups and/or principals recognized by the container to security roles specified in the deployment descriptor. Security roles have to be mapped by the deployer before the component is installed in the server.

**rollback**   The point in a transaction when all updates to any resources involved in the transaction are reversed.

**scalability**   The extent to which developers can apply a solution to problems of different sizes. Ideally, a solution should work well across the entire range of complexity. In practice, however, there are usually simpler solutions for problems of lower complexity.

**schema**   A description of the tables in a database, their attributes, and their relationships. Every database is an instance of some schema.

**Secure Sockets Layer (SSL)**   A protocol that allows communication between a Web browser and a server to be encrypted for privacy.

**security attributes**   A set of properties associated with a principal. Security attributes can be associated with a principal by an authentication protocol and/or by a J2EE product provider.

**security context**   An object that encapsulates the shared state information regarding security between two entities.

**security permission**   A mechanism, defined by J2SE, used by the J2EE platform to express the programming restrictions imposed on application component providers.

**security policy**   The data that defines what protection a system's security service must provide. There are many kinds of security policies. For example, access control policy and audit policy.

**serialize**   A way to pass objects from one JVM to another. Objects must be serialized before they are sent.

**servlet**   A server-side Java component that is usually executed in response to an HTTP request and produces its output in a browser.

**servlet container**   A container that provides the network services over which requests and responses are sent, decodes requests, and formats responses. All servlet containers must support HTTP as a protocol for requests and responses, but may also support additional request-response protocols, such as HTTPS.

**servlet context**   An object that contains a servlet's view of the Web application within which the servlet is running. Using the context, a servlet can log events, obtain URL references to resources, and set and store attributes that other servlets in the context can use.

**session**   An object used by a servlet to track a user's interaction with a Web application across multiple HTTP requests.

**session bean**   A session bean is a transient EJB instance that serves a single client. Session beans tend to implement procedural logic.

**Simple API for XML (SAX)**   An event-driven, serial-access mechanism for accessing XML documents.

**Simple Object Access Protocol (SOAP)**   SOAP provides a way for applications to communicate with each other over the Internet, independent of platform. Unlike OMG's IIOP, SOAP uses XML over HTTP in order to penetrate server firewalls. SOAP relies on XML to define the format of the information and then adds the necessary HTTP headers to send it.

**single-byte character set**   A set of characters in which each character is represented by a one-byte code, commonly called ASCII.

**skeleton**   A server-side representation of a remote object that takes serialized requests from a stub, deserializes and unpacks it, and submits it as a method call to be invoked on the object's implementation. The server-side skeleton is responsible for deserializing and unpacking the request from its companion client-side stub.

**socket**   A low-level endpoint of communication to which a name may be bound. The logical endpoint of a TCP/IP connection. An application accesses a TCP/IP connection through a socket.

**SQL/J**   A set of standards that includes specifications for embedding SQL statements in methods in the Java programming language and specifications for calling Java static methods as SQL stored procedures and user-defined functions.

**SQL-93**   The version of SQL standardized by ANSI in 1993. Sometimes called *SQL-3*.

**stack trace**   Java exceptions can be logged to a stack trace file that can be used for debugging.

**Standardized Generalized Markup Language (SGML)**   An ISO/ANSI/ECMA standard that specifies a way to annotate text documents with information about types of sections of a document.

**stateful session bean**   This Java bean maintains state on behalf of a specific client. It can be used to manage a process through multiple interactions.

**stateless session bean**   A session bean with no conversational state. All instances of a stateless session bean are identical.

**stored procedure**   A procedure that is part of a relational database.

**Structured Query Language (SQL)**   The standardized relational database language for defining database objects and manipulating data.

**stub**   A client-side representation of a remote object that is used to invoke methods on the implementation of the remote object. Defines the interface to the remote object implementation of an object. The stub is responsible for packaging up the client request, serializing it, and shipping it to the companion skeleton on the server side.

**subclass**   A class that is derived from a particular class, perhaps with one or more classes in between. See also *base class*, *parent class*, and *superclass*.

**subject**   Represents a grouping of related information for a single entity, such as a person. Such information includes the subject's identities as well as its security-related attributes (for example, passwords and cryptographic keys). Subjects may potentially have multiple identities.

**superclass**   A class from which a particular class is derived, perhaps with one or more classes in between. See also *subclass* and *subtype*.

**system administrator**   An EJB role that is responsible for configuring and administering the enterprise's computers, networks, and software systems.

**thin client**   A system that runs a very light operating system with no local system administration and executes applications delivered over the network.

**thread**   The basic unit of program execution. A process can have several threads running concurrently, each performing a different job, such as waiting for events or performing a time-consuming job that the program doesn't need to complete before going on.

**three-tier JDBC driver**   A driver that implements the JDBC API by making calls to a middle-tier server that translates the calls into DBMS-specific protocols and makes the calls to the DBMS server.

**throws**   A Java programming language keyword used in method declarations that specify which exceptions are not handled within the method but rather passed to the next higher level of the program.

**time-to-live (TTL)**   An attribute of a JMS message that specifies how long the message will survive, before it expires, and then will be removed from the system.

**transaction**   A complete unit of work that transforms a database from one consistent state to another.

**transaction attribute**   A value specified in an EJB's deployment descriptor that is used by the EJB container to control the transaction scope when the enterprise bean's methods are invoked. A transaction attribute can have the following values: `Required`, `RequiresNew`, `Supports`, `NotSupported`, `Mandatory`, `Never`.

**transaction isolation level**   The degree to which the intermediate state of the data being modified by a transaction is visible to other concurrent transactions and data being modified by other transactions is visible to it.

**transaction manager**   Provides the services and management functions required to support transaction demarcation, transactional resource management, synchronization, and transaction context propagation, among different resource managers using XA two-phase commit protocol (2PC).

**Transmission Control Protocol based on IP (TCP/IP)**   This is an Internet protocol that provides for the reliable delivery of streams of data from one host to another. See also *IP*.

**two-phase commit (2PC)**   A method of coordinating a single transaction across more than one resource manager. 2PC guarantees data integrity by ensuring that transactional updates are committed in all the participating databases, or are fully rolled back out of all the databases, reverting to the state prior to the start of the transaction.

**two-tier architecture**   A client/server relationship in which the user interface runs on the client and the database is stored on the server. The actual application logic can run on either the client or the server.

**two-tier JDBC driver**   A JDBC driver that translates JDBC calls directly into a DBMS vendor's specific protocol.

**Unicode**   A 16-bit character encoding scheme used to display, process, and exchange text written in most of the world's languages. In Java, strings are Unicode by default.

**Unified Modeling Language (UML)**   A widely used notation for analysis, design, implementation, and test of object oriented software.

**uniform resource identifier (URI)** A compact string of characters for identifying an abstract or physical resource. A URI is either a URL or a URN.

**uniform resource locator (URL)** Used for identifying and locating resources over the Internet.

**uniform resource name (URN)** A unique identifier that identifies an entity but doesn't tell where it is located. A system can use a URN to look up an entity locally before trying to find it on the Web.

**unit of work (UOW)** Synonym of *transaction*.

**Universal Description Discovery and Integration (UDDI)** Provides a global, public, XML-based, online business registry where businesses register and advertise their web services. UDDI defines an Internet version of the white and yellow pages in a telephone directory.

**university registration system (URS)** Sample J2EE application provided on Day 21 of this book. Excerpts from URS are used to demonstrate the examples written for some lessons.

**View bean** A type of JavaBean component used to transfer data between the Web tier and the Client tier.

**warning** An exceptional condition that does not interrupt execution of an application program, such as truncation of data values. JDBC provides a `getWarnings()` method to obtain this information.

**Web application** An application written for the Internet, including HTML, and those built with Java technologies such as JavaServer Pages and servlets.

**Web Archive (WAR) file** A JAR archive that contains a Web module.

**Web component** A component that provides services in response to requests; either a servlet, a JSP page, or a Tag Library.

**Web container** A container that implements the Web component contract of the J2EE architecture. This contract specifies a runtime environment for Web components that includes security, concurrency, life cycle management, transaction, deployment, and other services.

**Web module** A unit that consists of one or more Web components and a Web deployment descriptor.

**Web server** Software that provides services to access the Internet, an intranet, or an extranet. A Web server hosts Web sites, provides support for HTTP and other protocols,

E

and executes server-side programs (such as CGI scripts or servlets) that perform certain functions. In the J2EE architecture, a Web server provides services to a Web container.

**Web Services**   Loosely coupled software components capable of collaborating with each other over multiple networks to deliver a specific result to an end user. In the process, they leverage an emerging group of standards that govern their description and interaction, including SOAP (Simple Object Access Protocol), UDDI (Universal Discovery and Description Initiative), XML (Extensible Markup Language), and WSDL (Web Services Description Language).

**Web Services Description Language (WSDL)**   An XML-based specification to describe Web services.

**World Wide Web (WWW)**   The web of systems and the data in them that is the Internet. See also *Internet*.

**X.509**   A standard that specifies the format of certificates, which provide a way to securely associate a name to a public key, providing strong authentication.

**XA interface**   The XA interface is the bi-directional interface between a transaction manager and resource managers. The XA interface within JTA allows a transaction manager to control transaction boundaries for operations performed by multiple resource managers using the two-phase commit X/Open XA protocol.

**XML (Extensible Markup Language)**   A markup language that allows you to define the tags (markup) needed to identify the data and text in XML documents. J2EE deployment descriptors are expressed in XML.

**XML schema**   A document that defines valid contents for an XML document. A schema definition is more specific than a DTD, and provides much finer-grained control over content.

# INDEX

## Symbols

**2PC protocol (two-phase commit protocol), 384-386**

## A

**abstract persistent schema, 163**
  CMP entity beans, 254
**Access Control Lists.**
  *See* ACLs
**accessing**
  EJB (servlets), 136
  entity beans (clients), 239-240
  MDB, 336
  stateless session beans, 98

**accessor methods (container-managed relationships), 274**
**ACID properties, 378**
  atomic, 378
  consistent, 378
  durable, 378
**ACID properties, isolated, 378**
**ACLs (Access Control Lists), 78, 465**
**activation, 57**
  entity beans, 166
**adding JNDI entries, 70**
**Address class (JavaMail), 494, 497**
**administered objects (JMS)**
  ConnectionFactory, 306
  Destination, 306
**administration**
  approving orders, 532
  permissions, 465
  security, 469

**aggregation/composition relationship notation (UML), 561**
**algorithms (session beans), 32, 52**
**analyzing enterprise applications, 524**
**API (application-level programming), 68**
  J2EE, 365
  JavaMail, 494
  JNDI, 68
**Applet container (J2EE), 361**
**applets, 13**
**application assembler, 26**
**application client modules (J2EE), 371**
**application development roles, 26**

object view, 158
passivation, 166
persistent fields, 162
queries, 164
relational databases, 159
relationship fields, 163
removing, 171
sharing, 158
SQL statements, 230
synchronizing, 170
**environment parameters (JNDI), 77**
**errors (JMS), 306**
**examples**
abstract persistent schema, 163
architecting applications, 524
BMP deployment descriptors, 237-238
BMT, 458
client accessing entity beans, 264-265
CMP entity beans, 250, 259-263
CMT rollbacks, 416
component interface, 36
components, 527
container-managed relationships, 299
container-managed transactions, 393
creating university enrollment cart (stateful session beans), 55-56
DAO, 222, 231-235
developing with BMT, 450
developing with CMT, 421-430

distributed transactions, 388, 394-401
ejb-jar.xml file, 42
enterprise application, 521-534
Enterprise JavaBean classes, 36-37
entity bean business logic, 169
entity bean methods, 172-173
home interface, 35
implementing EJB bean classes, 251-253
JAAS (Java Authentication and Authorization Service), 484
JavaBeans, 147
JavaMail application, 507-512, 514
JDBC skeleton code, 201, 208
JMS body types, 326
JMS headers, 324
JMS local transactions, 321
JNDI context operations, 73, 75
JSP, 137-138
JSP taglibs, 143
local transaction, 198
looking up EJB components (JNDI), 81
looking up JavaMail sessions (JNDI), 82
looking up JDBC connection pools (JNDI), 81
looking up JMS destination (JNDI), 81

looking up JTA user transactions (JNDI), 82
MDB, 327, 343-346
MDB deployment descriptor, 339-341
message-driven beans, 34
PTP messaging models, 307
running BMP, 242
servlets, 126-128
session bean algorithms, 52
stateful session beans, 54, 107, 119
University Registration System application, 28, 530-533
user authentication (JNDI), 78
verifying orders, 337-339
XML tags, 552
**exception handling**
JDBC, 190
JMS, 318
JTA, 389
**exception implicit object (JSP), 142**
**exceptions (JSP), 143**
application exceptions, 90
BMT, 449
system-level, 449
handling, 143
predefined, 224
stateless session beans, 92
system exceptions, 90
**execute() method, 193**
**executeQuery() method, 195-196**
**expressions, executing, 141**
**Extensible Markup Language. *See* XML**

remote interfaces, 38-39
  BMP, 221-223
  BMT, 450
  calling semantics, 41
  CMP entity beans, 250
  CMT, 422
  comparing with local, 40
  container-managed rela-
    tionships, 282-283
  javax.ejb.EJBObject inter-
    face, 39
  stateful session beans,
    108-110
  stateless session beans, 89
remote method invocation
  (common vertical ser-
  vices), 23
remote objects (RMI), 38
remove method, 171
removing
  entity beans, 171
  servlets, 126
  session beans, 32
  stateful session beans, 63,
    121
repeatable read (transac-
  tions), 381
replication, 363
replying (JavaMail mes-
  sages), 502
Request implicit object
  (JSP), 142
resource adapter modules
  (J2EE), 371
resource factory, subcon-
  texts, 79
resource managers (trans-
  actions), 387
resource pooling, common
  vertical services, 23

resources (security), 464
Response implicit object
  (JSP), 142
restoring beans, 57
restrictions
  containers, 44
ResultSet interface
  (JDBC), 185
ResultSet methods, 194
ResultSetMetaData inter-
  face (JDBC), 185
RMI (Java Remote Method
  Invocation), 16, 38, 361
  interfaces, 89, 110
  invoking remote methods,
    38
  J2EE, 364
  skeletons, 38
  stubs, 38
RMI/IIOP (RMI over
  IIOP), 24
  J2EE, 365
roles, 25, 466
  application development,
    26
  container and server
    provider, 26
  deployer, 27
  deployment, 26
  infrastructure, 26
  system administrator, 27
rolling back, CMT, 416
running
  applications, 533
  BMP, 242
  BMT, 458
  clients (stateless session
    beans), 99
  JavaMail applications,
    517
  JBoss, 549
  MDB example, 343-346

## S

schema (XML), 556
scripting tags (JSP), 140
scriptlets (JSP), 141
  tags, 142
security, 463
  ACLs, 465
  administration, 469
  auditing, 469
  authentication, 466
  building sound architec-
    ture, 485
  certificate-related classes,
    469
  common vertical services,
    22
  credentials, 467
  delegating, 480
  digital signing, 468
  EIS tier, 481
  EJB tier, 476-480
  filtering, 469
  J2EE, 470, 485
    client tier, 470
    Web tier, 471-473
  JAAS, 482-484
  JMS, 306
  JNDI, 78
  PAM (Pluggable
    Authentication Model),
    482-484
  permissions, 464
  principals, 466
  realms, 465
  resources, 464
  roles, 466, 477-480
  servlets, 126
  Web applications, 475

# Other Related Titles

**Java 2 Micro Edition Application Development**
*Michael Kroll, Stefan Haustein*
0672320959
$49.99 US/
$77.99 CAN

**EJB 2.0, Rapid Working Knowledge**
*Peter Thaggard*
0672321785
$49.99 US/$77.99 CAN

**Sams Teach Yourself JavaServer Pages in 21 Days**
*Steve Holzner*
0672324490
$39.99 US/$59.95 CAN

**Aspect-Oriented Programming with AspectJ**
*Ivan Kiselev*
0672324105
$34.99 US/$52.95 CAN

**Sams Teach Yourself Extreme Programming in 24 Hours**
*Stewart Baird*
0672324415
$29.99 US/$44.95 CAN

**JSTL—JSP Standard Tag Library**
*Jeff Heaton*
0672324504
$34.99 US/$52.95 CAN

**JAX: Java APIs for XML**
*Aoyon Chowdhury, Parag Chaudhary*
0672324342
$34.99 US/$52.95 CAN

**Java Connector Architecture: Building Enterprise Adapters**
*Atul Apte*
0672323109
$49.99 US/
$77.99 CAN

**Java Deployment with JNLP and WebStart**
*Mauro Marinilli*
0672321823
$39.99 US/
$59.95 CAN

## SAMS

www.samspublishing.com

All prices are subject to change.